MCSA

Windows Server® 2012 R2

Installation and Configuration
Study Guide

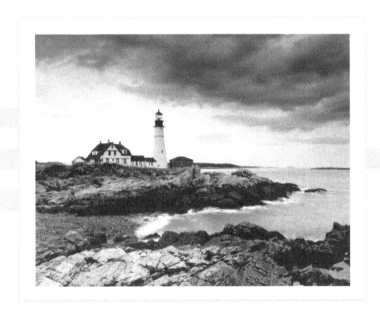

MCSA
Windows Server® 2012 R2
Installation and Configuration
Study Guide

William Panek

SYBEX®
A Wiley Brand

Senior Acquisitions Editor: Jeff Kellum
Development Editor: Gary Schwartz
Technical Editors: Rodney Fournier and Michael Rice
Production Editor: Eric Charbonneau
Copy Editor: Kim Wimpsett
Editorial Manager: Pete Gaughan
Production Manager: Kathleen Wisor
Professional Technology and Strategy Director: Barry Pruett
Associate Publisher: Jim Minatel
Media Project Manager 1: Laura Moss-Hollister
Media Associate Producer: Marilyn Hummel
Media Quality Assurance: Josh Frank
Book Designer: Judy Fung
Proofreader: Josh Chase, Word One New York
Indexer: Ted Laux
Project Coordinator, Cover: Patrick Redmond
Cover Designer: Wiley

This book is dedicated to the three ladies of my life: Crystal, Alexandria, and Paige.

Acknowledgments

I would like to thank my wife and best friend, Crystal. She is always the light at the end of my tunnel. I want to thank my two daughters, Alexandria and Paige, for all of their love and support during the writing of all my books. They make it all worthwhile.

I want to thank my family, and especially my brothers, Rick, Gary, and Rob. They have always been there for me. I want to thank my father, Richard, who helped me become the man I am today, and my mother, Maggie, for all of her love and support.

I would like to thank all of my friends and co-workers, especially Vic, Catherine, Jeff, Stephanie, Don, Jason, Doug, Dave, Steve, Pat, Mike (all of them), Tommy, George, Greg, Becca, Deb, Jeri, Lisa, Scotty, and all of the field guys. I want to also thank my team and everyone who works with my group including Moe, Jimmy, Paul, Dana, Dean, Reanna, Todd, and Will F. Because of all your hard work, you make me look good every day and make it a pleasure to go to work. Thanks to all of you for everything you do.

I want to thank everyone on my Sybex team, especially my development editor, Gary Schwartz, who helped me make this the best book possible, and Rodney R. Fournier, who is the technical editor of many of my books. It's always good to have the very best technical guy backing you up.

I want to thank Eric Charbonneau, who was my production editor, and my acquisitions editor, Jeff Kellum, who served as lead for the entire book. He has always been there for me, and it is always great to write for him.

Finally, I want to thank everyone else behind the scenes that helped make this book possible. It's truly an amazing thing to have so many people work on my books to help make them the very best. I can't thank you all enough for your hard work.

About the Authors

William Panek holds the following certifications: MCP, MCP+I, MCSA, MCSA+ Security and Messaging, MCSE-NT (3.51 and 4.0), MCSE 2000 and 2003, MCSE+Security and Messaging, MCDBA, MCT, MCTS, MCITP, CCNA, and CHFI. Will is also a Microsoft MVP.

After many successful years in the computer industry and a degree in computer programming, Will decided that he could better use his talents and his personality as an instructor. He began teaching for schools such as Boston University, Clark University, and the University of Maryland, just to name a few. He has done consulting and training work for some of the biggest government and corporate companies in the world including the U.S. Secret Service, Cisco, the U.S. Air Force, and the U.S. Army.

In January 2015, Will is now teaching for StormWind (www.stormwind.com). He currently lives in New Hampshire with his wife and two daughters. Will was also a representative in the New Hampshire House of Representatives from 2010 to 2012. In his spare time, he likes to golf, ski, shoot, and go snowmobiling. Will is also a commercially rated helicopter pilot.

Contents at a Glance

Contents

Table of Exercises

Introduction

This book is drawn from more than 20 years of IT experience. I have taken that experience and translated it into a Windows Server 2012 R2 book that will help you not only prepare for the MCSA: Windows Server 2012 R2 exams but also develop a clear understanding of how to install and configure Windows Server 2012 R2 while avoiding all of the possible configuration pitfalls.

Many Microsoft books just explain the Windows operating system, but with *MCSA: Windows Server 2012 R2 Complete Study Guide*, I go a step further by providing many in-depth, step-by-step procedures to support my explanations of how the operating system performs at its best.

Microsoft Windows Server 2012 R2 is the newest version of Microsoft's server operating system software. Microsoft has taken the best of Windows Server 2003, Windows Server 2008, and Windows Server 2012 and combined them into the latest creation, Windows Server 2012 R2.

Windows Server 2012 R2 eliminates many of the problems that plagued the previous versions of Windows Server, and it includes a much faster boot time and shutdown. It is also easier to install and configure, and it barely stops to ask the user any questions during installation. In this book, I will show you what features are installed during the automated installation and where you can make changes if you need to be more in charge of your operating system and its features.

This book takes you through all the ins and outs of Windows Server 2012 R2, including installation, configuration, Group Policy objects, auditing, backups, and so much more.

Windows Server 2012 R2 has improved on Microsoft's desktop environment, made networking easier, enhanced searching capability, and improved performance—and that's only scratching the surface.

When all is said and done, this is a technical book for IT professionals who want to take Windows Server 2012 R2 to the next step and get certified. With this book, you will not only learn Windows Server 2012 R2 and ideally pass the exams, but you will also become a Windows Server 2012 R2 expert.

The Microsoft Certification Program

Since the inception of its certification program, Microsoft has certified more than 2 million people. As the computer network industry continues to increase in both size and complexity, this number is sure to grow—and the need for proven ability will also increase. Certifications can help companies verify the skills of prospective employees and contractors.

The Microsoft certification tracks for Windows Server 2012 R2 include the following:

MCSA: Windows Server 2012 R2   The MCSA is now the lowest-level certification you can achieve with Microsoft in relation to Windows Server 2012 R2. It requires passing three exams: 70-410, 70-411, and 70-412. Or, if you qualify, you can take an Upgrading exam: Exam 70-417. This book assists in your preparation for all four exams.

MCSE: Server Infrastructure or MCSE: Desktop Infrastructure   The MCSE certifications, in relation to Windows Server 2012 R2, require that you become an MCSA first and then pass two additional exams. The additional exams will vary depending on which of the two MCSE tracks you choose. For more information, visit Microsoft's website at www.microsoft.com/learning.

MCSM: Directory Services   The MCSM certification takes things to an entirely new level. It requires passing a knowledge exam (in addition to having the MCSE in Windows Server 2012 R2) and a lab exam. This is now the elite-level certification in Windows Server 2012 R2.

How Do You Become Certified on Windows Server 2012 R2?

Attaining Microsoft certification has always been a challenge. In the past, students have been able to acquire detailed exam information—even most of the exam questions—from online "brain dumps" and third-party "cram" books or software products. For the new generation of exams, this is simply not the case.

Microsoft has taken strong steps to protect the security and integrity of its new certification tracks. Now prospective candidates must complete a course of study that develops detailed knowledge about a wide range of topics. It supplies them with the true skills needed, derived from working with the technology being tested.

The new generations of Microsoft certification programs are heavily weighted toward hands-on skills and experience. It is recommended that candidates have troubleshooting skills acquired through hands-on experience and working knowledge.

Fortunately, if you are willing to dedicate the time and effort to learn Windows Server 2012 R2, you can prepare yourself well for the exam by using the proper tools. By working through this book, you can successfully meet the requirements to pass the Windows Server 2012 R2 exams.

MCSA Exam Requirements

Candidates for MCSA certification on Windows Server 2012 R2 must pass at least the following three Windows Server 2012 R2 exams:

- 70-410: Installing and Configuring Windows Server 2012 R2
- 70-411: Administering Windows Server 2012 R2
- 70-412: Configuring Advanced Windows Server 2012 R2 Services

For those who have a qualifying certification, they can take the Upgrading Your Skills to MCSA Windows Server 2012 R2 exam (Exam 70-417). The objectives for this exam span the three individual exams. This book covers all of the objectives for the Upgrading exam. For details about the exam, visit Microsoft's website at www.microsoft.com/learning.

Microsoft provides exam objectives to give you a general overview of possible areas of coverage on the Microsoft exams. Keep in mind, however, that exam objectives are subject to change at any time without prior notice and at Microsoft's sole discretion. Visit the Microsoft Learning website (www.microsoft.com/learning) for the most current listing of exam objectives. The published objectives and how they map to this book are listed later in this introduction.

For a more detailed description of the Microsoft certification programs, including a list of all the exams, visit the Microsoft Learning website at: www.microsoft.com/learning.

Tips for Taking the Windows Server 2012 R2 Exams

Here are some general tips for achieving success on your certification exam:

- Arrive early at the exam center so that you can relax and review your study materials. During this final review, you can look over tables and lists of exam-related information.

- Read the questions carefully. Do not be tempted to jump to an early conclusion. Make sure you know exactly what the question is asking.

- Answer all questions. If you are unsure about a question, mark it for review and come back to it at a later time.

- On simulations, do not change settings that are not directly related to the question. Also, assume the default settings if the question does not specify or imply which settings are used.

- For questions about which you're unsure, use a process of elimination to get rid of the obviously incorrect answers first. This improves your odds of selecting the correct answer when you need to make an educated guess.

Exam Registration

At the time this book was released, Microsoft exams are given using Prometric testing centers (800-755-EXAM (800-755-3926)). As of December 31, 2014, Microsoft will be ending its relationship with Prometric, and all exams will be delivered through the more than 1,000 Authorized VUE Testing Centers around the world. For the location of a testing center near you, go to VUE's website at www.vue.com. If you are outside of the United States and Canada, contact your local VUE registration center.

Find out the number of the exam that you want to take and then register with the Prometric registration center nearest to you. At this point, you will be asked for advance payment for the exam. The exams are $125 each, and you must take them within one year of payment. You can schedule exams up to six weeks in advance or as late as one working day prior to the date of the exam. You can cancel or reschedule your exam if you contact the center at least two working days prior to the exam. Same-day registration is available in some locations, subject to space availability. Where same-day registration is available, you must register a minimum of two hours before test time.

When you schedule the exam, you will be provided with instructions regarding appointment and cancellation procedures, ID requirements, and information about the testing center location. In addition, you will receive a registration and payment confirmation letter from Prometric.

Microsoft requires certification candidates to accept the terms of a nondisclosure agreement before taking certification exams.

Who Should Read This Book?

This book is intended for individuals who want to earn their MCSA: Windows Server 2012 R2 certification.

This book will not only help anyone who is looking to pass the Microsoft exams, it will also help anyone who wants to learn the real ins and outs of the Windows Server 2012 R2 operating system.

What's Inside?

Here is a glance at what's in each chapter:

Chapter 1: Install Windows Server 2012 R2   In the first chapter, I explain the requirements and steps required to install and configure Windows Server 2012 R2.

Chapter 2: Configure Network Services   This chapter shows you how to install and configure DNS. I also explain the different types of DNS records and DNS zone types.

Chapter 3: Plan and Install Active Directory   I take you through the advantages and benefits of Windows Server 2012 R2 Active Directory.

Chapter 4: Configure Windows Server 2012 R2   I show you how to manage file systems, print servers, and file and share access.

Chapter 5: Administer Active Directory This chapter takes you through the different ways to create and manage your users and groups on the Windows Server 2012 R2 operating system.

Chapter 6: Manage GPOs You will see how to configure different types of Group Policy objects (GPOs) in Active Directory.

Chapter 7: Manage Security I show you how to secure Windows Server 2012 R2.

Chapter 8: Configure TCP/IP This chapter shows you how to configure IPv4 and IPv6. You'll look at IPv4 subnetting and how to manage a TCP/IP network.

Chapter 9: Use Virtualization in Windows Server 2012 This chapter will show you how to implement and configure Windows Server Hyper-V and virtual machines. You will learn about virtual networking, virtual hard disks, migration types, and Integration Services.

What's Included with the Book

This book includes many helpful items intended to prepare you for the MCSA: Windows Server 2012 R2 certification.

Assessment Test There is an assessment test at the conclusion of the introduction that can be used to evaluate quickly where you are with Windows Server 2012 R2. This test should be taken prior to beginning your work in this book, and it should help you identify areas in which you are either strong or weak. Note that these questions are purposely more simple than the types of questions you may see on the exams.

Objective Map and Opening List of Objectives Later in this introduction, I include a detailed exam objective map showing you where each of the exam objectives are covered. Each chapter also includes a list of the exam objectives that are covered.

Helpful Exercises Throughout the book, I have included step-by-step exercises of some of the more important tasks that you should be able to perform. Some of these exercises have corresponding videos that can be downloaded from the book's website. Also, in the following section I have a recommended home lab setup that will be helpful in completing these tasks.

Exam Essentials The end of each chapter also includes a listing of exam essentials. These are essentially repeats of the objectives, but remember that any objective on the exam blueprint could show up on the exam.

Chapter Review Questions Each chapter includes review questions. These are used to assess your understanding of the chapter and are taken directly from the chapter. These questions are based on the exam objectives, and they are similar in difficulty to items you might actually receive on the MCSA: Windows Server 2012 R2 exams.

The Sybex Test Engine, flashcards, videos, and glossary can be obtained at www.sybex.com/go/mcsawin2012r2install.

Sybex Test Engine Readers can access the Sybex Test Engine, which includes the assessment test and chapter review questions in electronic format. In addition, there are a total of three practice exams included with the Sybex test engine: one each for Exams 70-410, 70-411, and 70-412.

Electronic Flashcards Flashcards are included for quick reference. They are a great tool for learning important facts quickly. You may even consider these as additional simple practice questions, which is essentially what they are.

Videos Some of the exercises include corresponding videos. These videos show you how I do the exercises. There is also a video that shows you how to set up virtualization so that you can complete the exercises within a virtualized environment. This same video also shows you how to install Windows Server 2012 Datacenter on that virtualized machine.

PDF of Glossary of Terms There is a glossary included that covers the key terms used in this book.

Recommended Home Lab Setup

To get the most out of this book, you will want to make sure you complete the exercises throughout the chapters. To complete the exercises, you will need one of two setups. First, you can set up a machine with Windows Server 2012 R2 and complete the labs using a regular Windows Server 2012 R2 machine.

The second way to set up Windows Server 2012 R2 (the way I set up Server 2012 R2) is by using virtualization. I set up Windows Server 2012 R2 as a virtual hard disk (VHD), and I did all the labs this way. The advantages of using virtualization are that you can always just wipe out the system and start over without losing a real server. Plus, you can set up multiple virtual servers and create a full lab environment on one machine.

I created a video for this book showing you how to set up a virtual machine and how to install Windows Server 2012 R2 onto that virtual machine.

How to Contact Sybex

Sybex strives to keep you supplied with the latest tools and information you need for your work. Please check the website at www.sybex.com/go/mcsawin2012r2install, where I'll post additional content and updates that supplement this book should the need arise.

You can contact me by going to my website at www.willpanek.com.

Certification Objectives Maps

In addition to the book chapters, you will find coverage of exam objectives in the flashcards, practice exams, and videos on the book's companion website: www.sybex.com/go/mcsawin2012r2install

 Exam objectives are subject to change at any time without prior notice and at Microsoft's sole discretion. Please visit Microsoft's website (www.microsoft.com/learning) for the most current listing of exam objectives.

Objectives

Exam 70-410: Installing and Configuring Windows Server 2014

Install servers, Chapter 1

Plan for a server installation

Plan for server roles

Plan for a server upgrade

Install Server Core

Optimize resource utilization by using Features on Demand

Migrate roles from previous versions of Windows Server

Configure servers, Chapter 1

Configure Server Core

Delegate administration

Add and remove features in offline images

Deploy roles on remote servers

Convert Server Core to/from full GUI

Configure services

Configure NIC teaming

Configure local storage, Chapter 1

    Design storage spaces

    Configure basic and dynamic disks

    Configure MBR and GPT disks

    Manage volumes

    Create and mount virtual hard disks

    Configure storage pools and disk pools

Deploy and configure DNS service, Chapter 2

    Configure Active Directory integration of primary zones

    Configure forwarders

    Configure Root Hints

    Manage DNS cache

    Create A and PTR resource records

Deploy and configure Dynamic Host Configuration Protocol (DHCP) service, Chapter 2

    Create and configure scopes

    Configure a DHCP reservation

    Configure DHCP options

    Configure client and server for PXE boot

    Configure DHCP relay agent

    Authorize DHCP server

Install domain controllers, Chapter 3

    Add or remove a domain controller from a domain

    Upgrade a domain controller

    Install Active Directory Domain Services (AD DS) on a Server Core installation

    Install a domain controller from Install from Media (IFM)

    Resolve DNS SRV record registration issues

    Configure a global catalog server

    Deploy Active Directory iaas in Windows Azure

Configure file and share access, Chapter 4

    Create and configure shares

    Configure share permissions

    Configure offline files

    Configure NTFS permissions

    Configure access-based enumeration (ABE)

Configure Volume Shadow Copy Service (VSS)

Configure NTFS quotas

Create and configure Work Folders

Configure print and document services, Chapter 4

Configure the Easy Print print driver

Configure Enterprise Print Management

Configure drivers

Configure printer pooling

Configure print priorities

Configure printer permissions

Configure servers for remote management, Chapter 4

Configure WinRM

Configure down-level server management

Configure servers for day-to-day management tasks

Configure multi-server management

Configure Server Core

Configure Windows Firewall

Manage non-domain joined servers

Create and manage Active Directory users and computers, Chapter 5

Automate the creation of Active Directory accounts

Create, copy, configure, and delete users and computers

Configure templates

Perform bulk Active Directory operations

Configure user rights

Offline domain join

Manage inactive and disabled accounts

Create and manage Active Directory groups and organizational units (OUs), Chapter 5

Configure group nesting

Convert groups including security, distribution, universal, domain local, and domain global

Manage group membership using Group Policy

Enumerate group membership

Delegate the creation and management of Active Directory objects

Manage default Active Directory containers

Create, copy, configure, and delete groups and OUs

Create Group Policy Objects (GPOs), Chapter 6

    Configure a Central Store

    Manage starter GPOs

    Configure GPO links

    Configure multiple local group policies

    Configure security filtering

Configure application restriction policies, Chapter 6

    Configure rule enforcement

    Configure applocker rules

    Configure Software Restriction Policies

Configuring security policies, Chapter 7

    Configure User Rights Assignment

    Configure Security Options settings

    Configure Security templates

    Configure Audit Policy

    Configure Local Users and Groups

    Configure User Account Control (UAC)

Configuring Windows Firewall, Chapter 7

    Configure rules for multiple profiles using Group Policy

    Configure connection security rules

    Configure Windows Firewall to allow or deny applications, scopes, ports, and users

    Configure authenticated firewall exceptions

    Import and export settings

Configure IPv4 and IPv6 addressing, Chapter 8

    Configure IP address options

    Configure IPv4 or IPv6 subnetting

    Configure supernetting

    Configure interoperability between IPv4 and IPv6

    Configure ISATAP

    Configure Teredo

Create and configure virtual machine settings, Chapter 9

Configure dynamic memory , Chapter 9

Configure smart paging, Chapter 9

Configure Resource Metering, Chapter 9

Configure guest integration services, Chapter 9

Create and configure Generation 1 and 2 virtual machines, Chapter 9

Configure and use extended session mode, Chapter 9

Configure remoteFX, Chapter 9

Create and configure virtual machine storage, Chapter 9

    Create VHDs and VHDX

    Configure differencing drives

    Modify VHDs

    Configure pass-through disks

    Manage checkpoints

    Implement a virtual Fibre Channel adapter

    Configure storage Quality of Service

Create and configure virtual networks, Chapter 9

    Configure Hyper-V virtual switches

    Optimize network performance

    Configure MAC addresses

    Configure network isolation

    Configure synthetic and legacy virtual network adapters

    Configure NIC teaming in virtual machines

Assessment Test

1. Which of the following is a valid role for a Windows Server 2012 R2 computer?

    A. Stand-alone server

    B. Member server

    C. Domain controller

    D. All of the above

2. Which of the following is a benefit of using Active Directory? (Choose all that apply.)

    A. Hierarchical object structure

    B. Fault-tolerant architecture

    C. Ability to configure centralized and distributed administration

    D. Flexible replication

3. Which of the following features of the Domain Name System (DNS) can be used to improve performance? (Choose all that apply.)

    A. Caching-only servers

    B. DNS forwarding

    C. Secondary servers

    D. Zone delegation

4. Which of the following pieces of information should you have before you begin the Active Directory Installation Wizard? (Choose all that apply.)

    A. Active Directory domain name

    B. Administrator password for the local computer

    C. NetBIOS name for the server

    D. DNS configuration information

5. An Active Directory environment consists of three domains. What is the maximum number of sites that can be created for this environment?

    A. Two

    B. Three

    C. Nine

    D. Unlimited

6. Which of the following is *not* a valid Active Directory object?

    A. User

    B. Group

C. Organizational unit

D. Computer

E. None of the above

7. Which of the following is *not* considered a security principal?

   A. Users

   B. Security groups

   C. Distribution groups

   D. Computers

8. Which of the following should play the *least* significant role in planning an OU structure?

   A. Network infrastructure

   B. Domain organization

   C. Delegation of permissions

   D. Group Policy settings

9. How can the Windows Server 2012 R2 file and printer resources be made available from within Active Directory?

   A. A system administrator can right-click the resource and select Publish.

   B. A system administrator can create Printer and Shared Folder objects that point to these resources.

   C. The Active Directory Domains and Trusts tool can be used to make resources available.

   D. Only resources on a Windows 2000 or newer server can be accessed from within Active Directory.

10. The process by which a higher-level security authority assigns permissions to other administrators is known as which of the following?

   A. Inheritance

   B. Delegation

   C. Assignment

   D. Trust

11. What is the minimum amount of information you need to create a Shared Folder Active Directory object?

   A. The name of the share

   B. The name of the server

   C. The name of the server and the name of the share

   D. The name of the server, the server's IP address, and the name of the share

12. Which of the following operations is not supported by Active Directory?

   A. Assigning applications to users

   B. Assigning applications to computers

   C. Publishing applications to users

   D. Publishing applications to computers

13. Which of the following filename extensions is used primarily for Windows Installer setup programs?

   A. .msi

   B. .mst

   C. .zap

   D. .aas

14. A system administrator wants to allow a group of users to add computer accounts to a specific organizational unit (OU). What is the easiest way to grant only the required permissions?

   A. Delegate control of a user account

   B. Delegate control at the domain level

   C. Delegate control of an OU

   D. Delegate control of a computer account

   E. Create a Group Policy object (GPO) at the OU level

15. A Group Policy object (GPO) at the domain level sets a certain option to Disabled, while a GPO at the OU level sets the same option to Enabled. All other settings are left at their default. Which setting will be effective for objects within the OU?

   A. Enabled

   B. Disabled

   C. No effect

   D. None of the above

16. Which of the following tools can be used to create Group Policy object (GPO) links to Active Directory?

   A. Active Directory Users and Computers

   B. Active Directory Domains and Trusts

   C. Active Directory Sites and Services

   D. Group Policy Management Console

17. To test whether a DNS server is answering queries properly, you can use which of the following tools?

   A. The ping tool

   B. The nslookup tool

   C. The tracert tool

   D. The ipconfig tool

18. Which of the following is true about the time to live (TTL) attached to a DNS record?

   A. A resolver cannot use it; only servers making recursive queries can use it.

   B. Only resolvers use it.

   C. It is used to determine how long to cache retrieved results.

   D. It is refreshed each time the record is modified.

19. Which of the following statements about Windows Server 2012 Dynamic DNS (DDNS) is true?

   A. DDNS requires a Microsoft DHCP server to work.

   B. The Windows Server 2012 DDNS server can interoperate with recent versions of BIND.

   C. DDNS clients may not register their own addresses.

   D. DDNS works only with Microsoft clients and servers.

20. You have been given a server that contains three HBAs. Each card can access the storage over a separate path. The application that runs on the server can exceed the usage of a single path. Which of the following MPIO options should be selected to provide the needed bandwidth as well as minimal redundancy?

   A. Failover

   B. Dynamic Least Queue Depth

   C. Weighted path

   D. Round robin

Answers to Assessment Test

1. D. Based on the business needs of an organization, a Windows 2012 R2 Server computer can be configured in any of the roles listed. See Chapter 1 for more information.

2. A, B, C and D. All of the options listed are benefits of using Active Directory. See Chapter 3 for more information.

3. A, B, C and D. One of the major design goals for DNS was support for scalability. All of the features listed can be used to increase the performance of DNS. See Chapter 2 for more information.

4. A, B, C and D. Before beginning the installation of a domain controller, you should have all the information listed. See Chapter 3 for more information.

5. D. The number of sites in an Active Directory environment is independent of the domain organization. An environment that consists of three domains may have one or more sites, based on the physical network setup. See Chapter 3 for more information.

6. E. All of the choices are valid types of Active Directory objects, and all can be created and managed using the Active Directory Users and Computers tool. See Chapter 5 for more information.

7. C. Permissions and security settings cannot be made on distribution groups. Distribution groups are used only for sending email. See Chapter 4 for more information.

8. A. In general, you can accommodate your network infrastructure through the use of Active Directory sites. All of the other options should play a significant role when you design your OU structure. Permissions and Group Policy can both be applied at the domain or OU level. See Chapter 4 for more information.

9. B. Printer and Shared Folder objects within Active Directory can point to Windows Server 2012 R2 file and printer resources. See Chapter 4 for more information.

10. B. Delegation is the process by which administrators can assign permissions on the objects within an OU. This is useful when administrators want to give other users more control over administrative functions in Active Directory. See Chapter 4 for more information.

11. C. The name of the server and the name of the share make up the Universal Naming Convention (UNC) information required to create a Shared Folder object. See Chapter 4 for more information.

12. D. Applications cannot be published to computers, but they can be published to users and assigned to computers. See Chapter 5 for more information.

13. A. MSI files (.msi) are native Windows Installer files used with Windows Installer setup programs. The other file types do not apply to this situation. See Chapter 5 for more information.

14. E. To allow this permission at the OU level, the system administrator must create a GPO with the appropriate settings and link it to the OU. See Chapter 5 for more information.

15. A. Assuming that the default settings are left in place, the Group Policy setting at the OU level will take effect. See Chapter 5 for more information.

16. D. In Windows Server 2012 R2, you can create GPOs only by using the Group Policy Management Console. See Chapter 5 for more information.

17. B. The nslookup tool allows you to look up name and address information. See Chapter 2 for more information.

18. C. The TTL indicates how long the record may be safely cached; it may or may not be modified when the record is created. See Chapter 2 for more information on TTL.

19. B. DDNS works with BIND 8.2 and newer. See Chapter 2 for more information on DDNS.

20. D. A round-robin configuration uses all of the available active paths and will distribute I/O in a balanced round-robin fashion. Failover uses only the primary and standby paths, allowing for link failure. Weighted path assigns requests to the path with the least weight value. Dynamic Least Queue Depth routes requests to the path with the least number of outstanding requests. See Chapter 2 for more information.

Chapter

1

Install Windows Server 2012 R2

THE FOLLOWING 70-410 EXAM OBJECTIVES ARE COVERED IN THIS CHAPTER:

✓ **Install servers**

- Plan for a server installation
- Plan for server roles
- Plan for a server upgrade
- Install Server Core
- Optimize resource utilization by using Features on Demand
- Migrate roles from previous versions of Windows Server
- Configure Server Core
- Add and remove features in offline images
- Deploy roles on remote servers
- Convert Server Core to/from full GUI
- Configure NIC teaming

✓ **Configure local storage**

- Design storage spaces
- Configure basic and dynamic disks
- Configure MBR and GPT disks
- Manage volumes
- Create and mount virtual hard disks
- Configure storage pools and disk pools

This chapter covers the installation of Windows Server 2012 R2. It shows how to install both the full version of Windows Server 2012 R2 and the Server Core version. It also shows you how to use some PowerShell commands in Windows Server 2012 R2 Server Core.

Let's dive right into the server by talking about some of the new features and advantages of Windows Server 2012 R2.

Features and Advantages of Windows Server 2012 and Server 2012 R2

Before I show how to install and configure Windows Server 2012 R2, let's take a look at some of the new features and the advantages it offers.

 Since many of you will be upgrading from Windows Server 2003 and Windows Server 2008/2008 R2, these are the new features introduced by Microsoft since then. I will specifically identify any new features or advantages that are new to Windows Server 2012 R2 only.

I will talk about all of these features in greater detail throughout this book. What follows are merely brief descriptions.

Active Directory Certificate Services *Active Directory Certificate Services (AD CS)* provides a customizable set of services that allow you to issue and manage *public key infrastructure (PKI) certificates*. These certificates can be used in software security systems that employ public key technologies.

Active Directory Domain Services *Active Directory Domain Services (AD DS)* includes new features that make deploying domain controllers simpler and that let you implement them faster. AD DS also makes the domain controllers more flexible, both to audit and to authorize for access to files. Moreover, AD DS has been designed to make performing administrative tasks easier through consistent graphical and scripted management experiences.

Active Directory Rights Management Services *Active Directory Rights Management Services (AD RMS)* provides management and development tools that let you work with industry security technologies, including encryption, certificates, and authentication. Using these technologies allows organizations to create reliable information protection solutions.

BitLocker *BitLocker* is a tool that allows you to encrypt the hard drives of your computer. By encrypting the hard drives, you can provide enhanced protection against data theft or unauthorized exposure of your computers or removable drives that are lost or stolen.

BranchCache *BranchCache* allows data from files and web servers on a wide area network (WAN) to be cached on computers at a local branch office. By using BranchCache, you can improve application response times while also reducing WAN traffic. Cached data can be either distributed across peer client computers (distributed cache mode) or centrally hosted on a server (hosted cache mode). BranchCache is included with Windows Server 2012 R2 and Windows 8.

In this book, I will refer to *Windows 8*, which includes both Windows 8 and Windows 8.1. This is also true for *Windows Server 2008*. It will be used for both Windows Server 2008 and Windows Server 2008 R2. If, for some reason, both versions of Server 2008 did not cover an item, I will actually say 2008 R2.

DHCP *Dynamic Host Configuration Protocol (DHCP)* is an Internet standard that allows organizations to reduce the administrative overhead of configuring hosts on a TCP/IP-based network. Some of the new features are DHCP failover, policy-based assignment, and the ability to use Windows PowerShell for DHCP Server.

DNS *Domain Name System (DNS)* services are used in TCP/IP networks. DNS will convert a computer name or fully qualified domain name (FQDN) to an IP address. DNS also has the ability to do a reverse lookup and convert an IP address to a computer name. DNS allows you to locate computers and services through user-friendly names.

Failover Clustering *Failover Clustering* gives an organization the ability to provide high availability and scalability to networked servers. Failover clusters can include file share storage for server applications, such as Hyper-V and Microsoft SQL Server, and those that run on physical servers or virtual machines.

File Server Resource Manager *File Server Resource Manager* is a set of tools that allows administrators to manage and control the amount and type of data stored on the organization's servers. By using File Server Resource Manager, administrators have the ability to set up file management tasks, use quota management, get detailed reports, set up a file classification infrastructure, and configure file-screening management.

Hyper-V *Hyper-V* is one of the most changed features in Windows Server 2012 R2. Microsoft's new slogan is "Windows Server 2012 R2, built from the cloud up," and this has a lot to do with Hyper-V. It allows an organization to consolidate servers by creating and managing a virtualized computing environment. It does this by using virtualization technology that is built into Windows Server 2012 R2.

Hyper-V allows you to run multiple operating systems simultaneously on one physical computer. Each virtual operating system runs in its own virtual machine environment. I cover Hyper-V in detail in Chapter 9: "Use Virtualization in Windows Server 2012."

IPAM   *IP Address Management (IPAM)* is one of the features introduced with Windows Server 2012 R2. IPAM allows an administrator to customize and monitor the IP address infrastructure on a corporate network.

Kerberos Authentication   Windows Server 2012 R2 uses the *Kerberos authentication* (version 5) protocol and extensions for password-based and public key authentication. The Kerberos client is installed as a *security support provider (SSP)*, and it can be accessed through the *Security Support Provider Interface (SSPI)*.

Managed Service Accounts (gMSAs)   Stand-alone *managed service accounts*, originally created for Windows Server 2008 R2 and Windows 7, are configured domain accounts that allow automatic password management and *service principal names* (SPNs) management, including the ability to delegate management to other administrators.

Networking   There are many networking technologies and features in Windows Server 2012 R2, including BranchCache, Data Center Bridging (DCB), NIC Teaming, and many more.

Remote Desktop Services   Before Windows Server 2008, we used to refer to this as Terminal Services. *Remote Desktop Services* allows users to connect to virtual desktops, RemoteApp programs, and session-based desktops. Using Remote Desktop Services allows users to access remote connections from within a corporate network or from the Internet.

Security Auditing   *Security auditing* gives an organization the ability to help maintain the security of an enterprise. By using security audits, you can verify authorized or unauthorized access to machines, resources, applications, and services. One of the best advantages of security audits is to verify regulatory compliance.

Smart Cards   Using *smart cards* (referred to as *two-factor authentication*) and their associated *personal identification numbers (PINs)* is a popular, reliable, and cost-effective way to provide authentication. When using smart cards, the user not only must have the physical card but also must know the PIN to be able to gain access to network resources. This is effective because even if the smart card is stolen, thieves can't access the network unless they know the PIN.

TLS/SSL (Schannel SSP)   *Schannel* is a security support provider (SSP) that uses the *Secure Sockets Layer (SSL)* and *Transport Layer Security (TLS)* Internet standard authentication protocols together. The Security Support Provider Interface is an API used by Windows systems to allow security-related functionality, including authentication.

Windows Deployment Services   *Windows Deployment Services* allows an administrator to install Windows operating systems remotely. Administrators can use Windows Deployment Services to set up new computers by using a network-based installation.

Planning the Windows Server 2012 R2 Installation

Before you install Windows Server 2012 R2, you must first ask yourself these important questions: What type of server do I need? Will the server be a domain controller? What roles do I need to install on this server?

Once you have figured out what you need the server to do, you can make a game plan for the installation. So, let's start by looking at some of the server roles and technologies that can be installed on a Windows Server 2012 R2 computer.

Server Roles in Windows Server 2012 R2

When you install Windows Server 2012 R2, you have to decide which roles and features are going to be installed onto that server. This is an important decision in the computer world. Many administrators not only overuse a server but also underutilize servers in their organization.

For example, many administrators refuse to put any other roles or features on a domain controller. This may not be a good use of a server. Domain controllers help authenticate users onto the network, but after that the domain controllers are really not very busy all day long. Domain controllers have tasks that they must perform all day, but the server on which they reside is not heavily used when compared to a SQL Server machine or an Exchange mail server. This is where monitoring your server can be useful.

Now let's take a look at some of the roles and features you can install onto a Windows Server 2012 R2 machine. Knowing the different roles and features you can install will help you to design, deploy, manage, and troubleshoot technologies in Windows Server 2012 R2. Figure 1.1 shows the Add Roles And Features Wizard in Server Manager. It shows you just some of the roles that can be installed on a Windows Server 2012 R2 machine.

Roles and Features

Many of these features were discussed in the section "Features and Advantages of Windows Server 2012 and Server 2012 R2." I include them here again because they are also *roles* that can also be installed on Windows Server 2012 R2.

The following roles are available in Windows Server 2012 R2:

Active Directory Certificate Services The AD CS server role in Windows Server 2012 R2 allows you to build a PKI and provide public key cryptography, digital certificates, and digital signature capabilities for your organization.

FIGURE 1.1 Available roles in Windows Server 2012 R2

Feature AD CS provides a customizable set of services that allows you to issue and manage PKI certificates. These certificates can be used in software security systems that employ public key technologies.

Role AD CS in Windows Server 2012 R2 is the server role that allows you to build a PKI and provide public key cryptography, digital certificates, and digital signature capabilities for your organization.

Active Directory Domain Services The AD DS server role allows you to create a scalable, secure, and manageable infrastructure for user and resource management and to provide support for directory-enabled applications, such as Microsoft Exchange Server.

Active Directory Federation Services *Active Directory Federation Services (AD FS)* provides Internet-based clients with a secure identity access solution that works on both Windows and non-Windows operating systems. AD FS gives users the ability to do a *single sign-on (SSO)* and access applications on other networks without needing a secondary password.

Active Directory Lightweight Directory Services *Active Directory Lightweight Directory Services (AD LDS)* is a *Lightweight Directory Access Protocol (LDAP)* directory service that provides flexible support for directory-enabled applications, without the dependencies and domain-related restrictions of AD DS.

Active Directory Rights Management Services   Active Directory Rights Management Services (AD RMS) in Windows Server 2012 R2 is the server role that provides you with management and development tools that work with industry security technologies including encryption, certificates, and authentication to help organizations create reliable information protection solutions.

Application Server   *Application Server* provides an integrated environment for deploying and running custom, server-based business applications.

Failover Clustering   The Failover Clustering feature provides a way to create, configure, and manage failover clusters for up to 4,000 virtual machines or up to 64 physical nodes.

File and Storage Services   *File and Storage Services* allows an administrator to set up and manage one or more file servers. These servers can provide a central location on your network where you can store files and then share those files with network users. If users require access to the same files and applications or if centralized backup and file management are important issues for your organization, administrators should set up network servers as a file server.

Group Policy   *Group policies* are a set of rules and management configuration options that you can control through the Group Policy settings. These policy settings can be placed on users' computers throughout the organization.

Hyper-V   The Hyper-V role allows administrators to create and manage a virtualized environment by taking advantage of the technology built into the Windows Server 2012 R2 operating system. When an administrator installs the Hyper-V role, all required virtualization components are installed.

Some of the required components include the Windows hypervisor, Virtual Machine Management Service, the virtualization WMI provider, the virtual machine bus (VMbus), the virtualization service provider (VSP), and the virtual infrastructure driver (VID).

Networking   This feature allows administrators to design, deploy, and maintain a Windows Server 2012 R2 network. The networking features include 802.1X authenticated wired and wireless access, BranchCache, Data Center Bridging, low-latency workload technologies, and many more.

Network Load Balancing   The *Network Load Balancing (NLB)* feature dispenses traffic across multiple servers by using the TCP/IP networking protocol. By combining two or more computers that are running applications in Windows Server 2012 R2 into a single virtual cluster, NLB provides reliability and performance for mission-critical servers.

Network Policy and Access Services   Use the *Network Policy and Access Services* server role to install and configure *Network Access Protection (NAP)*, secure wired and wireless access points, and RADIUS servers and proxies.

Print and Document Services   *Print and Document Services* allows an administrator to centralize print server and network printer tasks. This role also allows you to receive scanned documents from network scanners and route the documents to a shared network resource, Windows SharePoint Services site, or email addresses. Print and Document

Services also provides fax servers with the ability to send and receive faxes while also giving the administrator the ability to manage fax resources such as jobs, settings, reports, and fax devices on the fax server.

Remote Desktop Services   Remote Desktop Services allows for faster desktop and application deployments to any device, improving remote user effectiveness while helping to keep critical data secure. Remote Desktop Services allows for both a *virtual desktop infrastructure (VDI)* and session-based desktops, allowing users to connect from anywhere.

Security and Protection   Windows Server 2012 R2 has many new and improved security features for your organization. These security features include Access Control, AppLocker, BitLocker, Credential Locker, Kerberos, NTLM, passwords, security auditing, smart cards, and Windows Biometric Framework (WBF).

Telemetry   The *Telemetry* service allows the Windows Feedback Forwarder to send feedback to Microsoft automatically by deploying a Group Policy setting to one or more organizational units. Windows Feedback Forwarder is available on all editions of Windows Server 2012 R2, including Server Core.

Volume Activation   Windows Server 2012 R2 *Volume Activation* will help your organization benefit from using this service to deploy and manage volume licenses for a medium to large number of computers.

Web Server (IIS)   The *Web Server (IIS)* role in Windows Server 2012 R2 allows an administrator to set up a secure, easy-to-manage, modular, and extensible platform for reliably hosting websites, services, and applications.

Windows Deployment Services   Windows Deployment Services allows an administrator to install a Windows operating system over the network. Administrators do not have to install each operating system directly from a CD or DVD.

Windows Server Backup Feature   The *Windows Server Backup* feature gives an organization a way to back up and restore Windows servers. You can use Windows Server Backup to back up the entire server (all volumes), selected volumes, the system state, or specific files or folders.

Windows Server Update Services   *Windows Server Update Services (WSUS)* allows administrators to deploy application and operating system updates. By deploying WSUS, administrators have the ability to manage updates that are released through Microsoft Update to computers in their network. This feature is integrated with the operating system as a server role on a Windows Server 2012 R2 system.

Migrating Roles and Features to Windows Server 2012 R2

Once you decide on which roles and features you are going to install onto your Windows Server 2012 R2 system, then you either have to install those roles and features from scratch or migrate them from a previous version of Windows server.

Windows Server 2012 R2 includes a set of migration tools that administrators can use to help ease the process of migrating server roles, features, operating system settings, and data. Administrators can migrate this data from an existing server that is running Windows Server 2003, Windows Server 2003 R2, Windows Server 2008, Windows Server 2008 R2, or Windows Server 2012 R2 to a computer that is running Windows Server 2012 R2.

Using Windows Server Migration Tools to migrate roles, role services, and features can simplify the deployment of new servers. You can migrate roles and features on servers running the Server Core installation option of Windows Server 2012 R2 and virtual servers. By using Windows Server Migration Tools, an administrator can reduce migration downtime, increase the accuracy of the migration process, and help eliminate conflicts that could otherwise occur during the migration process.

One advantage of using the migration tools is that most of them support cross-architecture migrations (x86-based to x64-based computing platforms), migrations between physical and virtual environments, and migrations between both the full and Server Core installation options of the Windows Server operating system. In Windows Server 2012 R2, Windows Server Migration Tools also supports cross-subnet migrations.

To use Windows Server Migration Tools, the feature must be installed on both the source and destination computers. Windows Server Migration Tools installation and preparation can be divided into the following stages:

1. Installing Windows Server Migration Tools on destination servers that run Windows Server 2012 R2

2. Creating deployment folders on destination servers that run Windows Server 2012 R2 for copying to source servers

3. Copying deployment folders from destination servers to source servers

4. Registering Windows Server Migration Tools on source servers

If you plan to use Windows Server Migration Tools, you must be a member of the Administrators group on both the source and destination servers to install, remove, or set up the tools.

Administrators can install Windows Server Migration Tools by using either the Add Roles Or Features Wizard in Server Manager or Windows PowerShell deployment cmdlets for Server Manager.

To install Windows Server Migration Tools on a Server Core installation of Windows Server 2012 R2, you would complete the following steps:

1. Open a Windows PowerShell session by typing **powershell.exe** in the current command prompt session and then pressing Enter.

2. In the Windows PowerShell session, install Windows Server Migration Tools by using the Windows PowerShell `Install-WindowsFeature` cmdlet for Server Manager. In the Windows PowerShell session, type the following, and then press Enter. (Omit the `ComputerName` parameter if you are installing the Windows Server Migration Tools on the local server.)

```
Install-WindowsFeature Migration -ComputerName computer_name
```

Roles and Features That Have Been Reduced in Windows Server 2012 R2

One thing that we want to look at is which Roles and Features are being deprecated or removed from Windows Server 2012 and Windows Server 2012 R2. Table 1.1 was taken directly from Microsoft's website (http://technet.microsoft.com/en-us/library/dn303411.aspx), and this table may change at any time. Thus I would recommend that you go out to Microsoft's website to see the current list of Roles and Features.

Table 1.1 lists the features and functionalities in Windows Server 2012 and Windows Server 2012 R2 that either have been removed from the product in the current release or are planned for potential removal in subsequent releases (shown as *deprecated*).

TABLE 1.1   Roles and Features Updates

	Windows Server 2012		Windows Server 2012 R2	
	Removed	Deprecated	Removed	Deprecated
AD FS v1 Web Agent			X	
AD FS in-place upgrade from AD FS 1.0 or "out-of-the-box" AD FS 2.0	X			
AD FS support for "Resource Group"	X			
AD FS support for NT Token mode	X			
AD FS support for using AD LDS as an authentication store	X			
AD RMS license revocation				X
AD RMS SDK				X
Application Server role				X
Built-in drivers for tape drives				X
Cluster Automation Server COM API	X (Optional)		X (Optional)	
Cluster.exe command-line interface	X (Optional)		X (Optional)	

CertObj COM and InetInfo interfaces of the Web Server role				X
Dcpromo.exe		X		
Dfscmd.exe				X
Drivers for Jet Red RDBMS and ODBC		X		X
File Replication Service				X
Internet Information Service (IIS) 6.0 Manager				X
Layered Service Providers		X		X
LPR/LPD protocol		X		X
Namespace for version 1.0 of WMI; WMIC (in WMI)		X	X	
NDIS version 5.0, 5.1, and 5.2 APIs		X	X	
Net DMA	X			
Network Access Protection (NAP)				X
Network Information Service (NIS) and Tools (in RSAT)				X
Nfsshare.exe				X
NFSv2 support				X
Oclist.exe	X			
ODBC support for 16- and 32-bit applications and drivers		X		X
ODBC/OLEDB support for Microsoft Oracle		X		
ODBC/OLEDB support for SQL beyond SQL Server 7 and SQL 2000		X		X

TABLE 1.1   Roles and Features Updates *(continued)*

	Windows Server 2012		Windows Server 2012 R2	
	Removed	Deprecated	Removed	Deprecated
Providers for SNMP, Win32_ ServerFeature API, Active Directory, MSClus WMI1.0 (in WMI)		X		X
Recovery disk creation			X	
Remote Data Service		X		
Role Collector (Ceiprole.exe) and associated API	X			
SCSIport host-bus adapter	X			
Servermanagercmd.exe		X	X	
SIS Limited API				X
Slmgr.vbs options			X	
SMB 1.0				X
SMB.sys	X			
SMTP and associated management tools		X		X
SQLXMLX		X		X
Storage Explorer snap-in for MMC	X			
Storage Manager for SANs snap-in for MMC	X			
Subsystem for UNIX-based applications		X	X	
Support for 32-bit cluster resource DLLs	X			
Support for hardware drivers for XDDM	X			

Feature				
Support for Microsoft SQL Server prior to 7.0	X			
Support for native VGA via the PC/AT BIOS or UEFI CSM	X			
Support for Static VMQ	X			
Support for Token Rings	X			
Support for Visual Studio Analyzer 2003 over ODBC, OLEDB, and ADO	X			
System Image Backup ("Windows 7 File Recovery")			X	
Telnet server				X
VM Chimney (also called TCP Offload) in Hyper-V	X			
Windows Server 2003 domain and functional levels of Active Directory				X
Windows Authorization Manager (AzMan)		X	X	
Windows Help executable (WinHlp32.exe)	X			
Windows Identity Foundation 3.5				X
Windows Server Resource Manager		X	X	
Winsock Direct		X	X	
WMI root/virtualization namespace v1 (in Hyper-V)		X	X	
XDR schema elements, XSI pattern feature of MSXML3 (in XML)		X		X

Deciding Which Windows Server 2012 R2 Versions to Use

You may be wondering which version of Windows Server 2012 R2 is best for your organization. After all, Microsoft offers the following four versions of Windows Server 2012 R2.

Windows Server 2012 R2 Datacenter   This version is designed for organizations that are looking to migrate to a highly virtualized, private cloud environment. Windows Server 2012 R2 Datacenter has full Windows Server functionality with unlimited virtual instances.

Windows Server 2012 R2 Standard   This version is designed for organizations with physical or minimally virtualized environments. Windows Server 2012 R2 Standard has full Windows Server functionality with two virtual instances.

Windows Server 2012 R2 Essentials   This version is ideal for small businesses that have as many as 25 users and 50 devices. Windows Server 2012 R2 Essentials has a simpler interface and preconfigured connectivity to cloud-based services but no virtualization rights.

Windows Server 2012 R2 Foundation   This version is designed for smaller companies that need a Windows Server experience for as few as 15 users. Windows Server 2012 R2 Foundation is a general-purpose server with basic functionality but no virtualization rights.

Once you choose what roles are going on your server, you must then decide how you're going to install Windows Server 2012 R2. There are two ways to install Windows Server 2012 R2. You can upgrade a Windows Server 2008 R2 with SP1 or Windows Server 2012 machine to Windows Server 2012 R2, or you can do a clean install of Windows Server 2012 R2. If you decide that you are going to upgrade, there are specific upgrade paths you must follow.

Your choice of Windows Server 2012 R2 version is dictated by how your current network is designed. If you are building a network from scratch, then it's pretty straightforward. Just choose the Windows Server 2012 R2 version based on your server's tasks. However, if you already have a version of Windows Server 2008 installed, you should follow the recommendations in Table 1.2, which briefly summarize the supported upgrade paths to Windows Server 2012 R2.

If your version of Microsoft Windows Server is not listed in the left column, upgrading to Windows Server 2012 R2 is not supported. If there is more than one edition listed in the right column, you can then choose either edition.

TABLE 1.2   Supported Windows Server 2012 R2 upgrade path recommendations

Current System	Upgraded System
Windows Server 2008 R2 Datacenter with SP1	Windows Server 2012 R2 Datacenter
Windows Server 2008 R2 Enterprise with SP1	Windows Server 2012 R2 Standard or Windows Server 2012 R2 Datacenter

Windows Server 2008 R2 Standard with SP1	Windows Server 2012 R2 Standard or Windows Server 2012 R2 Datacenter
Windows Web Server 2008 R2 with SP1	Windows Server 2012 R2 Standard
Windows Server 2012 Datacenter	Windows Server 2012 R2 Datacenter
Windows Server 2012 Standard	Windows Server 2012 R2 Standard or Windows Server 2012 R2 Datacenter
Hyper-V Server 2012	Hyper-V Server 2012 R2
Windows Storage Server 2012 Standard	Windows Storage Server 2012 R2 Standard
Windows Storage Server 2012 Workgroup	Windows Storage Server 2012 R2 Workgroup

Deciding on the Type of Installation

One of the final choices you must make before installing Windows Server 2012 R2 is what type of installation you want. There are three ways to install Windows Server 2012 R2.

Windows Server 2012 R2 with the Graphical User Interface (GUI)   This is the version with which most administrators are familiar. This is the version that uses *Microsoft Management Console (MMC)* windows, and it is the version that allows the use of a mouse to navigate through the installation.

Windows Server 2012 R2 Server Core   This is a bare-bones installation of Windows Server 2012 R2. You can think of it this way: If Windows Server 2012 R2 is a top-of-the-line luxury car, then Windows Server 2012 R2 Server Core is the stripped-down model with no air-conditioning, manual windows, and cloth seats. It might not be pretty to look at, but it gets the job done.

Windows Server 2012 R2 MinShell   This is the best of both installation types mentioned previously. Minimum Shell (MinShell) gives you the advantage of using the GUI management tools, but MinShell does not actually install the GUI. It gives administrators the ability to use tools with which they are familiar but still provides a small attack surface and the advantages of Server Core.

In Windows Server 2012 R2, an administrator has the ability to remove the GUI shell after a GUI shell install has been completed. This removes Internet Explorer 10, Windows Explorer, the desktop, and the Start screen. Microsoft Management Console (MMC), Server Manager, and a subset of Control Panel are still present, giving you a MinShell installation plus PowerShell.

⊕ Real World Scenario

Server Core

Here is an explanation of Server Core that I have used ever since it was introduced in Windows Server 2008.

I am a *huge* sports fan. I love watching sports on TV, and I enjoy going to games. If you have ever been to a hockey game, you know what a hockey goal looks like. Between hockey periods, the stadium workers often bring out a huge piece of Plexiglas onto the ice. There is a tiny square cut out of the bottom of the glass. The square is just a bit bigger than a hockey puck itself.

Now they pick some lucky fan out of the stands, give them a puck at center ice, and then ask them to shoot the puck into the net with the Plexiglas in front of it. If they get it through that tiny little square at the bottom of the Plexiglas, they win a car or some such great prize.

Well, Windows Server 2012 R2 with the GUI is like regular hockey with a net, and Windows Server 2012 R2 Server Core is the Plexiglas version.

Server Core supports a limited number of roles.

- Active Directory Certificate Services (AD CS)
- Active Directory Domain Services (AD DS)
- Active Directory Federation Services (AD FS)
- Active Directory Lightweight Directory Services (AD LDS)
- Active Directory Rights Management Services (AD RMS)
- Application Server
- DHCP Server
- DNS Server
- Fax Server
- File and Storage Services
- BITS Server
- BranchCache
- Hyper-V
- Network Policy and Access Services
- Print and Document Services
- Remote Access
- Remote Desktop Services

- Volume Activation Services
- Web Server (IIS)
- Windows Deployment Services
- Windows Server Update Services
- .NET Framework 3.5 Features
- .NET Framework 4.5 Features
- Streaming Media Services
- Failover Clustering
- iSCSI
- Network Load Balancing
- MPIO
- qWave
- Telnet Server/Client
- Windows Server Migration Tools
- Windows PowerShell 4.0

Server Core does not have the normal Windows interface or GUI. Almost everything has to be configured via the command line or, in some cases, using the Remote Server Administration Tools from a full version of Windows Server 2012 R2. While this might scare off some administrators, it has the following benefits:

Reduced Management   Because Server Core has a minimum number of applications installed, it reduces management effort.

Minimal Maintenance   Only basic systems can be installed on Server Core, so it reduces the upkeep you would need to perform in a normal server installation.

Smaller Footprint   Server Core requires only 1GB of disk space to install and 2GB of free space for operations.

Tighter Security   With only a few applications running on a server, it is less vulnerable to attacks.

The prerequisites for Server Core are basic. It requires the Windows Server 2012 R2 installation media, a product key, and the hardware on which to install it.

After you install the base operating system, you use PowerShell or the remote administrative tools to configure the network settings, add the machine to the domain, create and format disks, and install roles and features. It takes only a few minutes to install Server Core, depending on the hardware.

One of the new things to keep in mind is that you can upgrade or downgrade to Server Core or MinShell. In Windows Server 2008 R2 and Windows Server 2008, if you wanted to switch your Windows Server GUI to Server Core, or vice versa, there was no way to convert to a full Windows Server installation or a Server Core installation without reinstalling the operating system. In Windows Server 2012 R2, the Server Core or GUI installation options are no longer an irreversible selection made during setup. An administrator now has the ability to convert between a Server Core installation and a full installation as needed.

 Real World Scenario

Better Security

When I started in this industry more than 20 years ago, I was a programmer. I used to program computer hospital systems. When I switched to the networking world, I continued to work under contract with hospitals and with doctors' offices.

One problem I ran into is that many doctors are affiliated with hospitals, but they don't actually have offices within the hospital. Generally, they have offices either near the hospital or, in some cases, right across the street.

Here is the issue: Do we put servers in the doctors' offices, or do we make the doctor log into the hospital network through a remote connection? Doctors' offices normally don't have computer rooms, and we don't want to place a domain controller or server on someone's desk. It's just unsafe!

This is where Windows Server 2012 R2 Server Core can come into play. Since it is a slimmed-down version of Windows and there is no GUI, it makes it harder for anyone in the office to hack into the system. Also, Microsoft introduced a new domain controller in Windows Server 2008 called a *read-only domain controller (RODC)*. As its name suggests, it is a read-only version of a domain controller (explained in detail later in this book).

With Server Core and an RODC, you can feel safer placing a server on someone's desk or in any office. Server Core systems allow you to place servers in areas that you would never have placed them before. This can be a great advantage to businesses that have small, remote locations without full server rooms.

If you have a server that is running Server Core, there may be a situation in which you need to use the graphical user interfaces available only in Windows Server 2012 R2 with a GUI mode. Windows Server 2012 and Windows Server 2012 R2 allow you to switch the Server Core system to a Server with a GUI mode, or vice versa.

To convert from a Windows 2012 or Windows Server 2012 R2 Server Core system to Server with a GUI mode, run this code snippet (a restart is required):

```
Install-WindowsFeature Server-Gui-Mgmt-Infra,Server-Gui-Shell -Restart
```

To convert from Server Core mode to Server with a GUI mode, follow these steps when the server is initially installed in Server Core mode:

1. Determine the index number for a server with a GUI image (for example, SERVERDATA-CENTER, not SERVERDATACENTERCORE) using this cmdlet:

   ```
   Get-WindowsImage -ImagePath path to wim\install.wim
   ```

2. Run this line of code:

   ```
   Install-WindowsFeature Server-Gui-Mgmt-Infra,Server-Gui-Shell -Restart
   -Source wim: path to wim\install.wim: Index # from step 1
   ```

3. Alternatively, if you want to use Windows Update as the source instead of a WIM file, use this Windows PowerShell cmdlet:

   ```
   Install-WindowsFeature Server-Gui-Mgmt-Infra,Server-Gui-Shell -Restart
   ```

After you have completed the management tasks, you can switch the server back to Server Core mode whenever it is convenient (a restart is required) with this Windows PowerShell cmdlet:

```
Uninstall-WindowsFeature Server-Gui-Mgmt-Infra -restart
```

NIC Teaming

NIC Teaming, also known as *load balancing and failover (LBFO)*, gives an administrator the ability to allow multiple network adapters on a system to be placed into a team. Independent hardware vendors (IHVs) have required NIC Teaming, but until Windows Server 2012, NIC Teaming was *not* part of the Windows Server Operating System.

To be able to use NIC Teaming, the computer system must have at least one Ethernet adapter. If you want to provide fault protection, an administrator must have a minimum of two Ethernet adapters. One advantage of Windows Server 2012 R2 is that an administrator can setup 32 network adapters in a NIC Team.

NIC Teaming is a very common practice when setting up virtualization. It is one way that you can have load balancing with Hyper-V.

NIC Teaming gives an administrator the ability to allow a virtual machine to use virtual network adapters in Hyper-V. The advantage of using NIC Teaming in Hyper-V is that the administrator can use it to connect to more than one Hyper-V switch. This allows Hyper-V to maintain connectivity even if the network adapter under the Hyper-V switch gets disconnected.

An administrator can configure NIC Teaming in either Server Manager or PowerShell.

Installing Windows Server 2012 R2

In the following sections, I am going to walk you through two different types of installs. I will show you how to do a full install of Windows 2012 Server with the GUI, and then I will show you how to install the Server Core version of the same software.

 For these labs, I am using the full release of Windows Server 2012 R2 Datacenter, but you can use Windows Server 2012 R2 Standard.

Installing with the GUI

In Exercise 1.1, I will show you how to install Windows Server 2012 R2 Datacenter with the GUI. The GUI represents the Windows applications on the Desktop and the operating system functions that you can control and navigate with a mouse. The Server Core version is a command-line version only—you cannot use a mouse with Server Core unless you are going to use the mouse wheel for scrolling.

Windows Installation

At the time of this writing, I used the first full release of Windows Server 2012 R2 Datacenter. For this reason, there may be screens that have changed somewhat since this book was published.

EXERCISE 1.1

Installing Windows Server 2012 R2 with the GUI

1. Insert the Windows Server 2012 R2 installation DVD, and restart the machine from the installation media.

2. At the first screen, Windows Server 2012 R2 will ask you to configure your language, time and currency, and keyboard. Make your selections, and click Next.

3. At the next screen, click Install Now.

4. Depending on what version of Windows Server 2012 R2 you have (MSDN, TechNet, and so on), you may be asked to enter a product key. If this screen appears, enter your product key and click Next. If this screen does not appear, just go to step 5.

5. The Select The Operating System That You Want To Install screen then appears. Choose the Windows Server 2012 R2 Datacenter (Server With A GUI) selection and click Next.

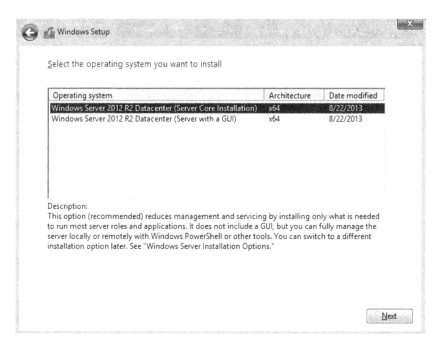

6. The license terms screen appears. After reading the Windows Server 2012 R2 license agreement, check the I Accept The License Terms check box and click Next.

7. On the Which Type Of Installation Do You Want? screen, choose Custom: Install Windows Only (Advanced).

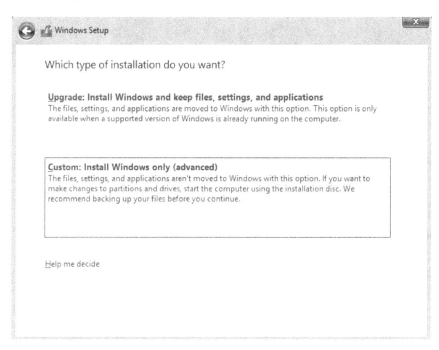

8. The next screen will ask you where you want to install Windows. If your hard disk is already formatted as NTFS, click the drive and then click Next. If the hard disk is not yet set up or formatted, choose the New link and create a partition. After creating the partition, click the Format link. Once the format is done, make sure you choose the new partition and click Next.

9. The Installing Windows screen will appear next. This is where the files from your media will be installed onto the system. The machine will reboot during this installation.

10. After the machine is finished rebooting, a screen requesting the administrator password will appear. Type in your password. (**P@ssword** is used in this exercise.) Your password must meet the password complexity requirements (one capitalized letter, one number, and/or one special character). Click Finish.

11. Next, log into the system. Press Ctrl+Alt+Del, and type in the administrator password. The machine will set up the properties of the administrator account.

12. Notice that the Server Manager dashboard automatically appears. Your Windows Server 2012 R2 installation is now complete.

13. Close Server Manager.

After you have logged into the Windows Server 2012 R2 Datacenter system, you will notice some big changes. The first is that the Start button in the lower-left corner of the screen has changed its look. Also, you can get to a Start button by clicking the Windows key (see Figure 1.2).

FIGURE 1.2   Windows key on a standard keyboard

Installing Windows Server 2012 R2 Server Core

In Exercise 1.2, you will learn how to install Windows Server 2012 R2 Server Core. You'll notice that the steps are similar to the ones in Exercise 1.1, with a couple of exceptions. As mentioned earlier, Server Core is a command-line configuration of Windows Server 2012 R2.

EXERCISE 1.2

Installing Windows Server 2012 R2 Using Server Core

1. Insert the Windows Server 2012 R2 installation DVD, and restart the machine from the installation media.

2. At the first screen, Windows Server 2012 R2 will prompt you to configure your language, time and currency, and keyboard. Make your selections, and click Next.

3. At the next screen, click Install Now.

4. Depending on what version of Windows Server 2012 R2 you have (MSDN, TechNet, and so on), you may be asked to enter a product key. If this screen appears, enter your product key and click Next. If this screen does not appear, just go to step 5.

5. The Select The Operating System That You Want To Install screen then appears. Choose the Windows Server 2012 R2 Datacenter (Server Core Installation) selection and click Next.

6. The license terms screen appears. After reading the Windows Server 2012 R2 license agreement, check the I Accept The License Terms check box and click Next.

7. At the Which Type Of Installation Do You Want? screen, choose Custom: Install Windows Only (Advanced).

8. The next screen will ask you where you want to install Windows. If your hard disk is already formatted as NTFS, click the drive and then click Next. If the hard disk is not set up or formatted, choose the New link and create a partition. After creating the partition, click the Format link. Once the format is done, make sure you choose the new partition and click Next.

9. The Installing Windows screen will appear next. This is where the files from your media will be installed onto the system. The machine will reboot during this installation.

10. After the machine is finished rebooting, a screen requesting the administrator password will appear. Type in your password. (**P@ssword** is used in this exercise.) Your password must meet the password complexity requirements (one capitalized letter, one number, and/or one special character).

11. Log into the system. Press Ctrl+Alt+Del, and type in the administrator password. The machine will set up the properties of the administrator account.

12. You will notice that the command prompt will automatically appear. Your Windows Server 2012 R2 Server Core installation is now complete.

13. To log out or turn off the machine, press Ctrl+Alt+Del and then click Sign Out.

After Windows Server 2012 R2 server is installed, you need to look at how to manage and configure the server. In the next section, you will learn how to manage a server remotely and with Windows PowerShell.

Using Windows Deployment Services

Another way that many IT departments deploy operating systems has been through the use of Windows Deployment Services (WDS). WDS allows an IT administrator to install a Windows operating system without using an installation disc. Using WDS allows you to deploy the operating system through a network installation. WDS can deploy Windows XP, Windows Server 2003, Windows Vista, Windows 7, Windows 8, Windows Server 2008/2008 R2, Microsoft Windows 2012, and Microsoft Windows Server 2012 R2.

The following are some of the advantages of using WDS for automated installation:

- You can remotely install Windows 7/Windows 8.

- The procedure simplifies management of the server image by allowing you to access Windows 7/8 distribution files from a distribution server.

- You can quickly recover the operating system in the event of a computer failure.

Here are the basic steps of the WDS process from a PXE-enabled WDS client:

1. The WDS client initiates a special boot process through the PXE network adapter (and the computer's BIOS configured for a network boot). On a PXE client, the user presses F12 to start the PXE boot process and to indicate that they want to perform a WDS installation.

2. A list of available Windows PE boot images is displayed. The user should select the appropriate Windows PE boot image from the boot menu.

3. The Windows Welcome screen is displayed. The user should click the Next button.

4. The WDS user is prompted to enter credentials for accessing and installing images from the WDS server.

5. A list of available operating system images is displayed. The user should select the appropriate image file to install.

6. The WDS user is prompted to enter the product key for the selected image.

7. The Partition And Configure The Disk screen is displayed. This screen provides the ability to install a mass storage device driver, if needed, by pressing F6.

8. The image copy process is initiated, and the selected image is copied to the WDS client computer.

The following sections describe how to set up the WDS server and the WDS clients and how to install Windows 7/8 through WDS.

Preparing the WDS Server

With the WDS server, you can manage and distribute Windows 7/8 operating system images to WDS client computers. The WDS server contains any files necessary for PXE booting, Windows PE boot images, and the Windows 7/8 images to be deployed.

The following steps for preparing the WDS server are discussed in the upcoming sections:

1. Make sure that the server meets the requirements for running WDS.

2. Install WDS.

3. Configure and start WDS.

4. Configure the WDS server to respond to client computers (if this was not configured when WDS was installed).

For WDS to work, the server on which you will install WDS must meet the requirements for WDS and be able to access the required network services.

WDS Server Requirements

The WDS server must meet these requirements:

- The computer must be a domain controller or a member of an Active Directory domain.

- At least one partition on the server must be formatted as NTFS.

- WDS must be installed on the server.

- The operating system must be Windows Server 2003, Windows Server 2008/2008 R2, Windows Server 2012, or Windows Server 2012 R2.

- A network adapter must be installed.

Network Services

The following network services must be running on the WDS server or be accessible to the WDS server from another network server:

- TCP/IP installed and configured.

- A DHCP server, which is used to assign DHCP addresses to WDS clients. (Ensure that your DHCP scope has enough addresses to accommodate all of the WDS clients that will need IP addresses.)

- A DNS server, which is used to locate the Active Directory controller.

- Active Directory, which is used to locate WDS servers and WDS clients as well as authorize WDS clients and manage WDS configuration settings and client installation options.

Installing the WDS Server Components

You can configure WDS on a Windows Server 2003/2008/2008 R2, Windows Server 2012, or Windows Server 2012 R2 computer by using the Windows Deployment Services Configuration Wizard or by using the WDSUTIL command-line utility. Table 1.3 describes the WDSUTIL command-line options.

TABLE 1.3 WDSUTIL command-line options

WDSUTIL Option	Description
/initialize-server	Initializes the configuration of the WDS server
/uninitialized-server	Undoes any changes made during the initialization of the WDS server
/add	Adds images and devices to the WDS server
/convert-ripimage	Converts Remote Installation Preparation (RIPrep) images to WIM images
/remove	Removes images from the server
/set	Sets information in images, image groups, WDS servers, and WDS devices
/get	Gets information from images, image groups, WDS servers, and WDS devices
/new	Creates new capture images or discover images
/copy- image	Copies images from the image store
/export-image	Exports to WIM files images contained within the image store
/start	Starts WDS services
/stop	Stops WDS services
/disable	Disables WDS services
/enable	Enables WDS services
/approve-autoadddevices	Approves Auto-Add devices
/reject-autoadddevices	Rejects Auto-Add devices
/delete-autoadddevices	Deletes records from the Auto-Add database
/update	Uses a known good resource to update a server resource

The first step in setting up WDS to deploy operating systems to the clients is to install the WDS role. You do this by using Server Manager.

One of the advantages of using the Windows deployment server is that WDS can work with Windows image (.wim) files. Windows image files can be created through the use of the Windows Sysprep utility.

One component to which you need to pay attention when using the Windows deployment server is *Preboot Execution Environment (PXE)* network devices. PXE boot devices are network interface cards (NICs) that can talk to a network without the need for an operating system. PXE boot NIC adapters are network adapters that have a set of preboot commands within the boot firmware.

This is important when using WDS because PXE boot adapters connect to a WDS server and request the data needed to load the operating system remotely. Remember, most of the machines for which you are using WDS do not have an operating system on the computer. You need NIC adapters that can connect to a network without the need for an operating system for WDS to work properly.

For the same reason, you must set up DHCP to accept PXE machines. Those machines need a valid TCP/IP address so that they can connect to the WDS server.

Preparing the WDS Client

The WDS client is the computer on which Windows 7/8 will be installed. WDS clients rely on a technology called PXE, which allows the client computer to boot remotely and connect to a WDS server.

To act as a WDS client, the computer must meet all of the hardware requirements for Windows 7/Windows 8 and have a PXE-capable network adapter installed, and a WDS server must be present on the network. Additionally, the user account used to install the image must be a member of the Domain Users group in Active Directory.

After the WDS server has been installed and configured, you can install Windows 7/Windows 8 on a WDS client that uses a PXE-compliant network card.

To install Windows 7/Windows 8 on the WDS client, follow these steps:

1. Start the computer. When prompted, press F12 for a network service boot. The Windows PE appears.

2. The Windows Welcome screen appears. Click the Next button to start the installation process.

3. Enter the username and password of an account that has permissions to access and install images from the WDS server.

4. A list of available operating system images stored on the WDS server appears. Select the image to install and click Next.

5. Enter the product key for the selected Windows 7/8 image and click Next.

6. The Partition And Configure The Disk screen appears. Select the desired disk-partitioning options, or click OK to use the default options.

7. Click Next to initiate the image-copying process. The Windows Setup process will begin after the image is copied to the WDS client computer.

Understanding Features On Demand

One of the problems in previous versions of Windows Server was how roles and features were stored on the hard disk. Before the introduction of Windows Server 2012, even if a server role or feature was disabled on a server, the binary files for that role or feature were still present on the disk. The problem with this approach is that, even if you disable the role, it still consumes space on your hard drive.

Features On Demand in Windows Server 2012 R2 solves this issue because not only can administrators disable a role or feature, they can also completely remove the role or feature's files.

Once this is done, a state of Removed is shown in Server Manager, or the state of Disabled With Payload Removed is shown in the Dism.exe utility. To reinstall a role or feature that has been completely removed, you must have access to the installation files.

If you want to remove a role or feature completely from the system, use -Remove with the Uninstall-WindowsFeature cmdlet of Windows PowerShell. For example, if you want to remove Windows Explorer, Internet Explorer, and all dependent components completely, run the following Windows PowerShell command:

```
Uninstall-WindowsFeature Server-Gui-Shell -Remove
```

If you want to reinstall a role or feature that has been removed completely, use the Windows PowerShell -Source option of the Install-WindowsFeature Server Manager cmdlet. Using the -Source option states the path where the WIM image files and the index number of the image will be located. If an administrator decides not to use the -Source option, Windows will use Windows Update by default.

When you're using the Features On Demand configuration, if feature files are not available on the server computer and the installation requires those feature files, Windows Server 2012 R2 can be directed to get those files from a side-by-side feature store, which is a shared folder that contains feature files. It is available to the server on the network, from Windows Update, or from installation media. This can be overwritten using the -Source option in the Windows PowerShell utility.

Source Files for Roles or Features

Offline virtual hard disks (VHDs) cannot be used as a source for installing roles or features that have been completely removed. Only sources for the same version of Windows Server 2012 R2 are supported.

To install a removed role or feature using a WIM image, follow these steps:

1. Run the following command:

    ```
    Get-windowsimage -imagepath \install.wim
    ```

In step 1, *imagepath* is the path where the WIM files are located.

2. Run the following command:

   `Install-WindowsFeature featurename -Source wim: path:index`

   In step 2, *featurename* is the name of the role or feature from `Get-WindowsFeature`. *path* is the path to the WIM mount point, and *index* is the index of the server image from step 1.

To add or remove a role or feature, you must have administrative rights to the Windows Server 2012 R2 machine.

Storage in Windows Server 2012 R2

As an IT administrator, you'll need to ask many questions before you start setting up a server. What type of disks should be used? What type of RAID sets should be made? What type of hardware platform should be purchased? These are all questions you must ask when planning for storage in a Windows Server 2012 R2 server. In the following sections, I will answer these questions so that you can make the best decisions for storage in your network's environment.

Initializing Disks

To begin, I must first discuss how to add disk drives to a server. Once a disk drive has been physically installed, it must be initialized by selecting the type of partition. Different types of partition styles are used to initialize disks: *Master Boot Record (MBR)* and *GUID Partition Table (GPT)*.

MBR has a partition table that indicates where the partitions are located on the disk drive, and with this particular partition style, only volumes up to 2TB (2,048GB) are supported. An MBR drive can have up to four primary partitions or can have three primary partitions and one extended partition that can be divided into unlimited logical drives.

Windows Server 2012 R2 can only boot off an MBR disk unless it is based on the Extensible Firmware Interface (EFI); then it can boot from GPT. An Itanium server is an example of an EFI-based system. GPT is not constrained by the same limitations as MBR. In fact, a GPT disk drive can support volumes of up to 18EB (18,874,368 million terabytes) and 128 partitions. As a result, GPT is recommended for disks larger than 2TB or disks used on Itanium-based computers. Exercise 1.3 demonstrates the process of initializing additional disk drives to an active computer running Windows Server 2012 R2. If you're not adding a new drive, then stop after step 4. I am completing this exercise using Computer Management, but you also can do this exercise using Server Manager.

EXERCISE 1.3

Initializing Disk Drives

1. Open Computer Management under Administrative Tools.

2. Select Disk Management.

3. After disk drives have been installed, right-click Disk Management and select Rescan Disks.

4. A pop-up box appears indicating that the server is scanning for new disks. If you did not add a new disk, go to step 9.

5. After the server has completed the scan, the new disk appears as Unknown.

6. Right-click the Unknown disk, and select Initialize Disk.

7. A pop-up box appears asking for the partition style. For this exercise, choose MBR.

8. Click OK.

9. Close Computer Management.

The disk will now appear online as a basic disk with unallocated space.

Configuring Basic and Dynamic Disks

Windows Server 2012 R2 supports two types of disk configurations: basic and dynamic. Basic disks are divided into partitions and can be used with previous versions of Windows. Dynamic disks are divided into volumes and can be used with Windows 2000 Server and newer releases.

When a disk is initialized, it is automatically created as a basic disk, but when a new fault-tolerant (RAID) volume set is created, the disks in the set are converted to dynamic disks. Fault-tolerance features and the ability to modify disks without having to reboot the server are what distinguish dynamic disks from basic disks.

 Fault tolerance (RAID) is discussed in detail later in this chapter in the "Redundant Array of Independent Disks" section.

A basic disk can simply be converted to a dynamic disk without loss of data. When a basic disk is converted, the partitions are automatically changed to the appropriate volumes. However, converting a dynamic disk back to a basic disk is not as simple. First, all the data on the dynamic disk must be backed up or moved. Then, all the volumes on the dynamic disk have to be deleted. The dynamic disk can then be converted to a basic disk. Partitions and logical drives can be created, and the data can be restored.

The following are actions that can be performed on basic disks:

- Formatting partitions
- Marking partitions as active
- Creating and deleting primary and extended partitions
- Creating and deleting logical drives
- Converting from a basic disk to a dynamic disk

The following are actions that can be performed on dynamic disks:

- Creating and deleting simple, striped, spanned, mirrored, or RAID-5 volumes
- Removing or breaking a mirrored volume
- Extending simple or spanned volumes
- Repairing mirrored or RAID-5 volumes
- Converting from a dynamic disk to a basic disk after deleting all volumes

In Exercise 1.4, you'll convert a basic disk to a dynamic disk.

EXERCISE 1.4

Converting a Basic Disk to a Dynamic Disk

1. Open Computer Management under Administrative Tools.

2. Select Disk Management.

3. Right-click a basic disk that you want to convert and select Convert To Dynamic Disk.

4. The Convert To Dynamic Disk dialog box appears. From here, select all of the disks that you want to convert to dynamic disks. In this exercise, only one disk will be converted.

5. Click OK.

6. The Convert To Dynamic Disk dialog box changes to the Disks To Convert dialog box and shows the disk/disks that will be converted to dynamic disks.

7. Click Convert.

8. Disk Management will warn that if you convert the disk to dynamic, you will not be able to start the installed operating system from any volume on the disk (except the current boot volume). Click Yes.

9. Close Computer Management.

The converted disk will now show as Dynamic in Disk Management.

Managing Volumes

A *volume set* is created from volumes that span multiple drives by using the free space from those drives to construct what will appear to be a single drive. The following list includes the various types of volume sets and their definitions:

- *Simple volume* uses only one disk or a portion of a disk.

- *Spanned volume* is a simple volume that spans multiple disks, with a maximum of 32. Use a spanned volume if the volume needs are too great for a single disk.

- *Striped volume* stores data in stripes across two or more disks. A striped volume gives you fast access to data but is not fault tolerant, nor can it be extended or mirrored. If one disk in the striped set fails, the entire volume fails.

- *Mirrored volume* duplicates data across two disks. This type of volume is fault tolerant because if one drive fails, the data on the other disk is unaffected.

- *RAID-5 volume* stores data in stripes across three or more disks. This type of volume is fault tolerant because if a drive fails, the data can be re-created from the parity off of the remaining disk drives. Operating system files and boot files cannot reside on the RAID-5 disks.

Exercise 1.5 illustrates the procedure for creating a volume set.

Creating a Volume Set

1. Open Computer Management under Administrative Tools.

2. Select Disk Management.

3. Select and right-click a disk that has unallocated space. If there are no disk drives available for a particular volume set, that volume set will be grayed out as a selectable option. In this exercise, you'll choose a spanned volume set, but the process after the volume set selection is the same regardless of which kind you choose. The only thing that differs is the number of disk drives chosen.

4. The Welcome page of the New Spanned Volume Wizard appears and explains the type of volume set chosen. Click Next.

5. The Select Disks page appears. Select the disk that will be included with the volume set and click Add. Repeat this process until all of the desired disks have been added. Click Next.

6. The Assign Drive Letter Or Path page appears. From here you can select the desired drive letter for the volume, mount the volume in an empty NTFS folder, or choose not to assign a drive letter. The new volume is labeled as E. Click Next.

7. The Format Volume page appears. Choose to format the new volume. Click Next.

8. Click Finish.

9. If the disks have not been converted to dynamic, you will be asked to convert the disks. Click Yes.

The new volume will appear as a healthy spanned dynamic volume with the new available disk space of the new volume set.

Storage Spaces in Windows Server 2012 R2

Windows Server 2012 R2 includes a technology called *Storage Spaces*. Windows Server 2012 R2 allows an administrator to virtualize storage by grouping disks into storage pools. These storage pools can then be turned into virtual disks called *storage spaces*.

The Storage Spaces technology allows an administrator to have a highly available, scalable, low-cost, and flexible solution for both physical and virtual installations. Storage Spaces allows you to set up this advantage on either a single server or in scalable multinode mode. So, before going any further, let's look at these two terms that you must understand.

Storage Pools   *Storage pools* are a group of physical disks that allows an administrator to delegate administration, expand disk sizes, and group disks together.

Storage Spaces   *Storage spaces* allow an administrator to take free space from storage pools and create virtual disks called storage spaces. Storage spaces give administrators the ability to have precise control, resiliency, and storage tiers.

Storage spaces and storage pools can be managed by an administrator through the use of the Windows Storage Management API, Server Manager, or Windows PowerShell.

One of the advantages of using the Storage Spaces technology is the ability to set up resiliency. There are three types of Storage Space resiliency: mirror, parity, and simple (no resiliency).

Fault tolerance (RAID) is discussed in detail in the "Redundant Array of Independent Disks" section.

Now that you understand what storage spaces and storage pools do, let's take a look at some of the other advantages of using these features in Windows Server 2012 R2.

Availability   One advantage to the Storage Spaces technology is the ability to fully integrate the storage space with failover clustering. This advantage allows administrators to achieve service deployments that are continuously available. Administrators have the ability to set up storage pools to be clustered across multiple nodes within a single cluster.

Tiered Storage   The Storage Spaces technology allows virtual disks to be created with a two-tier storage setup. For data that is used often, you have an SSD tier; for data that is not used often, you use an HDD tier. The Storage Spaces technology will automatically transfer data at a subfile level between the two different tiers based on how often the data is used. Because of tiered storage, performance is greatly increased for data that is used most often, and data that is not used often still gets the advantage of being stored on a low-cost storage option.

Delegation   One advantage of using storage pools is that administrators have the ability to control access by using access control lists (ACLs). What is nice about this advantage is that each storage pool can have its own unique access control lists. Storage pools are fully integrated with Active Directory Domain Services.

Redundant Array of Independent Disks

The ability to support drive sets and arrays using *Redundant Array of Independent Disks (RAID)* technology is built into Windows Server 2012 R2. RAID can be used to enhance data performance, or it can be used to provide fault tolerance to maintain data integrity in case of a hard disk failure. Windows Server 2012 R2 supports three types of RAID technologies: RAID-0, RAID-1, and RAID-5.

RAID-0 (Disk Striping)   *Disk striping* is using two or more volumes on independent disks created as a single striped set. There can be a maximum of 32 disks. In a striped set, data is divided into blocks that are distributed sequentially across all of the drives in the set. With RAID-0 disk striping, you get very fast read and write performance because multiple blocks of data can be accessed from multiple drives simultaneously. However, RAID-0 does not offer the ability to maintain data integrity during a single disk failure. In other words, RAID-0 is not fault tolerant; a single disk event will cause the entire striped set to be lost, and it will have to be re-created through some type of recovery process, such as a tape backup.

RAID-1 (Disk Mirroring)   *Disk mirroring* is two logical volumes on two separate identical disks created as a duplicate disk set. Data is written on two disks at the same time; that way, in the event of a disk failure, data integrity is maintained and available. Although this fault tolerance gives administrators data redundancy, it comes with a price because it diminishes the amount of available storage space by half. For example, if an administrator wants to create a 300GB mirrored set, they would have to install two 300GB hard drives into the server, thus doubling the cost for the same available space.

RAID-5 Volume (Disk Striping with Parity)   With a RAID-5 volume, you have the ability to use a minimum of three disks and a maximum of 32 disks. RAID-5 volumes allow data to be striped across all of the disks with an additional block of error-correction called parity. *Parity* is used to reconstruct the data in the event of a disk failure. RAID-5 has slower write performance than the other RAID types because the OS must calculate the parity information for each stripe that is written, but the read performance is equivalent to a stripe set, RAID-0, because the parity information is not read. Like RAID-1, RAID-5 comes with additional cost considerations. For every RAID-5 set, roughly an entire hard disk is consumed for storing the parity information. For example, a minimum RAID-5 set requires three hard disks, and if those disks are 300GB each, approximately 600GB of disk space is available to the OS and 300GB is consumed by parity information, which equates to 33.3 percent of the available space. Similarly, in a five-disk RAID-5 set of 300GB disks, approximately 1,200GB of disk space is available to the OS, which means that 20 percent of the total available space is consumed by the parity information. The words *roughly* and *approximately* are used when calculating disk space because a 300GB disk will really be only about 279GB of space. This is because vendors define a gigabyte as 1 billion bytes, but the OS defines it as 2^{30} (1,073,741,824) bytes. Also, remember that file systems and volume managers have overhead as well.

Software RAID is a nice option for a small company, but hardware RAID is definitely a better option if the money is available.

Table 1.4 breaks down the various aspects of the supported RAID types in Window Server 2012 R2.

TABLE 1.4   Supported RAID-level properties in Windows Server 2012 R2

RAID Level	RAID Type	Fault Tolerant	Advantages	Minimum Number of Disks	Maximum Number of Disks
0	Disk striping	No	Fast reads and writes	2	32
1	Disk mirroring	Yes	Data redundancy and faster writes than RAID-5	2	2
5	Disk striping with parity	Yes	Data redundancy with less overhead and faster reads than RAID-1	3	32

Creating RAID Sets

Now that you understand the concepts of RAID and how to use it, you can look at the creation of RAID sets in Windows Server 2012 R2. The process of creating a RAID set is the same as the process for creating a simple or spanned volume set, except for the minimum disk requirements associated with each RAID type.

Creating a mirrored volume set is basically the same as creating a volume set, as shown in Exercise 1.6, except that you will select New Mirrored Volume. It is after the disk select wizard appears that you'll begin to see the difference. Since a new mirrored volume is being created, the volume requires two disks.

During the disk select process, if only one disk is selected, the Next button will be unavailable because the disk minimum has not been met. Refer to Figure 1.3 to view the Select Disks page of the New Mirrored Volume Wizard during the creation of a new mirrored volume, and notice that the Next button is not available.

FIGURE 1.3   Select Disks page of the New Mirrored Volume Wizard

To complete the process, you must select a second disk by highlighting the appropriate disk and adding it to the volume set. Once the second disk has been added, the Add button becomes unavailable, and the Next button is available to complete the mirrored volume set creation (see Figure 1.4).

FIGURE 1.4   Adding the second disk to complete a mirrored volume set

After you click Next, the creation of the mirrored volume set is again just like the rest of the steps in Exercise 1.5. A drive letter will have to be assigned, and the volume will need to be formatted. The new mirrored volume set will appear in Disk Management. In Figure 1.5, notice that the capacity of the volume equals one disk even though two disks have been selected.

FIGURE 1.5   Newly created mirrored volume set

To create a RAID-5 volume set, you use the same process that you use to create a mirrored volume set. The only difference is that a RAID-5 volume set requires that a minimum of three disks be selected to complete the volume creation. The process is simple: Select New RAID-5 Volume, select the three disks that will be used in the volume set, assign a drive letter, and format the volume. Figure 1.6 shows a newly created RAID-5 volume set in Disk Management.

FIGURE 1.6   Newly created RAID-5 volume set

Mount Points

With the ever-increasing demands of storage, mount points are used to surpass the limitation of 26 drive letters and to join two volumes into a folder on a separate physical disk drive. A *mount point* allows you to configure a volume to be accessed from a folder on another existing disk.

Through Disk Management, a mount point folder can be assigned to a drive instead of using a drive letter, and it can be used on basic or dynamic volumes that are formatted with NTFS. However, mount point folders can be created only on empty folders within a volume. Additionally, mount point folder paths cannot be modified; they can be removed only once they have been created. Exercise 1.6 shows the steps to create a mount point.

EXERCISE 1.6

Creating Mount Points

1. Open Server Manager.

2. Click and then expand Storage.

3. Select Disk Management.

4. Right-click the volume where the mount point folder will be assigned, and select Change Drive Letter And Paths.

5. Click Add.

6. Either type the path to an empty folder on an NTFS volume or click Browse to select or make a new folder for the mount point.

When you explore the drive, you'll see the new folder created. Notice that the icon indicates that it is a mount point.

Microsoft MPIO

Multipath I/O (MPIO) is associated with high availability because a computer will be able to use a solution with redundant physical paths connected to a storage device. Thus, if one path fails, an application will continue to run because it can access the data across the other path.

The MPIO software provides the functionality needed for the computer to take advantage of the redundant storage paths. MPIO solutions can also load-balance data traffic across both paths to the storage device, virtually eliminating bandwidth bottlenecks to the computer. What allows MPIO to provide this functionality is the new native *Microsoft Device Specific Module (Microsoft DSM)*. The Microsoft DSM is a driver that communicates with storage devices—iSCSI, Fibre Channel, or SAS—and it provides the chosen load-balancing policies. Windows Server 2012 R2 supports the following load-balancing policies:

Failover In a failover configuration, there is no load balancing. There is a primary path that is established for all requests and subsequent standby paths. If the primary path fails, one of the standby paths will be used.

Failback This is similar to failover in that it has primary and standby paths. However, with failback you designate a preferred path that will handle all process requests until it fails, after which the standby path will become active until the primary reestablishes a connection and automatically regains control.

Round Robin In a round-robin configuration, all available paths will be active and will be used to distribute I/O in a balanced round-robin fashion.

Round Robin with a Subset of Paths In this configuration, a specific set of paths will be designated as a primary set and another as standby paths. All I/O will use the primary set of paths in a round-robin fashion until all of the sets fail. Only at this time will the standby paths become active.

Dynamic Least Queue Depth In a dynamic least queue depth configuration, I/O will route to the path with the least number of outstanding requests.

Weighted Path In a weighted path configuration, paths are assigned a numbered weight. I/O requests will use the path with the least weight—the higher the number, the lower the priority.

Exercise 1.7 demonstrates the process of installing the Microsoft MPIO feature for Windows Server 2012 R2.

EXERCISE 1.7

Installing Microsoft MPIO

1. Choose Server Manager by clicking the Server Manager icon on the Taskbar.

2. Click number 2, Add Roles And Features.

3. Choose role-based or feature-based installation and click Next.

4. Choose your server and click Next.

5. Click Next on the Roles screen.

6. On the Select Features screen, choose the Multipath I/O check box. Click Next.

7. On the Confirm Installation Selections page, verify that Multipath I/O is the feature that will be installed. Click Install.

8. After the installation completes, the Installation Results page appears stating that the server must be rebooted to finish the installation process.

9. Click Close.

10. Restart the system.

Typically, most storage arrays work with the Microsoft DSM. However, some hardware vendors require DSM software that is specific to their products. Third-party DSM software is installed through the MPIO utility as follows:

1. Open Administrative Tools ➢ MPIO.

2. Select the DSM Install tab (see Figure 1.7).

FIGURE 1.7   The DSM Install tab in the MPIO Properties dialog box

3. Add the path of the INF file and click Install.

iSCSI

Internet Small Computer System Interface (iSCSI) is an interconnect protocol used to establish and manage a connection between a computer (initiator) and a storage device (target). It does this by using a connection through TCP port 3260, which allows it to be used over a LAN, a WAN, or the Internet. Each initiator is identified by its iSCSI Qualified Name (iqn), and it is used to establish its connection to an iSCSI target.

iSCSI was developed to allow block-level access to a storage device over a network. This is different from using a network attached storage (NAS) device that connects through the use of Common Internet File System (CIFS) or Network File System (NFS).

Block-level access is important to many applications that require direct access to storage. Microsoft Exchange and Microsoft SQL are examples of applications that require direct access to storage.

By being able to leverage the existing network infrastructure, iSCSI was also developed as an alternative to Fibre Channel storage by alleviating the additional hardware costs associated with a Fibre Channel storage solution.

iSCSI also has another advantage over Fibre Channel in that it can provide security for the storage devices. iSCSI can use Challenge Handshake Authentication Protocol (CHAP or MS-CHAP) for authentication and Internet Protocol Security (IPsec) for encryption. Windows Server 2012 R2 is able to connect an iSCSI storage device out of the box with no additional software needing to be installed. This is because the Microsoft iSCSI initiator is built into the operating system.

Windows Server 2012 R2 supports two different ways to initiate an iSCSI session.

- Through the native Microsoft iSCSI software initiator that resides on Windows Server 2012 R2

- Using a hardware iSCSI host bus adapter (HBA) that is installed in the computer

Both the Microsoft iSCSI software initiator and iSCSI HBA present an iSCSI qualified name that identifies the host initiator. When the Microsoft iSCSI software initiator is used, the CPU utilization may be as much as 30 percent higher than on a computer with a hardware iSCSI HBA. This is because all of the iSCSI process requests are handled within the operating system. Using a hardware iSCSI HBA, process requests can be offloaded to the adapter, thus freeing the CPU overhead associated with the Microsoft iSCSI software initiator. However, iSCSI HBAs can be expensive, whereas the Microsoft iSCSI software initiator is free.

It is worthwhile to install the Microsoft iSCSI software initiator and perform load testing to see how much overhead the computer will have prior to purchasing an iSCSI HBA or HBAs, depending on the redundancy level. Exercise 1.8 explains how to install and configure an iSCSI connection.

EXERCISE 1.8

Configuring iSCSI Storage Connection

1. Click the Windows key or Start button in the left-hand corner ➢ Administrative Tools ➢ iSCSI Initiator.

2. If a dialog box appears, click Yes to start the service.

3.   Click the Discovery tab.

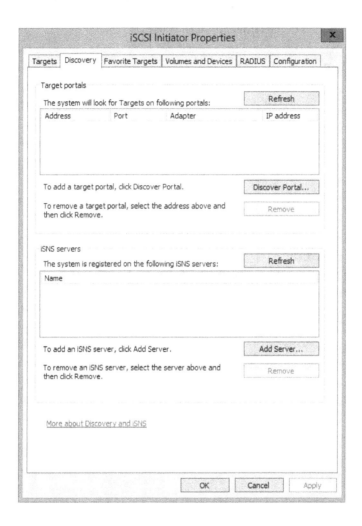

4.   In the Target Portals portion of the page, click Discover Portal.

5. Enter the IP address of the target portal and click OK.

6. The IP address of the target portal appears in the Target Portals box.

7. Click OK.

To use the storage that has now been presented to the server, you must create a volume on it and format the space. Refer to Exercise 1.3 to review this process.

Internet Storage Name Service

Internet Storage Name Service (iSNS) allows for central registration of an iSCSI environment because it automatically discovers available targets on the network. The purpose of iSNS is to help find available targets on a large iSCSI network.

The Microsoft iSCSI initiator includes an iSNS client that is used to register with the iSNS. The iSNS feature maintains a database of clients that it has registered either through

DCHP discovery or through manual registration. iSNS DHCP is available after the installation of the service, and it is used to allow iSNS clients to discover the location of the iSNS. However, if iSNS DHCP is not configured, iSNS clients must be registered manually with the iscsicli command.

To execute the command, launch a command prompt on a computer hosting the Microsoft iSCSI and type **iscsicli addisnsserver *server_name*,** where ***server_name*** is the name of the computer hosting iSNS. Exercise 1.9 walks you through the steps required to install the iSNS feature on Windows Server 2012 R2, and then it explains the different tabs in iSNS.

EXERCISE 1.9

Installing the iSNS Feature on Windows Server 2012 R2

1. Choose Server Manager by clicking the Server Manager icon on the Taskbar.

2. Click number 2 ➢ Add Roles And Features.

3. Choose role-based or featured-based installation and click Next.

4. Choose your server and click Next.

5. Click Next on the Roles screen.

6. On the Select Features screen, choose the iSNS Server Service check box. Click Next.

7. On the Confirmation screen, click the Install button.

8. Click the Close button. Close Server Manager and reboot.

9. Log in and open the iSNS server under Administrative Tools.

10. Click the General tab. This tab displays the list of registered initiators and targets. In addition to their iSCSI qualified name, it lists storage node type (Target or Initiator), alias string, and entity identifier (the Fully Qualified Domain Name [FQDN] of the machine hosting the iSNS client).

11. Click the Discovery Domains tab. The purpose of Discovery Domains is to provide a way to separate and group nodes. This is similar to zoning in Fibre Channel. The following options are available on the Discovery Domains tab:

- *Create* is used to create a new discovery domain.

- *Refresh* is used to repopulate the Discovery Domain drop-down list.

- *Delete* is used to delete the currently selected discovery domain.

- *Add* is used to add nodes that are already registered in iSNS to the currently selected discovery domain.

- *Add New* is used to add nodes by entering the iSCSI Qualified Name (iQN) of the node. These nodes do not have to be currently registered.

- *Remove Used* is used to remove selected nodes from the discovery domain.

12. Click the Discovery Domain Sets tab. The purpose of discovery domain sets is to separate further discovery domains. Discovery domains can be enabled or disabled, giving administrators the ability to restrict further the visibility of all initiators and targets. The options on the Discovery Domain Sets tab are as follows:

- The *Enable* check box is used to indicate the status of the discovery domain sets and to turn them off and on.

- *Create* is used to create new discovery domain sets.

- *Refresh* is used to repopulate the Discovery Domain Sets drop-down list.

- *Delete* is used to delete the currently selected discovery domain set.

- *Add* is used to add discovery domains to the currently selected discovery domain set.

- *Remove* is used to remove selected nodes from the discovery domain sets.

13. Close the iSNS server.

Fibre Channel

Fibre Channel storage devices are similar to iSCSI storage devices in that they both allow block-level access to their data sets and can provide MPIO policies with the proper hardware configurations. However, Fibre Channel requires a Fibre Channel HBA, fiber-optic cables, and Fibre Channel switches to connect to a storage device.

A *World Wide Name (WWN)* from the Fibre Channel HBA is used from the host and device so that they can communicate directly with each other, similar to using a NIC's MAC address. In other words, a logical unit number (LUN) is presented from a Fibre

Channel storage device to the WWN of the host's HBA. Fibre Channel has been the preferred method of storage because of the available connection bandwidth between the storage and the host.

Fibre Channel devices support 1Gb/s, 2Gb/s, and 4Gb/s connections, and they soon will support 8Gb/s connections, but now that 10Gb/s Ethernet networks are becoming more prevalent in many datacenters, iSCSI can be a suitable alternative. It is important to consider that 10Gb/s network switches can be more expensive than comparable Fibre Channel switches.

N-Port Identification Virtualization (NPIV) is a Fibre Channel facility allowing multiple n-port IDs to share a single physical N-Port. This allows multiple Fibre Channel initiators to occupy a single physical port. By using a single port, this eases hardware requirements in storage area network (SAN) design.

Network Attached Storage

The concept of a *network attached storage (NAS)* solution is that it is a low-cost device for storing data and serving files through the use of an Ethernet LAN connection. A NAS device accesses data at the file level via a communication protocol such as NFS, CIFS, or even HTTP, which is different from iSCSI or FC Fibre Channel storage devices that access the data at the block level. NAS devices are best used in file-storing applications, and they do not require a storage expert to install and maintain the device. In most cases, the only setup that is required is an IP address and an Ethernet connection.

Virtual Disk Service

Virtual Disk Service (VDS) was created to ease the administrative efforts involved in managing all of the various types of storage devices. Many storage hardware providers used their own applications for installation and management, and this made administering all of these various devices very cumbersome.

VDS is a set of application programming interfaces (APIs) that provides a centralized interface for managing all of the various storage devices. The native VDS API enables the management of disks and volumes at an OS level, and hardware vendor-supplied APIs manage the storage devices at a RAID level. These are known as software and hardware providers.

A *software provider* is host based, and it interacts with Plug and Play Manager because each disk is discovered and operates on volumes, disks, and disk partitions. VDS includes two software providers: basic and dynamic. The basic software provider manages basic disks with no fault tolerance, whereas the dynamic software providers manage dynamic disks with fault management. A hardware provider translates the VDS APIs into instructions specific to the storage hardware. This is how storage management applications are able to communicate with the storage hardware to create LUNs or Fibre Channel HBAs to view the WWN. The following are Windows Server 2012 R2 storage management applications that use VDS:

- The *Disk Management snap-in* is an application that allows you to configure and manage the disk drives on the host computer. You have already seen this application in use when you initialized disks and created volume sets.

- DiskPart is a command-line utility that configures and manages disks, volumes, and partitions on the host computer. It can also be used to script many of the storage management commands. DiskPart is a robust tool that you should study on your own because it is beyond the scope of this book. Figure 1.8 shows the various commands and their function in the DiskPart utility.

FIGURE 1.8   DiskPart commands

- DiskRAID is also a scriptable command-line utility that configures and manages hardware RAID storage systems. However, at least one VDS hardware provider must be installed for DiskRAID to be functional. DiskRAID is another useful utility that you should study on your own because it's beyond the scope of this book.

Booting from a VHD

Once you have installed each operating system, you can choose the operating system that you will boot to during the boot process. You will see a boot selection screen that asks you to choose which operating system you want to boot.

The Boot Configuration Data (BCD) store contains boot information parameters that were previously found in boot.ini in older versions of Windows. To edit the boot options in the BCD store, use the bcdedit utility, which can be launched only from a command prompt. To open a command prompt window, do the following:

1. Launch \Windows\system32\cmd.exe.

2. Open the Run command by pressing the Windows key plus the R key and then entering **cmd**.

3. Type **cmd.exe** in the Search Programs And Files box and press Enter.

After the command prompt window is open, type **bcdedit** to launch the bcdedit utility. You can also type **bcdedit /?** to see all of the different bcdedit commands.

Virtualization is covered in greater detail in Chapter 9: "Use Virtualization in Windows Server 2012."

Summary

In this chapter, you studied the latest advantages of using Windows Server 2012 R2. You also learned about the different roles and features you can install on a Windows Server 2012 R2 machine. You also explored how to migrate those roles and features from a Windows Server 2008, 2008 R2, and Windows Server 2012 machine to a Windows Server 2012 R2 machine.

I discussed the different upgrade paths that are available and which upgrades are best for your current network setup. You learned that another important issue to decide when installing Windows Server 2012 R2 is whether to use Server Core or the GUI installation.

You learned how to install Windows Server 2012 R2 Datacenter with GUI, and you installed the Windows Server 2012 R2 Server Core. Remember, Server Core is a slimmed-down version of Windows Server. With no GUI desktop available, it's a safer alternative to a normal Windows install. As discussed, a nice advantage of Windows Server 2012 R2 is that you can change from Server Core to the GUI version and back again.

I discussed a feature called Features On Demand. This feature allows you to remove roles and features from the operating system and remove the associated files completely from the hard drive, thus saving disk space.

You examined the various aspects of Windows Server 2012 R2 storage services as well as the various types of storage technologies and native Windows Server 2012 R2 storage management tools. I started the chapter by discussing initializing disks and choosing a partition type: MBR or GPT. I then discussed the types of disk configurations, dynamic and basic, that are supported in Windows Server 2012 R2. You learned that various properties are associated with each type of configuration. Then I discussed the different types of RAID and the properties of each.

The next section explored storage technologies, namely, iSCSI, Fibre Channel, and NAS. I primarily focused on iSCSI because of the native support in Window Server 2012 R2. You learned how to configure an iSCSI initiator and a connection to an iSCSI target. After that, you looked at its iSNS server and how to configure it.

The chapter concluded by looking at Storage Manager for SANs and Storage Explorer, which are built-in management tools in Windows Server 2012 R2 for storage devices and firewall settings.

Exam Essentials

Understand the upgrade paths.   It's important to make sure you understand the different upgrade paths from Windows Server 2008 R2 with SP1 and Windows Server 2012 to Windows Server 2012 R2.

Understand Windows Server 2012 R2 server roles.   Understand what the Windows Server 2012 R2 server roles do for an organization and its users.

Understand Windows Server 2012 R2 GUI vs. Server Core.   Understand the difference between the Windows Server 2012 R2 GUI version and the Windows Server 2012 R2 Server Core version. Know the benefits of using Server Core, and know that you can convert between the two different versions.

Understand Features On Demand.   Understand the new feature called Features On Demand. Microsoft loves to ask exam questions about its new features, and this will be no exception. Understand how features and roles stay on the system until you physically remove them from the hard drive.

Know disk types.   Know how to initialize disks and the type of partitioning to choose. Also know the difference between dynamic and basic disks and when to use them.

Understand RAID.   Know the various RAID types, the requirements for each, and when it is appropriate to use each type.

Know storage technologies.   Understand how to use the storage technologies Fibre Channel, iSCSI, and NAS. Know how to configure an iSCSI initiator and how to establish a connection to a target. Know the various MPIO policies.

Understand how to manage storage.   Know what type of administrative features are available for Storage Manager for SANs and Storage Explorer.

Review Questions

1. You are the administrator for the ABC Company. You are looking to install Windows Server 2012 R2, and you need to decide which version to install. You need to install a version of Windows that is just for logon authentication and nothing else. You want the most secure option and cost is not an issue. What should you install?

    A. Windows Server 2012 R2 Datacenter with GUI

    B. Windows Server 2012 R2 Datacenter Server Core

    C. Windows Server 2012 R2 Standard with GUI

    D. Windows Server 2012 R2 Web Server Core

2. You are the IT manager for a large organization. One of your co-workers installed a new Windows Server 2012 R2 Datacenter Server Core machine, but now the IT team has decided that it should be a Windows Server 2012 R2 Datacenter with GUI. What should you do?

    A. Reinstall Windows Server 2012 R2 Datacenter Server Core on the same machine.

    B. Install a new machine with Windows Server 2012 R2 Datacenter Server Core.

    C. Convert the current Windows Server 2012 R2 Datacenter Server Core to the Windows Server 2012 R2 Datacenter with GUI version.

    D. Dual-boot the machine with both Windows Server 2012 R2 Datacenter Server Core and Windows Server 2012 R2 Datacenter with GUI.

3. You are the administrator for your company, and you are looking at upgrading your Windows Server 2008 web server to Windows Server 2012 R2. Which version of Windows Server 2012 R2 does Microsoft recommend you use?

    A. Windows Server 2012 R2 Datacenter

    B. Windows Server 2012 R2 Standard

    C. Windows Server 2012 R2 Essentials

    D. Windows Server 2012 R2 Foundation

4. You are looking at upgrading your Windows Server 2008 R2 Enterprise with SP2 machine to Windows Server 2012 R2. Your organization is considering virtualizing its entire server room, which has 25 servers. To which version of Windows Server 2012 R2 would you upgrade?

    A. Windows Server 2012 R2 Datacenter

    B. Windows Server 2012 R2 Standard

    C. Windows Server 2012 R2 Essentials

    D. Windows Server 2012 R2 Foundation

5. You have been hired to help a small company set up its first Windows network. It has had the same 13 users for the entire two years it has been open, and the company has no plans to expand. What version of Windows Server 2012 R2 would you recommend?

   A. Windows Server 2012 R2 Datacenter

   B. Windows Server 2012 R2 Standard

   C. Windows Server 2012 R2 Essentials

   D. Windows Server 2012 R2 Foundation

6. You have been hired to help a small company set up its Windows network. It has 20 users, and it has no plans to expand. What version of Windows Server 2012 R2 would you recommend?

   A. Windows Server 2012 R2 Datacenter

   B. Windows Server 2012 R2 Standard

   C. Windows Server 2012 R2 Essentials

   D. Windows Server 2012 R2 Foundation

7. Which of the following are benefits of using Windows Server 2012 R2 Server Core? (Choose all that apply.)

   A. Reduced management

   B. Minimal maintenance

   C. Smaller footprint

   D. Tighter security

8. You are a server administrator, and you are trying to save hard drive space on your Windows Server 2012 R2 Datacenter machine. Which feature can help you save hard disk space?

   A. HDSaver.exe

   B. Features On Demand

   C. ADDS

   D. WinRM

9. You have a server named SRV1 that runs Windows Server 2012 R2. You want to remove Windows Explorer, Windows Internet Explorer, and all components and files from this machine. Which command should you run?

   A. msiexec.exe /uninstall iexplore.exe /x

   B. msiexec.exe /uninstall explorer.exe /x

   C. Uninstall-WindowsFeature Server-Gui-Mgmt-Infra Remove

   D. Uninstall-WindowsFeature Server-Gui-Shell Remove

10. What type of domain controller would you install into an area where physical security is a concern?

    A. Primary domain controller

    B. Backup domain controller

    C. Read-only domain controller

    D. Locked-down domain controller

Chapter

2

Configure Network Services

THE FOLLOWING 70-410 EXAM OBJECTIVES ARE COVERED IN THIS CHAPTER:

✓ **Deploy and configure DNS service**

- Configure Active Directory integration of primary zones
- Configure forwarders
- Configure Root Hints
- Manage DNS cache
- Create A and PTR resource records

✓ **Deploy and configure Dynamic Host Configuration Protocol (DHCP) service**

- Create and configure scopes
- Configure a DHCP reservation
- Configure DHCP options
- Configure client and server for PXE boot
- Configure DHCP relay agent
- Authorize DHCP server

The Domain Name System (DNS) is one of the key topics that you'll need to understand if you plan to take any of the Microsoft Windows Server 2012 R2 administration exams (70-410, 70-411, 70-412, and so forth).

It's also imperative that you understand DNS to work with Active Directory because it requires DNS to function properly, and many important system functions (including Kerberos authentication and finding domain controllers) are handled through DNS lookups. Windows 2000, Windows XP, Windows Vista, Windows 7, and Windows 8 clients use DNS for name resolution and to find Kerberos key distribution centers (KDCs), global catalog servers, and other services that may be registered in DNS.

By the time you complete this chapter, you will have a deeper understanding of how DNS works and how to set up, configure, manage, and troubleshoot DNS in Microsoft Windows Server 2012 R2.

In this chapter, you'll also learn how to install and manage DHCP, including how to set up plain DHCP scopes, superscopes, and multicast scopes. You'll also learn how to set up integration between Dynamic DNS and DHCP and how to authorize a DHCP server to integrate with Active Directory.

There are two versions of DHCP: DHCP v4 and DHCP v6. In this chapter, I will just say "DHCP server" when referring to the physical DHCP server. If I am referring to a specific version of DHCP, I will specify the version.

Introducing DNS

The *Domain Name System (DNS)* is a service that allows you to resolve a hostname to an Internet Protocol (IP) address. One of the inherent complexities of operating in networked environments is working with multiple protocols and network addresses. Owing largely to the tremendous rise in the popularity of the Internet, however, most environments have transitioned to use *Transmission Control Protocol/Internet Protocol (TCP/IP)* as their primary networking protocol. Microsoft is no exception when it comes to supporting TCP/IP in its workstation and server products. All current versions of Microsoft's operating systems support TCP/IP, as do most other modern operating systems.

An easy way to understand DNS is to think about making a telephone call. If you wanted to call Microsoft and did not know the phone number, you could call information, tell them the name (Microsoft), and get the telephone number. You would then make the call. Now think about trying to connect to Server1. You don't know the TCP/IP number (the computer's telephone number), so your computer asks DNS (information) for the number of Server1. DNS returns the number, and your system makes the connection (call). DNS is your network's 411, or information, and it returns the TCP/IP data for your network.

TCP/IP is actually a collection of different technologies (protocols and services) that allow computers to function together on a single, large, and heterogeneous network. Some of the major advantages of this protocol include widespread support for hardware, software, and network devices; reliance on a system of standards; and scalability. TCP handles tasks such as sequenced acknowledgments. IP involves many jobs, such as logical subnet assignment and routing.

The Form of an IP Address

To understand DNS, you must first understand how TCP/IP addresses are formed. Because DNS is strictly on a network to support TCP/IP, understanding the basics of TCP/IP is extremely important.

 Microsoft exams cover TCP/IP. The TCP/IP material will be covered in Chapter 8, "Configure TCP/IP."

An *IP address* is a logical number that uniquely identifies a computer on a TCP/IP network. TCP/IP allows a computer packet to reach the correct host. Windows Server 2012 R2 works with two versions of TCP/IP: IPv4 and IPv6. An IPv4 address takes the form of four octets (eight binary bits), each of which is represented by a decimal number between 0 and 255. The four numbers are separated by decimal points. For example, all of the following are valid IP addresses:

- 128.45.23.17
- 230.212.43.100
- 10.1.1.1

The dotted decimal notation was created to make it easier for users to deal with IP addresses, but this idea did not go far enough. As a result, another abstraction layer was developed, which used names to represent the dotted decimal notation—the domain name. For example, the IP address 11000000 10101000 00000001 00010101 maps to 192.168.1.21, which in turn might map to server1.company.org, which is how the computer's address is usually presented to the user or application.

As stated earlier, IPv4 addresses are made up of octets, or the decimal (base 10) representation of 8 bits. It takes four octets to add up to the 32 bits required. IPv6 expands the address space to 128 bits. The address is usually represented in hexadecimal notation as follows:

```
2001:0DB8:0000:0000:1234:0000:A9FE:133E
```

You can tell that the implementation of DNS would make life a lot easier for everyone, even those of us who like to use alphanumeric values. (For example, some of us enjoy pinging the address in lieu of the name.) Fortunately, DNS already has the ability to handle IPv6 addresses using an AAAA record. An A record in IPv4's addressing space is 32 bits, and an AAAA record (4 *A*s) in IPv6's is 128 bits.

Nowadays, most computer users are quite familiar with navigating to DNS-based resources, such as www.microsoft.com. To resolve these "friendly" names to TCP/IP addresses that the network stack can use, you need a method for mapping them. Originally, ASCII flat files (often called HOSTS files, as shown in Figure 2.1) were used for this purpose. In some cases, they are still used today in small networks, and they can be useful in helping to troubleshoot name resolution problems.

FIGURE 2.1 HOSTS file

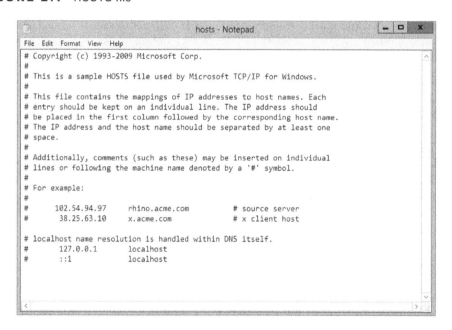

As the number of machines and network devices grew, it became unwieldy for administrators to manage all of the manual updates required to enter new mappings to a master HOSTS file and distribute it. Clearly, a better system was needed.

As you can see from the sample HOSTS file in Figure 2.1, you can conduct a quick test of the email server's name resolution as follows:

1. Open the HOSTS file: C:\Windows\Systems32\drivers\etc.

2. Add the IP-address-to-hostname mapping.

3. Try to ping the server using the hostname to verify that you can reach it using an easy-to-remember name.

Following these steps should drive home the concept of DNS for you because you can see it working to make your life easier. Now you don't have to remember 10.0.0.10; you only need to remember exchange03. However, you can also see how this method can become unwieldy if you have many hosts that want to use easy-to-remember names instead of IP addresses to locate resources on your network.

When dealing with large networks, users and network administrators must be able to locate the resources they require with minimal searching. Users don't care about the actual physical or logical network address of the machine; they just want to be able to connect to it using a simple name that they can remember.

From a network administrator's standpoint, however, each machine must have its own logical address that makes it part of the network on which it resides. Therefore, some scalable and easy-to-manage method for resolving a machine's logical name to an IP address and then to a domain name is required. DNS was created just for this purpose.

DNS is a hierarchically distributed database. In other words, its layers are arranged in a definite order, and its data is distributed across a wide range of machines, each of which can exert control over a portion of the database. DNS is a standard set of protocols that defines the following:

- A mechanism for querying and updating address information in the database

- A mechanism for replicating the information in the database among servers

- A schema of the database

 NOTE   DNS is defined by a number of requests for comments (RFCs), though primarily by RFC 1034 and RFC 1035.

DNS was originally developed in the early days of the Internet (called ARPAnet at the time) when it was a small network created by the Department of Defense for research purposes. Before DNS, computer names, or hostnames, were manually entered into a HOSTS file located on a centrally administered server. Each site that needed to resolve hostnames outside of its organization had to download this file. As the number of computers on the Internet grew, so did the size of this HOSTS file—and along with it the problems of its management. The need for a new system that would offer features such as scalability, decentralized administration, and support for various data types became more and more obvious. DNS, introduced in 1984, became this new system.

With DNS, the hostnames reside in a database that can be distributed among multiple servers, decreasing the load on any one server and providing the ability to administer this naming system on a per-partition basis. DNS supports hierarchical names and allows for the registration of various data types in addition to the hostname-to-IP-address mapping used in HOSTS files. Database performance is ensured through its distributed nature as well as through caching.

The DNS distributed database establishes an inverted logical tree structure called the *domain namespace*. Each node, or domain, in that space has a unique name. At the top of the tree is the root. This may not sound quite right, which is why the DNS hierarchical model is described as being an inverted tree, with the root at the top. The root is represented by the null set "". When written, the root node is represented by a single dot (.).

Each node in the DNS can branch out to any number of nodes below it. For example, below the root node are a number of other nodes, commonly referred to as *top-level domains (TLDs)*. These are the familiar .com, .net, .org, .gov, .edu, and other such names. Table 2.1 lists some of these TLDs.

TABLE 2.1   Common top-level DNS domains

Common top-level domain names	Type of organization
com	Commercial (for example, stellacon.com for Stellacon Training Corporation).
edu	Educational (for example, gatech.edu for the Georgia Institute of Technology)
gov	Government (for example, whitehouse.gov for the White House in Washington, D.C.)
int	International organizations (for example, nato.int for NATO); this top-level domain is fairly rare
mil	Military organizations (for example, usmc.mil for the Marine Corps); there is a separate set of root name servers for this domain
net	Networking organizations and Internet providers (for example, hiwaay.net for HiWAAY Information Systems); many commercial organizations have registered names under this domain too
org	Noncommercial organizations (for example, fidonet.org for FidoNet)
au	Australia
uk	United Kingdom
ca	Canada
us	United States
jp	Japan

Each of these nodes then branches out into another set of domains, and they combine to form what we refer to as domain names, such as microsoft.com. A *domain name* identifies the domain's position in the logical DNS hierarchy in relation to its parent domain by separating each branch of the tree with a dot. Figure 2.2 shows a few of the top-level domains, where the Microsoft domain fits, and a host called Tigger within the microsoft .com domain. If someone wanted to contact that host, they would use the *fully qualified domain name (FQDN)*, tigger.microsoft.com.

An FQDN includes the trailing dot (.) to indicate the root node, but it's commonly left off in practice.

FIGURE 2.2 The DNS hierarchy

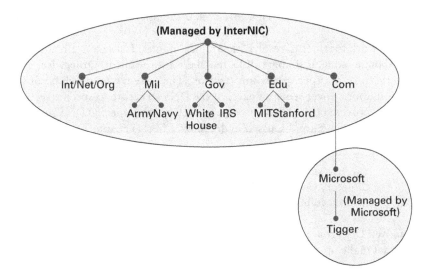

As previously stated, one of the strengths of DNS is the ability to delegate control over portions of the DNS namespace to multiple organizations. For example, the Internet Corporation for Assigned Names and Numbers (ICANN) assigns the control over TLDs to one or more organizations. In turn, those organizations delegate portions of the DNS namespace to other organizations. For example, when you register a domain name, let's call it example.com, you control the DNS for the portion of the DNS namespace within example.com. The registrar controlling the .com TLD has delegated control over the example.com node in the DNS tree. No other node can be named example directly below the .com within the DNS database.

Within the portion of the domain namespace that you control (example.com), you could create host and other records (more on these later). You could also further subdivide example.com and delegate control over those divisions to other organizations or departments. These divisions are called *subdomains*. For example, you might create subdomains named for the cities in which the company has branch offices and then delegate control over those subdomains to the branch offices. The subdomains might be named losangeles.example.com, chicago.example.com, portsmouth.example.com, and so on.

Each domain (or delegated subdomain) is associated with DNS name servers. In other words, for every node in the DNS, one or more servers can give an authoritative answer to queries about that domain. At the root of the domain namespace are the root servers. More on these later.

> Domain names and hostnames must contain only characters a to z, A to Z, 0 to 9, and – (hyphen). Other common and useful characters, such as the & (ampersand), / (slash), . (period), and _ (underscore), are not allowed. This is in conflict with NetBIOS's naming restrictions. However, you'll find that Windows Server 2012 R2 is smart enough to take a NetBIOS name, like Server_1, and turn it into a legal DNS name, like server1.example.com.

DNS servers work together to resolve hierarchical names. If a server already has information about a name, it simply fulfills the query for the client. Otherwise, it queries other DNS servers for the appropriate information. The system works well because it distributes the authority over separate parts of the DNS structure to specific servers. A *DNS zone* is a portion of the DNS namespace over which a specific DNS server has authority (DNS zone types are discussed in detail later in this chapter).

> There is an important distinction to make between DNS zones and Active Directory (AD) domains. Although both use hierarchical names and require name resolution, DNS zones do not map directly to AD domains.

Within a given DNS zone, resource records (RRs) contain the hosts and other database information that make up the data for the zone. For example, an RR might contain the host entry for www.example.com, pointing it to the IP address 192.168.1.10.

Understanding Servers, Clients, and Resolvers

You will need to know a few terms and concepts in order to manage a DNS server. Understanding these terms will make it easier to understand how the Windows Server 2012 R2 DNS server works.

DNS Server   Any computer providing domain name services is a *DNS name server*. No matter where the server resides in the DNS namespace, it's still a DNS name server. For example, 13 root name servers at the top of the DNS tree are responsible for delegating the TLDs. The *root servers* provide referrals to name servers for the TLDs, which in turn provide referrals to an authoritative name server for a given domain.

> The Berkeley Internet Name Domain (BIND) was originally the only software available for running the root servers on the Internet. However, a few years ago the organizations responsible for the root servers undertook an effort to diversify the software running on these important machines. Today, root servers run multiple types of name server software. BIND is still primarily on Unix-based machines, and it is also the most popular for Internet providers. No root servers run Windows DNS.

Any DNS server implementation supporting Service Location Resource Records (see RFC 2782) and Dynamic Updates (RFC 2136) is sufficient to provide the name service for any operating system running Windows 2003 software and newer.

DNS Client   A *DNS client* is any machine that issues queries to a DNS server. The client hostname may or may not be registered in a DNS database. Clients issue DNS requests through processes called *resolvers*. You'll sometimes see the terms *client* and *resolver* used synonymously.

Resolver   *Resolvers* are software processes, sometimes implemented in software libraries that handle the actual process of finding the answers to queries for DNS data. The resolver is also built into many larger pieces of software so that external libraries don't have to be called to make and process DNS queries. Resolvers can be what you'd consider client computers or other DNS servers attempting to resolve an answer on behalf of a client (for example, Internet Explorer).

Query   A *query* is a request for information sent to a DNS server. Three types of queries can be made to a DNS server: recursive, inverse, and iterative. I'll discuss the differences between these query types in the section "DNS Queries," a bit later in the chapter.

Understanding the DNS Process

To help you understand the DNS process, I will start by covering the differences between Dynamic DNS and Non-Dynamic DNS. During this discussion, you will learn how Dynamic DNS populates the DNS database. You'll also see how to implement security for Dynamic DNS. I will then talk about the workings of different types of DNS queries. Finally, I will discuss caching and time to live (TTL). You'll learn how to determine the best setting for your organization.

Dynamic DNS and Non-Dynamic DNS

To understand Dynamic DNS and Non-Dynamic DNS, you must go back in time. (Here is where the TV screen always used to get wavy.) Many years ago when many of us worked on Windows NT 3.51 and Windows NT 4.0, almost all Microsoft networks used Windows Internet Name Service (WINS) to do their TCP/IP name resolution. Windows versions 95/98 and NT 4.0 Professional were all built on the idea of using WINS. This worked out well for administrators because WINS was dynamic (which meant that once it was installed, it automatically built its own database). Back then, there was no such thing as Dynamic DNS; administrators had to enter DNS records into the server manually. This is important to know even today. If you have clients still running any of these older operating systems (95/98 or NT 4), these clients cannot use Dynamic DNS.

Now let's move forward in time to the release of Windows Server 2000. Microsoft announced that DNS was going to be the name resolution method of choice. Many administrators (myself included) did not look forward to the switch. Because there was no such thing as Dynamic DNS, most administrators had nightmares about manually entering records. However, luckily for us, when Microsoft released Windows Server 2000, DNS had the ability to operate dynamically. Now when you're setting up Windows Server 2012 R2 DNS, you can choose what type of dynamic update you would like to use, if any. Let's talk about why you would want to choose one over the other.

The *Dynamic DNS (DDNS) standard*, described in RFC 2136, allows DNS clients to update information in the DNS database files. For example, a Windows Server 2012 R2 DHCP server can automatically tell a DDNS server which IP addresses it has assigned to what machines. Windows 2000, 2003, 2008, XP Pro, Vista, Windows 7, and Windows 8 DHCP clients can do this too. For security reasons, however, it's better to let the DHCP server do it. The result: IP addresses and DNS records stay in sync so that you can use DNS and DHCP together seamlessly. Because DDNS is a proposed Internet standard, you can even use the Windows Server 2012 R2 DDNS-aware parts with Unix/Linux-based DNS servers.

Non-Dynamic DNS (NDDNS) does not automatically populate the DNS database. The client systems do not have the ability to update to DNS. If you decide to use Non-Dynamic DNS, an administrator will need to populate the DNS database manually. Non-Dynamic DNS is a reasonable choice if your organization is small to midsized and you do not want extra network traffic (clients updating to the DNS server) or if you need to enter the computer's TCP/IP information manually because of strict security measures.

Dynamic DNS has the ability to be secure, and the chances are slim that a rogue system (a computer that does not belong in your DNS database) could update to a secure DNS server. Nevertheless, some organizations have to follow stricter security measures and are not allowed to have dynamic updates.

The major downside to entering records into DNS manually occurs when the organization is using the *Dynamic Host Configuration Protocol (DHCP)*. When using DHCP, it is possible for users to end up with different TCP/IP addresses every day. This means an administrator has to update DNS manually each day to keep it accurate.

If you choose to allow Dynamic DNS, you need to decide how you want to set it up. When setting up dynamic updates on your DNS server, you have three choices (see Figure 2.3).

None   This means your DNS server is Non-Dynamic.

Nonsecure and Secure   This means that any machine (even if it does not have a domain account) can register with DNS. Using this setting could allow rogue systems to enter records into your DNS server.

Secure Only   This means that only machines with accounts in Active Directory can register with DNS. Before DNS registers any account in its database, it checks Active Directory to make sure that account is an authorized domain computer.

FIGURE 2.3 Setting the Dynamic Updates option

How Dynamic DNS Populates the DNS Database

TCP/IP is the protocol used for network communications on a Microsoft Windows Server 2012 R2 network. Users have two ways to receive a TCP/IP number:

- Static (administrators manually enter the TCP/IP information)
- Dynamic (using DHCP)

When an administrator sets up TCP/IP, DNS can also be configured.

Once a client gets the address of the DNS server, if that client is allowed to update with DNS, the client sends a registration to DNS or requests DHCP to send the registration. DNS then does one of two things, depending on which Dynamic Updates option is specified:

- Check with Active Directory to see whether that computer has an account (Secure Only updates), and if it does, enter the record into the database.
- Enter the record into its database (Nonsecure and Secure updates).

What if you have clients that cannot update DNS? Well, there is a solution—DHCP. In the DNS tab of the IPv4 Properties window, check the option labeled "Dynamically update DNS A and PTR records for DHCP clients that do not request updates (for example, clients running Windows NT 4.0)," which is shown in Figure 2.4.

DHCP, along with Dynamic DNS clients, allows an organization to update its DNS database dynamically without the time and effort of having an administrator manually enter DNS records.

FIGURE 2.4 DHCP settings for DNS

DNS Queries

As stated earlier, a client can make three types of queries to a DNS server: recursive, inverse, and iterative. Remember that the client of a DNS server can be a resolver (what you'd normally call a client) or another DNS server.

Iterative Queries

Iterative queries are the easiest to understand: A client asks the DNS server for an answer, and the server returns the best answer. This information likely comes from the server's cache. The server never sends out an additional query in response to an iterative query. If the server doesn't know the answer, it may direct the client to another server through a referral.

Recursive Queries

In a *recursive query*, the client sends a query to a name server, asking it to respond either with the requested answer or with an error message. The error states one of two things:

- The server can't come up with the right answer.
- The domain name doesn't exist.

In a recursive query, the name server isn't allowed just to refer the client to some other name server. Most resolvers use recursive queries. In addition, if your DNS server uses a forwarder, the requests sent by your server to the forwarder will be recursive queries.

Figure 2.5 shows an example of both recursive and iterative queries. In this example, a client within the Microsoft Corporation is querying its DNS server for the IP address for www.whitehouse.gov.

FIGURE 2.5   A sample DNS query

Here's what happens to resolve the request:

1. The resolver sends a recursive DNS query to its local DNS server asking for the IP address of www.whitehouse.gov. The local name server is responsible for resolving the name, and it cannot refer the resolver to another name server.

2. The local name server checks its zones, and it finds no zones corresponding to the requested domain name.

3. The root name server has authority for the root domain, and it will reply with the IP address of a name server for the .gov top-level domain.

4. The local name server sends an iterative query for www.whitehouse.gov to the Gov name server.

5. The Gov name server replies with the IP address of the name server servicing the whitehouse.gov domain.

6. The local name server sends an iterative query for www.whitehouse.gov to the whitehouse.gov name server.

7. The whitehouse.gov name server replies with the IP address corresponding to www.whitehouse.gov.

8. The local name server sends the IP address of www.whitehouse.gov back to the original resolver.

Inverse Queries

Inverse queries use pointer (PTR) records. Instead of supplying a name and then asking for an IP address, the client first provides the IP address and then asks for the name. Because there's no direct correlation in the DNS namespace between a domain name and its associated IP address, this search would be fruitless without the use of the in-addr.arpa domain. Nodes in the in-addr.arpa domain are named after the numbers in the dotted-octet representation of IP addresses. However, because IP addresses get more specific from left to right and domain names get less specific from left to right, the order of IP address octets must be reversed when building the in-addr.arpa tree. With this arrangement, administration of the lower limbs of the DNS in-addr.arpa tree can be given to companies as they are assigned their Class A, B, or C subnet address or delegated even further down thanks to Variable Length Subnet Masking (VLSM).

Once the domain tree is built into the DNS database, a special PTR record is added to associate the IP addresses with the corresponding hostnames. In other words, to find a hostname for the IP address 206.131.234.1, the resolver would query the DNS server for a PTR record for 1.234.131.206.in-addr.arpa. If this IP address is outside of the local domain, the DNS server will start at the root and sequentially resolve the domain nodes until arriving at 234.131.206.in-addr.arpa, which would contain the PTR record for the desired host.

Caching and Time to Live

When a name server is processing a recursive query, it may be required to send out several queries to find the definitive answer. Name servers, acting as resolvers, are allowed to cache all of the received information during this process; each record contains information called *time to live (TTL)*. The TTL specifies how long the record will be held in the local cache until it must be resolved again. If a query comes in that can be satisfied by this cached data, the TTL that's returned with it equals the current amount of time left before the data is flushed.

There is also a negative cache TTL. The *negative cache TTL* is used when an authoritative server responds to a query indicating that the record queried doesn't exist, and it indicates the amount of time that this negative answer may be held. Negative caching is quite helpful in preventing repeated queries for names that don't exist.

The administrator for the DNS zone sets TTL values for the entire zone. The value can be the same across the zone, or the administrator can set a separate TTL for each RR within the zone. Client resolvers also have data caches and honor the TTL value so that they know when to flush.

Choosing Appropriate TTL Values

For zones that you administer, you can choose the TTL values for the entire zone, for negative caching, and for individual records. Choosing an appropriate TTL depends on a number of factors, including the following:

- Amount of change you anticipate for the records within the zone

- Amount of time you can withstand an outage that might require changing an IP address

- Amount of traffic you believe the DNS server can handle

Resolvers query the name server every time the TTL expires for a given record. A low TTL, say 60 seconds, can burden the name server, especially for popular DNS records. (DNS queries aren't particularly intensive for a server to handle, but they can add up quickly if you mistakenly use 60 seconds instead of 600 seconds for the TTL on a popular record.) Set a low TTL only when you need to respond quickly to a changing environment.

A high TTL, say 604,800 seconds (that's one week), means that if you need to make a change to the DNS record, clients might not see the change for up to a week. This consideration is especially important when making changes to the network, and it's one that's all too frequently overlooked. I can't count the number of times I've worked with clients who had recently made a DNS change to a new IP for their email or website only to ask why it's not working for some clients. The answer can be found in the TTL value. If the record is being cached, then the only thing that can solve their problem is time.

You should choose a TTL that's appropriate for your environment. Take the following factors into account:

- The amount of time that you can afford to be offline if you need to make a change to a DNS record that's being cached

- The amount of load that a low TTL will cause on the DNS server

In addition, you should plan well ahead of any major infrastructure changes and change the TTL to a lower value to lessen the effect of the downtime by reducing the amount of time that the record(s) can be cached.

Introducing DNS Database Zones

As mentioned earlier in this chapter, a DNS zone is a portion of the DNS namespace over which a specific DNS server has authority. Within a given DNS zone, there are resource records (RRs) that define the hosts and other types of information that make up the database for the zone. You can choose from several different zone types. Understanding the characteristics of each will help you choose which is right for your organization.

 The DNS zones discussed in this book are all Microsoft Windows Server 2012 / 2012 R2 zones. Non-Windows (for example, Unix) systems set up their DNS zones differently.

In the following sections, I will discuss the different zone types and their characteristics.

Understanding Primary Zones

When you're learning about zone types, things can get a bit confusing. But it's really not difficult to understand how they work and why you would want to choose one type of zone over the other. Zones are databases that store records. By choosing one zone type over another, you are basically just choosing how the database works and how it will be stored on the server.

The primary zone is responsible for maintaining all of the records for the DNS zone. It contains the primary copy of the DNS database. All record updates occur on the primary zone. You will want to create and add primary zones whenever you create a new DNS domain.

There are two types of primary zones:

- Primary zone
- Primary zone with Active Directory Integration (Active Directory DNS)

 From this point forward, I refer to a primary zone with Active Directory Integration as an *Active Directory DNS*. When I use only the term *primary zone*, Active Directory is not included.

To install DNS as a primary zone, you must first install DNS using the Server Manager MMC. Once DNS is installed and running, you create a new zone and specify it as a primary zone.

 The process of installing DNS and its zones will be discussed later in this chapter. In addition, there will be step-by-step exercises to walk you through how to install these components.

Primary zones have advantages and disadvantages. Knowing the characteristics of a primary zone will help you decide when you need the zone and when it fits into your organization.

Local Database

Primary DNS zones get stored locally in a file (with the suffix .dns) on the server. This allows you to store a primary zone on a domain controller or a member server. In addition, by loading DNS onto a member server, you can help a small organization conserve resources. Such an organization may not have the resources to load DNS on an Active Directory domain controller.

Unfortunately, the local database has many disadvantages:

Lack of Fault Tolerance   Think of a primary zone as a contact list on your smartphone. All of the contacts in the list are the records in your database. The problem is that, if you lose your phone or the phone breaks, you lose your contact list. Until your phone gets fixed or you swap out your phone card, the contacts are unavailable.

It works the same way with a primary zone. If the server goes down or you lose the hard drive, DNS records on that machine are unreachable. An administrator can install a secondary zone (explained later in the next section), and that provides temporary fault tolerance. Unfortunately, if the primary zone is down for an extended period of time, the secondary server's information will no longer be valid.

Additional Network Traffic   Let's imagine that you are looking for a contact number for John Smith. John Smith is not listed in your smartphone directory, but he is listed in your partner's smartphone. You have to contact your partner to get the listing. You cannot directly access your partner's phone's contacts.

When a resolver sends a request to DNS to get the TCP/IP address for Jsmith (in this case Jsmith is a computer name) and the DNS server does not have an answer, it does not have the ability to check the other server's database directly to get an answer. Thus it forwards the request to another DNS. When DNS servers are replicating zone databases with other DNS servers, this causes additional network traffic.

No Security   Staying with the smartphone example, let's say that you call your partner looking for John Smith's phone number. When your partner gives you the phone number over your wireless phone, someone with a scanner can pick up your conversation. Unfortunately, wireless telephone calls are not very secure.

Now a resolver asks a primary zone for the Jsmith TCP/IP address. If someone on the network has a packet sniffer, they can steal the information in the DNS packets being sent over the network. The packets are not secure unless you implement some form of secondary security. Also, the DNS server has the ability to be dynamic. A primary zone accepts all updates from DNS servers. You cannot set it to accept secure updates only.

Understanding Secondary Zones

In Windows Server 2012 R2 DNS, you have the ability to use secondary DNS zones. Secondary zones are noneditable copies of the DNS database. You use them for *load balancing* (also referred to as *load sharing*), which is a way of managing network overloads on a single server. A secondary zone gets its database from a primary zone.

A *secondary zone* contains a database with all of the same information as the primary zone, and it can be used to resolve DNS requests. Secondary zones have the following advantages:

- A secondary zone provides fault tolerance, so if the primary zone server becomes unavailable, name resolution can still occur using the secondary zone server.

- Secondary DNS servers can also increase network performance by offloading some of the traffic that would otherwise go to the primary server.

Secondary servers are often placed within the parts of an organization that have high-speed network access. This prevents DNS queries from having to run across slow wide area network (WAN) connections. For example, if there are two remote offices within the stellacon.com organization, you may want to place a secondary DNS server in each remote office. This way, when clients require name resolution, they will contact the nearest server for this IP address information, thus preventing unnecessary WAN traffic.

Having too many secondary zone servers can actually cause an increase in network traffic because of replication (especially if DNS changes are fairly frequent). Therefore, you should always weigh the benefits and drawbacks and properly plan for secondary zone servers.

Understanding Active Directory Integrated DNS

Windows Server 2000 introduced *Active Directory Integrated DNS* to the world. This zone type was unique and was a separate choice during setup. In Windows Server 2003, this zone type became an add-on to a primary zone. In Windows Server 2012 R2, it works the same way. After choosing to set up a primary zone, you check the box labeled Store The Zone In Active Directory (see Figure 2.6).

FIGURE 2.6   Setting up an Active Directory Integrated zone

Disadvantages of Active Directory Integrated DNS

The main disadvantage of Active Directory Integrated DNS is that it has to reside on a domain controller because the DNS database is stored in Active Directory. As a result, you cannot load this zone type on a member server, and small organizations might not have the resources to set up a dedicated domain controller.

Advantages of Active Directory Integrated DNS

The advantages of using an Active Directory Integrated DNS zone well outweigh the disadvantage just discussed. The following are some of the major advantages to an Active Directory Integrated zone:

Full Fault Tolerance   Think of an Active Directory Integrated zone as a database on your server that stores contact information for all your clients. If you need to retrieve John Smith's phone number, as long as it was entered, you can look it up on the software.

If John Smith's phone number was stored only on your computer and your computer stopped working, no one could access John Smith's phone number. But since John Smith's phone number is stored in a database to which everyone has access, if your computer stops working, other users can still retrieve John Smith's phone number.

An Active Directory Integrated zone works the same way. Since the DNS database is stored in Active Directory, all Active Directory DNS servers can have access to the same data. If one server goes down or you lose a hard drive, all other Active Directory DNS servers can still retrieve DNS records.

No Additional Network Traffic   As previously discussed, an Active Directory Integrated zone is stored in Active Directory. Since all records are now stored in Active Directory, when a resolver needs a TCP/IP address for Jsmith, any Active Directory DNS server can access Jsmith's address and respond to the resolver.

When you choose an Active Directory Integrated zone, DNS zone data can be replicated automatically to other DNS servers during the normal Active Directory replication process.

DNS Security   An Active Directory Integrated zone has a few security advantages over a primary zone:

- An Active Directory Integrated zone can use secure dynamic updates.
- As explained earlier, the Dynamic DNS standard allows secure-only updates or dynamic updates, not both.
- If you choose secure updates, then only machines with accounts in Active Directory can register with DNS. Before DNS registers any account in its database, it checks Active Directory to make sure that it is an authorized domain computer.
- An Active Directory Integrated zone stores and replicates its database through Active Directory replication. Because of this, the data gets encrypted as it is sent from one DNS server to another.

Background Zone Loading   Background zone loading (discussed in more detail later in this chapter) allows an Active Directory Integrated DNS zone to load in the background. As a result, a DNS server can service client requests while the zone is still loading into memory.

Understanding Stub Zones

Stub zones work a lot like secondary zones—the database is a noneditable copy of a primary zone. The difference is that the stub zone's database contains only the information necessary (three record types) to identify the authoritative DNS servers for a zone (see Figure 2.7). You should not use stub zones to replace secondary zones, nor should you use them for redundancy and load balancing.

FIGURE 2.7   DNS stub zone type

     Stub zone databases contain only three record types: name server (NS), start of authority (SOA), and glue host (A) records. Understanding these records will help you on the Microsoft certification exams. Microsoft asks many questions about stub zones on all DNS-related exams.

When to Use Stub Zones

Stub zones become particularly useful in a couple of different scenarios. Consider what happens when two large companies merge: example.com and example.net. In most cases, the DNS zone information from both companies must be available to every employee. You could set up a new zone on each side that acts as a secondary for the other side's primary zone, but administrators tend to be very protective of their DNS databases, and they probably wouldn't agree to this plan.

A better solution is to add to each side a stub zone that points to the primary server on the other side. When a client in example.com (which you help administer) makes a request for a name in example.net, the stub zone on the example.com DNS server would send the client to the primary DNS server for example.net without actually resolving the name. At this point, it would be up to example.net's primary server to resolve the name.

An added benefit is that, even if the administrators over at example.net change their configuration, you won't have to do anything because the changes will automatically replicate to the stub zone, just as they would for a secondary server.

Stub zones can also be useful when you administer two domains across a slow connection. Let's change the previous example a bit and assume that you have full control over example.com and example.net but that they connect through a 56Kbps line. In this case, you wouldn't necessarily mind using secondary zones because you personally administer the entire network. However, it could get messy to replicate an entire zone file across that slow line. Instead, stub zones would refer clients to the appropriate primary server at the other site.

GlobalName Zones

Earlier in this chapter, I talked about organizations using WINS to resolve NetBIOS names (also referred to as *computer names*) to TCP/IP addresses. Even today, many organizations still use WINS along with DNS for name resolution. Unfortunately, WINS is slowly becoming obsolete.

To help organizations move forward with an all-DNS network, Microsoft Windows Server 2012 R2 DNS supports *GlobalName zones*. These use single-label names (DNS names that do not contain a suffix such as .com, .net, and so on). GlobalName zones are not intended to support peer-to-peer networks and workstation name resolution, and they don't support dynamic DNS updates.

GlobalName zones are designed to be used with servers. Because GlobalName zones are not dynamic, an administrator has to enter the records into the zone database manually. In most organizations, the servers have static TCP/IP addresses, and this works well with the GlobalName zone design. GlobalName zones are usually used to map single-label CNAME (alias) resource records to an FQDN.

Zone Transfers and Replication

DNS is such an important part of the network that you should not just use a single DNS server. With a single DNS server, you also have a single point of failure, and in fact, many domain registrars encourage the use of more than two name servers for a domain. Secondary servers or multiple primary Active Directory Integrated servers play an integral role in providing DNS information for an entire domain.

As previously stated, secondary DNS servers receive their zone databases through zone transfers. When you configure a secondary server for the first time, you must specify the primary server that is authoritative for the zone and that will send the zone transfer. The primary server must also permit the secondary server to request the zone transfer.

Zone transfers occur in one of two ways: *full zone transfers (AXFR)* and *incremental zone transfers (IXFR)*.

When a new secondary server is configured for the first time, it receives a full zone transfer from the primary DNS server. The full zone transfer contains all of the information in the DNS database. Some DNS implementations always receive full zone transfers.

After the secondary server receives its first full zone transfer, subsequent zone transfers are incremental. The primary name server compares its zone version number with that of the secondary server, and it sends only the changes that have been made in the interim. This significantly reduces network traffic generated by zone transfers.

The secondary server typically initiates zone transfers when the refresh interval time for the zone expires or when the secondary or stub server boots. Alternatively, you can configure notify lists on the primary server that send a message to the secondary or stub servers whenever any changes to the zone database occur.

When you consider your DNS strategy, you must carefully consider the layout of your network. If you have a single domain with offices in separate cities, you want to reduce the number of zone transfers across the potentially slow or expensive WAN links, although this is becoming less of a concern because of continuous increases in bandwidth.

Active Directory Integrated zones do away with traditional zone transfers altogether. Instead, they replicate across Active Directory with all of the other AD information. This replication is secure and encrypted because it uses the Active Directory security.

How DNS Notify Works

Windows Server 2012 R2 supports DNS Notify. *DNS Notify* is a mechanism that allows the process of initiating notifications to secondary servers when zone changes occur (RFC 1996). DNS Notify uses a push mechanism for communicating to a select set of secondary zone servers when their zone information is updated. (DNS Notify does not allow you to configure a notify list for a stub zone.)

After being notified of the changes, secondary servers can then start a pull zone transfer and update their local copies of the database.

Many different mechanisms use the push/pull relationship. Normally, one object pushes information to another, and the second object pulls the information from the first. Most applications push replication on a change value and pull it on a time value. For example, a system can push replication after 10 updates, or it can be pulled every 30 minutes.

To configure the DNS Notify process, you create a list of secondary servers to notify. List the IP address of the server in the primary master's Notify dialog box (see Figure 2.8). The Notify dialog box is located under the Zone Transfers tab, which is located in the zone Properties dialog box (see Figure 2.9).

FIGURE 2.8   DNS Notify dialog box

FIGURE 2.9   DNS Zone Transfers tab

Configuring Stub Zone Transfers with Zone Replication

In the preceding section, I talked about how to configure secondary server zone transfers. What if you wanted to configure settings for stub zone transfers? This is where zone replication scope comes in.

Only Active Directory–Integrated primary and stub zones can configure their replication scope. Secondary servers do not have this ability.

You can configure zone replication scope configurations in two ways. An administrator can set configuration options through the DNS snap-in or through a command-line tool called DNSCmd.

To configure zone replication scope through the DNS snap-in, follow these steps:

1. Click Start ➢ Administrative Tools ➢ DNS.

2. Right-click the zone you want to set up.

3. Choose Properties.

4. In the Properties dialog box, click the Change button next to Replication (see Figure 2.10).

FIGURE 2.10 DNS zone replication scope

5. Choose the replication scope that fits your organization.

Advantages of DNS in Windows Server 2012 R2

DNS in Microsoft Windows Server 2012 R2 has some great advantages over many other versions of Microsoft DNS. Here are some of the improvements of DNS in Windows Server 2012 R2 (some of these became available in Windows Server 2008, but they have been improved upon):

- Background zone loading
- Support for TCP/IP version 6 (IPv6)
- Read-only domain controllers
- GlobalName zone
- DNS Socket Pool
- DNS Cache Locking
- DNS Security Extensions (DNSSEC)
- DNS Devolution
- Zone Level Statistics
- Record Weighting
- Netmask Ordering
- DnsUpdateProxy Group
- Windows PowerShell Support

Background Zone Loading

If an organization had to restart a DNS server with an extremely large Active Directory Integrated DNS zones database in the past, DNS had a common problem with an Active Directory Integrated DNS zone. After the DNS restart, it could take hours for DNS data to be retrieved from Active Directory. During this time, the DNS server was unable to service any client requests.

Microsoft Windows Server 2008 DNS addressed this problem by implementing background zone loading, and Windows Server 2012 R2 has taken it a step further. As the DNS restarts, the Active Directory zone data populates the database in the background. This allows the DNS server to service client requests for data from other zones almost immediately after a restart.

Background zone loading accomplishes this task by loading the DNS zone using separate threads. This allows a DNS server to service requests while still loading the rest of the zone. If a client sends a request to the DNS server for a computer that has not yet loaded into memory, the DNS server retrieves the data from Active Directory and updates the record.

Support for IPv6 Addresses

Over the past few years, the Internet has starting running into a problem that was not foreseen when it was first created—it started running out of TCP/IP addresses. As you probably know, when the Internet was created, it was used for government and academic purposes only. Then, seemingly overnight, it grew to be the information superhighway. Nowadays, asking someone for his or her email address is almost as common as asking for their phone number.

Version 4 (IPv4) was the common version of TCP/IP. The release of TCP/IP version 6 (IPv6) has solved the lack-of-IP-addresses problem. IPv4 addresses are 32 bits long, but IPv6 addresses are 128 bits in length. The longer lengths allow for a much greater number of globally unique TCP/IP addresses.

Microsoft Windows Server 2012 R2 DNS has built-in support to accommodate both IPv4 and IPv6 address records. (DNS records are explained later in this chapter.) DHCP can also issue IPv6 addresses, which lets administrators allow DHCP to register the client with DNS, or the IPv6 client can register their address with the DNS server.

Support for Read-Only Domain Controllers

Windows Server 2008 introduced a new type of domain controller called the *read-only domain controller (RODC)*. This is a full copy of the Active Directory database without the ability to write to Active Directory. The RODC gives an organization the ability to install a domain controller in a location (onsite or offsite) where security is a concern.

Microsoft Windows Server 2012 R2 DNS has implemented a type of zone to help support an RODC. A primary read-only zone allows a DNS server to receive a copy of the application partition (including ForestDNSZones and DomainDNSZones) that DNS uses. This allows DNS to support an RODC because DNS now has a full copy of all DNS zones stored in Active Directory.

A primary, read-only zone is just what it says—a read-only zone; so to make any changes to it, you have to change the primary zones located on the Active Directory Integrated DNS server.

DNS Socket Pools

If your server is running Windows Server 2012 R2, you will be able to take advantage of DNS socket pools. *DNS socket pools* allow source port randomization to protect against DNS cache-poisoning attacks.

If you choose to use source port randomization, when the DNS service starts, the DNS server will randomly pick a source port from a pool of available sockets. This is an advantage because, instead of DNS using a well-known source port when issuing queries, the DNS server uses a random port selected from the socket pool. This helps guard against attacks because a hacker must correctly access the source port of the DNS query. The socket pool is automatically enabled in DNS with the default settings.

When using the DNS Socket Pool, the default size of the DNS socket pool is 2,500. When configuring the socket pool, you have the ability to choose a size value from 0 to 10,000. The larger the value, the greater the protection you will have against DNS spoofing attacks. If you decide to configure your socket pool size with a zero value, only a single socket for remote DNS queries will be used.

DNS Cache Locking

Windows Server 2012 R2 *DNS cache locking* allows cached DNS records to remain safe for the duration of the record's time to live (TTL) value. This means that the cached DNS records cannot be overwritten or changed. Because of this new DNS feature, it's tougher for hackers to perform cache-poisoning attacks against your DNS server.

DNS administrators can set how long a record will remain safe in cache. The configuration is based on a percent value. For example, if you set your cache locking value to 50 percent, then the cached records cannot be overwritten until half of the TTL has been reached. DNS cache locking is set to 100 percent by default. This means that the cached records never get overwritten.

DNS Security Extensions

One major issue that you must always look at is keeping your DNS safe. Think about it—DNS is a database of computer names and IP addresses. As a hacker, if I control DNS, I can control your company. In organizations that do not support extra security like IPsec, DNS security is even more important. This is where DNSSEC can help.

Windows Server 2012 R2 can use a suite of extensions that will help add security to DNS, and that suite is called *Domain Name System Security Extensions (DNSSEC)*, which was introduced in Windows Server 2008 R2. The DNSSEC protocol allows your DNS servers to be secure by validating DNS responses. DNSSEC secures your DNS resource records by accompanying the records with a digital signature.

To allow your DNS resource records to receive digital signatures, DNSSEC is applied to your DNS server by a procedure called *zone signing*. This process begins when a DNS resolver initiates a DNS query for a resource record in a signed DNS zone. When a response is returned, a digital signature (RRSIG) accompanies the response, and this allows the response to be verified. If the verification is successful, then the DNS resolver knows that the data has not been modified or tampered with in any way.

Once you implement a zone with DNSSEC, all of the records that are contained within that zone get individually signed. Since all of the records in the zone get individually signed, this gives administrators the ability to add, modify, or delete records without resigning the entire zone. The only requirement is to resign any updated records.

Trust Anchors

Trust anchors are an important part of the DNSSEC process because trust anchors allow the DNS servers to validate the DNSKEY resource records. *Trust anchors* are preconfigured public keys that are linked to a DNS zone. For a DNS server to perform validation, one or more trust anchors must be configured. If you are running an Active Directory Integrated zone, trust anchors can be stored in the Active Directory Domain Services directory partition of the forest. If you decide to store the trust anchors in the directory partition, then all DNS servers that reside on a domain controller get a copy of this trust anchor. On DNS servers that reside on stand-alone servers, trust anchors are stored in a file called `TrustAnchors.dns`.

If your servers are running Windows Server 2012 R2, then you can view trust anchors in the DNS Manager Console tree in the Trust Points container. You can also use Windows PowerShell or Dnscmd.exe to view trust anchors. Windows PowerShell is the recommended command-line method for viewing trust anchors. The following line is a PowerShell command to view the trust anchors for Contoso.com:

```
get-dnsservertrustanchor sec.contoso.com
```

DNSSEC Clients

Windows 7, Windows 8, Windows Server 2008/2008 R2, and Windows Server 2012/2012 R2 are all DNS clients that receive a response to a DNS query, examine the response, and then evaluate whether the response has been validated by a DNS server. The DNS client itself is nonvalidating, and the DNS client relies on the local DNS server to indicate that validation was successful. If the server doesn't perform validation, then the DNS client service can be configured to return no results.

If you are interested in learning how to set up DNSSEC in a lab environment, Microsoft has a website that explains all about DNSSEC and how to set up the lab environment. Visit http://technet.microsoft.com/en-us/library/hh831411.aspx.

DNS Devolution

Using *DNS devolution*, if a client computer is a member of a child namespace, the client computer will be able to access resources in the parent namespace without the need to provide explicitly the fully qualified domain name (FQDN) of the resource. DNS devolution removes the leftmost label of the namespace to get to the parent suffix. DNS devolution allows the DNS resolver to create the new FQDNs. DNS devolution works by appending the single-label, unqualified domain name with the parent suffix of the primary DNS suffix name.

Zone Level Statistics

DNS zone level server statistics are available in Windows Server 2012 R2 by using the Windows PowerShell cmdlet Get-DnsServerStatistics. This powerful Windows PowerShell cmdlet retrieves statistics and data for the DNS server. The following is an example of the Get-DnsServerStatistics cmdlet:

```
Get-DnsServerStatistics -ZoneName <String[]> [-AsJob][-CimSession
<CimSession[]> ][-Clear][-ComputerName <String> ][-ThrottleLimit <Int32> ]
[ <CommonParameters>]
```

The ZoneName parameter allows an administrator to get specific statistics for the DNS zone that you have specified. If the ZoneName parameter is not specified during the

PowerShell cmdlet, the server-level statistics are retrieved and shown. If an administrator uses the Clear parameter in the PowerShell cmdlet along with the ZoneName parameter, the statistics for the specified zone will be cleared. So, use this cmdlet carefully.

Record Weighting

Weighting DNS records will allow an administrator to place a value on DNS SRV records. Clients will then randomly choose SRV records proportional to the weight value assigned.

Netmask Ordering

If round robin is enabled, when a client requests name resolution, the first address entered in the database is returned to the resolver, and it is then sent to the end of the list. The next time a client attempts to resolve the name, the DNS server returns the second name in the database (which is now the first name) and then sends it to the end of the list, and so on. Round robin is enabled by default.

Netmask ordering is part of the round-robin process. When an administrator configures netmask ordering, the DNS server will detect the subnet of the querying client. The DNS server will then return a host address available for the same subnet. Netmask ordering is enabled through the DNS Manager console on the Advanced tab of the server Properties dialog box.

DnsUpdateProxy Group

As mentioned previously, the DHCP server can be configured to register host (A) and pointer (PTR) resource records dynamically on behalf of DHCP clients. Because of this, the DNS server can end up with stale resources. To help solve this issue, an administrator can use the built-in security group called *DnsUpdateProxy.*

To use the DnsUpdateProxy group, an administrator must first create a dedicated user account and configure the DHCP servers with its credentials. This will protect against the creation of unsecured records. Also, when you create the dedicated user account, members of the DnsUpdateProxy group will be able to register records in zones that allow only secured dynamic updates. Multiple DHCP servers can use the same credentials of one dedicated user account.

Now that you have looked at some of the new features of Windows Server 2012 R2 DNS, let's take a look at some of the DNS record types.

Windows PowerShell Support

Microsoft has more than 100 PowerShell cmdlets specifically for DNS. While in Windows PowerShell, you can list all of the DNS cmdlets that are available. To see the entire list, use the following PowerShell command:

```
Get-Command -Module DnsServer cmdlet.
```

For an entire list of all of the Windows PowerShell DNS cmdlets, go to `http://technet` `.microsoft.com/en-us/library/jj649850.aspx`.

Introducing DNS Record Types

No matter where your zone information is stored, you can rest assured that it contains a variety of DNS information. Although the DNS snap-in makes it unlikely that you'll ever need to edit these files by hand, it's good to know exactly what data is contained there.

As stated previously, zone files consist of a number of resource records. You need to know about several types of resource records to manage your DNS servers effectively. They are discussed in the following sections.

Part of the resource record is its class. *Classes* define the type of network for the resource record. There are three classes: Internet, Chaosnet, and Hesoid. By far, the Internet class is the most popular. In fact, it's doubtful that you'll see either Chaosnet or Hesoid classes in the wild.

The following are some of the more important resource records in a DNS database. For a listing of records in a Microsoft DNS database, visit Microsoft's website at `http://technet.microsoft.com/en-us/library/` `cc958958.aspx`.

Start of Authority Records

The first record in a database file is the *start of authority (SOA) record*. The SOA defines the general parameters for the DNS zone, including the identity of the authoritative server for the zone.

The SOA appears in the following format:

```
@ IN SOA primary_mastercontact_e-mailserial_number
refresh_timeretry_timeexpiration_timetime_to_live
```

Here is a sample SOA from the domain example.com:

```
@ IN SOA win2k3r2.example.com. hostmaster.example.com. (
                    5            ; serial number
                    900          ; refresh
                    600          ; retry
                    86400        ; expire
                    3600     ) ; default TTL
```

Table 2.2 lists the attributes stored in the SOA record.

TABLE 2.2   The SOA record structure

Field	Meaning
Current zone	The current zone for the SOA. This can be represented by an @ symbol to indicate the current zone or by naming the zone itself. In the example, the current zone is example.com. The trailing dot (.com.) indicates the zone's place relative to the root of the DNS.
Class	This will almost always be the letters *IN* for the Internet class.
Type of record	The type of record follows. In this case, it's SOA.
Primary master	The primary master for the zone on which this file is maintained.
Contact email	The Internet email address for the person responsible for this domain's database file. There is no @ symbol in this contact email address because @ is a special character in zone files. The contact email address is separated by a single dot (.). So the email address of root@example.com would be represented by root.example.com in a zone file.
Serial number	This is the "version number" of this database file. It increases each time the database file is changed.
Refresh time	The amount of time (in seconds) that a secondary server will wait between checks to its master server to see if the database file has changed and a zone transfer should be requested.
Retry time	The amount of time (in seconds) that a secondary server will wait before retrying a failed zone transfer.
Expiration time	The amount of time (in seconds) that a secondary server will spend trying to download a zone. Once this time limit expires, the old zone information will be discarded.
Time to live	The amount of time (in seconds) that another DNS server is allowed to cache any resource records from this database file. This is the value that is sent out with all query responses from this zone file when the individual resource record doesn't contain an overriding value.

Name Server Records

Name server (NS) records list the name servers for a domain. This record allows other name servers to look up names in your domain. A zone file may contain more than one name server record. The format of these records is simple:

```
example.com.    IN    NS    Hostname.example.com
```

Table 2.3 explains the attributes stored in the NS record.

TABLE 2.3   The NS record structure

Field	Meaning
Name	The domain that will be serviced by this name server. In this case, I used example.com.
AddressClass	Internet (IN)
RecordType	Name server (NS)
Name Server Name	The FQDN of the server responsible for the domain

 Any domain name in the database file that is not terminated with a period will have the root domain appended to the end. For example, an entry that just has the name *sales* will be expanded by adding the root domain to the end, whereas the entry sales.example.com. won't be expanded.

Host Record

A *host record* (also called an *A record* for IPv4 and *AAAA record* for IPv6) is used to associate statically a host's name to its IP addresses. The format is pretty simple:

```
host_nameoptional_TTL IN  A  IP_Address
```

Here's an example from my DNS database:

```
www  IN  A  192.168.0.204
SMTP IN  A  192.168.3.144
```

The A or AAAA record ties a hostname (which is part of an FQDN) to a specific IP address. This makes these records suitable for use when you have devices with statically assigned IP addresses. In this case, you create these records manually using the DNS snap-in. As it turns out, if you enable DDNS, your DHCP server can create these for you. This automatic creation is what enables DDNS to work.

Notice that an optional TTL field is available for each resource record in the DNS. This value is used to set a TTL that is different from the default TTL for the domain. For example, if you wanted a 60-second TTL for the www A or AAAA record, it would look like this:

```
www 60 IN  A  192.168.0.204
```

Alias Record

Closely related to the host record is the *alias record*, or *canonical name (CNAME) record*. The syntax of an alias record is as follows:

```
aliasoptional_TTL  IN  CNAME  hostname
```

Aliases are used to point more than one DNS record toward a host for which an A record already exists. For example, if the hostname of your web server was actually chaos, you would likely have an A record such as this:

```
chaos IN A 192.168.1.10
```

Then you could make an alias or CNAME for the record so that www.example.com would point to chaos:

```
www IN CNAME chaos.example.com.
```

Note the trailing dot (.) on the end of the CNAME record. This means the root domain is not appended to the entry.

Pointer Record

A or AAAA records are probably the most visible component of the DNS database because Internet users depend on them to turn FQDNs like www.microsoft.com into the IP addresses that browsers and other components require to find Internet resources. However, the host record has a lesser-known but still important twin: the *pointer (PTR) record*. The format of a PTR record appears as follows:

```
reversed_address.in-addr.arpa. optional_TTL IN PTR targeted_domain_name
```

The A or AAAA record maps a hostname to an IP address, and the PTR record does just the opposite—mapping an IP address to a hostname through the use of the in-addr.arpa zone.

The PTR record is necessary because IP addresses begin with the least-specific portion first (the network) and end with the most-specific portion (the host), whereas hostnames begin with the most-specific portion at the beginning and the least-specific portion at the end.

Consider the example 192.168.1.10 with a subnet mask 255.255.255.0. The portion 192.168.1 defines the network and the final .10 defines the host, or the most-specific portion of the address. DNS is just the opposite: The hostname www.example.com. defines the most-specific portion, www, at the beginning and then traverses the DNS tree to the least-specific part, the dot (.), at the root of the tree.

Reverse DNS records, therefore, need to be represented in this most-specific-to-least-specific manner. The PTR record for mapping 192.168.1.10 to www.example.com would look like this:

```
10.1.168.192.in-addr.arpa. IN PTR www.example.com.
```

Now a DNS query for that record can follow the logical DNS hierarchy from the root of the DNS tree all the way to the most-specific portion.

Mail Exchanger Record

The *mail exchanger (MX) record* is used to specify which servers accept mail for this domain. Each MX record contains two parameters—a preference and a mail server, as shown in the following example:

```
domain IN MX preference mailserver_host
```

The MX record uses the preference value to specify which server should be used if more than one MX record is present. The preference value is a number. The lower the number, the more preferred the server. Here's an example:

```
example.com.    IN  MX  0  mail.example.com.
example.com.    IN  MX  10 backupmail.example.com.
```

In the example, `mail.example.com` is the default mail server for the domain. If that server goes down for any reason, emailers then use the `backupmail.example.com` mail server.

Service (SRV) Record

Windows Server 2012 R2 depends on some other services, like the Lightweight Directory Access Protocol (LDAP) and Kerberos. Using a service record, which is another type of DNS record, a Windows 2000, XP, Vista, Windows 7, Windows 8, and all Windows Server products can query DNS servers for the location of a domain controller. This makes it much easier (for both the client and the administrator) to manage and distribute logon traffic in large-scale networks. For this approach to work, Microsoft has to have some way to register the presence of a service in DNS. Enter the service (SRV) record.

Service (SRV) records tie together the location of a service (like a domain controller) with information about how to contact the service. SRV records provide seven items of information. Let's review an example to help clarify this powerful concept. (Table 2.4 explains the fields in the following example.)

```
ldap.tcp.example.com.  86400 IN SRV  10  100  389  hsv.example.com
ldap.tcp.example.com.  86400 IN SRV  20  100  389  msy.example.com
```

TABLE 2.4 The SRV record structure

Field	Meaning
Domain name	Domain for which this record is valid (`ldap.tcp.example.com.`).
TTL	Time to live (86,400 seconds).
Class	This field is always IN, which stands for Internet.

Record type	Type of record (SRV).
Priority	Specifies a preference, similar to the Preference field in an MX record. The SRV record with the lowest priority is used first (10).
Weight	Service records with equal priority are chosen according to their weight (100).
Port number	The port where the server is listening for this service (389).
Target	The FQDN of the host computer (hsv.example.com and msy.example.com).

 You can define other types of service records. If your applications support them, they can query DNS to find the services they need.

Configuring DNS

In the following sections, you'll begin to learn about the actual DNS server. You will start by installing DNS. Then I will talk about different zone configuration options and what they mean. Finally, you'll complete an exercise that covers configuring Dynamic DNS, delegating zones, and manually entering records.

DNS requires that you use a static IP address on the server. The reason for this is that clients access the DNS server by using its TCP/IP address, and that's why DNS servers need to install a static IP address.

If you are currently using DHCP on your server, change your DNS server to have a static IP address before completing this exercise. I know that most of you already know how to change your IP address, but for anyone new to Microsoft Server 2012 R2, click the Start button and go into Control Panel. Make sure that the VIEW BY in the upper-right corner is set to large icons, and then choose Network and Sharing Center. On the right side of the windows under Access Type, click the access type link you have (Ethernet, Wireless, and so forth). Choose Properties, and then click Internet Protocol Version 4 (TCP/IPv4) and choose Properties. Choose the radio button for Use The Following IP Address and enter your local TCP/IP settings. Click OK to change it from DHCP to a static TCP/IP address.

Installing DNS

Let's start by installing DNS. Installing DNS is an important part of running a network. Exercise 2.1 walks you through the installation of a DNS server.

EXERCISE 2.1

Installing and Configuring the DNS Service

1. Open Server Manager.

2. On the Server Manager dashboard, click the Add Roles And Features link.

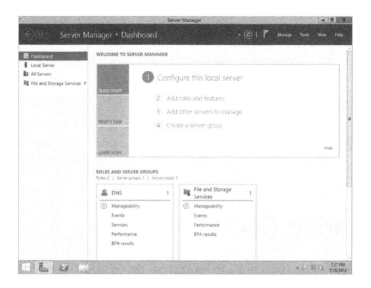

3. If a Before You Begin screen appears, click Next.

4. On the Selection type page, choose Role-Based Or Feature-Based Installation and click Next.

5. Click the Select A Server From The Server Pool radio button and choose the server under the Server Pool section. Click Next.

6. Click the DNS Server Item in the Server Role list. If a pop-up window appears telling you that you need to add additional features, click the Add Features button. If you did not give your system a static TCP/IP address, a window appears stating that you need a static TCP/IP address; just click the Continue button to bypass the error. Click Next to continue.

7. On the Add Features page, just click Next.

8. Click Next on the DNS Server information screen.

9. On the Confirm Installation screen, choose the Restart The Destination Server Automatically If Required check box and then click the Install button.

10. At the Installation progress screen, click Close after the DNS server is installed.

11. Close Server Manager.

Load Balancing with Round Robin

Like other DNS implementations, the Windows Server 2012 R2 implementation of DNS supports load balancing through the use of round robin. Load balancing distributes the network load among multiple network hosts if they are available. You set up round-robin load balancing by creating multiple resource records with the same hostname but different IP addresses for multiple computers. Depending on the options you select, the DNS server responds with the addresses of one of the host computers.

If round robin is enabled, when a client requests name resolution, the first address entered in the database is returned to the resolver and is then sent to the end of the list. The next time a client attempts to resolve the name, the DNS server returns the second name in the database (which is now the first name) and then sends it to the end of the list, and so on. Round robin is enabled by default.

Configuring a Caching-Only Server

Although all DNS name servers cache queries that they have resolved, caching-only servers are DNS name servers that only perform queries, cache the answers, and return the results. They are not authoritative for any domains, and the information that they contain is limited to what has been cached while resolving queries. Accordingly, they don't have any zone files, and they don't participate in zone transfers. When a caching-only server is first started, it has no information in its cache; the cache is gradually built over time.

Caching-only servers are easy to configure. After installing the DNS service, simply make sure the root hints are configured properly:

1. Right-click your DNS server and choose the Properties command.

2. When the Properties dialog box appears, switch to the Root Hints tab (see Figure 2.11).

FIGURE 2.11   The Root Hints tab of the DNS server's Properties dialog box

3. If your server is connected to the Internet, you should see a list of root hints for the root servers maintained by ICANN and the Internet Assigned Numbers Authority (IANA). If not, click the Add button to add root hints as defined in the cache.dns file.

   You can obtain current cache.dns files on the Internet by using a search engine. Just search for *cache.dns* and download one. (I always try to get cache.dns files from a university or a company that manages domain names.)

Setting Zone Properties

There are six tabs on the Properties dialog box for a forward or reverse lookup zone. You only use the Security tab to control who can change properties and to make dynamic updates to records on that zone. The other tabs are discussed in the following sections.

 Secondary zones don't have a Security tab, and their SOA tab shows you the contents of the master SOA record, which you can't change.

General Tab

The General tab includes the following:

- The Status indicator and the associated Pause button let you see and control whether this zone can be used to answer queries. When the zone is running, the server can use it to answer client queries; when it's paused, the server won't answer any queries it gets for that particular zone.

- The Type indicator and its Change button allow you to select the zone type. The options are Standard Primary, Standard Secondary, and AD-Integrated. (See "Introducing DNS Database Zones" earlier in this chapter.) As you change the type, the controls you see below the horizontal dividing line change too. For primary zones, you'll see a field that lets you select the zone filename; for secondary zones, you'll get controls that allow you to specify the IP addresses of the primary servers. But the most interesting controls are the ones you see for AD Integrated zones. When you change to the AD Integrated zones, you have the ability to make the dynamic zones Secure Only.

- The Replication indicator and its Change button allow you to change the replication scope if the zone is stored in Active Directory. You can choose to replicate the zone data to any of the following:
  - All DNS servers in the Active Directory forest
  - All DNS servers in a specified domain
  - All domain controllers in the Active Directory domain (required if you use Windows 2000 domain controllers in your domain)
  - All domain controllers specified in the replication scope of the application directory partition

- The Dynamic Updates field gives you a way to specify whether you want to support Dynamic DNS updates from compatible DHCP servers. As you learned earlier in the section "Dynamic DNS and Non-Dynamic DNS," the DHCP server or DHCP client must know about and support Dynamic DNS in order to use it, but the DNS server has to participate too. You can turn dynamic updates on or off, or you can require that updates be secured.

Start Of Authority (SOA) Tab

The options on the Start Of Authority (SOA) tab, shown in Figure 2.12, control the contents of the SOA record for this zone.

FIGURE 2.12   The Start Of Authority (SOA) tab of the zone Properties dialog box

- The Serial Number field indicates which version of the SOA record the server currently holds. Every time you change another field, you should increment the serial number so that other servers will notice the change and get a copy of the updated record.

- The Primary Server and Responsible Person fields indicate the location of the primary name server (NS) for this zone and the email address of the administrator responsible for the maintenance of this zone, respectively. The standard username for this is host-master.

- The Refresh Interval field controls how often any secondary zones of this zone must contact the primary zone server and get any changes that have been posted since the last update.

- The Retry Interval field controls how long secondary servers will wait after a zone transfer fails before they try again. They'll keep trying at the interval you specify (which should be shorter than the refresh interval) until they eventually succeed in transferring zone data.

- The Expires After field tells the secondary servers when to throw away zone data. The default of 1 day (24 hours) means that a secondary server that hasn't gotten an update in 24 hours will delete its local copy of the zone data.

- The Minimum (Default) TTL field sets the default TTL for all RRs created in the zone. You can assign specific TTLs to individual records if you want.

- The TTL For This Record field controls the TTL for the SOA record itself.

Name Servers Tab

The *name server (NS) record* for a zone indicates which name servers are authoritative for the zone. That normally means the zone primary server and any secondary servers you've configured for the zone. (Remember, secondary servers are authoritative read-only copies of the zone.) You edit the NS record for a zone using the Name Servers tab (see Figure 2.13). The tab shows you which servers are currently listed, and you use the Add, Edit, and Remove buttons to specify which name servers you want included in the zone's NS record.

FIGURE 2.13 The Name Servers tab of the zone Properties dialog box

WINS Tab

The WINS tab allows you to control whether this zone uses WINS forward lookups. These lookups pass on queries that DNS can't resolve to WINS for action. This is a useful setup if you're still using WINS on your network. You must explicitly turn this option on with the Use WINS Forward Lookup check box on the WINS tab for a particular zone.

Zone Transfers Tab

Zone transfers are necessary and useful because they're the mechanism used to propagate zone data between primary and secondary servers. For primary servers (whether AD Integrated or not), you can specify whether your servers will allow zone transfers and, if so, to whom.

You can use the following controls on the Zone Transfers tab to configure these settings per zone:

- The Allow Zone Transfers check box controls whether the server answers zone transfer requests for this zone at all; when it's not checked, no zone data is transferred. The Allow Zone Transfers selections are as follows:

  - To Any Server allows any server anywhere on the Internet to request a copy of your zone data.

  - Only To Servers Listed On The Name Servers Tab (the default) limits transfers to servers you specify. This is a more secure setting than To Any Server because it limits transfers to other servers for the same zone.

  - Only To The Following Servers allows you to specify exactly which servers are allowed to request zone transfers. This list can be larger or smaller than the list specified on the Name Servers tab.

- The Notify button is for setting up automatic notification triggers that are sent to secondary servers for this zone. Those triggers signal the secondary servers that changes have occurred on the primary server so that the secondary servers can request updates sooner than their normally scheduled interval. The options in the Notify dialog box are similar to those in the Zone Transfers tab. You can enable automatic notification and then choose either Servers Listed On The Name Servers Tab or The Following Servers.

Configuring Zones for Dynamic Updates

In Exercise 2.2, you will create and then modify the properties of a forward lookup zone. In addition, you'll configure the zone to allow dynamic updates. You are installing this DNS zone as a primary zone *without* AD integration. Even if you installed this DNS server onto a domain controller, do not choose the check box for AD integration.

EXERCISE 2.2

Configuring a Zone for Dynamic Updates

1. Open the DNS management snap-in by selecting Server Manager. Once in Server Manager, click DNS on the left side. In the Servers window (center screen), right-click your server name and choose DNS Manager.

2. Click the DNS server to expand it and then click the Forward Lookup Zones folder. Right-click the Forward Lookup Zones folder and choose New Zone.

3. At the New Zone Welcome screen, click Next.

4. At the Zone Type screen, choose the Primary Zone option. Again, if your DNS server is also a domain controller, do not check the box to store the zone in Active Directory. Click Next when you are ready.

5. Enter a new zone name in the Zone Name field and click Next. (I used my last name— Panek.com.)

6. Leave the default zone filename and click Next.

7. Select the Do Not Allow Dynamic Updates radio button and click Next.

8. Click Finish to end the wizard.

9. Right-click the zone you just created and choose the Properties command.

10. Click the down arrow next to Dynamic Updates. Notice that there are only two options (None and Nonsecure And Secure). The Secure Only option is not available because you are not using Active Directory Integrated. Make sure Nonsecure And Secure is chosen.

11. Click OK to close the Properties box.

12. Close the DNS management snap-in.

13. Close the Server Manager snap-in.

Delegating Zones for DNS

DNS provides the ability to divide the namespace into one or more zones, which can then be stored, distributed, and replicated to other DNS servers. When deciding whether to divide your DNS namespace to make additional zones, consider the following reasons to use additional zones:

- A need to delegate management of part of your DNS namespace to another location or department within your organization.

- A need to divide one large zone into smaller zones for distributing traffic loads among multiple servers, for improving DNS name-resolution performance, or for creating a more fault-tolerant DNS environment.

- A need to extend the namespace by adding numerous subdomains at once, such as to accommodate the opening of a new branch or site.

Each newly delegated zone requires a primary DNS server just as a regular DNS zone does. When delegating zones within your namespace, be aware that for each new zone you create, you need to place delegation records in other zones that point to the authoritative DNS servers for the new zone. This is necessary both to transfer authority and to provide correct referral to other DNS servers and clients of the new servers being made authoritative for the new zone.

In Exercise 2.3, you'll create a delegated subdomain of the domain you created back in Exercise 2.2. Note that the name of the server to which you want to delegate the subdomain must be stored in an A or CNAME record in the parent domain.

EXERCISE 2.3

Creating a Delegated DNS Zone

1. Open the DNS management snap-in by selecting Server Manager. Once in Server Manager, click DNS on the left side. In the Servers window (center screen), right-click your server name and choose DNS Manager.

2. Expand the DNS server and locate the zone you created in Exercise 2.2.

3. Right-click the zone and choose the New Delegation command.

4. The New Delegation Wizard appears. Click Next to dismiss the initial wizard page.

5. Enter **ns1** (or whatever other name you like) in the Delegated Domain field of the Delegated Domain Name page. This is the name of the domain for which you want to delegate authority to another DNS server. It should be a subdomain of the primary domain (for example, to delegate authority for farmington.example.net, you'd enter **farmington** in the Delegated Domain field). Click Next to complete this step.

6. When the Name Servers page appears, click the Add button to add the name(s) and IP address(es) of the servers that will be hosting the newly delegated zone. For the purpose of this exercise, enter the server name you used in Exercise 2.2. Click the Resolve button to resolve this domain name's IP address automatically into the IP address field. Click OK when you are finished. Click Next to continue with the wizard.

7. Click the Finish button. The New Delegation Wizard disappears, and you'll see the new zone you just created appear beneath the zone you selected in step 3. The newly delegated zone's folder icon is drawn in gray to indicate that control of the zone is delegated.

DNS Forwarding

If a DNS server does not have an answer to a DNS request, it may be necessary to send that request to another DNS server. This is called *DNS forwarding*. You need to understand the two main types of forwarding:

External Forwarding   When a DNS server forwards an external DNS request to a DNS server outside of your organization, this is considered *external forwarding*. For example, a resolver requests the host www.microsoft.com. Most likely, your internal DNS server is not going to have Microsoft's web address in its DNS database. So, your DNS server is going to send the request to an external DNS (most likely your ISP).

Conditional Forwarding   *Conditional forwarding* is a lot like external forwarding except that you are going to forward requests to specific DNS servers based on a condition. Usually, this is an excellent setup for internal DNS resolution. For example, let's say you have two companies, stellacon.com and stellatest.com. If a request comes in for Stellacon.com, it gets forwarded to the Stellacon DNS server, and any requests for Stellatest.com will get forwarded to the Stellatest DNS server. Requests are forwarded to a specific DNS server depending on the condition that an administrator sets up.

Manually Creating DNS Records

From time to time, you may find it necessary to add resource records manually to your Windows Server 2012 R2 DNS servers. Although Dynamic DNS frees you from the need to fiddle with A and PTR records for clients and other such entries, you still have to create other resource types (including MX records, required for the proper flow of SMTP email) manually. You can manually create A, PTR, MX, SRV, and many other record types.

There are only two important things to remember for manually creating DNS records:

- You must right-click the zone and choose either the New Record command or the Other New Records command.

- You must know how to fill in the fields of whatever record type you're using.

    For example, to create an MX record, you need three pieces of information (the domain, the mail server, and the priority). To create an SRV record, however, you need several more pieces of information.

In Exercise 2.4, you will manually create an MX record for a mailtest server in the zone you created in Exercise 2.2.

EXERCISE 2.4

 Manually Creating DNS RRs

1. Open the DNS management snap-in by selecting Server Manager. Once in Server Manager, click DNS on the left side. In the Servers window (center screen), right-click your server name and choose DNS Manager.

2. Expand your DNS server, right-click its zone and choose New Host (A record).

3. Enter **mailtest** in the Name field. Enter a TCP/IP number in the IP Address field. (You can use any number for this exercise, for example, 192.168.1.254.) Click the Add Host button.

4. A dialog box appears stating that the host record was created successfully. Click OK. Click Done.

5. Right-click your zone name and choose New Mail Exchanger (MX).

6. Enter **mailtest** in the Host Or Child Domain field and enter **mailtest.yourDomain**
   .com (or whatever domain name you used in Exercise 2.2) in the Fully-Qualified Domain
   Name (FQDN) Of Mail Server field; then click OK. Notice that the new record is already
   visible.

7. Next create an alias (or CNAME) record to point to the mail server. (It is assumed that
   you already have an A record for mailtest in your zone.) Right-click your zone, and
   choose New Alias (CNAME).

8. Type **mail** into the Alias Name field.

9. Type **mailtest.yourDomain.com** into the Fully-Qualified Domain Name (FQDN) For Target Host field.

10. Click the OK button.

11. Close the DNS management snap-in.

DNS Aging and Scavenging

When using dynamic updates, computers (or DHCP) will register a resource record with
DNS. These records get removed when a computer is shut down properly. A major problem
in the industry is that laptops are frequently removed from the network without a proper
shutdown. Therefore, their resource records continue to live in the DNS database.

Windows Server 2012 R2 DNS supports two features called *DNS aging* and *DNS*
scavenging. These features are used to clean up and remove stale resource records of a
primary DNS zone. DNS aging and DNS scavenging flags old resource records that have

not been updated in a certain amount of time (determined by the scavenging interval). These stale records will be scavenged at the next cleanup interval. DNS uses time stamps on the resource records to determine how long they have been listed in the DNS database.

DNS allows an administrator to set up and configure aging and scavenging through the use of the DNS snap-in. DNS aging and scavenging allows an administrator to perform some of the following related tasks for your DNS servers and any of the Active Directory–Integrated zones that they load:

- Administrators can enable or disable the use of scavenging at a DNS server and/or for selected zones at the DNS server.

- You can modify the no-refresh/refresh interval, either as a server default or by specifying an overriding value at selected zones.

- Administrators can specify when periodic scavenging occurs automatically at the DNS server for any of its eligible zones and how often these operations are repeated.

- Manually initiate a single scavenging operation for all eligible zones at the DNS server.

Enabling Scavenging of Stale Records

When you install Windows Server 2012 R2 DNS aging and scavenging features on all DNS servers and any of their zones, administrators should consider the following settings before using these features:

Determine whether you should use aging and scavenging for server-wide settings.   When using these settings, you are choosing to affect every one of the zone-level properties for all Active Directory–Integrated zones that are loaded at the server.

Determine whether you should use aging and scavenging for zone settings.   When using these settings, you are choosing to use them for zone-specific properties for just the selected zones and not the entire server. These settings apply only to the applicable zone and its resource records, and they do not apply to any other zone on the DNS server. Unless these zone-level properties are otherwise configured, they inherit their defaults from comparable settings that are maintained in server aging and scavenging properties.

Enabling aging and scavenging for use with standard primary zones modifies the format of zone files. This change does not affect zone replication to secondary servers, but the modified zone files cannot be loaded by other versions of DNS servers.

Monitoring and Troubleshooting DNS

Now that you have set up and configured your DNS name server and created some resource records, you will want to confirm that it is resolving and replying to client DNS requests. A couple of tools allow you to do some basic monitoring and managing. Once you are able to monitor DNS, you'll want to start troubleshooting.

The simplest test is to use the `ping` command to make sure that the server is alive. A more thorough test would be to use `nslookup` to verify that you can actually resolve addresses for items on your DNS server.

In the following sections, you'll look at some of these monitoring and management tools and how to troubleshoot DNS.

Monitoring DNS with the DNS Snap-In

You can use the DNS snap-in to do some basic server testing and monitoring. More important, you use the snap-in to monitor and set logging options. On the Event Logging tab of the server's Properties dialog box (see Figure 2.14), you can pick which events you want logged. The more events you select, the more logging information you'll get. This is useful when you're trying to track what's happening with your servers, but it can result in a very large log file if you're not careful.

FIGURE 2.14   The Event Logging tab of the server's Properties dialog box

The Monitoring tab (see Figure 2.15) gives you some testing tools. When the check box labeled A Simple Query Against This DNS Server is checked, a test is performed that asks for a single record from the local DNS server. It's useful for verifying that the service is running and listening to queries, but not much else. When the check box labeled A Recursive Query To Other DNS Servers is checked, the test is more sophisticated—a recursive query checks whether forwarding is working okay. The Test Now button and the Perform Automatic Testing At The Following Interval check box allow you to run these tests now or later as you require.

FIGURE 2.15   The Monitoring tab of the server's Properties dialog box

Another tab in the server's properties that allows you to monitor the activity of the DNS server is the Debug Logging tab. The Debug Logging tab allows you to monitor all outbound and inbound DNS traffic, packet content, packet type, and which transport protocol (TCP or UDP) that you want to monitor on the DNS server.

 If the simple query fails, check that the local server contains the zone 1.0.0.127.in-addr.arpa. If the recursive query fails, check that your root hints are correct and that your root servers are running.

In Exercise 2.5, you will enable logging, use the DNS MMC to test the DNS server, and view the contents of the DNS log.

EXERCISE 2.5

Simple DNS Testing

1. Open the DNS management snap-in by selecting Server Manager. Once in Server Manager, click DNS on the left side. In the Servers window (center screen), right-click your server name and choose DNS Manager.

2. Right-click the DNS server name on the top left and select Properties.

3. Switch to the Debug Logging tab, check all of the debug logging options except Filter Packets By IP Address, and enter a full path and filename in the File Path And Name field. Click the Apply button.

4. Switch to the Monitoring tab and check both A Simple Query Against This DNS Server and A Recursive Query To Other DNS Servers.

5. Click the Test Now button several times and then click OK.

6. Press the Windows key on the keyboard (left side between the Ctrl and Alt keys) and then choose Computer. Navigate to the folder that you specified in step 3 and use Word-Pad or Notepad to view the contents of the log file.

Troubleshooting DNS

When troubleshooting DNS problems, ask yourself the following basic questions:

- What application is failing? What works? What doesn't work?

- Is the problem basic IP connectivity, or is it name resolution? If the problem is name resolution, does the failing application use NetBIOS names, DNS names, or host-names?

- How are the things that do and don't work related?

- Have the things that don't work ever worked on this computer or network? If so, what has changed since they last worked?

Windows Server 2012 R2 provides several useful tools, discussed in the following sections, which can help you answer these questions:

- Nslookup is used to perform DNS queries and to examine the contents of zone files on local and remote servers.

- DNSLint is a command-line utility used for troubleshooting many common DNS issues.

- Ipconfig allows you to perform the following tasks:
    - View DNS client settings
    - Display and flush the resolver cache
    - Force a dynamic update client to register its DNS records
- The DNS log file monitors certain DNS server events and logs them for your edification.

Using *Nslookup*

Nslookup is a standard command-line tool provided in most DNS server implementations, including Windows Server 2012 R2. Windows Server 2012 R2 gives you the ability to launch nslookup from the DNS snap-in.

When nslookup is launched from the DNS snap-in, a command prompt window opens automatically. You enter nslookup commands in this window.

Nslookup offers you the ability to perform query testing of DNS servers and to obtain detailed responses at the command prompt. This information can be useful for diagnosing and solving name resolution problems, for verifying that resource records are added or updated correctly in a zone, and for debugging other server-related problems. You can do a number of useful things with nslookup:

- Use it in noninteractive mode to look up a single piece of data
- Enter interactive mode and use the debug feature
- Perform the following from within interactive mode:
    - Set options for your query
    - Look up a name
    - Look up records in a zone
    - Perform zone transfers
    - Exit nslookup

When you are entering queries, it is generally a good idea to enter FQDNs so that you can control what name is submitted to the server. However, if you want to know which suffixes are added to unqualified names before they are submitted to the server, you can enter nslookup in debug mode and then enter an unqualified name.

Using Nslookup on the Command Line

To use nslookup in plain-old command-line mode, enter the following in the command prompt window:

```
nslookup DNS_name_or_IP_address server_IP_address
```

This command will look up a DNS name or address using a server at the IP address you specify.

Using *Nslookup* in Interactive Mode

Nslookup is a lot more useful in interactive mode because you can enter several commands in sequence. Entering **nslookup** by itself (without specifying a query or server) puts it in interactive mode, where it will stay until you type **exit** and press Enter. Before that point, you can look up lots of useful stuff. The following are some of the tasks you can perform with nslookup in interactive mode:

Setting Options with the set Command   While in interactive mode, you can use the set command to configure how the resolver will carry out queries. Table 2.5 shows a few of the options available with set.

TABLE 2.5   Command-line options available with the set command

Option	Purpose
set all	Shows all the options available.
set d2	Puts nslookup in debug mode so that you can examine the query and response packets between the resolver and the server.
set domain=*domain name*	Tells the resolver what domain name to append for unqualified queries.
set timeout=*timeout*	Tells the resolver how long to keep trying to contact the server. This option is useful for slow links where queries frequently time out and the wait time must be lengthened.
set type=*record type*	Tells the resolver which type of resource records to search for (for example, A, PTR, or SRV). If you want the resolver to query for all types of resource records, type **settype=all**.

Looking Up a Name   While in interactive mode, you can look up a name just by typing it: **stellacon.com**. In this example, stellacon is the owner name for the record for which you are searching, and .com is the server you want to query.

You can use the wildcard character (*) in your query. For example, if you want to look for all resource records that have *k* as the first letter, just type **k*** as your query.

Looking Up a Record Type   If you want to query a particular type of record (for instance, an MX record), use the set type command. The command set type=mx tells nslookup you're interested only in seeing MX records that meet your search criteria.

Listing the Contents of a Domain   To get a list of the contents of an entire domain, use the ls command. To find all of the hosts in your domain, you'd type **set type=a** and then type **ls -t yourdomain.com**.

Troubleshooting Zone Transfers   You can simulate zone transfers by using the ls command with the -d switch. This can help you determine whether the server you are querying allows zone transfers to your computer. To do this, type **ls -d domain__name**.

Nslookup Responses and Error Messages

A successful nslookup response looks like this:

```
Server: Name_of_DNS_server
Address: IP_address_of_DNS_server
Response_data
```

Nslookup might also return an error message. Some common messages are listed in Table 2.6.

TABLE 2.6   Common nslookup error messages

Error message	Meaning
DNS request timed out. Timeout was *x* seconds. *** Can't find server name for address *IP_Address*: Timed out *** Default servers are not available Default Server: Unknown Address: *IP_address_of_DNS_server*	The resolver did not locate a PTR resource record (containing the hostname) for the server IP address you specified. Nslookup can still query the DNS server, and the DNS server can still answer queries.
*** Request to Server timed-out	A request was not fulfilled in the allotted time. This might happen, for example, if the DNS service was not running on the DNS server that is authoritative for the name.
*** Server can't find *Name_or_IP_address_queried_for*: No response from server	The server is not receiving requests on User Datagram Protocol (UDP) port 53.
*** Server can't find *Name_or_IP_address_queried_for:* Non-existent domain	The DNS server was unable to find the name or IP address in the authoritative domain. The authoritative domain might be on the remote DNS server or on another DNS server that this DNS server is unable to reach.

| *** Server can't find *Name_or_TP_ address_queried_for*: Server failed | The DNS server is running, but it is not working properly. For example, it might include a corrupted packet, or the zone in which you are querying for a record might be paused. However, this message can also be returned if the client queries for a host in a domain for which the DNS server is not authoritative. You will also receive the error if the DNS server cannot contact its root servers, it is not connected to the Internet, or it has no root hints. |

In Exercise 2.6, you'll get some hands-on practice with the nslookup tool. You can run this exercise from Windows 7, Windows 8, and Windows Server 2012 R2.

EXERCISE 2.6

Using the nslookup **Command**

1. Click the Start button and in the Search Programs And Files box (above the Start button), type **CMD**. Then hit Enter.

2. Type **nslookup** and press the Enter key. (For the rest of the exercise, use the Enter key to terminate each command.)

3. Try looking up a well-known address: Type **www.microsoft.com**.

4. Try looking up a nonexistent host: Type **www.example.ccccc**. Notice that your server indicates that it can't find the address and times out. This is normal behavior.

5. Type **exit** at the prompt. Type **exit** again to leave the command prompt.

Using *DNSLint*

Microsoft Windows Server 2012 R2 DNS can use the DNSLint command-line utility to help diagnose some common DNS name-resolution issues and to help diagnose potential problems of incorrect delegation. You need to download DNSLint from the Microsoft Download Center.

DNSLint uses three main functions to verify DNS records and to generate a report in HTML:

dnslint/d This function helps diagnose the reasons for "lame delegation" and other related DNS problems.

dnslint/ql This function helps verify a user-defined set of DNS records on multiple DNS servers.

dnslint/ad This function helps verify DNS records pertaining to Active Directory replication.

Here is the syntax for DNSLint:

```
dnslint /d domain_name | /ad [LDAP_IP_address] | /ql input_file
[/c [smtp,pop,imap]] [/no_open] [/r report_name]
[/t] [/test_tcp] [/s DNS_IP_address] [/v] [/y]
```

The following are some sample queries:

```
dnslint /d stellacon.com
dnslint /ad /s 192.168.36.201
dnslint /ql dns_server.txt
dnslint /ql autocreate
dnslint /v /d stellacon.com
dnslint /r newfile /d stellacon.com
dnslint /y /d stellacon.com
dnslint /no_open /d stellacon.com
```

Table 2.7 explains the command options.

TABLE 2.7 DNSLint command options

Command option	Meaning
/d	Domain name that is being tested.
/ad	Resolves DNS records that are used for Active Directory forest replication.
/s	TCP/IP address of host.
/ql	Requests DNS query tests from a list. This switch sends DNS queries specified in an input file.
/v	Turns on verbose mode.
/r filename	Allows you to create a report file.
/y	Overwrites an existing report file without being prompted.
/no_open	Prevents a report from opening automatically.

Using *Ipconfig*

You can use the command-line tool ipconfig to view your DNS client settings, to view and reset cached information used locally for resolving DNS name queries, and to register the resource records for a dynamic update client. If you use the ipconfig command with no parameters, it displays DNS information for each adapter, including the domain name and

DNS servers used for that adapter. Table 2.8 shows some command-line options available with `ipconfig`.

TABLE 2.8 Command-line options available for the `ipconfig` command

Command	What It Does
`ipconfig /all`	Displays additional information about DNS, including the FQDN and the DNS suffix search list.
`ipconfig /flushdns`	Flushes and resets the DNS resolver cache. For more information about this option, see the section "Configuring DNS" earlier in this chapter.
`ipconfig /displaydns`	Displays the contents of the DNS resolver cache. For more information about this option, see the section "Configuring DNS" earlier in this chapter.
`ipconfig /registerdns`	Refreshes all DHCP leases and registers any related DNS names. This option is available only on Windows 2000 and newer computers that run the DHCP client service.

You should know and be comfortable with the `ipconfig` commands related to DNS for the exam.

Using *DNSCmd*

`DNSCmd` allows you to display and change the properties of DNS servers, zones, and resource records through the use of command-line commands. The `DNSCmd` utility allows you to modify, create, and delete resource records and/or zones manually, and it allows you to force replication between two DNS servers.

Table 2.9 lists some of the `DNSCmd` commands and their explanations.

TABLE 2.9 DNSCmd command-line options

Command	Explanation
`dnscmd /clearcache`	Clears the DNS server cache
`dnscmd /config`	Resets DNS server or zone configuration
`dnscmd /createdirectorypartition`	Creates a DNS application directory partition
`dnscmd /deletedirectorypartition`	Deletes a DNS application directory partition
`dnscmd /enumrecords`	Shows the resource records in a zone

TABLE 2.9 DNSCmd command-line options *(continued)*

Command	Explanation
dnscmd /exportsettings	Creates a text file of all server configuration information
dnscmd /info	Displays server information
dnscmd /recordadd	Adds a resource record to a zone
dnscmd /recorddelete	Deletes a resource record from a zone
dnscmd /zoneadd	Creates a new DNS zone
dnscmd /zonedelete	Deletes a DNS zone
dnscmd /zoneexport	Creates a text file of all resource records in the zone
dnscmd /zoneinfo	Displays zone information
dnscmd /zonerefresh	Forces replication of the master zone to the secondary zone

Using the DNS Log File

You can configure the DNS server to create a log file that records the following information:

- Queries
- Notification messages from other servers
- Dynamic updates
- Content of the question section for DNS query messages
- Content of the answer section for DNS query messages
- Number of queries this server sends
- Number of queries this server has received
- Number of DNS requests received over a UDP port
- Number of DNS requests received over a TCP port
- Number of full packets sent by the server
- Number of packets written through by the server and back to the zone

The DNS log appears in systemroot\System32\dns\Dns.log. Because the log is in RTF format, you must use WordPad or Word to view it.

Once the log file reaches the maximum size, Windows Server 2012 R2 writes over the beginning of the file. You can change the maximum size of the log. If you increase the size value, data persists for a longer time period, but the log file consumes more disk space. If you decrease the value, the log file uses less disk space, but the data persists for a shorter time period.

> Do not leave DNS logging turned on during normal operation because it sucks up both processing and hard disk resources. Enable it only when diagnosing and solving DNS problems.

Troubleshooting the *.(root)* Zone

The *DNS root zone* is the top-level DNS zone in the DNS hierarchy. Windows Server 2012 R2-based DNS servers will build a .(root) zone when a connection to the Internet can't be found.

Because of this, the .(root) zone may prevent access to the Internet. The DNS forwarding option and DNS root hints will not be configurable. If you want your DNS to work as a DNS forwarder or you want to use root hints, you must remove the .(root) zone.

Issues with Non-Microsoft DNS Servers

Another troubleshooting problem that you may run into is working with both Microsoft DNS servers and non-Microsoft DNS servers. One of the most common non-Microsoft DNS servers is the Unix-based BIND DNS server.

If you need to complete a zone transfer from Microsoft DNS to a BIND DNS server, you need to enable BIND Secondaries on the Microsoft DNS server (see Figure 2.16).

FIGURE 2.16   Enabling BIND secondaries

If you need to enable Bind Secondaries, complete the following steps:

1. Open DNS management.
2. Right-click the server name and choose Properties.
3. Click the Advanced tab.
4. Check the Enable BIND Secondaries box.
5. Click OK.

Overview of DHCP

As you will see in Chapter 7, TCP/IP is the priority protocol for Windows Server 2012 R2. There are two ways to have clients and servers get TCP/IP addresses:

- You can manually assign the addresses.
- The addresses can be assigned automatically.

Manually assigning addresses is a fairly simple process. An administrator goes to each of the machines on the network and assigns TCP/IP addresses. The problem with this method arises when the network becomes midsized or larger. Think of an administrator trying to individually assign 4,000 TCP/IP addresses, subnet masks, default gateways, and all other configuration options needed to run the network.

DHCP's job is to centralize the process of IP address and option assignment. You can configure a DHCP server with a range of addresses (called a *pool*) and other configuration information and let it assign all of the IP parameters—addresses, default gateways, DNS server addresses, and so on.

 DHCP is defined by a series of request for comments documents, notably 2131 and 2132.

Introducing the DORA Process

An easy way to remember how DHCP works is to learn the acronym DORA. *DORA* stands for Discover, Offer, Request, and Acknowledge. In brief, here is DHCP's DORA process:

1. *Discover*: When IP networking starts up on a DHCP-enabled client, a special message called a DHCPDISCOVER is broadcast within the local physical subnet.
2. *Offer*: Any DHCP server that hears the request checks its internal database and replies with a message called a DHCPOFFER, which contains an available IP address.

The contents of this message depend on how the DHCP server is configured—there are numerous options aside from an IP address that you can specify to pass to the client on a Windows Server DHCP server.

3. *Request*: The client receives one or more DHCPOFFERs (depending on how many DHCP servers exist on the local subnet), chooses an address from one of the offers, and sends a DHCPREQUEST message to the server to signal acceptance of the DHCPOF-FER.

   This message might also request additional configuration parameters.

   Other DHCP servers that sent offers take the request message as an acknowledgment that the client didn't accept their offer.

4. *Acknowledge*: When the DHCP server receives the DHCPREQUEST, it marks the IP address as being in use (that is, usually, though it's not required). Then it sends a DHC-PACK to the client.

   The acknowledgment message might contain requested configuration parameters.

   If the server is unable to accept the DHCPREQUEST for any reason, it sends a DHCPNAK message. If a client receives a DHCPNAK, it begins the configuration process over again.

5. When the client accepts the IP offer, the address is assigned to the client for a specified period of time, called a *lease*. After receiving the DHCPACK message, the client performs a final check on the parameters (sometimes it sends an ARP request for the offered IP address) and makes note of the duration of the lease. The client is now configured. If the client detects that the address is already in use, it sends a DHCPDECLINE.

   If the DHCP server has given out all of the IP addresses in its pool, it won't make an offer. If no other servers make an offer, the client's IP network initialization will fail, and the client will use Automatic Private IP Addressing (APIPA).

DHCP Lease Renewal

No matter how long the lease period, the client sends a new lease request message directly to the DHCP server when the lease period is half over (give or take some randomness required by RFC 2131). This period goes by the name *T1* (not to be confused with the T1 type of network connection). If the server hears the request message and there's no reason to reject it, it sends a DHCPACK to the client. This resets the lease period.

If the DHCP server isn't available, the client realizes that the lease can't be renewed. The client continues to use the address, and once 87.5 percent of the lease period has elapsed (again, give or take some randomness), the client sends out another renewal request. This interval is known as *T2*. At that point, any DHCP server that hears the renewal can respond to this *DHCP request message* (which is a request for a lease renewal) with a DHCPACK and renew the lease. If at any time during this process the client gets a negative DHCPNACK message, it must stop using its IP address immediately and start the leasing process over from the beginning by requesting a new lease.

When a client initializes its IP networking, it always attempts to renew its old address. If the client has time left on the lease, it continues to use the lease until its end. If the client is unable to get a new lease by that time, all IP functions stop until a new, valid address can be obtained.

DHCP Lease Release

Although leases can be renewed repeatedly, at some point they might run out. Furthermore, the lease process is "at will." That is, the client or server can cancel the lease before it ends. In addition, if the client doesn't succeed in renewing the lease before it expires, the client loses its lease and reverts to APIPA. This release process is important for reclaiming extinct IP addresses used by systems that have moved or switched to a non-DHCP address.

Advantages and Disadvantages of DHCP

DHCP was designed from the start to simplify network management. It has some significant advantages, but it also has some drawbacks.

Advantages of DHCP

The following are advantages of DHCP:

- Configuration of large and even midsized networks is much simpler. If a DNS server address or some other change is necessary to the client, the administrator doesn't have to touch each device in the network physically to reconfigure it with the new settings.

- Once you enter the IP configuration information in one place—the server—it's automatically propagated to clients, eliminating the risk that a user will misconfigure some parameters and require you to fix them.

- IP addresses are conserved because DHCP assigns them only when requested.

- IP configuration becomes almost completely automatic. In most cases, you can plug in a new system (or move one) and then watch as it receives a configuration from the server. For example, when you install new network changes, such as a gateway or DNS server, the client configuration is done at only one location—the DHCP server.

- It allows a preboot execution environment (PXE) client to get a TCP/IP address from DHCP. PXE clients (also called Microsoft Windows Deployment Services [WDS] clients) can get an IP address without needing to have an operating system installed. This allows WDS clients to connect to a WDS server through the TCP/IP protocol and download an operating system remotely.

Disadvantages of DHCP

Unfortunately, there are a few drawbacks with DHCP:

- DHCP can become a single point of failure for your network. If you have only one DHCP server and it's not available, clients can't request or renew leases.

- If the DHCP server contains incorrect information, the misinformation will automatically be delivered to all of your DHCP clients.

- If you want to use DHCP on a multisegment network, you must put either a DHCP server or a relay agent on each segment, or you must ensure that your router can forward Bootstrap Protocol (BOOTP) broadcasts.

Ipconfig Lease Options

The ipconfig command-line tool is useful for working with network settings. Its /renew and /release switches make it particularly handy for DHCP clients. These switches allow you to request renewal of, or give up, your machine's existing address lease. You can do the same thing by toggling the Obtain An IP Address Automatically button in the Internet Protocol (TCP/IP) Properties dialog box, but the command-line option is useful especially when you're setting up a new network.

For example, I spend about a third of my time teaching MCSA or MCSE classes, usually in temporary classrooms set up at conferences, hotels, and so on. Laptops are used in these classes, with one brawny one set up as a DNS/DHCP/DC server. Occasionally, a client will lose its DHCP lease (or not get one, perhaps because a cable has come loose). The quickest way to fix it is to pop open a command-line window and type **ipconfig/renew**.

You can configure DHCP to assign options only to certain classes. *Classes*, defined by an administrator, are groups of computers that require identical DHCP options. The /setclassid*classID* switch of ipconfig is the only way to assign a machine to a class.

More specifically, the switches do the following:

ipconfig /renew   Instructs the DHCP client to request a lease renewal. If the client already has a lease, it requests a renewal from the server that issued the current lease. This is equivalent to what happens when the client reaches the half-life of its lease. Alternatively, if the client doesn't currently have a lease, it is equivalent to what happens when you boot a DHCP client for the first time. It initiates the DHCP mating dance, listens for lease offers, and chooses one it likes.

ipconfig /release   Forces the client to give up its lease immediately by sending the server a DHCP release notification. The server updates its status information and marks the client's old IP address as "available," leaving the client with no address bound to its network interface. When you use this command, most of the time it will be immediately followed by ipconfigrenew. The combination releases the existing lease and gets a new one, probably with a different address. (It's also a handy way to force your client to get a new set of settings from the server before the lease expiration time.)

ipconfig /setclassid*classID*   Sets a new class ID for the client. You will see how to configure class options later in the section "Setting Scope Options for IPv4." For now, you should know that the only way to add a client machine to a class is to use this command. Note that you need to renew the client lease for the class assignment to take effect.

If you have multiple network adapters in a single machine, you can provide the name of the adapter (or adapters) upon which you want the command to work, including an asterisk (*) as a wildcard. For example, one of my servers has two network cards: an Intel EtherExpress (ELNK1) and a generic 100Mbps card. If you want to renew DHCP settings for both adapters, you can type **ipconfig /renew ***. If you just want to renew the Intel EtherExpress card, you can type **ipconfig /renew ELNK'**.

Understanding Scope Details

By now you should have a good grasp of what a lease is and how it works. To learn how to configure your servers to hand out those leases, however, you need to have a complete understanding of some additional topics: scopes, superscopes, exclusions, reservations, address pool, and relay agents.

Scope

Let's start with the concept of a *scope*, which is a contiguous range of addresses. There's usually one scope per physical subnet, and a scope can cover a Class A, Class B, or Class C network address or a TCP/IP v6 address. DHCP uses scopes as the basis for managing and assigning IP addressing information.

Each scope has a set of parameters, or scope options, that you can configure. *Scope options* control what data is delivered to DHCP clients when they're completing the DHCP negotiation process with a particular server. For example, the DNS server name, default gateway, and default network time server are all separate options that can be assigned. These settings are called *option types*. You can use any of the types provided with Windows Server 2012 R2, or you can specify your own.

Superscope

A *superscope* enables the DHCP server to provide addresses from more than one scope to clients on the same physical subnet. This is helpful when clients within the same subnet have more than one IP network and thus need IPs from more than one address pool. Microsoft's DHCP snap-in allows you to manage IP address assignment in the superscope, though you must still configure other scope options individually for each child scope.

Exclusions and Reservations

The scope defines what IP addresses could potentially be assigned, but you can influence the assignment process in two additional ways by specifying exclusions and reservations:

Exclusions   These are IP addresses within the range that you never want automatically assigned. These excluded addresses are off-limits to DHCP. You'll typically use exclusions to tag any addresses that you never want the DHCP server to assign at all. You might use exclusions to set aside addresses that you want to assign permanently to servers that play a vital role in your organization.

Reservations   These are IP addresses within the range for which you want a permanent DHCP lease. They essentially reserve a particular IP address for a particular device. The device still goes through the DHCP process (that is, its lease expires and it asks for a new one), but it always obtains the same addressing information from the DHCP server.

Exclusions are useful for addresses that you don't want to participate in DHCP at all. *Reservations* are helpful for situations in which you want a client to get the same settings each time they obtain an address.

An address cannot be simultaneously reserved and excluded. Be aware of this fact for the exam, possibly relating to a troubleshooting question.

 Real World Scenario

Using Reservations and Exclusions

Deciding when to assign a reservation or exclusion can sometimes be confusing. In practice, you'll find that certain computers in the network greatly benefit by having static IP network information. Servers such as DNS servers, the DHCP server itself, SMTP servers, and other low-level infrastructure servers are good candidates for static assignment. There are usually so few of these servers that the administrator is not overburdened if a change in network settings requires going out to reconfigure each individually. Chances are that the administrator would still need to reconfigure these servers manually (by using ipconfig /release and then ipconfig /renew), even if they did not have IP addresses reserved. Even in large installations, I find it preferable to manage these vital servers by hand rather than to rely on DHCP.

Reservations are also appropriate for application servers and other special but nonvital infrastructure servers. With a reservation in DHCP, the client device will still go through the DHCP process but will always obtain the same addressing information from the DHCP server. The premise behind this strategy is that these nonvital servers can withstand a short outage if DHCP settings change or if the DHCP server fails.

Address Pool

The range of IP addresses that the DHCP server can assign is called its *address pool*. For example, let's say you set up a new DHCP scope covering the 192.168.1 subnet. That gives you 255 IP addresses in the pool. After adding an exclusion from 192.168.1.240 to 192.168.1.254, you're left with 241 (255 − 14) IP addresses in the pool. That means (in theory, at least) that you can service 241 unique clients at a time before you run out of IP addresses.

DHCP Relay Agent

By design, DHCP is intended to work only with clients and servers on a single IP network to communicate. But RFC 1542 sets out how BOOTP (on which DHCP is based) should work in circumstances in which the client and server are on different IP networks. If no DHCP server is available on the client's network, you can use a DHCP relay agent to forward DHCP broadcasts from the client's network to the DHCP server. The relay agent acts like a radio repeater, listening for DHCP client requests and retransmitting them through the router to the server.

Installing and Authorizing DHCP

Installing DHCP is easy using the Windows Server 2012/2012 R2 installation mechanism. Unlike some other services discussed in this book, the installation process installs just the service and its associated snap-in, starting it when the installation is complete. At that point, it's not delivering any DHCP service, but you don't have to reboot.

Installing DHCP

Exercise 2.7 shows you how to install DHCP Server using Server Manager. This exercise was completed on a Windows Server 2012 R2 Member Server since Active Directory is not installed yet.

EXERCISE 2.7

Installing the DHCP Service

1. Choose Server Manager by clicking the Server Manager icon on the taskbar.

2. Click Add Roles And Features.

3. Choose role-based or feature-based installation and click Next.

4. Choose your server and click Next.

5. Choose DHCP and click Next.

6. At the Features screen, click Next.

7. Click Next at the DHCP screen.

8. At the DHCP confirmation screen, click the Install button.

9. When the installation is complete, click the Close button.

10. On the left side, click the DHCP link.

11. Click the More link next to Configuration Required For DHCP Server.

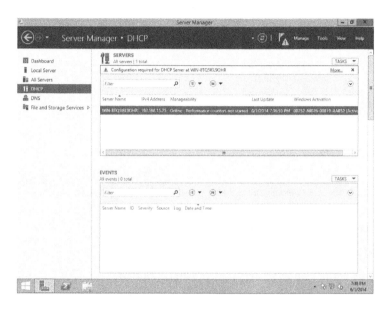

12. Under Action, click Complete DHCP Configuration.

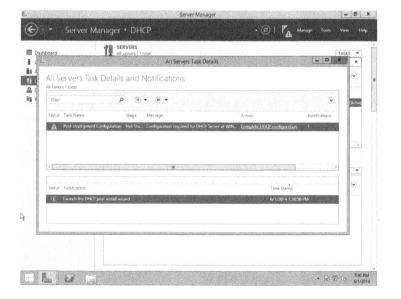

13. At the DHCP Description page, click Commit.

14. Click Close at the Summary screen.

15. Close Server Manager.

Introducing the DHCP Snap-In

When you install the DHCP server, the DHCP snap-in is also installed. You can open it by selecting Administrative Tools ➢ DHCP. Figure 2.17 shows the snap-in.

As you can see, the snap-in follows the standard MMC model. The left pane displays IPv4 and IPv6 sections and which servers are available; you can connect to servers other than the one to which you're already connected. A Server Options folder contains options that are specific to a particular DHCP server. Each server contains subordinate items grouped into folders. Each scope has a folder named after the scope's IP address range. Within each scope, four subordinate views show you interesting things about the scope, such as the following:

- The Address Pool view shows what the address pool looks like.

- The Address Leases view shows one entry for each current lease. Each lease shows the computer name to which the lease was issued, the corresponding IP address, and the current lease expiration time.

FIGURE 2.17   DHCP snap-in

- The Reservations view shows the IP addresses that are reserved and which devices hold them.
- The Scope Options view lists the set of options you've defined for this scope.

Authorizing DHCP for Active Directory

Authorization creates an Active Directory object representing the new server. It helps keep unauthorized servers off your network. Unauthorized servers can cause two kinds of problems. They may hand out bogus leases, or they may fraudulently deny renewal requests from legitimate clients.

When you install a DHCP server using Windows Server 2012/2012 R2 and Active Directory is present on your network, the server won't be allowed to provide DHCP services to clients until it has been authorized. If you install DHCP on a member server in an Active Directory domain or on a stand-alone server, you'll have to authorize the server manually. When you authorize a server, you're adding its IP address to the Active Directory object that contains the IP addresses of all authorized DHCP servers.

You also have the ability to authorize a DHCP server during the installation of DHCP if you are installing DHCP onto an Active Directory machine.

At start time, each DHCP server queries the directory, looking for its IP address on the "authorized" list. If it can't find the list or if it can't find its IP address on the list, the DHCP service fails to start. Instead, it adds a message to the event log, indicating that it couldn't service client requests because the server wasn't authorized.

Exercise 2.8 and Exercise 2.9 show you how to authorize and unauthorize a DHCP server onto a network with Active Directory. If you installed DHCP onto a network with a domain, you can complete the following two exercises, but if you are still on a member server, you *cannot* do these exercises. These are here to show you how to do it after you have Active Directory on your network.

EXERCISE 2.8

Unauthorizing a DHCP Server

1. From Administrative Tools, choose DHCP to open the DHCP snap-in.

2. Right-click the server you want to unauthorize and choose the Unauthorize command.

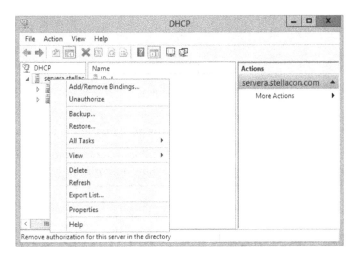

3. Click Yes on the dialog box asking if you are sure you want to complete this action.

EXERCISE 2.9

Authorizing a DHCP Server

1. From Administrative Tools, choose DHCP to open the DHCP snap-in.

2. Right-click the server you want to authorize and choose the Authorize command.

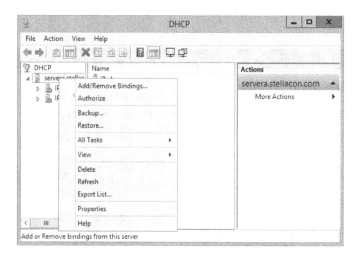

3. Wait a short time (30 to 45 seconds) to allow the authorization to take place.

4. Right-click the server again. Verify that the Unauthorize command appears in the pop-up menu. This indicates that the server is now authorized.

Creating and Managing DHCP Scopes

You can use any number of DHCP servers on a single physical network if you divide the range of addresses that you want assigned into multiple scopes. Each scope contains a number of useful pieces of data, but before you can understand them, you need to know some additional terminology.

You can perform the following management tasks on DHCP scopes:

- Create a scope
- Configure scope properties
- Configure reservations and exclusions
- Set scope options

- Activate and deactivate scopes
- Create a superscope
- Create a multicast scope
- Integrate Dynamic DNS and DHCP

I will cover each task in the following sections.

Creating a New Scope in IPv4

Like many other things in Windows Server 2012 R2, a wizard drives the process of creating a new scope. You will most likely create a scope while installing DHCP, but you may need to create more than one. The overall process is simple, as long as you know beforehand what the wizard is going to ask. If you think about what defines a scope, you'll be well prepared. You need to know the following:

- The IP address range for the scope you want to create.
- Which IP addresses, if any, you want to exclude from the address pool.
- Which IP addresses, if any, you want to reserve.
- Values for the DHCP options you want to set, if any. This item isn't strictly necessary for creating a scope. However, to create a useful scope, you'll need to have some options to specify for the clients.

To create a scope, under the server name, right-click the IPv4 option in the DHCP snap-in, and use the Action ➢ New Scope command. This starts the New Scope Wizard (see Figure 2.18). You will look at each page of the wizard in the following sections.

FIGURE 2.18   Welcome page of the New Scope Wizard

Setting the Screen Name

The Scope Name page allows you to enter a name and description for your scope. These will be displayed by the DHCP snap-in.

It's a good idea to pick sensible names for your scopes so that other administrators will be able to figure out the purpose of the scope. For example, the name DHCP is likely not very helpful, whereas a name like 1st Floor Subnet is more descriptive and can help in troubleshooting.

Defining the IP Address Range

The IP Address Range page (see Figure 2.19) is where you enter the start and end IP addresses for your range. The wizard does minimal checking on the addresses you enter, and it automatically calculates the appropriate subnet mask for the range. You can modify the subnet mask if you know what you're doing.

FIGURE 2.19   IP Address Range page of the New Scope Wizard

Adding Exclusions and Delay

The Add Exclusions And Delay page (see Figure 2.20) allows you to create exclusion ranges. Exclusions are TCP/IP numbers that are in the pool, but they do not get issued to clients. To exclude one address, put it in the Start IP Address field. To exclude a range, also fill in the End IP Address field. The delay setting is a time duration by which the server will delay the transmission of a DHCPOFFER message.

Although you can always add exclusions later, it's best to include them when you create the scope so that no excluded addresses are ever passed out to clients.

FIGURE 2.20   Add Exclusions And Delay page of the New Scope Wizard

Setting a Lease Duration

The Lease Duration page (see Figure 2.21) allows you to set how long a device gets to use an assigned IP address before it has to renew its lease. The default lease duration is eight days. You may find that a shorter or longer duration makes sense for your network. If your network is highly dynamic, with lots of arrivals, departures, and moving computers, set a shorter lease duration; if it's less active, make it longer.

FIGURE 2.21   Lease Duration page of the New Scope Wizard

Remember that renewal attempts begin when approximately half of the lease period is over (give or take a random interval), so don't set them too short.

Configuring Basic DHCP Options

The Configure DHCP Options page (see Figure 2.22) allows you to choose whether you want to set up basic DHCP options such as default gateway and DNS settings. The options are described in the following sections. If you choose not to configure options, you can always do so later. However, you should not activate the scope until you've configured the options you want assigned.

FIGURE 2.22   Configure DHCP Options page of the New Scope Wizard

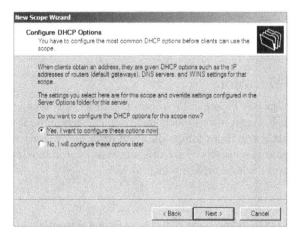

Configuring a Router

The first option configuration page is the Router (Default Gateway) page (see Figure 2.23), in which you enter the IP addresses of one or more routers (more commonly referred to as *default gateways*) that you want to use for outbound traffic. After entering the IP addresses of the routers, use the Up and Down buttons to order the addresses. Clients will use the routers in the order specified when attempting to send outgoing packets.

Providing DNS Settings

On the Domain Name And DNS Servers page (see Figure 2.24), you specify the set of DNS servers and the parent domain you want passed down to DHCP clients. Normally, you'll want to specify at least one DNS server by filling in its DNS name or IP address. You can also specify the domain suffix that you want clients to use as the base domain for all connections that aren't fully qualified. For example, if your clients are used to navigating based on server name alone rather than the fully qualified domain name (FQDN) of server.willpanek.com, then you'll want to place your domain here.

FIGURE 2.23   Router (Default Gateway) page of the New Scope Wizard

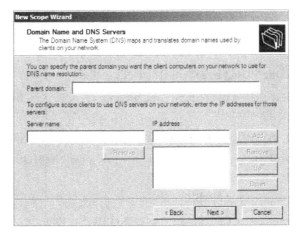

FIGURE 2.24   Domain Name And DNS Servers page of the New Scope Wizard

Providing WINS Settings

If you're still using Windows Internet Name Service (WINS) on your network, you can configure DHCP so that it passes WINS server addresses to your Windows clients. (If you want the Windows clients to honor it, you'll also need to define the WINS/NBT Node Type option for the scope.) As on the DNS server page, on the WINS Servers page (see Figure 2.25) you can enter the addresses of several servers and move them into the order in which you want clients to try them. You can enter the DNS or NetBIOS name of each server, or you can enter an IP address.

FIGURE 2.25   WINS Servers page of the New Scope Wizard

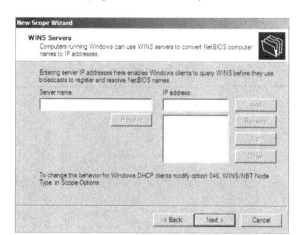

Here are some of the more common options you can set on a DHCP server:

003 Router   Used to provide a list of available routers or default gateways on the same subnet.

006 DNS Servers   Used to provide a list of DNS servers.

015 DNS Domain Name   Used to provide the DNS suffix.

028 Broadcast Address   Used to configure the broadcast address, if different than the default, based on the subnet mask.

44 WINS/NBNS Servers   Used to configure the IP addresses of WINS servers.

46 WINS/NBT Node Type   Used to configure the preferred NetBIOS name resolution method. There are four settings for node type:

B node (0x1)   Broadcast for NetBIOS resolution

P node (0x2)   Peer-to-peer (WINS) server for NetBIOS resolution

M node (0x4)   Mixed node (does a B node and then a P node)

H node (0x8)   Hybrid node (does a P node and then a B node)

051 Lease   Used to configure a special lease duration.

Activating the Scope

The Activate Scope page (see Figure 2.26) gives you the option to activate the scope immediately after creating it. By default, the wizard assumes that you want the scope activated unless you select the No, I Will Activate This Scope Later radio button, in which case the scope will remain dormant until you activate it manually.

FIGURE 2.26 Activate Scope page of the New Scope Wizard

 Be sure to verify that there are no other DHCP servers assigned to the address range you choose!

In Exercise 2.10, you will create a new scope for the 192.168.0.xprivate Class C network. First you need to complete Exercise 2.7 before beginning this exercise.

EXERCISE 2.10

 Creating a New Scope

1. Open the DHCP snap-in by selecting Administrative Tools ➢ DHCP.

2. Right-click the IPv4 folder and choose New Scope. The New Scope Wizard appears.

3. Click the Next button on the welcome page.

4. Enter a name and a description for your new scope and click the Next button.

5. On the IP Address Range page, enter **192.168.0.2** as the start IP address for the scope and **192.168.0.250** as the end IP address. Leave the subnet mask controls alone (though when creating a scope on a production network, you might need to change them). Click the Next button.

6. On the Add Exclusions And Delay page, click Next without adding any excluded addresses or delays.

7. On the Lease Duration page, set the lease duration to 3 days and click the Next button.

8. On the Configure DHCP Options page, click the Next button to indicate you want to configure default options for this scope.

9. On the Router (Default Gateway) page, enter **192.168.0.1** for the router IP address and then click the Add button. Once the address is added, click the Next button.

10. On the Domain Name And DNS Servers page, enter the IP address of a DNS server on your network in the IP Address field (for example, you might enter **192.168.0.251**) and click the Add button. Click the Next button.

11. On the WINS Servers page, click the Next button to leave the WINS options unset.

12. On the Activate Scope page, if your network is currently using the 192.168.0.*x* range, select Yes, I Want To Activate This Scope Now. Click the Next button.

13. When the wizard's summary page appears, click the Finish button to create the scope.

Creating a New Scope in IPv6

Now that you have seen how to create a new scope in IPv4, I'll go through the steps to create a new scope in IPv6.

To create a scope, right-click the IPv6 option in the DHCP snap-in under the server name and select the Action ➢ New Scope command. This starts the New Scope Wizard. Just as with creating a scope in IPv4, the welcome page of the wizard tells you that you've launched the New Scope Wizard. You will look at each page of the wizard in the following sections.

Setting the Screen Name

The Scope Name page (see Figure 2.27) allows you to enter a name and description for your scope. These will be displayed by the DHCP snap-in.

FIGURE 2.27   IPv6 Scope Name page of the New Scope Wizard

It's a good idea to pick a sensible name for your scopes so that other administrators will be able to figure out what the scope is used for.

Scope Prefix

The Scope Prefix page (see Figure 2.28) gets you started creating the IPv6 scope. IPv6 has three types of addresses, which can be categorized by type and scope.

FIGURE 2.28   Scope Prefix page of the New Scope Wizard

Unicast Addresses   *One-to-one.* A packet from one host is delivered to another host. The following are some examples of IPv6 unicast:

- The unicast prefix for site-local addresses is FEC0::/48.
- The unicast prefix for link-local addresses is FE80::/64.

The 6to4 address allows communication between two hosts running both IPv4 and IPv6. The way to calculate the 6to4 address is by combining the global prefix 2002::/16 with the 32 bits of a public IPv4 address of the host. This gives you a 48-bit prefix. 6to4 is described in RFC 3056.

Multicast addresses   *One-to-many.* A packet from one host is delivered to multiple hosts (but not everyone). The prefix for multicast addresses is FF00::/8.

Anycast addresses   A packet from one host is delivered to the nearest of multiple hosts (in terms of routing distance).

Adding Exclusions

As with the IPv4 New Scope Wizard, the Add Exclusions page (see Figure 2.29) allows you to create exclusion ranges. *Exclusions* are TCP/IP numbers that are in the pool but do not get issued to clients. To exclude one address, put it in the Start IPv6 Address field. To exclude a range, also fill in the End IPv6 Address field.

FIGURE 2.29 Add Exclusions page of the New Scope Wizard

Setting a Lease Duration

The Scope Lease page (see Figure 2.30) allows you to set how long a device gets to use an assigned IP address before it has to renew its lease. You can set two different lease durations. The section labeled Non Temporary Address (IANA) is the lease time for your more permanent hosts (such as printers and server towers). The one labeled Temporary Address (IATA) is for hosts that might disconnect at any time, such as laptops.

Activating the Scope

The Completing The New Scope Wizard page (see Figure 2.31) gives you the option to activate the scope immediately after creating it. By default, the wizard will assume you want the scope activated. If you want to wait to activate the scope, choose No in the Activate Scope Now box.

Changing Scope Properties (IPv4 and IPv6)

Each scope has a set of properties associated with it. Except for the set of options assigned by the scope, you can find these properties on the General tab of the scope's Properties

FIGURE 2.30 Scope Lease page of the New Scope Wizard

FIGURE 2.31 Completing The New Scope Wizard page of the New Scope Wizard

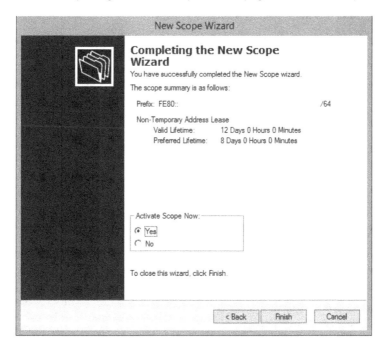

dialog box (see Figure 2.32). Some of these properties, such as the scope name and description, are self-explanatory. Others require a little more explanation.

FIGURE 2.32   General tab of the scope's Properties dialog box for an IPv4 scope

- The Start IP Address and End IP Address fields allow you to set the range of the scope.
- For IPv4 scopes, the settings in the section Lease Duration For DHCP Clients control how long leases in this scope are valid.

  The IPv6 scope dialog box includes a Lease tab where you set the lease properties.

When you make changes to these properties, they have no effect on existing leases. For example, say you create a scope from 172.30.1.1 to 172.30.1.199. You use that scope for a while and then edit its properties to reduce the range from 172.30.1.1 to 172.30.1.150. If a client has been assigned the address 172.30.1.180, which was part of the scope before you changed it, the client will retain that address until the lease expires but will not be able to renew it.

Changing Server Properties

Just as each scope has its own set of properties, so too does the server itself. You access the server properties by right-clicking the IPv4 or IPv6 object within the DHCP management console and selecting Properties.

IPv4 Server Properties

Figure 2.33 shows the IPv4 Properties dialog box.

FIGURE 2.33   General tab of the IPv4 Properties dialog box for the server

The IPv4 Properties dialog box has four tabs: General, DNS, Network Access Protection, and Advanced.

The Advanced tab, shown in Figure 2.34, contains the following configuration parameters:

- Audit Log File Path is where you enter the location for log files.

- Conflict Detection Attempts specifies how many ICMP echo requests (pings) the server sends for an address it is about to offer. The default is 0. Conflict detection is a way to verify that the DHCP server is not issuing IP addresses that are already being used on the network.

The Network Access Protection tab (see Figure 2.35) allows you to set up *Network Access Protection (NAP)*. With NAP, which is a Windows Server 2012 R2 service, an administrator can perform the following tasks:

- Carry out computer health policy validation

- Ensure ongoing compliance with health policies

- Optionally restrict the access of computers that do not meet the computer health requirements

FIGURE 2.34   The Advanced tab of the IPv4 Properties dialog box for the server

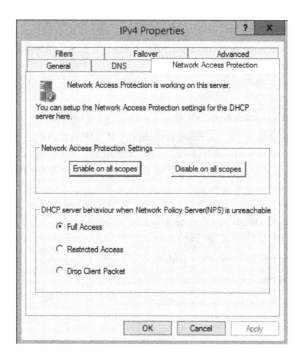

FIGURE 2.35   The Network Access Protection tab of the IPv4 Properties dialog box for the server

IPv6 Server Properties

The IPv6 Properties dialog box for the server has two tabs: General and Advanced. On the General tab (see Figure 2.36), you can configure the following settings:

- Frequency with which statistics are updated
- DHCP auditing

FIGURE 2.36   Server's IPv6 Properties, General tab

The Advanced tab (see Figure 2.37) allows you to configure the following settings:

- Database path for the audit log file path.
- Connection bindings.
- Registration credentials for dynamic DNS. The registration credential is the user account that DHCP will use to register clients with Active Directory.

Managing Reservations and Exclusions

After defining the address pool for your scope, the next step is to create reservations and exclusions, which reduce the size of the pool. In the following sections, you will learn how to add and remove exclusions and reservations.

FIGURE 2.37   Server's IPv6 Properties, Advanced tab

Adding and Removing Exclusions

When you want to exclude an entire range of IP addresses, you need to add that range as an exclusion. Ordinarily, you'll want to do this before you enable a scope because that prevents any of the IP addresses you want excluded from being leased before you have a chance to exclude them. In fact, you can't create an exclusion that includes a leased address—you have to get rid of the lease first.

Adding an Exclusion Range

Here's how to add an exclusion range:

1. Open the DHCP snap-in and find the scope to which you want to add an exclusion (either IPv4 or IPv6).

2. Expand the scope so that you can see its Address Pool item for IPv4 or the Exclusion section for IPv6.

3. Right-click the Address Pool or Exclusion section and choose the New Exclusion Range command.

4. When the Add Exclusion dialog box appears (see Figure 2.38), enter the IP addresses you want to exclude. To exclude a single address, type it in the Start IP Address field. To exclude a range of addresses, also fill in the End IP Address field.

5. Click the Add button to add the exclusion.

When you add exclusions, they appear in the Address Pool node, which is under the Scope section for IPv4 and under the Exclusion section of IPv6.

FIGURE 2.38 Add Exclusion dialog boxes for IPv4 and IPv6

IPv4 Add Exclusion dialog box   IPv6 Add Exclusion dialog box

Removing an Exclusion Range

To remove an exclusion, just right-click it and choose the Delete command. After confirming your command, the snap-in removes the excluded range and the addresses become immediately available for issuance.

Adding and Removing Reservations

Adding a reservation is simple as long as you have the MAC address of the device for which you want to create a reservation. Because reservations belong to a single scope, you create and remove them within the Reservations node beneath each scope.

Adding a Reservation

To add a reservation, perform the following tasks:

1. Right-click the scope and select New Reservation.

   This displays the New Reservation dialog box, shown in Figure 2.39.

FIGURE 2.39 New Reservation dialog boxes for IPv4 and IPv6

IPv4 New Reservation dialog box   IPv6 New Reservation dialog box

2. Enter the IP address and MAC address or ID for the reservation.

> To find the MAC address of the local computer, use the `ipconfig` command. To find the MAC address of a remote machine, use the `nbtstat-a`*computername* command.

3. If you want, you can also enter a name and description.

4. For IPv4, in the Supported Types section, choose whether the reservation will be made by DHCP only, BOOTP only (useful for remote-access devices), or both.

Removing a Reservation

To remove a reservation, right-click it and select Delete. This removes the reservation but does nothing to the client device.

> There's no way to change a reservation once it has been created. If you want to change any of the associated settings, you'll have to delete and re-create the reservation.

Setting Scope Options for IPv4

Once you've installed a server, authorized it in Active Directory, and fixed up the address pool, the next step is to set scope options that you want sent out to clients, such as router (that is, default gateway) and DNS server addresses. You must configure the options you want sent out before you activate a scope. If you don't, clients may register in the scope without getting any options, rendering them virtually useless. Thus, configure the scope options, along with the IP address and subnet mask that you configured earlier in this chapter.

In the following sections, you will learn how to configure and assign scope options on the DHCP server.

Understanding Option Assignment

You can control which DHCP options are doled out to clients in five (slightly overlapping) ways:

Predefined Options   *Predefined options* are templates that are available in the Server, Scope, or Client Options dialog box.

Server Options   *Server options* are assigned to all scopes and clients of a particular server. That means if there's some setting you want all clients of a DHCP server to have, no matter what scope they're in, this is where you assign it. Specific options (those that are set at the class, scope, or client level) will override server-level options. That gives you an escape valve; it's a better idea, though, to be careful about which options you assign if your server manages multiple scopes.

Scope Options   If you want a particular option value assigned only to those clients in a certain subnet, you should assign it as a *scope option*. For example, it's common to specify different routers for different physical subnets; if you have two scopes corresponding to different subnets, each scope would probably have a separate value for the router option.

Class Options   You can assign different options to clients of different types, that is, *class options*. For example, Windows 2000, XP, Vista, Windows 7, Windows 8, Server 2003, Server 2003 R2, Server 2008, Server 2008 R2, and Server 2012/2012 R2 machines recognize a number of DHCP options that Windows 98, Windows NT, and Mac OS machines ignore, and vice versa. By defining a Windows 2000 or newer class (using the `ipconfig /setclassid` command you saw earlier), you could assign those options only to machines that report themselves as being in that class.

Client Options   If a client is using DHCP reservations, you can assign certain options to that specific client. You attach *client options* to a particular reservation. Client options override scope, server, and class options. The only way to override a client option is to configure the client manually. The DHCP server manages client options.

> Client options override class options, class options override scope options, and scope options override server options.

Assigning Options

You can use the DHCP snap-in to assign options at the scope, server, reserved address, or class level. The mechanism you use to assign these options is the same for each; the only difference is where you set the options.

When you create an option assignment, remember that it applies to all of the clients in the server or the scope from that point forward. Option assignments aren't retroactive, and they don't migrate from one scope to another.

Creating and Assigning a New Option

To create a new option and have it assigned, follow these steps:

1.   Select the scope or server where you want the option assigned.

2.   Select the corresponding Options node and choose Action ➤ Configure Options.

   To set options for a reserved client, right-click its entry in the Reservations node and select Configure Options.

   Then you'll see the Scope Options dialog box (see Figure 2.40), which lists all of the options that you might want to configure.

3.   To select an individual option, check the box next to it and then use the controls in the Data Entry control group to enter the value you want associated with the option.

FIGURE 2.40 The Scope Options dialog box

4. Continue to add options until you've specified all of the ones you want attached to the server or scope. Then click OK.

Configuring the DHCP Server for Classes

You saw how to assign classes to individual machines earlier in the chapter. Now you will learn how to configure the DHCP server to recognize your customized classes and configure options for them. In Exercise 2.11, you will create a new user class and configure options for the new class. Before you begin, make sure that the computers you want to use in the class have been configured with the `ipconfig /setclassid` command, as described in the section "Ipconfig Lease Options" earlier in this chapter.

EXERCISE 2.11

Configuring User Class Options

1. Open the DHCP snap-in by selecting Administrative Tools ➢ DHCP.

2. Right-click the IPv4 item and select Define User Classes.

3. Click the Add button in the DHCP User Classes dialog box.

4. In the New Class dialog box, enter a descriptive name for the class in the Display Name field. Enter a class ID in the ID field. (Typically, you will enter the class ID in the ASCII portion of the ID field.) When you have finished, click OK.

5. The new class appears in the DHCP User Classes dialog box. Click the Close button to return to the DHCP snap-in.

6. Right-click the Scope Options node and select Configure Options.

7. Click the Advanced tab. Select the class you defined in step 4 from the User Class pop-up menu.

8. Configure the options you want to set for the class. Click OK when you have finished. Notice that the options you configured (and the class with which they are associated) appear in the right pane of the DHCP window.

About the Default Routing and Remote Access Predefined User Class

Windows Server 2012/2012 R2 includes a predefined user class called the *Default Routing and Remote Access class*. This class includes options important to clients connecting to Routing and Remote Access, notably the 051 Lease option.

Be sure to know that the 051 Lease option is included within this class and that it can be used to assign a shorter lease duration for clients connecting to Routing and Remote Access.

Activating and Deactivating Scopes

When you've completed the steps in Exercise 2.5 and you're ready to unleash your new scope so that it can be used to make client assignments, the final required step is activating the scope. When you activate a scope, you're just telling the server that it's OK to start handing out addresses from that scope's address pool. As soon as you activate a scope, addresses from its pool may be assigned to clients. Of course, this is a necessary precondition to getting any use out of your scope.

If you later want to stop using a scope, you can, but be aware that it's a permanent change. When you deactivate a scope, DHCP tells all clients registered with the scope that they need to release their leases immediately and renew them someplace else—the equivalent of a landlord who evicts tenants when the building is condemned!

Don't deactivate a scope unless you want clients to stop using it immediately.

Creating a Superscope for IPv4

A *superscope* allows the DHCP server to provide multiple logical subnet addresses to DHCP clients on a single physical network. You create superscopes with the New Superscope command, which triggers the New Superscope Wizard.

You can have only one superscope per server.

The steps in Exercise 2.12 take you through the process of creating a superscope.

EXERCISE 2.12

Creating a Superscope

1. Open the DHCP snap-in by selecting Administrative Tools ➢ DHCP.

2. Follow the instructions in Exercise 2.10 to create two scopes: one for 192.168.0.2 through 192.168.0.127 and one for 192.168.1.12 through 192.168.1.127.

3. Right-click IPv4 and choose the New Superscope command. The New Superscope Wizard appears. Click the Next button.

4. On the Superscope Name page, name your superscope and click the Next button.

5. The Select Scopes page appears, listing all scopes on the current server. Select the two scopes you created in step 2 and then click the Next button.

6. The wizard's summary page appears. Click the Finish button to create your scope.

7. Verify that your new superscope appears in the DHCP snap-in.

Deleting a Superscope

You can delete a superscope by right-clicking it and choosing the Delete command. A superscope is just an administrative convenience, so you can safely delete one at any time—it doesn't affect the "real" scopes that make up the superscope.

Adding a Scope to a Superscope

To add a scope to an existing superscope, find the scope you want to add, right-click it, and choose Action ➢ Add To Superscope. A dialog box appears, listing all of the superscopes known to this server. Pick the one to which you want the current scope appended and click the OK button.

Removing a Scope from a Superscope

To remove a scope from a superscope, open the superscope and right-click the target scope. The pop-up menu provides a Remove From Superscope command that will do the deed.

Activating and Deactivating Superscopes

Just as with regular scopes, you can activate and deactivate superscopes. The same restrictions and guidelines apply. You must activate a superscope before it can be used, and you must not deactivate it until you want all of your clients to lose their existing leases and be forced to request new ones.

To activate or deactivate a superscope, right-click the superscope name, and select Activate or Deactivate, respectively, from the pop-up menu.

Creating IPv4 Multicast Scopes

Multicasting occurs when one machine communicates to a network of subscribed computers rather than specifically addressing each computer on the destination network. It's much more efficient to multicast a video or audio stream to multiple destinations than it is to unicast it to the same number of clients, and the increased demand for multicast-friendly network hardware has resulted in some head scratching about how to automate the multicast configuration.

In the following sections, you will learn about MADCAP, the protocol that controls multicasting, and about how to build and configure a multicast scope.

Understanding the Multicast Address Dynamic Client Allocation Protocol

DHCP is usually used to assign IP configuration information for *unicast* (or one-to-one) network communications. With multicast, there's a separate type of address space assigned from 224.0.0.0 through 239.255.255.255. Addresses in this space are known as *Class D addresses*, or simply *multicast addresses*. Clients can participate in a multicast just by knowing (and using) the multicast address for the content they want to receive. However, multicast clients also need to have an ordinary IP address.

How do clients know what address to use? Ordinary DHCP won't help because it's designed to assign IP addresses and option information to one client at a time. Realizing this, the Internet Engineering Task Force (IETF) defined a new protocol: *Multicast Address Dynamic Client Allocation Protocol (MADCAP)*. MADCAP provides an analog to DHCP but for multicast use. A MADCAP server issues leases for multicast addresses only. MADCAP clients can request a multicast lease when they want to participate in a multicast.

DHCP and MADCAP have some important differences. First you have to realize that the two are totally separate. A single server can be a DHCP server, a MADCAP server, or both; no implied or actual relation exists between the two. Likewise, clients can use DHCP and/or MADCAP at the same time—the only requirement is that every MADCAP client has to get a unicast IP address from somewhere.

Remember that DHCP can assign options as part of the lease process but MADCAP cannot. The only thing MADCAP does is dynamically assign multicast addresses.

Building Multicast Scopes

Most of the steps you go through when creating a multicast scope are identical to those required for an ordinary unicast scope. Exercise 2.13 highlights the differences.

EXERCISE 2.13

Creating a New Multicast Scope

1. Open the DHCP snap-in by selecting Administrative Tools ➢ DHCP.

2. Right-click IPv4 and choose New Multicast Scope. The New Multicast Scope Wizard appears. Click the Next button on the welcome page.

3. In the Multicast Scope Name page, name your multicast scope (and add a description if you'd like). Click the Next button.

4. The IP Address Range page appears. Enter a start IP address of **224.0.0.0** and an end IP address of **224.255.0.0**. Adjust the TTL to 1 to make sure that no multicast packets escape your local network segment. Click the Next button when you're finished.

5. The Add Exclusions page appears; click its Next button.

6. The Lease Duration page appears. Since multicast addresses are used for video and audio, you'd ordinarily leave multicast scope assignments in place somewhat longer than you would with a regular unicast scope, so the default lease length is 30 days (instead of 8 days for a unicast scope). Click the Next button.

7. The wizard asks you if you want to activate the scope now. Click the No radio button and then the Next button.

8. The wizard's summary page appears; click the Finish button to create your scope.

9. Verify that your new multicast scope appears in the DHCP snap-in.

Setting Multicast Scope Properties

Once you create a multicast scope, you can adjust its properties by right-clicking the scope name and selecting Properties.

The Multicast Scope Properties dialog box has two tabs. The General tab (see Figure 2.41) allows you to change the scope's name, its start and end addresses, its Time To Live (TTL) value, its lease duration, and its description—in essence, all of the settings you provided when you created it in the first place.

The Lifetime tab (see Figure 2.42) allows you to limit how long your multicast scope will be active. By default, a newly created multicast scope will live forever, but if you're creating a scope to provide MADCAP assignments for a single event (or a set of events of limited duration), you can specify an expiration time for the scope. When that time is reached, the scope disappears from the server but not before making all of its clients give up their multicast address leases. This is a nice way to make sure that the lease cleans up after itself when you're finished with it.

FIGURE 2.41 General tab of the Multicast Scope Properties dialog box

FIGURE 2.42 Lifetime tab of the Multicast Scope Properties dialog box

Integrating Dynamic DNS and IPv4 DHCP

DHCP integration with Dynamic DNS is a simple concept but powerful in action. By setting up this integration, you can pass addresses to DHCP clients while still maintaining the integrity of your DNS services.

The DNS server can be updated in two ways. One way is for the DHCP client to tell the DNS server its address. Another way is for the DHCP server to tell the DNS server when it registers a new client.

Neither of these updates will take place, however, unless you configure the DNS server to use Dynamic DNS. You can make this change in two ways:

- If you change it at the scope level, it will apply only to the scope.

- If you change it at the server level, it will apply to all scopes and superscopes served by the server.

Which of these options you choose depends on how widely you want to support Dynamic DNS; most of the sites I visit have enabled DNS updates at the server level.

To update the settings at either the server or scope level, you need to open the scope or server properties by right-clicking the appropriate object and choosing Properties. The DNS tab of the Properties dialog box (see Figure 2.43) includes the following options:

Enable DNS Dynamic Updates According To The Settings Below   This check box controls whether this DHCP server will attempt to register lease information with a DNS server. It must be checked to enable Dynamic DNS.

> **Dynamically Update DNS A And PTR Records Only If Requested By The DHCP Clients**   This radio button (which is on by default) tells the DHCP server to register the update only if the DHCP client asks for DNS registration. When this button is active, DHCP clients that aren't hip to DDNS won't have their DNS records updated. However, Windows 2000, XP, Vista, Windows 7, Windows 8, Server 2003/2003 R2, Server 2008/2008 R2, and Server 2012/2012 R2 DHCP clients are smart enough to ask for the updates.

> **Always Dynamically Update DNS A And PTR Records**   This radio button forces the DHCP server to register any client to which it issues a lease. This setting may add DNS registrations for DHCP-enabled devices that don't really need them, such as print servers. However, it allows other clients (such as Mac OS, Windows NT, and Linux machines) to have their DNS information automatically updated.

Discard A And PTR Records When Lease Is Deleted   This check box has a long name but a simple function. When a DHCP lease expires, what should happen to the DNS registration? Obviously, it would be nice if the DNS record associated with a lease vanished when the lease expired. When this check box is checked (as it is by default), that's exactly what happens. If you uncheck this box, your DNS will contain entries for expired leases that are no longer valid. When a particular IP address is reissued on a new lease, the DNS will be updated, but in between leases you'll have incorrect data in your DNS—something that's always best to avoid.

Dynamically Update DNS A And PTR Records For DHCP Clients That Do Not Request Updates   This check box lets you handle these older clients graciously by making the updates using a separate mechanism.

In Exercise 2.14, you will enable a scope to participate in Dynamic DNS updates.

FIGURE 2.43   DNS tab of the scope's IPv4 Properties dialog box

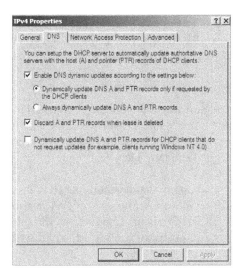

EXERCISE 2.14

Enabling DHCP-DNS Integration

1. Open the DHCP snap-in by selecting Administrative Tools ➢ DHCP.

2. Right-click the IPv4 item and select Properties.

3. The Server Properties dialog box appears. Click the DNS tab.

4. Verify that the check box labeled Enable DNS Dynamic Updates According To The Settings Below is checked and verify that the radio button labeled Dynamically Update DNS A And PTR Records Only If Requested By The DHCP Clients is selected.

5. Verify that the check box labeled Discard A And PTR Records When Lease Is Deleted is checked. If not, then check it.

6. Click the OK button to apply your changes and close the Server Properties dialog box.

Using Multiple DHCP Servers

DHCP can become a single point of failure within a network if there is only one DHCP server. If that server becomes unavailable, clients will not be able to obtain new leases or renew existing leases. For this reason, it is recommended that you have more than one DHCP server in the network. However, more than one DHCP server can create problems if they both are configured to use the same scope or set of addresses. Microsoft recommends the 80/20 rule for redundancy of DHCP services in a network.

Implementing the 80/20 rule calls for one DHCP server to make approximately 80 percent of the addresses for a given subnet available through DHCP while another server makes the remaining 20 percent of the addresses available. For example, with a /24 network of 254 addresses, say 192.168.1.1 to 192.168.1.254, you might have Server 1 offer 192.168.1.10 to 192.168.1.210 while Server 2 offers 192.168.1.211 to 192.168.254.

DHCP Load Sharing

Load sharing is the normal default way that you use multiple DHCP servers (as explained earlier). Both servers cover the same subnets (remember that a DHCP server can handle multiple subnets at the same time) simultaneously, and both servers assign IP addresses and options to clients on the assigned subnets. The client requests are load balanced and shared between the two servers.

This is a good option for a company that has multiple DHCP servers in the same physical location. The DHCP servers are set up in a failover relationship at the same site, and both servers respond to all DHCP client requests from the subnets to which they are associated. The DHCP server administrator can set the load distribution ratio between the multiple DHCP servers.

DHCP Hot Standby

When thinking of a DHCP hot standby setup, think of the old server failover cluster. You have two servers where one server does all of the work and the other server is a standby server in the event that the first server crashes or goes down.

In a DHCP hot standby situation, the two DHCP servers operate in a failover relationship where one server acts as an active server and is responsible for leasing IP addresses to all clients in a scope or subnet. The secondary DHCP server assumes the standby role, and it is ready to go in the event that the primary DHCP server becomes unavailable. If the primary server becomes unavailable, the secondary DHCP server is given the role of the primary DHCP server and takes over all the responsibilities of the primary DHCP server.

This failover situation is best suited to DHCP deployments where a company has DHCP servers in multiple locations.

To learn more about DHCP failover situations, please visit Microsoft at http://technet.microsoft.com/en-us/library/hh831385.aspx. Microsoft has been known for taking questions right off its websites, and this website is the perfect solution for doing this.

Working with the DHCP Database Files

DHCP uses a set of database files to maintain its knowledge of scopes, superscopes, and client leases. These files, which live in the *systemroot*\System32\DHCP folder, are always open when the DHCP service is running. DHCP servers use Joint Engine Technology (JET) databases to maintain their records.

 You shouldn't modify or alter the DHCP database files when the service is running.

The primary database file is dhcp.mdb—it has all of the scope data in it.
The following files are also part of the DHCP database:

Dhcp.tmp This is a backup copy of the database file created during reindexing of the database. You normally won't see this file, but if the service fails during reindexing, it may not remove the file when it should.

J50.log This file (plus a number of files named J50xxxxx.log, where xxxxx stands for 00001, 00002, 00003, and so on) is a log file that stores changes before they're written to the database. The DHCP database engine can recover some changes from these files when it restarts.

J50.chk This is a checkpoint file that tells the DHCP engine which log files it still needs to recover.

In the following sections, you will see how to manipulate the DHCP database files.

Removing the Database Files

If you're convinced that your database is corrupt because the lease information that you see doesn't match what's on the network, the easiest repair mechanism is to remove the database files and start over with an empty database.

 If you think the database is corrupt because the DHCP service fails at startup, you should check the event log.

To start over, follow these steps:

1. Stop the DHCP service by typing **net stop dhcpserver** at the command prompt.
2. Remove all of the files from the *systemroot*\system32\DHCP folder.
3. Restart the service (at command prompt type **net start dhcpserver**).
4. Reconcile the scope.

Changing the Database Backup Interval

By default, the DHCP service backs up its databases every 60 minutes. You can adjust this setting by editing the Backup Interval value under HKEY_LOCAL_MACHINE\SYSTEM\ CurrentControlSet\Services\DHCPServer\Parameters. This allows you to make backups either more frequently (if your database changes a lot or if you seem to have ongoing corruption problems) or less often (if everything seems to be on an even keel).

Moving the DHCP Database Files

You may find that you need to dismantle or change the role of your DHCP server and offload the DHCP functions to another computer. Rather than spend the time re-creating the DHCP database on the new machine by hand, you can copy the database files and use them directly. This is especially helpful if you have a complicated DHCP database with lots of reservations and option assignments.

By copying the files, you also minimize the amount of human error that could be introduced by reentering the information by hand.

Compacting the DHCP Database Files

There may be a time when you need to compact the DHCP database. Microsoft has a utility called jetpack.exe that allows you to compact the JET database. Microsoft JET databases are used for WINS and DHCP databases. If you wanted to use the jetpack command, the proper syntax is

```
JETPACK.EXE <database name><temp database name>
```

After you compact the database, you rename the temp database to dhcp.mdb.

Summary

DNS was designed to be a robust, scalable, and high-performance system for resolving friendly names to TCP/IP host addresses. This chapter presented an overview of the basics of DNS and how DNS names are generated. We then looked at the many new features available in the Microsoft Windows Server 2012 R2 version of DNS, and we focused on how to install, configure, and manage the necessary services. Microsoft's DNS is based on a widely accepted set of industry standards. Because of this, Microsoft's DNS can work with both Windows- and non-Windows-based networks.

This chapter also covered the DHCP lease process as it relates to TCP/IP configuration information for clients. The following stages were covered: IP discovery, IP lease offer, IP lease selection, and IP lease acknowledgment. You learned how to install and configure the DHCP server on Windows Server 2012 R2 and how to create and manage DHCP scopes and scope options. I also discussed the authorization of DHCP servers within Active Directory and scopes for IPv4 and IPv6 and showed how to create them. Finally, I covered superscopes as well as managing client leases with the options therein.

Exam Essentials

Understand the purpose of DNS. DNS is a standard set of protocols that defines a mechanism for querying and updating address information in the database, a mechanism for replicating the information in the database among servers, and a schema of the database.

Understand the different parts of the DNS database. The SOA record defines the general parameters for the DNS zone, including who is the authoritative server. NS records list the name servers for a domain; they allow other name servers to look up names in your domain. A host record (also called an address record or an A record) statically associates a host's name with its IP addresses. Pointer records (PTRs) map an IP address to a hostname, making it possible to do reverse lookups. Alias records allow you to use more than one name to point to a single host. The MX record tells you which servers can accept mail bound for a domain. SRV records tie together the location of a service (like a domain controller) with information about how to contact the service.

Know how DNS resolves names. With iterative queries, a client asks the DNS server for an answer, and the client, or resolver, returns the best kind of answer it has available. In a recursive query, the client sends a query to one name server, asking it to respond either with the requested answer or with an error. The error states either that the server can't come up with the right answer or that the domain name doesn't exist. With inverse queries, instead of supplying a name and then asking for an IP address, the client first provides the IP address and then asks for the name.

Understand the differences among DNS servers, clients, and resolvers. Any computer providing domain name services is a DNS server. A DNS client is any machine issuing queries to a DNS server. A resolver handles the process of mapping a symbolic name to an actual network address.

Know how to install and configure DNS. DNS can be installed before, during, or after installing the Active Directory service. When you install the DNS server, the DNS snap-in is installed too. Configuring a DNS server ranges from easy to difficult, depending on what you're trying to make it do. In the simplest configuration, for a caching-only server, you don't have to do anything except to make sure the server's root hints are set correctly. You can also configure a root server, a normal forward lookup server, and a reverse lookup server.

Know how to create new forward and reverse lookup zones. You can use the New Zone Wizard to create a new forward or reverse lookup zone. The process is basically the same for both types, but the specific steps and wizard pages differ somewhat. The wizard walks you through the steps, such as specifying a name for the zone (in the case of forward lookup zones) or the network ID portion of the network that the zone covers (in the case of reverse lookup zones).

Know how to configure zones for dynamic updates. The DNS service allows dynamic updates to be enabled or disabled on a per-zone basis at each server. This is easily done in the DNS snap-in.

Know how to delegate zones for DNS. DNS provides the ability to divide the namespace into one or more zones; these can then be stored, distributed, and replicated to other DNS servers. When delegating zones within your namespace, be aware that for each new zone you create, you need delegation records in other zones that point to the authoritative DNS servers for the new zone.

Understand the tools that are available for monitoring and troubleshooting DNS. You can use the DNS snap-in to do some basic server testing and monitoring. More important, you use the snap-in to monitor and set logging options. Windows Server 2012 R2 automatically logs DNS events in the event log under a distinct DNS server heading. Nslookup offers the ability to perform query testing of DNS servers and to obtain detailed responses at the command prompt. You can use the command-line tool ipconfig to view your DNS client settings, to view and reset cached information used locally for resolving DNS name queries, and to register the resource records for a dynamic update client. Finally, you can configure the DNS server to create a log file that records queries, notification messages, dynamic updates, and various other bits of DNS information.

Know how to install and authorize a DHCP server. You install the DHCP service using the Add/Remove Windows Components Wizard. You authorize the DHCP server using the DHCP snap-in. When you authorize a server, you're actually adding its IP address to the Active Directory object that contains a list of the IP addresses of all authorized DHCP servers.

Know how to create a DHCP scope. You use the New Scope Wizard to create a new scope for both IPv4 and IPv6. Before you start, you'll need to know the IP address range for the scope you want to create; which IP addresses, if any, you want to exclude from the address pool; which IP addresses, if any, you want to reserve; and the values for the DHCP options you want to set, if any.

Understand how relay agents help with multiple physical network segments. A question about relay agents on the exam may appear to be a DHCP-related question. Relay agents assist DHCP message propagation across network or router boundaries where such messages ordinarily wouldn't pass.

Understand the difference between exclusions and reservations. When you want to exclude an entire range of IP addresses, you need to add that range as an exclusion. Any IP addresses within the range for which you want a permanent DHCP lease are known as reservations. Remember that exclusions are TCP/IP numbers in a pool that do not get issued and reservations are numbers in a TCP/IP pool that get issued only to the same client each time.

Review Questions

1. You are the network administrator for the ABC Company. Your network consists of two DNS servers named *DNS1* and *DNS2*. The users who are configured to use DNS2 complain because they are unable to connect to Internet websites. The following table shows the configuration of both servers:

   DNS1   DNS2

   `_msdcs.abc.comabc.com`   `.(root)_msdcs.abc.comabc.com`

   The users connected to DNS2 need to be able to access the Internet. What needs to be done?

   A. Build a new Active Directory Integrated zone on DNS2.

   B. Delete the `.(root)` zone from DNS2 and configure conditional forwarding on DNS2.

   C. Delete the current `cache.dns` file.

   D. Update your `cache.dns` file and root hints.

2. You are the network administrator for a large company that has one main site and one branch office. Your company has a single Active Directory forest, `ABC.com`. You have a single domain controller (ServerA) in the main site that has the DNS role installed. ServerA is configured as a primary DNS zone. You have decided to place a domain controller (ServerB) in the remote site and implement the DNS role on that server. You want to configure DNS so that, if the WAN link fails, users in both sites can still update records and resolve any DNS queries. How should you configure the DNS servers?

   A. Configure ServerB as a secondary DNS server. Set replication to occur every five minutes.

   B. Configure ServerB as a stub zone.

   C. Configure ServerB as an Active Directory Integrated zone and convert ServerA to an Active Directory Integrated zone.

   D. Convert ServerA to an Active Directory Integrated zone and configure ServerB as a secondary zone.

3. You are the network administrator for a midsize computer company. You have a single Active Directory forest, and your DNS servers are configured as Active Directory Integrated zones. When you look at the DNS records in Active Directory, you notice that there are many records for computers that do not exist on your domain. You want to make sure that only domain computers register with your DNS servers. What should you do to resolve this issue?

   A. Set dynamic updates to None.

   B. Set dynamic updates to Nonsecure And Secure.

   C. Set dynamic updates to Domain Users Only.

   D. Set dynamic updates to Secure Only.

4. Your company consists of a single Active Directory forest. You have a Windows Server 2012 R2 domain controller that also has the DNS role installed. You also have a Unix-based DNS server at the same location. You need to configure your Windows DNS server to allow zone transfers to the Unix-based DNS server. What should you do?

   A. Enable BIND secondaries.

   B. Configure the Unix machine as a stub zone.

   C. Convert the DNS server to Active Directory Integrated.

   D. Configure the Microsoft DNS server to forward all requests to the Unix DNS server.

5. You are the network administrator for Stellacon Corporation. Stellacon has two trees in its Active Directory forest, stellacon.com and abc.com. Company policy does not allow DNS zone transfers between the two trees. You need to make sure that when anyone in abc.com tries to access the stellacon.com domain, all names are resolved from the stellacon.com DNS server. What should you do?

   A. Create a new secondary zone in abc.com for stellacon.com.

   B. Configure conditional forwarding on the abc.com DNS server for stellacon.com.

   C. Create a new secondary zone in stellacon.com for abc.com.

   D. Configure conditional forwarding on the stellacon.com DNS server for abc.com.

6. You are the network administrator for your organization. A new company policy states that all inbound DNS queries need to be recorded. What can you do to verify that the IT department is compliant with this new policy?

   A. Enable Server Auditing – Object Access.

   B. Enable DNS debug logging.

   C. Enable server database query logging.

   D. Enable DNS Auditing – Object Access.

7. You are the network administrator for a small company with two DNS servers: DNS1 and DNS2. Both DNS servers reside on domain controllers. DNS1 is set up as a standard primary zone, and DNS2 is set up as a secondary zone. A new security policy was written stating that all DNS zone transfers must be encrypted. How can you implement the new security policy?

   A. Enable the Secure Only setting on DNS1.

   B. Enable the Secure Only setting on DNS2.

   C. Configure Secure Only on the Zone Transfers tab for both servers.

   D. Delete the secondary zone on DNS2. Convert both DNS servers to use Active Directory Integrated zones.

8. You are responsible for DNS in your organization. You look at the DNS database and see a large number of older records on the server. These records are no longer valid. What should you do?

   A. In the zone properties, enable Zone Aging and Scavenging.

   B. In the server properties, enable Zone Aging and Scavenging.

   C. Manually delete all of the old records.

   D. Set Dynamic Updates to None.

9. Your IT team has been informed by the compliance team that it needs copies of the DNS Active Directory Integrated zones for security reasons. You need to give the Compliance department a copy of the DNS zone. How should you accomplish this goal?

   A. Run dnscmd /zonecopy.

   B. Run dnscmd /zoneinfo.

   C. Run dnscmd /zoneexport.

   D. Run dnscmd /zonefile.

10. You are the network administrator for a Windows Server 2012 R2 network. You have multiple remote locations connected to your main office by slow satellite links. You want to install DNS into these offices so that clients can locate authoritative DNS servers in the main location. What type of DNS servers should be installed in the remote locations?

    A. Primary DNS zones

    B. Secondary DNS zones

    C. Active Directory Integrated zones

    D. Stub zones

Chapter

3

Plan and Install Active Directory

THE FOLLOWING 70-410 EXAM OBJECTIVES ARE COVERED IN THIS CHAPTER:

✓ **Install domain controllers**

- Add or remove a domain controller from a domain
- Upgrade a domain controller
- Install Active Directory Domain Services (AD DS) on a Server Core installation
- Install a domain controller from Install from Media (IFM)
- Resolve DNS SRV record registration issues
- Configure a global catalog server
- Deploy Active Directory iaas in Windows Azure

Now that you are familiar with Domain Name System (DNS), you need to verify that the computer you upgrade to a domain controller (DC) meets the basic file system and network connectivity requirements so that Active Directory runs smoothly and efficiently in your organization.

Next, you'll explore the concept of *domain functional levels*, which essentially determine what sorts of domain controllers you can use in your environment. For instance, in the Windows Server 2003 domain functional level, you can include Server 2012/2012 R2, Server 2008 R2, Server 2008, and Server 2003 domain controllers, but the functionality of the domain is severely limited.

Once you understand how to plan properly for your domain environment, you will learn how to install Active Directory, which you will accomplish by promoting a Windows Server 2012 R2 computer to a domain controller. I will also discuss a feature in Windows Server 2012 R2 called a *read-only domain controller (RODC)*.

After you become familiar with the initial Active Directory installation, you will learn how to install and configure Application Directory partitions. These partitions provide replicable data repositories using the Active Directory paradigm, but they don't actually store any security principals, such as users or groups. As the name implies, you use Application Directory partitions primarily to store data generated by applications that need to be replicated throughout your network environments independent of the rest of Active Directory.

The final section of this chapter deals with integrating DNS with Active Directory. You learned about DNS in Chapter 2, "Configure Network Services," but in this chapter I will review how DNS implements with Active Directory.

For these exercises, I assume you are creating a Windows Server 2012 R2 machine in a test environment and not on a live network. If this Windows Server 2012 R2 machine is being added into a Windows Server 2012 or 2008 R2 domain, you will need to prep the domain (explained in the section "Adprep" later in this chapter).

Verifying the File system

When you're planning your Active Directory deployment, the file system that the operating system uses is an important concern for two reasons. First, the file system can provide the ultimate level of security for all the information stored on the server itself. Second, it is responsible for managing and tracking all of this data. The Windows Server 2012 R2 plat-form supports two file systems:

- Windows NT File System (NTFS)
- Resilient File System (ReFS)

Although ReFS was new to Windows Server 2012, NTFS has been around for many years, and NTFS in Windows Server 2012 R2 has been improved for better performance.

If you have been working with servers for many years, you may have noticed a few changes to the server file system choices. For example, in Windows Server 2003, you could choose between FAT, FAT32, and NTFS. In Windows Server 2008 R2, you could choose between FAT32 and NTFS. In Windows Server 2012 R2, you will notice that all versions of FAT have been removed (see Figure 3.1).

FIGURE 3.1   Format options on Windows Server 2012 R2

Resilient File System (ReFS)

Windows Server 2012 R2 now includes a new file system called *Resilient File System (ReFS)*. ReFS was created to help Windows Server 2012 R2 maximize the availability of data and online operation. ReFS allows the Windows Server 2012 R2 system to continue to function despite some errors that would normally cause data to be lost or the system to go down. ReFS uses data integrity to protect your data from errors and also to make sure that all of your important data is online when that data is needed.

One of the issues that IT members have had to face over the years is the problem of rapidly growing data sizes. As we continue to rely more and more on computers, our data continues to get larger and larger. This is where ReFS can help an IT department. ReFS was designed specifically with the issues of scalability and performance in mind, which resulted in some of the following ReFS features:

Availability   If your hard disk becomes corrupt, ReFS has the ability to implement a salvage strategy that removes the data that has been corrupted. This feature allows the healthy data to continue to be available while the unhealthy data is removed. All of this can be done without taking the hard disk offline.

Scalability   One of the main advantages of ReFS is the ability to support volume sizes up to 2^{78} bytes using 16KB cluster sizes, while Windows stack addressing allows 2^{64} bytes. ReFS also supports file sizes of $2^{64}-1$ bytes, 2^{64} files in a directory, and the same number of directories in a volume.

Robust Disk Updating   ReFS uses a disk updating system referred to as an *allocate-on-write transactional model* (also known as *copy on write*). This model helps to avoid many hard disk issues while data is written to the disk because ReFS updates data using disk writes to multiple locations in an atomic manner instead of updating data in place.

Data Integrity   ReFS uses a check-summed system to verify that all data that is being written and stored is accurate and reliable. ReFS always uses allocate-on-write for updates to the data, and it uses checksums to detect disk corruption.

Application Compatibility   ReFS allows for most NTFS features and also supports the Win32 API. Because of this, ReFS is compatible with most Windows applications.

NTFS

Let's start with some of the features of NTFS. There are many benefits to using NTFS, including support for the following:

Disk Quotas   To restrict the amount of disk space used by users on the network, system administrators can establish *disk quotas*. By default, Windows Server 2012 R2 supports disk quota restrictions at the volume level. That is, you can restrict the amount of storage space that a specific user uses on a single disk volume. Third-party solutions that allow more granular quota settings are also available.

File System Encryption   One of the fundamental problems with network operating systems (NOSs) is that system administrators are often given full permission to view all files and data stored on hard disks, which can be a security and privacy concern. In some cases, this is necessary. For example, to perform backup, recovery, and disk management functions, at least one user must have all permissions. Windows Server 2012 R2 and NTFS address these issues by allowing for *file system encryption*. Encryption essentially scrambles all of the data stored within files before they are written to the disk. When an authorized user requests the files, they are transparently decrypted and provided. By using encryption, you can prevent the data from being used in case it is stolen or intercepted by an unauthorized user—even a system administrator.

Dynamic Volumes   Protecting against disk failures is an important concern for production servers. Although earlier versions of Windows NT supported various levels of Redundant Array of Independent Disks (RAID) technology, software-based solutions had some short-comings. Perhaps the most significant was that administrators needed to perform server reboots to change RAID configurations. Also, you could not make some configuration changes without completely reinstalling the operating system. With Windows Server 2012 R2 support for *dynamic volumes*, system administrators can change RAID and other disk configuration settings without needing to reboot or reinstall the server. The result is greater data protection, increased scalability, and increased uptime. Dynamic volumes are also included with ReFS.

Mounted Drives   By using *mounted drives*, system administrators can map a local disk drive to an NTFS directory name. This helps them organize disk space on servers and increase manageability. By using mounted drives, you can mount the C:\Users directory to an actual physical disk. If that disk becomes full, you can copy all of the files to another, larger drive without changing the directory path name or reconfiguring applications.

Remote Storage   System administrators often notice that as soon as they add more space, they must plan the next upgrade. One way to recover disk space is to move infrequently used files to external hard drives. However, backing up and restoring these files can be quite difficult and time-consuming. System administrators can use the *remote storage* features supported by NTFS to off-load seldom-used data automatically to a backup system or other devices. The files, however, remain available to users. If a user requests an archived file, Windows Server 2012 R2 can automatically restore the file from a remote storage device and make it available. Using remote storage like this frees up system administrators' time and allows them to focus on tasks other than micromanaging disk space.

Self-healing NTFS   In previous versions of the Windows Server operating system, if you had to fix a corrupted NTFS volume, you used a tool called Chkdsk.exe. The disadvantage of this tool is that the Windows Server's availability was disrupted. If this server was your domain controller, that could stop domain logon authentication.

To help protect the Windows Server 2012 R2 NTFS file system, Microsoft now uses a feature called self-healing NTFS. *Self-healing NTFS* attempts to fix corrupted NTFS file systems without taking them offline. Self-healing NTFS allows an NTFS file system to be corrected without running the Chkdsk.exe utility. New features added to the NTFS kernel code allow disk inconsistencies to be corrected without system downtime.

Security   NTFS allows you to configure not only folder-level security but also file-level security. NTFS security is one of the biggest reasons most companies use NTFS. ReFS also allows folder- and file-level security.

Setting Up the NTFS Partition

Although the features mentioned in the previous section likely compel most system administrators to use NTFS, additional reasons make using it mandatory. The most important reason is that the Active Directory data store must reside on an NTFS partition. Therefore, before you begin installing Active Directory, make sure you have at least one NTFS partition available. Also, be sure you have a reasonable amount of disk space available (at least 4GB). Because the size of the Active Directory data store will grow as you add objects to it, also be sure that you have adequate space for the future.

Exercise 3.1 shows you how to use the administrative tools to view and modify disk configuration.

 WARNING   Before you make any disk configuration changes, be sure you completely understand their potential effects; then perform the test in a lab environment and make sure you have good, verifiable backups handy. Changing partition sizes and adding and removing partitions can result in a total loss of all information on one or more partitions.

If you want to convert an existing partition from FAT or FAT32 to NTFS, you need to use the CONVERT command-line utility. For example, the following command converts the C: partition from FAT to NTFS:

```
CONVERT c: /fs:ntfs
```

EXERCISE 3.1

Viewing Disk Configuration

1. Press the Windows key on the keyboard (left side between the Ctrl and Alt keys) and then choose Administrative Tools.

2.   Double-click Computer Management.

3.   Under Storage, click Disk Management.

The Disk Management program shows you the logical and physical disks that are currently configured on your system. Note that information about the size of each partition is also displayed (in the Capacity column).

4.   Use the View menu to choose various depictions of the physical and logical drives in your system.

5.   To see the available options for modifying partition settings, right-click any of the disks or partitions. This step is optional.

6.   Close Computer Management.

Verifying Network Connectivity

Although a Windows Server 2012 R2 computer can be used by itself without connecting to a network, you will not harness much of the potential of the operating system without network connectivity. Because the fundamental purpose of a network operating system is to provide resources to users, you must verify network connectivity.

Basic Connectivity Tests

Before you begin to install Active Directory, you should perform several checks of your current configuration to ensure that the server is configured properly on the network. You should test the following:

Network Adapter   At least one network adapter should be installed and properly configured on your server. A quick way to verify that a network adapter is properly installed is to use the Computer Management administrative tool. Under Device Manager, Network Adapters branch, you should have at least one network adapter listed. If you do not, use the Add Hardware icon in Control Panel to configure hardware.

TCP/IP   Make sure that TCP/IP is installed, configured, and enabled on any necessary network adapters. The server should also be given a valid IP address and subnet mask. Optionally, you may need to configure a default gateway, DNS servers, WINS servers, and other network settings. If you are using DHCP, be sure that the assigned information is correct. It is always a good idea to use a static IP address for servers because IP address changes can cause network connectivity problems if they are not handled properly.

    You must understand TCP/IP to use Windows Server 2012 R2 and Active Directory. TCP/IP will be covered in greater detail in Chapter 8, "Configure TCP/IP."

Internet Access   If the server should have access to the Internet, verify that it is able to connect to external web servers and other machines outside of the local area network (LAN). If the server is unable to connect, you might have a problem with the TCP/IP configuration.

LAN Access   The server should be able to view other servers and workstations on the network. If other machines are not visible, make sure that the network and TCP/IP configurations are correct for your environment.

Client Access   Network client computers should be able to connect to your server and view any shared resources. A simple way to test connectivity is to create a share and test whether other machines are able to see files and folders within it. If clients cannot access the machine, make sure that both the client and the server are configured properly.

Wide Area Network Access   If you're working in a distributed environment, you should ensure that you have access to any remote sites or users who will need to connect to this machine. Usually, this is a simple test that can be performed by a network administrator.

Tools and Techniques for Testing Network Configuration

In some cases, verifying network access can be quite simple. You might have some internal and external network resources with which to test. In other cases, it might be more complicated. You can use several tools and techniques to verify that your network configuration is correct.

Using the `Ipconfig` Utility   By typing **`ipconfig/all`** at the command prompt, you can view information about the TCP/IP settings of a computer. Figure 3.2 shows the types of information you'll receive.

FIGURE 3.2 Viewing TCP/IP information with the **ipconfig** utility

Using the **Ping** Command   The ping command was designed to test connectivity to other computers. You can use the command simply by typing **ping** and then an IP address or hostname at the command line. The following are some steps for testing connectivity using the ping command.

Ping Other Computers on the Same Subnet   You should start by pinging a known active IP address on the network to check for a response. If you receive one, then you have connectivity to the network.

Next check to see whether you can ping another machine using its hostname. If this works, then local name resolution works properly.

Ping Computers on Different Subnets   To ensure that routing is set up properly, you should attempt to ping computers that are on other subnets (if any exist) on your network. If this test fails, try pinging the default gateway. Any errors may indicate a problem in the network configuration or a problem with a router.

When You Don't Receive a Response

Some firewalls, routers, or servers on your network or on the Internet might prevent you from receiving a successful response from a ping command. This is usually for security reasons (malicious users might attempt to disrupt network traffic using excessive pings as well as redirects and smurf attacks). If you do not receive a response, do not assume that the service is not available. Instead, try to verify connectivity in other ways. For example, you can use the TRACERT command to demonstrate connectivity beyond your subnet, even if other routers ignore Internet Control Message Protocol (ICMP) responses. Because the display of a second router implies connectivity, the path to an ultimate destination shows success even if it does not display the actual names and addresses.

Browsing the Network   To ensure that you have access to other computers on the network, be sure that they can be viewed by clicking Network. This verifies that your name resolution parameters are set up correctly and that other computers are accessible. Also, try connecting to resources (such as file shares or printers) on other machines.

By default, Network Discovery is turned off. To browse the network, you must first enable Network Discovery from the Control Panel in the Network and Sharing Center ➢ Advanced Sharing settings.

Browsing the Internet   You can quickly verify whether your server has access to the Internet by visiting a known website, such as www.microsoft.com. Success ensures that you have access outside of your network. If you do not have access to the Web, you might need to verify your proxy server settings (if applicable) and your DNS server settings.

By performing these simple tests, you can ensure that you have a properly configured network connection and that other network resources are available.

Understanding Domain and Forest Functionality

Windows Server 2012 R2 Active Directory uses a concept called *domain and forest functionality.* The functional level that you choose during the Active Directory installation determines which features your domain can use.

Windows Server 2008, Windows Server 2008 R2, Windows Server 2012, and Windows Server 2012 R2 include additional forest functionality compared to Windows Server 2003. Forest functionality applies to all of the domains within a forest.

About the Domain Functional Level

Windows Server 2012 R2 will support the following domain functional levels:

- Windows Server 2003
- Windows Server 2008
- Windows Server 2008 R2
- Windows Server 2012
- Windows Server 2012 R2

Which function level you use depends on the domain controllers you have installed on your network. This is an important fact to remember. You can use Windows Server 2003, Windows Server 2008/2008 R2, and Windows 2012 member servers in the Windows

Server 2012 R2 function level as long as all domain controllers are running Windows Server 2012 R2.

When you are deciding which function level you will use in your organization, you must choose the function level of your lowest domain controller. For example, if you have a Windows Server 2003 domain controller, your function levels should be Windows Server 2003. If you choose a higher level, the Windows Server 2003 domain controller will not function. Be careful—once a forest function level is upgraded, it cannot be downgraded lower than Windows Server 2008.

Table 3.1 shows the features available in Windows Server 2003, Windows Server 2008, Windows Server 2008 R2, Windows Server 2012, and Windows Server 2012 R2 domain function levels.

TABLE 3.1   Comparing domain functional levels

Domain functional feature	Windows Server 2003	Windows Server 2008	Windows Server 2008 R2	Windows Server 2012	Windows Server 2012 R2
Authentication assurance	Disabled	Disabled	Enabled	Enabled	Enabled
Fine-grained password policies	Disabled	Enabled	Enabled	Enabled	Enabled
Last interactive logon information	Disabled	Enabled	Enabled	Enabled	Enabled
Advanced Encryption Services (AES 128 and 256) support for the Kerberos protocol	Disabled	Enabled	Enabled	Enabled	Enabled
Distributed File System replication support for Sysvol	Disabled	Enabled	Enabled	Enabled	Enabled
Read-only domain controller (RODC)	Enabled	Enabled	Enabled	Enabled	Enabled
Ability to redirect the Users and Computers containers	Enabled	Enabled	Enabled	Enabled	Enabled
Ability to rename domain controllers	Enabled	Enabled	Enabled	Enabled	Enabled

TABLE 3.1   Comparing domain functional levels *(continued)*

Domain functional feature	Windows Server 2003	Windows Server 2008	Windows Server 2008 R2	Windows Server 2012	Windows Server 2012 R2
Logon time stamp updates	Enabled	Enabled	Enabled	Enabled	Enabled
Kerberos KDC key version numbers	Enabled	Enabled	Enabled	Enabled	Enabled
Passwords for InetOrgPerson objects	Enabled	Enabled	Enabled	Enabled	Enabled
Converts NT groups to domain local and global groups	Enabled	Enabled	Enabled	Enabled	Enabled
SID history	Enabled	Enabled	Enabled	Enabled	Enabled
Group nesting	Enabled	Enabled	Enabled	Enabled	Enabled
Universal groups	Enabled	Enabled	Enabled	Enabled	Enabled

About Forest Functionality

Windows Server 2012 R2 forest functionality applies to all of the domains in a forest. All domains have to be upgraded to Windows Server 2012 R2 before the forest can be upgraded to Windows Server 2012 R2.

There are five levels of forest functionality:

- Windows Server 2003
- Windows Server 2008
- Windows Server 2008 R2
- Windows Server 2012
- Windows Server 2012 R2

Windows Server 2003, Windows Server 2008, Windows Server 2008 R2, Windows Server 2012, and Windows Server 2012 R2 have many of the same forest features. Some of these features are described in the following list:

Global Catalog Replication Enhancements   When an administrator adds a new attribute to the global catalog, only those changes are replicated to other global catalogs in the forest. This can significantly reduce the amount of network traffic generated by replication.

Defunct Schema Classes and Attributes   You can never permanently remove classes and attributes from the Active Directory schema. However, you can mark them as defunct so that they cannot be used. With Windows Server 2003, Windows Server 2008, Windows Server 2008 R2, Windows Server 2012, and Windows Server 2012 R2 forest functionality, you can redefine the defunct schema attribute so that it occupies a new role in the schema.

Forest Trusts   Previously, system administrators had no easy way of granting permission on resources in different forests. Windows Server 2003, Windows Server 2008, Windows Server 2008 R2, Windows Server 2012, and Windows Server 2012 R2 resolve some of these difficulties by allowing trust relationships between separate Active Directory forests. Forest trusts act much like domain trusts, except that they extend to every domain in two forests. Note that all forest trusts are intransitive.

Linked Value Replication   Windows Server 2003, Windows Server 2008, Windows Server 2008 R2, Windows Server 2012, and Windows Server 2012 R2 use a concept called *linked value replication*. With linked value replication, only the user record that has been changed is replicated (not the entire group). This can significantly reduce network traffic associated with replication.

Renaming Domains   Although the Active Directory domain structure was originally designed to be flexible, there were several limitations. Because of mergers, acquisitions, corporate reorganizations, and other business changes, you may need to rename domains. In Windows Server 2003, Windows Server 2008, Windows Server 2008 R2, Windows Server 2012, and Windows Server 2012 R2 you can change the DNS and NetBIOS names for any domain. Note that this operation is not as simple as just issuing a rename command. Instead, there's a specific process that you must follow to make sure the operation is successful. Fortunately, when you properly follow the procedure, Microsoft supports domain renaming even though not all applications support it.

Other Features   Windows Server 2008, Windows Server 2008 R2, Windows Server 2012, and Windows Server 2012 R2 also support the following features:

- Improved replication algorithms and dynamic auxiliary classes are designed to increase performance, scalability, and reliability.

- *Active Directory Federation Services (AD FS)*, also known as *Trustbridge*, handles federated identity management. *Federated identity management* is a standards-based information technology process that enables distributed identification, authentication, and authorization across organizational and platform boundaries. The ADFS solution in Windows Server 2003 R2, Windows Server 2008, Windows Server 2008 R2, Windows Server 2012, and Windows Server 2012 R2 helps administrators address these challenges by enabling organizations to share a user's identity information securely.

- *Active Directory Lightweight Directory Services (AD LDS)* was developed for organizations that require flexible support for directory-enabled applications. AD LDS, which uses the Lightweight Directory Access Protocol (LDAP), is a directory service that adds flexibility and helps organizations avoid increased infrastructure costs.

- Active Directory Recycle Bin (Windows Server 2008 R2 Forest level or higher) provides administrators with the ability to restore deleted objects in their entirety while AD DS is running. Before this, if you deleted an Active Directory object, you needed to recover it from a backup. Now you can recover the object from the AD recycle bin.

Many of the concepts related to domain and forest functional features are covered in greater detail later in this book.

Planning the Domain Structure

Once you have verified the technical configuration of your server for Active Directory, it's time to verify the Active Directory configuration for your organization. Since the content of this chapter focuses on installing the first domain in your environment, you really need to know only the following information prior to beginning setup:

- The DNS name of the domain

- The computer name or the NetBIOS name of the server (which will be used by previous versions of Windows to access server resources)

- In which domain function level the domain will operate

- Whether other DNS servers are available on the network

- What type of and how many DNS servers are available on the network

However, if you will be installing additional domain controllers in your environment or will be attaching to an existing Active Directory structure, you should also have the following information:

- If this domain controller will join an existing domain, you should know the name of that domain. You will also either require a password for a member of the Enterprise Administrators group for that domain or have someone with those permissions create a domain account before promotion.

- You should know whether the new domain will join an existing tree and, if so, the name of the tree it will join.

- You should know the name of a forest to which this domain will connect (if applicable).

Installing Active Directory

Installing Active Directory is an easy and straightforward process as long as you plan adequately and make the necessary decisions beforehand. There are many ways that you can install Active Directory. You can install Active Directory by using the Windows Server 2012 R2 installation disk (Install from Media (IFM)), using Server Manager, or using Windows PowerShell. But before you can do the actual installation, you must first make sure that your network is ready for the install.

In the following sections, you'll look at the required steps to install the first domain controller in a given environment.

Adprep

When you are adding a new user to Active Directory, you fill in fields such as First Name, Last Name, and so on. These fields are called *attributes*. The problem is that when you go to install Windows Server 2012 R2, its version of Active Directory has newer attributes than the previous versions of Active Directory. Thus, you need to set up your current version of Active Directory so that it can accept the installation of Windows Server 2012 R2 Active Directory. This is why you use Adprep. Adprep is required to run in order to add the first Windows Server 2012 R2 domain controller to an existing domain or forest.

You would need to run `Adprep /forestprep` to add the first Windows Server 2012 R2 domain controller to an existing forest. `Adprep /forestprep` must be run by an administrator who is a member of the Enterprise Admins group, the Schema Admins group, and the Domain Admins group of the domain that hosts the schema master.

You would need to run `Adprep /domainprep` to add the first Windows Server 2012 R2 domain controller to an existing domain. Again, to achieve this command, you must be a member of the Domain Admins group of the domain where you are installing the Windows Server 2012 R2 domain controller.

`Adprep /rodcprep` must be run to add the first Windows Server 2012 R2 RODC to an existing forest. The administrator who runs this command must be a member of the Enterprise Admins group.

One feature that is new to the Windows Server 2012 R2 Active Directory installation process is that, if needed, Adprep will automatically be executed during the normal Active Directory Domain Services installation.

Active Directory Prerequisites

Before you install Active Directory into your network, you must first make sure that your network and the server meet some minimum requirements. Table 3.2 will show you the requirements needed for Active Directory.

TABLE 3.2 Active Directory requirements

Requirement	Description
Adprep	When adding the first Windows Server 20012 R2 domain controller to an existing Active Directory domain, Adprep commands run automatically as needed.
Credentials	When installing a new AD DS forest, the administrator must be set to local Administrator on the first server. To install an additional domain controller in an existing domain, you need to be a member of the Domain Admins group.
DNS	Domain Name System needs to be installed for Active Directory to function properly. You can install DNS during the Active Directory installation.
NTFS	The Windows Server 2012 R2 drives that store the database, log files, and SYSVOL folder must be placed on a volume that is formatted with the NTFS file system.
RODCs	Read Only Domain Controllers can be installed as long as another domain controller (Windows Server 2008 or newer) already exists on the domain. Also the Forest functional level must be at least Windows Server 2003.
TCP/IP	You must configure the appropriate TCP/IP settings on your domain, and you must configure the DNS server addresses.

The Installation Process

Windows Server 2012 R2 computers are configured as either member servers (if they are joined to a domain) or stand-alone servers (if they are part of a workgroup). The process of converting a server to a domain controller is known as *promotion*. Through the use of a simple and intuitive wizard in Server Manager, system administrators can quickly configure servers to be domain controllers after installation. Administrators also have the ability to promote domain controllers using Windows PowerShell.

The first step in installing Active Directory is promoting a Windows Server 2012 R2 computer to a domain controller. The first domain controller in an environment serves as the starting point for the forest, trees, domains, and the operations master roles.

Exercise 3.2 shows the steps you need to follow to promote an existing Windows Server 2012 R2 computer to a domain controller. To complete the steps in this exercise, you must have already installed and configured a Windows Server 2012 R2 computer. You also need a DNS server that supports SRV records. If you do not have a DNS server available, the Active Directory Installation Wizard automatically configures one for you.

Promoting a Domain Controller

1. Install the Active Directory Domain Services by clicking the Add Roles And Features link in Server Manager's Dashboard view.

2. At the Before You Begin screen, click Next.

3. The Select installation Type screen will be next. Make sure that the Role-Based radio button is selected and click Next.

4. At the Select Destination Server screen, choose the local machine. Click Next.

5. At the Select Server Roles screen, click the check box for Active Directory Domain Services.

EXERCISE 3.2 *(continued)*

6. After you check the Active Directory Domain Services box, a pop-up menu will appear asking you to install additional features. Click the Add Features button.

7. Click Next.

8. At the Select Features screen, accept the defaults and click Next.

9. Click Next at the information screen.

10. Click the Install button at the Confirmation Installation screen.

11. The Installation Progress screen will show you how the installation is progressing.

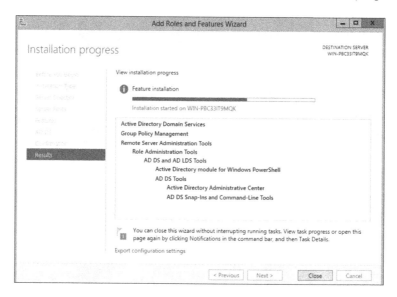

12. After the installation is complete, click the Close button.

13. On the left side window, click the AD DS link.

14. Click the More link next to Configuration Required for Active Directory Domain Services.

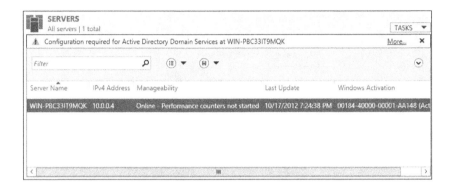

15. Under the Post-Deployment Configuration section, click the Promote This Server To A Domain Controller link.

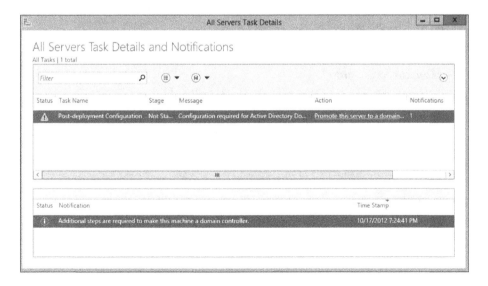

16. At this point, you will configure this domain controller. You are going to install a new domain controller in a new domain in a new forest. At the Deployment Configuration screen, choose the Add A New Forest radio button. You then need to add a root domain name. In this exercise, I will use Sybex.com. Click Next.

EXERCISE 3.2 *(continued)*

17. At the Domain Controller Options screen, set the following options:

   ▪ Function levels: Windows Server 2008 R2 (for both)

   ▪ Verify that the DNS and Global Catalog check boxes are checked

   ▪ Password: **P@ssw0rd**

   Then click Next.

18. At the DNS screen, click Next.

19. At the additional options screen, accept the default NetBIOS domain name and click Next.

20. At the Paths screen, accept the default file locations and click Next.

21. At the Review Options screen, verify your settings and click Next.

22. At the Prerequisites Check screen, click the Install button (as long as there are no errors).

23. After the installation completes, the machine will automatically reboot. Log in as the administrator.

24. Close Server Manager.

25. Click the Start button on the keyboard and choose Administrative Tools.

26. You should see new MMC snap-ins for Active Directory.

EXERCISE 3.2 *(continued)*

27. Close the Administrative Tools window.

In Exercise 3.3, you will learn how to install Active Directory on a Server Core installation. You will use Windows Server 2012 R2 Datacenter Server Core. Before actually installing AD DS, you will learn how to configure the computer name, the time, the administrator password, and a static TCP/IP address, and then you will install DNS.

EXERCISE 3.3

Installing AD DS on Server Core

1. At the Server Core command prompt, type **cd\windows\system32** and press Enter.

2. Type **timedate.cpl** and set your date, local time zone, and time. Click OK.

3. Type **Netsh** and press Enter.

4. Type **Interface**, and press Enter.

5. Type **IPv4**, and press Enter.

6. Type **Show IP** and press Enter. This will show you the current TCP/IP address and the interface with which the TCP/IP address is associated.

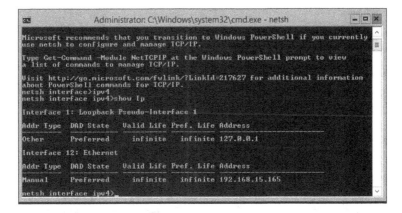

7. As you can see, interface 12 is my Ethernet interface. To change this interface, type the following command and press Enter:

```
Set address name="12" source=static address=192.168.15.165
mask=255.255.255.0 gateway=192.168.15.1
```

I used 192.168.15.x for my address. You can replace the address, mask, and gateway based on your local settings.

EXERCISE 3.3 *(continued)*

8. Type **Show IP** and press Enter. You should see that the new address is now manual and set to the IP address you set.

9. Type **Exit** and press Enter.

10. Type **Net User Administrator** ⋆ and press Enter.

11. Type in your password and then confirm the password. I used P@ssw0rd for my password.

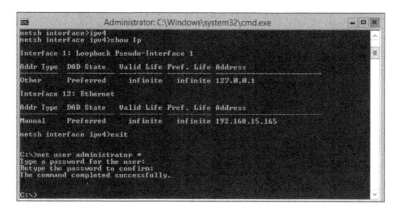

12. Type the following command and press Enter:

    Netdom renamecomputer %computername% /newname:ServerA

13. Type **Y** and press Enter.

14. Type **Shutdown /R /T 0** and press Enter. This will reboot the machine. After the reboot, log back into the system.

15. Type **PowerShell** and press Enter.

16. At the PowerShell prompt, type **Add-WindowsFeature DNS** and press Enter. This will add DNS to the server.

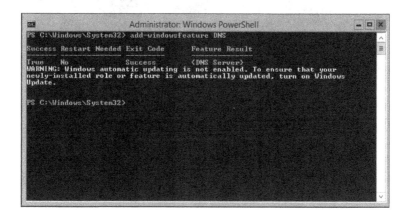

17. At the PowerShell prompt, type **Add-WindowsFeature AD-Domain-Services** and press Enter.

18. At the PowerShell prompt, type **Import-Module ADDSDeployment**.

19. At the PowerShell prompt, type **Install-ADDSForest**.

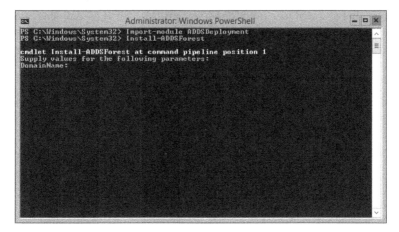

20. Type in your domain name and press Enter. I used Sybex.com.

21. Next you will be asked for your Safe mode administrator password. Type in **P@ssw0rd** and then confirm it.

22. Type **Y** and press Enter.

Active Directory will install, and the machine will automatically reboot.

Deploying Active Directory IaaS in Windows Azure

Well before I jump into this topic, I must first explain what I am talking about. Windows Azure is a Microsoft cloud platform that allows you to put your server data into the cloud. Deploying Active Directory with IaaS means you are using virtualization for the deployment.

So, to put this in a nutshell, when doing this type of install, it's actually not too far off from the install you already did. You create a virtual server and then install Active Directory. Then you upload that virtual server to the cloud.

 I understand that I have not explained virtualization, but Hyper-V and virtualization will be covered in detail in Chapter 9, "Use Virtualization in Windows Server 2012 R2."

Now that you understand what this section is about, let's talk about some of the tasks that are different from the normal way you install Active Directory virtually. There are three main differences when installing Active Directory IaaS on Windows Azure.

Windows Azure virtual machines may need to have connectivity to the corporate network.   Microsoft states that you don't have to have connectivity to your on-site corporate network, but you will lose functionality. Thus, Microsoft recommends that you set up connectivity, and to do that, you must use Windows Azure Virtual Network. Windows Azure Virtual Network includes a site-to-site or site-to-point virtual private network (VPN) component capable of seamlessly connecting Windows Azure virtual machines and on-site machines.

Static IP addresses are *not* supported on Windows Azure virtual machines.   Normally, when setting up a server, we all use static IP addresses. This is actually required on a DHCP server, DNS server, and so on. But when you deploy Active Directory IaaS in Windows Azure, you must use Dynamic TCP/IP addressing, and this requires that you set up Windows Azure Virtual Network.

IP addresses for Windows Azure virtual machines are attached to Windows Azure Virtual Network, and that TCP/IP address persists for the lifetime of the virtual machine. Because of this, the Windows Server Active Directory requirements for IP addressing are met, and the requirements for DNS are also met if you want the server to have both roles.

Windows Azure allows for two distinct disk types for virtual machines.   As you will learn in Chapter 9, the selection of the virtual machine disk type is important when deploying domain controllers. Windows Azure allows both "operating system disks" and "data disks." Most of the time you will use data disks when installing Active Directory on the virtual machine. Data disks use write-through caching, guaranteeing durability of writes, and this is important to the integrity of any Windows Server active machine. There are some other factors of which you should be aware when choosing your disk type. Please check Microsoft's website for more details when choosing a disk type.

Verifying Active Directory Installation

Once you have installed and configured Active Directory, you'll want to verify that you have done so properly. In the following sections, you'll look at methods for doing this.

Using Event Viewer

The first (and perhaps most informative) way to verify the operations of Active Directory is to query information stored in the Windows Server 2012 R2 event log. You can do this using the Windows Server 2012 R2 Event Viewer. Exercise 3.4 walks you through this procedure. Entries seen with the Event Viewer include errors, warnings, and informational messages.

To complete the steps in Exercise 3.4, you must have configured the local machine as a domain controller.

EXERCISE 3.4

Viewing the Active Directory Event Log

1. Open Administrative tools by pressing the Windows key and choosing Administrative Tools.

2. Open the Event Viewer snap-in from the Administrative Tools program group.

3. In the left pane, under Applications And Services Logs, select Directory Service.

4. In the right pane, you can sort information by clicking column headings. For example, you can click the Source column to sort by the service or process that reported the event.

5. Double-click an event in the list to see the details for that item. Note that you can click the Copy button to copy the event information to the Clipboard. You can then paste the data into a document for later reference. Also, you can move between items using the up and down arrows. Click OK when you have finished viewing an event.

6. Filter an event list by right-clicking the Directory Service item in the left pane and selecting Filter Current Log. Note that filtering does not remove entries from the event logs—it only restricts their display.

7. To verify Active Directory installation, look for events related to the proper startup of Active Directory, such as Event ID 1000 (Active Directory Startup Complete) and 1394 (Attempts To Update The Active Directory Database Are Succeeding). Also, be sure to examine any error or warning messages because they could indicate problems with DNS or other necessary services.

8. When you've finished viewing information in the Event Viewer, close the application.

Gaining Insight Through Event Viewer

Despite its simple user interface and somewhat limited GUI functionality, the Event Viewer tool can be your best ally in isolating and troubleshooting problems with Windows Server 2012 R2. The Event Viewer allows you to view information that is stored in various log files that are maintained by the operating system. This includes information from the following logs:

Application   Stores messages generated by programs running on your system. For example, SQL Server 2012 might report the completion of a database backup job within the Application log.

Security   Contains security-related information as defined by your auditing settings. For example, you could see when users have logged onto the system or when particularly sensitive files have been accessed.

System   Contains operating system-related information and messages. Common messages might include a service startup failure or information about when the operating system was last rebooted.

Directory Service   Stores messages and events related to how Active Directory functions. For example, you might find details related to replication here.

DNS Server   Contains details about the operations of the DNS service. This log is useful for troubleshooting replication or name-resolution problems.

Other Log Files   Contain various features of Windows Server 2012 R2 and the applications that may run on this operating system, which can create additional types of logs. These files allow you to view more information about other applications or services through the familiar Event Viewer tool.

Additionally, developers can easily send custom information from their programs to the Application log. Having all of this information in one place really makes it easy to analyze operating system and application messages. Also, many third-party tools and utilities are available for analyzing log files.

Although the Event Viewer GUI does a reasonably good job of letting you find the information you need, you might want to extract information to analyze other systems or applications. One especially useful feature of the Event Viewer is its ability to save a log file in various formats. You can access this feature by clicking Action ➢ Save As. You'll be given the option of saving in various formats, including tab- and comma-delimited text files. You can then open these files in other applications (such as Microsoft Excel) for additional data analysis.

Overall, in the real world, the Event Viewer can be an excellent resource for monitoring and troubleshooting your important servers and workstations.

In addition to providing information about the status of events related to Active Directory, the Event Viewer shows you useful information about other system services and applications. You should routinely use this tool.

Using Active Directory Administrative Tools

After a server has been promoted to a domain controller, you will see that various tools are added to the Administrative Tools program group, including the following:

Active Directory Administrative Center   This is a *Microsoft Management Console (MMC)* snap-in that allows you to accomplish many Active Directory tasks from one central location. This MMC snap-in allows you to manage your directory services objects, including doing the following tasks:

- Reset user passwords
- Create or manage user accounts
- Create or manage groups
- Create or manage computer accounts
- Create or manage organizational units (OUs) and containers
- Connect to one or several domains or domain controllers in the same instance of Active Directory Administrative Center
- Filter Active Directory data

Active Directory Domains and Trusts   Use this tool to view and change information related to the various domains in an Active Directory environment. This MMC snap-in also allows you to set up shortcut trusts.

Active Directory Sites and Services   Use this tool to create and manage Active Directory sites and services to map to an organization's physical network infrastructure. Sites and services are covered in detail in Chapter 5, "Administer Active Directory."

Active Directory Users and Computers   User and computer management is fundamental for an Active Directory environment. The Active Directory Users and Computers tool allows you to set machine- and user-specific settings across the domain. This tool is discussed throughout this book.

Active Directory Module for Windows PowerShell   *Windows PowerShell* is a command-line shell and scripting language. The Active Directory Module for Windows PowerShell is a group of cmdlets used to manage your Active Directory domains, Active Directory Lightweight Directory Services (AD LDS) configuration sets, and Active Directory Database Mounting Tool instances in a single, self-contained package.

A good way to make sure that Active Directory is accessible and functioning properly is to run the Active Directory Users and Computers tool. When you open the tool, you should see a configuration similar to that shown in Figure 3.3. Specifically, you should make sure the name of the domain you created appears in the list. You should also click the Domain Controllers folder and make sure that the name of your local server appears in the right pane. If your configuration passes these two checks, Active Directory is present and configured.

Testing from Clients

The best test of any solution is simply to verify that it works the way you had intended in your environment. When it comes to using Active Directory, a good test is to ensure that clients can view and access the various resources presented by Windows Server 2012 R2 domain controllers. In the following sections, you'll look at several ways to verify that Active Directory is functioning properly.

FIGURE 3.3   Viewing Active Directory information using the Active Directory Users and Computers tool

Verifying Client Connectivity

If you are unable to see the recently promoted server on the network, there is likely a network configuration error. If only one or a few clients are unable to see the machine, the problem is probably related to client-side configuration. To fix this, make sure that the client computers have the appropriate TCP/IP configuration (including DNS server settings) and that they can see other computers on the network.

If the new domain controller is unavailable from any of the other client computers, you should verify the proper startup of Active Directory using the methods mentioned earlier in this chapter. If Active Directory has been started, ensure that the DNS settings are correct. Finally, test network connectivity between the server and the clients by accessing the network or by using the ping command.

Joining a Domain

If Active Directory has been properly configured, clients and other servers should be able to join the domain. Exercise 3.5 outlines the steps you need to take to join a Windows 7 or Windows 8 computer to the domain.

To complete this exercise, you must have already installed and properly configured at least one Active Directory domain controller and a DNS server that supports SRV records in your environment. In addition to the domain controller, you need at least one other computer, not configured as a domain controller, running one of the following operating systems: Windows 2000, Windows XP Professional (Windows XP Home Edition cannot join a domain), Windows Vista, Windows 7, Windows 8, Windows Server 2003, Windows Server 2008, Windows Server 2008 R2, Windows Server 2012, or Windows Server 2012 R2.

Once clients are able to join the domain successfully, they should be able to view Active Directory resources using the Network icon. This test validates the proper functioning of Active Directory and ensures that you have connectivity with client computers.

 Exercise 3.5 is being done from a Windows 7 Enterprise computer.

EXERCISE 3.5

Joining a Computer to an Active Directory Domain

1. Right-click the Computer icon on the Start menu, and click Properties.

2. Go to the section called Computer Name. On the right side, click the Change Settings link.

3. Next to the section To Rename This Computer Or Change Its Domain Or Workgroup, click the Change button.

4. In the Member Of section, choose the Domain option. Type the name of the Active Directory domain that this computer should join. Click OK.

5. When prompted for the username and password of an account that has permission to join computers to the domain, enter the information for an administrator of the domain. Click OK to commit the changes. If you successfully joined the domain, you will see a dialog box welcoming you to the new domain.

6. You will be notified that you must reboot the computer before the changes take place. Select Yes when prompted to reboot.

Creating and Configuring Application Data Partitions

Organizations store many different kinds of information in various places. For the IT departments that support this information, it can be difficult to ensure that the right information is available when and where it is needed. Windows Server 2012 R2 uses a feature called *application data partitions*, which allows system administrators and application developers to store custom information within Active Directory. The idea behind application data partitions is that since you already have a directory service that can replicate all kinds of information, you might as well use it to keep track of your own information.

Developing distributed applications that can, for example, synchronize information across an enterprise is not a trivial task. You have to come up with a way to transfer data between remote sites (some of which are located across the world), and you have to ensure that the data is properly replicated. By storing application information in Active Directory, you can take advantage of its storage mechanism and replication topology. Application-related information stored on domain controllers benefits from having fault-tolerance features and availability.

Consider the following simple example to understand how this can work. Suppose your organization has developed a customer Sales Tracking and Inventory application. The company needs to make the information that is stored by this application available to all of its branch offices and users located throughout the world. However, the goal is to do this with the least amount of IT administrative effort. Assuming that Active Directory has already been deployed throughout the organization, developers can build support into the application for storing data within Active Directory. They can then rely on Active Directory to store and synchronize the information among various sites. When users request updated data from the application, the application can obtain this information from the nearest domain controller that hosts a replica of the Sales Tracking and Inventory data.

Other types of applications can also benefit greatly from the use of application data partitions. Now that you have a good understanding of the nature of application data partitions, let's take a look at how you can create and manage them using Windows Server 2012 R2 and Active Directory.

Creating Application Data Partitions

By default, after you create an Active Directory environment, you will not have any customer application data partitions. Therefore, the first step in making this functionality available is to create a new application data partition. You can use several tools to do this:

Third-Party Applications or Application-Specific Tools   Generally, if you are planning to install an application that can store information in the Active Directory database, you'll receive some method of administering and configuring that data along with the application. For example, the setup process for the application might assist you in the steps you need to take to set up a new application data partition and to create the necessary structures for storing data.

Creating and managing application data partitions are advanced Active Directory–related functions. Be sure that you have a solid understanding of the Active Directory schema, Active Directory replication, LDAP, and your applications' needs before you attempt to create new application data partitions in a live environment.

Active Directory Service Interfaces   ADSI is a set of programmable objects that can be accessed through languages such as Visual Basic Scripting Edition (VBScript), Visual C#, Visual Basic .NET, and many other language technologies that support the Component Object Model (COM) standard. Through the use of ADSI, developers can create, access, and update data stored in Active Directory and in any application data partitions.

The LDP Tool   You can view and modify the contents of the Active Directory schema using LDAP-based queries. The LDP tool allows you to view information about application data partitions.

Ldp.exe is a graphical user interface (GUI) tool that allows an administrator to configure Lightweight Directory Access Protocol (LDAP) directory service. Administrators have the ability to use the LDP tool to administer an Active Directory Lightweight Directory Services (AD LDS) instance. To use the LDP tool, you must be an administrator or equivalent.

Figure 3.4 shows an example of connecting to a domain controller and browsing Active Directory information.

FIGURE 3.4   Using the LDP tool to view Active Directory schema information

Ntdsutil   The ntdsutil utility is the main method by which system administrators create and manage application data partitions on their Windows Server 2012 R2 domain controllers. This utility's specific commands are covered later in this chapter.

Creating and managing application data partitions can be fairly complex. Such a project's success depends on the quality of the architecture design. This is a good example of where IT staff and application developers must cooperate to ensure that data is stored effectively and that it is replicated efficiently.

You can create an application data partition in one of three different locations within an Active Directory forest:

- As a new tree in an Active Directory forest
- As a child of an Active Directory domain partition

    For example, you can create an Accounting application data partition within the Finance.MyCompany.com domain.

- As a child of another application data partition

    This method allows you to create a hierarchy of application data partitions.

As you might expect, you must be a member of the Enterprise Admins or Domain Admins group to be able to create application data partitions. Alternatively, you can be delegated the appropriate permissions to create new partitions.

Now that you have a good idea of the basic ways in which you can create application data partitions, let's look at how replicas (copies of application data partition information) are handled.

Managing Replicas

A *replica* is a copy of any data stored within Active Directory. Unlike the basic information that is stored in Active Directory, application partitions cannot contain security principals. Also, not all domain controllers automatically contain copies of the data stored in an application data partition. System administrators can define which domain controllers host copies of the application data. This is an important feature because, if replicas are used effectively, administrators can find a good balance between replication traffic and data consistency. For example, suppose that three of your organization's 30 locations require up-to-date accounting-related information. You might choose to replicate the data only to domain controllers located in the places that require the data. Limiting replication of this data reduces network traffic.

Replication is the process by which replicas are kept up-to-date. Application data can be stored and updated on designated servers in the same way basic Active Directory information (such as users and groups) is synchronized between domain controllers. Application data partition replicas are managed using the *Knowledge Consistency Checker (KCC)*, which ensures that the designated domain controllers receive updated replica information. Additionally, the KCC uses all Active Directory sites and connection objects (covered in Chapter 5) that you create to determine the best method to handle replication.

Removing Replicas

When you perform a *demotion* on a domain controller, that server can no longer host an application data partition. If a domain controller contains a replica of application data partition information, you must remove the replica from the domain controller before you demote it. If a domain controller is the machine that hosts a replica of the application data partition, then the entire application data partition is removed and will be permanently lost. Generally, you want to do this only after you're absolutely sure that your organization no longer needs access to the data stored in the application data partition.

Using *ntdsutil* to Manage Application Data Partitions

The primary method by which system administrators create and manage application data partitions is through the ntdsutil command-line tool. You can launch this tool simply by entering **ntdsutil** at a command prompt. The ntdsutil command is both interactive and context sensitive. That is, once you launch the utility, you'll see an ntdsutil command prompt. At this prompt, you can enter various commands that set your context within the application. For example, if you enter the domain management command, you'll be able to use domain-related commands. Several operations also require you to connect to a domain, a domain controller, or an Active Directory object before you perform a command.

 For complete details on using ntdsutil, see the Windows Server 2012 R2 Help and Support Center.

Table 3.3 describes the domain management commands supported by the ntdsutil tool. You can access this information by typing in the following sequence of commands at a command prompt:

```
ntdsutil
domain management
Help
```

TABLE 3.3 ntdsutil domain management commands

ntdsutil domain management command	Purpose
Help or ?	Displays information about the commands that are available within the Domain Management menu of the ntdsutil command.
Connection or Connections	Allows you to connect to a specific domain controller. This will set the context for further operations that are performed on specific domain controllers.
Create NC *PartitionDistinguishedName DNSName*	Creates a new application directory partition.
Delete NC *PartitionDistinguishedName*	Removes an application data partition.
List NC Information *Partition DistinguishedName*	Shows information about the specified application data partition.
List NC Replicas *PartitionDistinguishedName*	Returns information about all replicas for the specific application data partition.
Precreate *PartitionDistinguished NameServerDNSName*	Pre-creates cross-reference application data partition objects. This allows the specified DNS server to host a copy of the application data partition.
Remove NC Replica *PartitionDistinguishedName DCDNSName*	Removes a replica from the specified domain controller.
Select Operation Target	Selects the naming context that will be used for other operations.

TABLE 3.3 ntdsutil domain management commands *(continued)*

ntdsutil domain management command	Purpose
Set NC Reference Domain *PartitionDistinguishedName DomainDistinguishedName*	Specifies the reference domain for an application data partition.
Set NC Replicate NotificationDelay *PartitionDistinguishedName FirstDCNotificationDelay OtherDCNotificationDelay*	Defines settings for how often replication will occur for the specified application data partition.

The ntdsutil commands are all case insensitive. Mixed case was used in the table to make them easier to read. NC in commands stands for "naming context," referring to the fact that this is a partition of the Active Directory schema.

Figure 3.5 provides an example of working with ntdsutil. The following commands were entered to set the context for further operations:

```
ntdsutil
domain management
connections
connect to server localhost
connect to domain ADTest
quit
list
```

FIGURE 3.5 Viewing naming contexts on the local domain controller

Configuring DNS Integration with Active Directory

There are many benefits to integrating Active Directory and DNS services:

- You can configure and manage replication along with other Active Directory components.

- You can automate much of the maintenance of DNS resource records through the use of dynamic updates.

- You will be able to set specific security options on the various properties of the DNS service.

Exercise 3.6 shows the steps that you must take to ensure that these integration features are enabled. You'll look at the various DNS functions that are specific to interoperability with Active Directory.

Before you begin this exercise, make sure that the local machine is configured as an Active Directory domain controller and that DNS services have been properly configured. If you instructed the Active Directory Installation Wizard to configure DNS automatically, many of the settings mentioned in this section may already be enabled. However, you should verify the configuration and be familiar with how the options can be set manually.

EXERCISE 3.6

Configuring DNS Integration with Active Directory

1. Open Administrative tools by pressing the Windows key and choosing Administrative Tools.

2. Open the DNS snap-in from the Administrative Tools program group.

3. Right-click the icon for the local DNS server and select Properties. Click the Security tab. Notice that you can now specify which users and groups have access to modify the configuration of the DNS server. Make any necessary changes and click OK.

4. Expand the local server branch and the Forward Lookup Zones folder.

5. Right-click the name of the Active Directory domain you created and select Properties.

6. On the General tab, verify that the type is Active Directory–Integrated and that the Data Is Stored In Active Directory message is displayed. If this option is not currently selected, you can change it by clicking the Change button next to Type and choosing the Store The Zone In Active Directory check box on the bottom.

7. Verify that the Dynamic Updates option is set to Secure Only. This ensures that all updates to the DNS resource records database are made through authenticated Active Directory accounts and processes.

The other options are Nonsecure And Secure (accepts all updates) and None (to disallow dynamic updates).

8. Finally, notice that you can define the security permissions at the zone level by clicking the Security tab. Make any necessary changes and click OK.

Summary

This chapter covered the basics of implementing an Active Directory forest and domain structure, creating and configuring application data partitions, and setting the functional level of your domain and forest.

You are now familiar with how you can implement Active Directory. We carefully examined all of the necessary steps and conditions that you need to follow to install Active Directory on your network. First you need to prepare for the Domain Name System because Active Directory cannot be installed without the support of a DNS server.

You also need to verify that the computer you upgrade to a domain controller meets some basic file system and network connectivity requirements so that Active Directory can run smoothly and efficiently in your organization. These are some of the most common things you will have to do when you deploy Active Directory.

The chapter also covered the concept of domain functional levels, which essentially determine the kinds of domain controllers you can use in your environment. For instance, in the Windows 2003 functional level, you can include Windows Server 2012 R2, Windows Server 2012, Windows Server 2008 R2, Windows Server 2008, and Windows Server 2003 domain controllers, but the functionality of the domain is severely limited.

In this chapter, you also learned how to install Active Directory, which you accomplish by promoting a Windows Server 2012 computer to a domain controller using Server Manager. You also learned how to verify the installation by testing Active Directory from a client computer.

This chapter was limited in scope to examining the issues related to installing and configuring the first domain in an Active Directory environment. In later chapters, you'll see how to create and manage more complex configurations.

Exam Essentials

Know the prerequisites for promoting a server to a domain controller.   You should understand the tasks that you must complete before you attempt to upgrade a server to a domain controller. Also, you should have a good idea of the information you need in order to complete the domain controller promotion process.

Understand the steps of the Active Directory Installation Wizard.   When you run the Active Directory Installation Wizard, you'll be presented with many different choices. You should understand the effects of the various options provided in each step of the wizard.

Be familiar with the tools that you will use to administer Active Directory.   Three main administrative tools are installed when you promote a Windows Server 2012 R2 to a domain controller. Be sure that you know which tools to use for which types of tasks.

Understand the purpose of application data partitions.   The idea behind application data partitions is that since you already have a directory service that can replicate all kinds of security information, you can also use it to keep track of application data. The main benefit of storing application information in Active Directory is that you can take advantage of its storage mechanism and replication topology. Application-related information stored on domain controllers benefits from having fault-tolerance features and availability.

Review Questions

1. You are the system administrator of a large organization that has recently implemented Windows Server 2012 R2. You have a few remote sites that do not have very tight security. You have decided to implement read-only domain controllers (RODCs). What forest and function levels does the network need for you to do the install? (Choose all that apply.)

    A. Windows 2000 Mixed

    B. Windows 2008 R2

    C. Windows 2003

    D. Windows 2008

2. What is the maximum number of domains that a Windows Server 2012 R2 computer configured as a domain controller may participate in at one time?

    A. Zero

    B. One

    C. Two

    D. Any number of domains

3. A system administrator is trying to determine which file system to use for a server that will become a Windows Server 2012 R2 file server and domain controller. The company has the following requirements:

    ▪ The file system must allow for file-level security from within Windows 2012 R2 Server.

    ▪ The file system must make efficient use of space on large partitions.

    ▪ The domain controller Sysvol must be stored on the partition.

    Which of the following file systems meets these requirements?

    A. FAT

    B. FAT32

    C. HPFS

    D. NTFS

4. For security reasons, you have decided that you must convert the system partition on your removable drive from the FAT32 file system to NTFS. Which of the following steps must you take in order to convert the file system? (Choose two.)

    A. Run the command CONVERT /FS:NTFS from the command prompt.

    B. Rerun Windows Server 2008 R2 Setup and choose to convert the partition to NTFS during the reinstallation.

C. Boot Windows Server 2008 R2 Setup from the installation CD-ROM and choose Rebuild File System.

D. Reboot the computer.

5. Windows Server 2012 R2 requires the use of which of the following protocols or services in order to support Active Directory? (Choose two.)

A. DHCP

B. TCP/IP

C. NetBEUI

D. IPX/SPX

E. DNS

6. You are promoting a Windows Server 2012 R2 computer to an Active Directory domain controller for test purposes. The new domain controller will be added to an existing domain. While you are using the Active Directory Installation Wizard, you receive an error message that prevents the server from being promoted. Which of the following might be the cause of the problem? (Choose all that apply.)

A. The system does not contain an NTFS partition on which the Sysvol directory can be created.

B. You do not have a Windows Server 2012 R2 DNS server on the network.

C. The TCP/IP configuration on the new server is incorrect.

D. The domain has reached its maximum number of domain controllers.

7. Your network contains a single Active Directory domain. The domain contains five Windows Server 2008 R2 domain controllers. You plan to install a new Windows Server 2012 R2 domain controller. Which two actions would you need to perform? (Each correct answer presents part of the solution. Choose two.)

A. Run `adprep.exe /rodcprep` at the command line.

B. Run `adprep.exe /forestprep` at the command line.

C. Run `adprep.exe /domainprep` at the command line.

D. From Active Directory Domains and Trusts, raise the functional level of the domain.

E. From Active Directory Users and Computers, prestage the RODC computer account.

8. You are the network administrator for a large company that creates widgets. Management asks you to implement a new Windows Server 2012 R2 system. You need to implement federated identity management. Which of the following will help you do this?

A. Active Directory Federation Services

B. Active Directory DNS Services

C. Active Directory IIS Services

D. Active Directory IAS Services

9. You are the system administrator responsible for your company's infrastructure. You think you have an issue with name resolution, and you need to verify that you are using the correct hostname. You want to test DNS on the local system and need to see whether the hostname server-1 resolves to the IP address 10.1.1.1. Which of the following actions provides a solution to the problem?

A. Add a DNS server to your local subnet.

B. Add the mapping for the hostname server-1 to the IP address 10.1.1.1 in the local system's HOSTS file.

C. Add an A record to your local WINS server.

D. Add an MX record to your local DNS server.

10. You have one Active Directory forest in your organization that contains one domain named Stellacon.com. You have two domain controllers configured with the DNS role installed. There are two Active Directory Integrated zones named Stellacon.com and Stellatest. com. One of your IT members (who is not an administrator) needs to be able to modify the Stellacon.com DNS server, but you need to prevent this user from modifying the Stellatest.com SOA record. How do you accomplish this?

A. Modify the permissions of the Stellacon.com zone from the DNS Manager snap-in.

B. Modify the permissions of the Stellatest.com zone from the DNS Manager snap-in.

C. Run the Delegation Of Control Wizard in Active Directory.

D. Run the Delegation Of Control Wizard in the DNS snap-in.

Chapter

4

Configure Windows Server 2012 R2

THE FOLLOWING 70-410 EXAM OBJECTIVES ARE COVERED IN THIS CHAPTER:

✓ **Configure file and share access**

- ▪ Create and configure shares
- ▪ Configure share permissions
- ▪ Configure offline files
- ▪ Configure NTFS permissions
- ▪ Configure access-based enumeration (ABE)
- ▪ Configure Volume Shadow Copy Service (VSS)
- ▪ Configure NTFS quotas
- ▪ Create and configure Work Folders

✓ **Configure print and document services**

- ▪ Configure the Easy Print print driver
- ▪ Configure Enterprise Print Management
- ▪ Configure drivers
- ▪ Configure printer pooling
- ▪ Configure print priorities
- ▪ Configure printer permissions

✓ **Configure servers for remote management**

- ▪ Configure WinRM
- ▪ Configure down-level server management
- ▪ Configure servers for day-to-day management tasks
- ▪ Configure multi-server management
- ▪ Configure Server Core
- ▪ Configure Windows Firewall
- ▪ Manage non-domain joined servers

This chapter explains how to set up your servers so that your network users have something to access. Before you can set up a server, you have to determine the purpose of it. Is it going to be a print server, a file storage server, a remote access server, or a domain controller?

After you have decided how the machine is going to help your network, you must implement your decision. In this chapter, I'll show you how to set up a print server and a file server. In addition, I will discuss how to set up permissions and security for these servers and how you can limit the amount of space your users can have on a server.

Microsoft Windows Server 2012 and Windows Server 2012 R2 are used for all of the server types in this chapter. Although other operating systems can be used, this chapter refers only to Windows Server 2012 and Windows Server 2012 R2.

Understanding File Servers

Before you configure a file server, you must understand what a file server actually does. *File servers* are machines on your network that store data files to share among network clients. The same machine can be a file server and another type of server. For example, a machine can both host network files and run Exchange Server 2013. Such a machine would have both file server and application server functions. (*Application servers* are machines that host applications used by network clients.)

🌐 **Real World Scenario**

Multiple Server Types on One Machine

More than ever, in today's world most IT departments have to worry about budgets. The problem is that the IT department often has the smallest budget in a company. You are typically stuck between a rock and a hard place because if your network is running well, people (including executives) forget about you. This makes it hard when you ask for anything that may impact the budget.

Because of the lack of funds, often you will leverage one machine to perform many server tasks. I have seen several companies where the IT department had to have the same machine running both as an application server and as a file server.

You must consider various factors before allowing a machine to run multiple server types. How many processors do you have? What are the processor speeds? How much RAM does the machine have? What is the hard drive speed? What type of applications will be hosted on the machine?

After you have gathered all of the information about the machine, then you can decide whether the machine can host multiple server types. Keep this one fact in mind, however—because of the requirements and demands on the computer system, it's always a good idea to host SQL Server on a dedicated machine.

When setting up a file server, one of the most important things you will do is to set up work and personal folders for your users. I have been consulting for many years, and one thing I always stress to all of my clients is to perform regular backups. After all, most organizations would not be able to recover after losing all of their data. Usually, companies back up only their servers, and this is why home folders are so important. *Home folders* are one of the most common file types on a file server; they are folders set up on the server for users to store information. Users have a location on the server to store their important data, and therefore that data will be backed up when the company does its regular backups.

Home folders are just one example of how to use work folders on a file server. I will be discussing other examples throughout this chapter.

Configuring File Servers

Now that you have an understanding of what a file server does, it's time to discuss how to configure these servers. Setting up a file server properly encompasses many steps. As always, one major concern is security. In the following sections, I will first describe how to share and publish online and offline files and folders. Then I will discuss the two types of security—shared permissions and NTFS security—that an administrator can set when sharing files or folders.

Sharing Folders

A file server is for sharing and storing data. To use one, you need to know how to set up a share, or a shared folder, on your server. A *shared folder* is exactly what it says; it's a folder that is shared on your network so that users can access the data within that folder. As an administrator, you have the ability to determine which users can access which files within a shared folder.

One of the main goals of Active Directory is to make resources easy to find. Active Directory also makes it easy to determine which files are available to users. That being said, I will explain how Active Directory manages to publish shared folders.

Making Active Directory Objects Available to Users

With Active Directory, a system administrator can control which objects users can see. The act of making an Active Directory object available is known as *publishing*. The two main publishable objects are Printer objects and Shared work folder objects. The reason I list Shared work folders here is because personal folders for users are not normally published in Active Directory. You publish an object in Active Directory because you want an easy way for everyone to find resources. Ordinarily, you don't want everyone accessing someone's home folder, and this is why you don't normally publish home folders.

The general process for creating server shares and shared printers has remained unchanged from previous versions of Windows. You create the various objects (printers or folders) and then enable them for sharing.

To make these resources available via Active Directory, however, there's an additional step: You must publish the resources. Once an object has been published in Active Directory, clients will be able to find it.

When you publish objects in Active Directory, you should know the server name and share name of the resource. This information, however, doesn't matter to your users. A system administrator can change the resource to which an object points without having to reconfigure or even notify clients. For example, if you move a share from one server to another, all you need to do is update the Shared Folder's object's properties to point to the new location. Active Directory clients still refer to the resource with the same path and name as they used before.

Exercise 4.1 will walk you through the steps for sharing and publishing a folder for use on your network.

Creating and Publishing a Shared Work Folder

1. Create a new folder in the root directory of your C: partition, and name it **Test Share**.

2. Right-click the Test Share folder, and choose Share With ➢ Specific People.

3. In the File Sharing dialog box, enter the names of users with whom you want to share this folder. In the upper box, enter **Everyone** and then click Add. Note that Everyone appears in the lower box. Click in the Permission Level column next to Everyone, and choose Read/Write from the drop-down menu. Then click Share.

4. You see a message that your folder has been shared. Click Done.

5. Open the Active Directory Users and Computers tool. Expand the current domain. Select New ➤ Shared Folder.

6. In the New Object – Shared Folder dialog box, type **Shared Folder Test** for the name of the folder. Then type the UNC path to the share (for example, **\\serverA\Test Share**). Click OK to create the share.

One of the main benefits of having all of your resource information in Active Directory is that you can easily find the information that you're seeking using the Find dialog box. When setting up objects in Active Directory, I recommend you always enter as much information as possible for the objects you're creating. The extra effort will pay off when your users start doing searches for these objects. The more information you enter, the more users can search to find the appropriate resource they need.

Access-Based Enumeration

Access-Based Enumeration (ABE) is a feature included with Windows Server 2012/2012 R2. ABE allows your domain users to list only the files and folders to which they have access when browsing content on the file server.

ABE helps eliminate domain users' issues that are caused by users connecting to file servers and seeing large numbers of files and folders the user cannot connect. ABE allows users only to see files and folders to which they have access.

Knowing that ABE is working on the Windows Server helps you set up your permissions properly. If you need to give a user the ability to see files and folders that they might not be able to change, you need to allow them at least to read or view the directories. As an administrator, it's important that you understand that Access-Based Enumeration is working on the server and what you need to do to get a user around it when needed.

Configuring Offline Files

If you have been in this industry long enough, you have seen a major change in end-user computers. Years ago, only a few select users had laptops. They were big and bulky, and they weighed almost as much as today's desktop computers.

The pendulum has swung in the opposite direction. It probably seems like every one of your end users now has a laptop. As an IT administrator, this gives you a whole new set of challenges and problems to address.

One challenge that you have to address is how users can work on files while outside of the office. If you have a user who wants to work at home, how do you give them the files they need to get their work done?

The answer is *offline folders*. These folders contain data that can be worked on by users while outside the office. An IT administrator can set up offline folders through the use of *Group Policy objects (GPOs)*.

When you decide to make folders available for offline use, these folders need to synchronize with the laptops so that all of the data matches between both systems. As an administrator, one decision that you will need to make is when the offline folders will be synchronized. There are three synchronization options that you can set in a GPO (see Figure 4.1).

FIGURE 4.1   Synchronization options in a GPO

You can set up any combination of these options:

- When you select Synchronize All Offline Files Before Logging Off, offline folders are synchronized when the user logs off the network.

- When you select Synchronize All Offline Files When Logging On, offline folders are synchronized when the user logs on to the network.

- When you select Synchronize Offline Files Before Suspend, offline folders are synchronized before the user does a system suspend.

In Exercise 4.2, I will show you the steps necessary to configure offline folder options by using a GPO. This exercise uses the Group Policy Management Console (GPMC). If your GPMC is not installed, use the Server Manager MMC (under Features) to install it.

Group Policy objects will be covered in full detail in Chapter 6 "Manage GPOs."

EXERCISE 4.2

Configuring Offline Folder Options

1. Open the Group Policy Management Console.

2. In the left pane, expand your forest and then your domain. Under your domain name, there should be a default domain policy.

3. Right-click the default domain policy and choose Edit.

4. In the User Configuration section, expand Policies ➢ Administrative Templates ➢ Network and then click Offline Files.

5. Right-click Synchronize All Offline Files Before Logging Off and choose Edit. The GPO setting dialog box appears. Choose the Enabled option and click OK.

6. Right-click Synchronize All Offline Files When Logging On and choose Edit. The GPO setting dialog box appears. Choose the Enabled option and click OK.

7. Right-click Synchronize Offline Files Before Suspend and choose Edit. The GPO setting dialog box appears. Choose the Enabled option. In the Action drop-down box, make sure Quick is selected. Click OK.

8. Close the GPMC.

Now that you have set up a GPO for synchronization, it's time to share a folder for offline usage. In Exercise 4.3, you will set up a folder for offline access. You must complete Exercise 4.1 before doing this exercise.

Configuring a Shared Network Folder for Offline Access

1. Right-click the Test Share folder that you created in Exercise 4.1 and choose Properties.

2. Click the Sharing tab and then click the Advanced Sharing button.

3. When the Advanced Sharing dialog box appears, click the Caching button.

4. When the Offline Settings dialog box appears, choose the All Files And Programs That Users Open From The Shares Will Be Automatically Available Offline option. Click OK.

5. Click OK twice more to close the Properties dialog box.

Volume Shadow Copy Services

Windows includes a feature that allows you to create a point-in-time image of one or more volumes. The *Volume Shadow Copy Service (VSS)* is the feature within Windows that allows an administrator take an image (shadow copy) of one or more volumes. Shadow copies have the ability to provide both file system and application.

Shadow copies allow an administrator to back up shared folders to a remote location. Shadow copies are designed to help recover files that were accidentally deleted, that were overwritten, or that have become corrupt. One major advantage to shadow copies is that open files can be backed up. This means that even if users are currently working on files in a shared folder that has shadow copies enabled, the shadow copies will continue to function.

Once administrators have configured and enabled shadow copies (using the Computer Management snap-in), network users can restore earlier versions of files. After the initial shadow copy of the shared folder is created, only changes are copied and not the entire file.

You can enable shadow copies of entire volumes.

The following are some of the settings that you can configure when setting up shadow copies:

Schedule   You have the ability to set the schedule of the shadow copies. You can set this schedule to run daily, weekly, monthly, once, at system startup, at logon, or when the system is idle. You can also set the time at which the shadow copy will run.

Storage Locations   An administrator needs to set the location of the shadow copy backup. If you are on a network, it is a good idea to place the shadow copy on a network drive.

Maximum Size   You can set a maximum size on your shadow copies, or you can specify that they have no size limit. One of the predetermined settings is 64 shadow copies per volume.

In Exercise 4.4, you'll set up a volume to make shadow copies every Monday at 7 a.m. To set up the shadow copies, you will use the Computer Management MMC snap-in.

EXERCISE 4.4

Configuring a Shadow Copy on a Volume

1.   Open Computer Management by pressing the Windows key and selecting Administrative Tools ➢ Computer Management.

2.   Expand Storage and then right-click Disk Management. Choose All Tasks ➢ Configure Shadow Copies.

3.   When the Shadow Copies dialog box appears, click the Settings button.

4.   When the Settings windows appears, click the Schedule button.

5.   In the Schedule window, set the schedule task to weekly and the start time for 7 a.m. Uncheck all of the days-of-the-week boxes except Mon. Click OK.

6.   When the Settings window reappears, click OK.

7.   If the Enable button is enabled, click it. Then click OK.

8.   Exit the Computer Management MMC.

To recover a previous version of a file from a shadow copy, you use the *server_name*\ *share_name* path. The operating system determines how you will gain access to the shared folders and shadow copies. Shadow copies are built into Windows XP (SP1), Windows Vista, Windows 7, Windows 8, Windows Server 2003, Windows Server 2008/2008 R2, and Windows Server 2012/2012 R2. If you are using a different Microsoft operating system, you need to download the Shadow Copy Client Pack from the Microsoft download center.

VssAdmin Command

Another way to create, configure, and manage shadow copies is by using the vssadmin.exe command-line utility. The vssadmin.exe command allows you to create, delete, list, and resize shadow copies and shadow storage.

One area where the VSS is very important is during backups. When you back up open files, the VSS copies the data and helps back up open files. For example, when you are backing up a Microsoft Exchange server using a Unitrends backup server, the VSS Exchange writer is used. To see if the VSS writers are functioning properly, you can open a command prompt (with administrative privileges) and type in the following statement:

```
VSSAdmin list writers
```

This command will show you all the different VSS service writers and how those VSS writers are functioning properly.

Table 4.1 describes the vssadmin.exe command and the different commands associated with the vssadmin utility.

TABLE 4.1   Vssadmin.exe commands

Command	Description
Add ShadowStorage	Adds a new volume shadow copy storage association
Create Shadow	Creates a new volume shadow copy
Delete Shadows	Deletes volume shadow copies
Delete ShadowStorage	Deletes the volume shadow copy storage associations
List Providers	Lists registered volume shadow copy providers
List Shadows	Lists existing volume shadow copies
List ShadowStorage	Lists volume shadow copy storage associations
List Volumes	Lists volumes eligible for shadow copies
List Writers	Lists subscribed volume shadow copy writers
Resize ShadowStorage	Resizes a volume shadow copy storage association
Revert Shadow	Reverts a volume to a shadow copy
Query Reverts	Queries the progress of in-progress revert operations

Configuring Permissions

You have gone through the steps necessary to set up a shared folder, publish it to Active Directory, and set it up for offline access. Now you will see how you can protect these files and folders by using permissions.

You can secure folders using permissions in two ways, and you can secure files in one way. You can set up permissions and security through NTFS or through sharing.

Understanding NTFS

NTFS is an option that you have when you are formatting a hard drive. You can format a hard drive for a Microsoft operating system in three ways.

- File Allocation Table (FAT) is supported on older operating systems only (Server 2003, Server 2000, XP, and so on).

- FAT32 is supported in Windows Server 2012 R2.

- NTFS is supported in Windows Server 2012 R2.

NTFS has many advantages over FAT and FAT32. They include the following:

Compression   Compression helps compact files or folders to allow for more efficient use of hard drive space. For example, a file that usually takes up 20MB of space might use only 13MB after compression. To enable compression, just open the Advanced Attributes dialog box for a folder and check the Compress Contents To Save Disk Space box (see Figure 4.2).

FIGURE 4.2   Setting up compression on a folder

Quotas   *Quotas* allow you to limit how much hard drive space users can have on a server. Quotas are discussed in greater detail in the section "Configuring Disk Quotas."

Encryption   *Encrypting File System (EFS)* allows a user or administrator to secure files or folders by using encryption. Encryption employs the user's security identification

(SID) number to secure the file or folder. To implement encryption, open the Advanced Attributes dialog box for a folder and check the Encrypt Contents To Secure Data box (see Figure 4.3).

FIGURE 4.3   Setting up encryption on a folder

If files are encrypted using EFS and an administrator has to unencrypt the files, there are two ways to do this. First, you can log in using the user's account (the account that encrypted the files) and unencrypt the files. Second, you can become a recovery agent and manually unencrypt the files.

If you use EFS, it's best not to delete users immediately when they leave a company. Administrators have the ability to recover encrypted files, but it is much easier to gain access to the user's encrypted files by logging in as the user who left the company and unchecking the encryption box.

Security   One of the biggest advantages of NTFS is security. Security is one of the most important aspects of an IT administrator's job. An advantage of NTFS security is that the security can be placed on individual files and folders. It does not matter whether you are local to the share (in front of the machine where the data is stored) or remote to the share (coming across the network to access the data); the security is always in place with NTFS.

The default security permission is Users = Read on new folders or shares.

NTFS security is *additive*. In other words, if you are a member of three groups (Marketing, Sales, and R&D) and these three groups have different security settings, you get the highest level of permissions. For example, let's say you have a user by the name of wpanek who belongs to all three groups (Marketing, Sales, and R&D).

Figure 4.4 shows this user's permissions. The Marketing group has Read and Execute permissions to the Stellacon Documents folder. The Sales group has Read and Write, and the R&D group has Full Control. Since wpanek is a member of all three groups, wpanek would get Full Control (the highest level).

FIGURE 4.4 Security settings on the Stellacon Documents folder

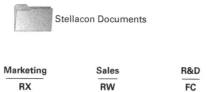

Marketing	Sales	R&D
RX	RW	FC

The only time this does not apply is with the Deny permission. Deny overrides any other group setting. Taking the same example, if Sales has Deny permission for the Stellacon Documents folder, the user wpanek would be denied access to that folder. The only way around this Deny is if you added wpanek directly to the folder and gave him individual permissions (see Figure 4.5). Individual permissions override a group Deny. In this example, the individual right of wpanek would override the Sales group's Deny. The user's security permission for the Stellacon Documents folder would be Full Control.

FIGURE 4.5 Individual permissions

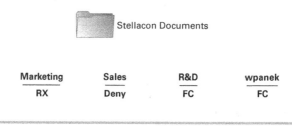

Marketing	Sales	R&D	wpanek
RX	Deny	FC	FC

Give users only the permissions necessary to do their jobs. Do not give them higher levels than they need.

Understanding Shared Permissions

When you set up a folder to be shared, you have the ability to assign that folder's permissions. *Shared permissions* can be placed only on the folder and not on individual files. Files have the ability to inherit their permissions from the parent folder.

Shared folder permissions are in effect only when users are remote to the shared data. In other words, if computer A shares a folder called Downloads and assigns that folder shared permissions, those permissions would apply only if you connected to that share from a machine other than computer A. If you were sitting in front of computer A, the shared permissions would not apply.

Like NTFS permissions (discussed in the previous section), shared permissions are additive, so users receive the highest level of permissions granted by the groups of which they are members.

Also, as with NTFS permissions, the Deny permission (see Figure 4.6) overrides any group permission, and an individual permission overrides a group Deny.

FIGURE 4.6 Setting up permissions on a shared folder

The default shared permission is Administrators = Full Control. The shared permissions going from lowest to highest are Read, Change, Full Control, and Deny. Table 4.2 compares the two different types of permissions and security.

TABLE 4.2 NTFS security vs. shared permissions

Description	NTFS	Shared
Folder-level security.	Yes	Yes
File-level security.	Yes	No
In effect when local to the data.	Yes	No
In effect when remote to the data.	Yes	Yes
Permissions are additive.	Yes	Yes
Group Deny overrides all other group settings.	Yes	Yes
Individual settings override group settings.	Yes	Yes

How NTFS Security and Shared Permissions Work Together

When you set up a shared folder, you need to set up shared permissions on that folder. If you're using NTFS, you will also need to set up NTFS security on the folder. Since both shared permissions and NTFS security are in effect when the user is remote, what happens when the two conflict?

These are the two basic rules of thumb:

- The local permission is the NTFS permission.

- The remote permission is the more restrictive set of permissions between NTFS and shared.

This is easy to do as long as you do it in steps. Let's look at Figure 4.7 and walk through the process of figuring out what wpanek has for rights.

FIGURE 4.7 NTFS security and shared permissions example

Shared permissions				NTFS security		
Marketing	**Sales**	**R&D**	Local = ?	**Marketing**	**Sales**	**R&D**
R	R	R	Remote = ?	RX	R	FC

wpanek

Marketing
Sales
R&D

As you can see, wpanek belongs to three groups (Marketing, Sales, and R&D), and all three groups have settings for the Stellacon Documents folder. In the figure, you will notice that there are two questions: Remote = ? and Local = ? That's what you need to figure out—what are wpanek's effective permissions when he is sitting at the computer that shares the folder, and what are his effective permissions when he connects to the folder from another computer (remotely)? To figure this out, follow these steps:

1. Add up the permissions on each side separately.

   Remember, permissions and security are *additive*. You get the highest permission. So, if you look at each side, the highest shared permission is the Read permission. The NTFS security side should add up to equal Full Control. Thus, now you have Read permission on shared and Full Control on NTFS.

2. Determine the local permissions.

   Shared permissions do not apply when you are local to the data. Only NTFS would apply. Thus, the local permission would be Full Control.

3. Determine the remote permissions.

   Remember, the remote permission is the most restrictive set of permissions between NTFS and shared. Since Read is more restrictive than Full Control, the remote permission would be Read.

   Let's try another. Look at Figure 4.8, and see whether you can come up with wpanek's local and remote permissions.

FIGURE 4.8 NTFS security and shared permissions

Shared permissions   Stellacon Documents   NTFS security

Marketing	Sales	R&D			Marketing	Sales	R&D
R	R	FC	Local = ?		R	R	R
			Remote = ?				

wpanek
Marketing
Sales
R&D

Your answer should match the following:

Local = Read

Remote = Read

Remember, first you add up each side to get the highest level of rights. NTFS would be Read, and shared would be Full Control. The local permission is always just NTFS (shared does not apply to local permissions), and remote permission is whichever permission (NTFS or shared) is the most restrictive (which would be Read on the NTFS side).

Exercise 4.5 walks you through the process of setting both NTFS and shared permissions. You must complete Exercise 4.1 before doing this exercise.

EXERCISE 4.5

Configuring Shared and NTFS Settings

1. Right-click the Test Share folder you created in Exercise 4.1 and choose Properties.

2. Click the Sharing tab and then click the Advanced Sharing button. (You will set the shared permissions first.)

3. Click the Permissions button. Click the Add button. When the Select User page appears, choose a group from Active Directory. (I used the Sales group.) Once you find your group, click OK.

4. The Permissions dialog box appears. With your group highlighted, click the Allow check box next to Full Control and click OK. (All of the other Allow check boxes will automatically become checked.)

5. On the Advanced Sharing page, click OK. Now click the Security tab. (This allows you to set the NTFS security settings.)

6. Click the Edit button. That takes you to the Permissions page. Now click the Add button. When the Select User page appears, choose a group from Active Directory. (I used the Everyone group.) Once you find your group, choose OK.

7. The Permissions dialog box appears. With your group highlighted, click the Allow check box next to Modify, and click OK. (All of the check boxes below Modify will automatically become checked.)

8. Click Close.

Configuring Disk Quotas

In this chapter so far, you have seen how to set up a share and publish it to Active Directory. You've also learned how to set up permissions and security and how NTFS and shared permissions work with each other. It's time to learn how to limit users' hard drive space on the servers.

Disk quotas give administrators the ability to limit how much storage space a user can have on a hard drive. As mentioned earlier in this chapter, disk quotas are an advantage of using NTFS over FAT32. If you decide to use FAT32 on a volume or partition, quotas will not be available.

You have a few options available to you when you set up disk quotas. You can set up disk quotas based on volume or on users.

 A good rule of thumb is to set up an umbrella quota policy that covers the entire volume and then let individual users exceed the umbrella as needed.

Setting Quotas by Volume   One way to set up disk quotas is by setting the quota by volume, on a per-volume basis. This means that if you have a hard drive with C:, D:, and E: volumes, you would have to set up three individual quotas—one for each volume. This is your umbrella. This is where you set up an entire disk quota based on the volume for all users.

Setting Quotas by User   You have the ability to set up quotas on volumes by user. Here is where you would individually let users have independent quotas that exceed your umbrella quota.

Specifying Quota Entries   You use quota entries to configure the volume and user quotas. You do this on the Quotas tab of the volume's Properties dialog box. (See Exercise 4.6.)

Creating Quota Templates   Quota templates are predefined ways to set up quotas. Templates allow you to set up disk quotas without needing to create a disk quota from scratch. One advantage of using a template is that when you want to set up disk quotas on multiple volumes (C:, D:, and E:) on the same hard drive, you do not need to re-create the quota on each volume.

Exercise 4.6 will show you how to set up an umbrella quota for all users and then have an individual account in your Active Directory exceed this quota.

EXERCISE 4.6

Configuring Disk Quotas

1. Open Windows Explorer.

2. Right-click the local disk (C:) and choose Properties.

3. Click the Quotas tab.

4. Check the Enable Quota Management check box. Also check the Deny Disk Space To Users Exceeding Quota Limit box.

5. Click the Limit Disk Space To option and enter **1000MB** in the box.

6. Enter **750MB** in the Set Warning Level To boxes.

7. Click the Apply button. If a warning box appears, click OK. This warning is just informing you that the disk may need to be rescanned for the quota.

8. Now that you have set up an umbrella quota to cover everyone, you'll set up a quota that exceeds the umbrella. Click the Quota Entries button.

9. The Quotas Entries for (C:) window appears. You will see some users already listed. These are users who are already using space on the volume. Click the Quota menu at the top and choose New Quota Entry.

    Notice the N/A entry in the Percent Used column. This belongs to the administrator account, which by default has no limit.

10. On the Select User page, choose a user that you want to allow to exceed the quota (for this example, I used the wpanek account). Click OK.

11. This opens the Add New Quota Entry dialog box. Click the Do Not Limit Disk Usage option and click OK.

12. You will notice that the new user has no limit. Close the disk quota tool.

Configuring Print Services

One of the most important components on a network is the printer. Printers today are almost as important as the computers themselves. Think about your network. What would your network be like without a printer? Even small networks or home networks have a printer today.

How many printers do you want on your network? It is not feasible to put a printer on every user's desk. What if some users need black and white while others need color? Do you give each user two printers? What if they need laser printing for reports but ink-jets will work fine for every other type of print job? These are all questions that you must answer before buying any printers for your networks.

This is also where network printers and print servers come into play. *Network printers* are printers that can be directly connected to the network through some form of network interface card. These printers usually have settings that can be configured for your network needs. For example, if your network uses DHCP, you can set the printer to be a DHCP client.

Print servers are servers that have a connected printer, where the server handles all printing issues. This is an excellent solution for printers that cannot directly connect to the network. Once the printer is connected to the network (through the use of a NIC or a server), the end user just connects to the printer and prints. To the end user, there is no real difference between the two options.

Before an end user can print to a network printer, an administrator must connect, set up, share, and publish the printer for use. An administrator must also set the permissions on the printer to allow users to print to that printer. The following sections will discuss these items in detail.

Creating and Publishing Printers

Once your printer is installed, you must share the printer and then publish the printer to Active Directory before users can print to it. Printers can be published easily within Active Directory. This makes them available to users in your domain.

Exercise 4.7 walks you through the steps you need to take to share and publish a Printer object by having you create and share a printer. To complete the printer installation, you need access to the Windows Server 2012 installation media (via the hard disk, a network share, or the CD/DVD drive). If you do not have a printer for this exercise, just choose one from the list and continue the exercise.

EXERCISE 4.7

Creating and Publishing a Printer

1. Press the Windows key and select ➢ Control Panel ➢ Devices and Printers ➢ Add Printer. This starts the Add Printer Wizard.

2. On the Add Printer page, click the link The Printer That I Want Isn't Listed.

3. Choose Add A Local Printer and click Next.

4. On the Choose A Printer Port page, select Use An Existing Port. From the drop-down list beside that option, make sure LPT1: (Printer Port) is selected. Click Next.

5. On the Install The Printer Driver page, select Generic for the manufacturer, and for the printer, highlight Generic/Text Only. Click Next.

6. If a driver page appears, choose Use The Driver That Is Currently Installed and click Next.

7. On the Type A Printer Name page, enter **Text Printer**. Uncheck the Set As The Default Printer box and then click Next.

8. The Installing Printer page appears. After the system is finished, the Printer Sharing page appears. Make sure the Share This Printer So That Others On Your Network Can Find And Use It box is selected, and accept the default share name of Text Printer.

9. In the Location section, type **Building 203**, and in the Comment section, add the following comment: **This is a text-only printer**. Click Next.

10. On the You've Successfully Added Text Printer page, click Finish.

11. Next you need to verify that the printer will be listed in Active Directory. Right-click the Text Printer icon, and select Text Printer Properties.

12. Next select the Sharing tab and make sure that the List In The Directory box is checked. Click OK to accept the settings.

13. Close the printer Properties box, and close Devices And Printers.

Note that when you create and share a printer this way, an Active Directory Printer object is not displayed within the Active Directory Users and Computers tool.

Configuring Printers

The printer has now been installed and published to Active Directory. It's time to set all of the different configuration options. To get to the options, right-click the Printer object and choose Properties.

The following are just some of the tabs you can configure:

The General Tab The General tab (see Figure 4.9) allows you to set some basic printer attributes.

- The field at the top of the dialog box contains the display name of the Printer object.

- The Location field should contain text that helps users physically locate the printer. This allows users to search for printers based on location (location-aware printing).

- The Comment field allows an administrator to put in any additional information, such as the printer type.

- The Printing Preferences button takes you to controls that allow you to change the layout and paper type of the printer.

FIGURE 4.9 The General tab of the printer's Properties dialog box

The Sharing Tab   The Sharing tab (see Figure 4.10) allows you to configure your printer for sharing on your network. This is what allows users to use a network printer (if they have the proper permissions on the printer).

- The Share This Printer check box allows you to share the printer on the network.

- Share Name is the name your users will see on the network.

- When Render Print Jobs On Client Computers is checked, the client computer caches the print job until the printer is ready to print. If unchecked, the print server will cache the entire job before it prints to the printer.

- When List In The Directory is checked, users can search the directory for the printer.

- The Additional Drivers button allows you to load additional drivers for your clients. It is especially useful for giving access to drivers for older client systems. One advantage of a print server is that the server will automatically download drivers to client computers.

FIGURE 4.10   The Sharing tab of the printer's Properties dialog box

The Ports Tab   The Ports tab (see Figure 4.11) allows you to configure the port to which your printer is connected. You can add ports or configure existing ports.

- The Port check boxes allow you to choose to which port your printer is connected. Options are the printer port, serial port, local port, and print to file port.

- The Add Port button allows you to add a custom port (for example, a TCP/IP port).

- The Delete Port button allows you to remove a port from the Port list.

- The Configure Port button gives you settings to configure an existing port. For example, if you use TCP/IP, this button allows you to change the TCP/IP options.

- Enable Bidirectional Support allows your printer and computer to communicate back and forth. If this check box is disabled, your printer cannot support two-way communications.

- A *printer pool* allows two or more identical printers to share the print load. When a document is sent to the printer pool, the first available printer receives the print job and prints it. Enable Printer Pooling allows a large department or organization to get print jobs done faster. Users do not have to wait for one printer to get their print job. You should follow these rules when setting up a printer pool:

    - All printers in the pool need to be the same model and type.

    - All printers in the pool should be in the same physical location. Print jobs will be printed to the first available printer. If these printers are located all over the company, it may take a user too long to find their print job.

FIGURE 4.11 The Ports tab of the printer's Properties dialog box

The Advanced Tab The Advanced tab (see Figure 4.12) is where you can set availability, priority, and many other options.

- The availability controls let you set the hours when this printer can be used. You can set it to be always available or available only between the hours you set.

- If multiple print shares are set up to go to the same printer, you can specify a printer priority with the Priority field for each share. The higher the number, the faster a print job sent to that share will access the printer. The highest priority is 99, and the default (lowest) is 1. If two users send jobs to the same printer at the same time, one with a 99 priority and the other with a 1 priority, the 99 priority would print first.

- Driver is the default printer driver that the printer is using.

- The print spooling controls let you decide how the print job will spool. You can choose to have the entire job spool first before printing (this ensures that the entire job is received by the print queue before printing), to start printing immediately while the job is still spooling, or to print directly to the printer without spooling. (The last option requires a printer with a large amount of RAM on the motherboard.)

- Hold Mismatched Documents allows the spooler to hold any print jobs that don't match the setup for the print device.

- Print Spooled Documents First allows a completely spooled printer job to be printed first even if it has a lower priority number than a job that is still spooling.

- Usually, after a print job has been printed, the print queue deletes the print job. If you check the Keep Printed Documents box, the print queue will not delete the print job after it is printed.

- Enable Advanced Printing Features allows you to set some advanced features such as the Page Order and Pages Per Sheet settings.

FIGURE 4.12   Advanced tab of the printer's Properties dialog box

The Color Management Tab   This tab allows you to adjust the color of your printing jobs.

The Security Tab   The Security tab (see Figure 4.13) is where you can set the permissions for your printer. This allows users to print, manage printers, manage documents, and take advantage of special permissions.

- The Add button allows you to add users and groups to the printer.

- The Remove button allows you to remove users and groups from the printer.

- The following controls, available in the Permissions For Everyone box, apply to everyone on your network:

  - Print gives everyone the right to print to this printer.

  - Manage Printers gives everyone the right to manage this printer, including deleting print jobs, setting priorities, setting availability, and so on.

  - Manage Documents gives everyone the right to manage print jobs.

  - Special Permissions allows you to set unique permissions such as Print, Manage Printers, Read permissions, Change permissions, and Take Ownership.

FIGURE 4.13   Security tab of the printer's Properties dialog box

Migrating Print Servers

In a network environment, an administrator may find it necessary to replace older print servers or to consolidate multiple print servers into one. To do this print server migration or replacement, you can use the Printer Migration Wizard or the `Printbrm.exe` command-line tool. These two utilities allow you to export print queues, printer settings, printer ports, and language monitors. These utilities then allow you to import these settings on another print server running Windows Server 2012 R2.

Printer Pooling

In a large organization, one issue that you may run into when you print a document to a print device is that you may have to wait a while for that document to print. If you have hundreds of print jobs being sent to a print device, it could take time until your print job appears on the print device. This is where printer pools can help.

A *printer pool* allows an administrator to associates multiple printers (identical print devices) with a single set of printer software. When you send a print job to a device, the print job will print to the first available device in the printer pool. This allows print jobs to print faster to multiple devices. For this to work, you must make sure that all devices are in the same physical area. You do not want a user traveling all over the company looking for their print job because they don't know which device printed the job.

To set up a printer to print to multiple devices, follow these steps:

1. Open Devices and Printers.
2. Right-click the printer you are using and then click Printer Properties.
3. On the Ports tab, select the Enable Printer Pooling check box.
4. Click each port where the printers you want to pool are connected.

Easy Print Driver

One printer configuration that is a little different from normal is when you are setting up a printer for a Remote Desktop server. However, Microsoft has included a feature to help. That feature is called the *Easy Print Driver*.

Remote Desktop Services gives you the ability to do printer redirection. What this means is Remote Desktop can route printing jobs from a server to a printer that is attached to a client computer. On an RD Session Host server, an administrator has the ability to use the Remote Desktop Easy Print printer driver to help simplify printer configuration.

The RD Session Host server first tries to use the Remote Desktop Easy Print driver, and if the RD client computer does not support this driver, the server looks for a matching printer driver on the server.

Configuring Remote Management

As an administrator, sometimes you might need to manage a server remotely. There are a few different tools you can use to do this task. You can use remote administration to help configure services on a Windows Server 2012 R2 system. The following sections cover Windows Remote Management and Windows PowerShell.

Windows PowerShell does not always have to be used remotely. For example, you can use Windows PowerShell when configuring a Windows Server 2012 R2 Server Core installation locally.

Windows Remote Management

The *Windows Remote Management (WinRM) utility* is Microsoft's version of the WS-Management protocol, an industry-standard protocol that allows different vendors' operating systems and hardware to work together. There are three main ways to access the WinRM utility:

- WinRM command-line tool
- WinRM scripting objects
- Windows Remote Shell command-line tool

The WinRM utility allows you to execute commands remotely and obtain management data from local and remote computers. You can use the WinRM utility on both Windows-based operating systems and non-Windows-based operating systems.

When using the WinRM utility, you can use the -machine switch to indicate the remote machine to which you are connecting. When connecting to a machine, you can connect using the localhost name, the NetBIOS name, the fully qualified domain name (FQDN), or the IP address of the remote machine. The following is an example of a WinRM command using a FQDN name on the secure port 443:

```
winrm get -machine:server.stellacon.local -port:443
```

Table 4.3 shows the command-line WinRM commands and descriptions of what each command does.

TABLE 4.3 WinRM commands and descriptions

Command	Description
WinRM g or WinRM get	Retrieves management information
WinRM s or WinRM set	Modifies management information
WinRM c or WinRM create	Creates a new instance on the managed resources
WinRM d or WinRM delete	Removes an instance from a managed resource
WinRM e or WinRM enumerate	Lists all instances of a managed resource
WinRM i or WinRM invoke	Executes a method on a managed resource
WinRM id or WinRM identity	Determines whether a WS-Management implementation is running on a remote machine

WinRM quickconfig	Configures a machine to accept WS-Management commands from a remote machine
WinRM configSDDL	Modifies an existing security descriptor for a Uniform Resource Identifier (URI)
WinRM helpmsg	Displays error messages for an error code

Now that you have looked at WinRM, let's take a look at how to use the Windows PowerShell utility.

Windows PowerShell

Windows PowerShell is a task-based, command-line scripting utility that allows you to execute commands locally or remotely on a Windows Server 2012 R2 machine. It was specifically designed for system administrators to allow for local or remote administration.

 Microsoft asks a lot of questions on the exam about Windows PowerShell. Therefore, I will be discussing PowerShell throughout this book because of its importance on all of the Windows Server 2012 R2 exams.

Most operating system shells, including Cmd.exe and the SH, KSH, CSH, and BASH Unix shells, work by running a command or utility in a new process and then presenting the results to the user as text. These system shells also have commands that are built into the shell and execute in the shell process. In most system shells, because there are only a few built-in commands, many utilities have been created over the years to complete tasks.

Windows PowerShell contains an interactive prompt and a scripting environment that can be used independently or in combination. Unlike the previously mentioned system shells, which accept and return text, Windows PowerShell is built using the *.NET Framework common language runtime (CLR)* and the .NET Framework. Because of this, Windows PowerShell accepts and returns .NET Framework objects. This important change in the shell allows you to use entirely new tools and methods to manage and configure Windows.

Windows PowerShell introduced the concept of using cmdlets (pronounced "command-lets"). Cmdlets are simple, single-function command-line tools built into the shell. Administrators can use the cmdlets independently, or they can combine these tools to execute complex tasks and harness the true power of PowerShell. Windows PowerShell includes more than a hundred core cmdlets, but the true advantage of PowerShell is that anyone can write their own cmdlets and share them with other users.

Administrators often automate the management of their multicomputer environments by running sequences of long-running tasks, or *workflows*, which can affect multiple managed computers or devices at the same time. Windows PowerShell can help administrators accomplish workflows in a more effective way. Windows PowerShell includes some of the following advantages:

Windows PowerShell Scripting Syntax   Administrators can use Windows PowerShell scripting expertise to create script-based tasks by using the extensible Windows PowerShell language. Windows PowerShell script-based tasks are easy to create, and IT members can share them easily by entering them into an email or publishing them on a web page.

Day-to-Day Management tasks   Windows PowerShell allows administrators to configure and maintain servers. PowerShell allows you to pre-create scripts or use ready-to-use scripts to handle day-to-day tasks. This way, an administrator can just run a script to complete server configurations or management.

Multiserver Management   Administrators can concurrently apply workflow tasks to hundreds of managed servers and computers. Windows PowerShell includes common parameters to set workflows automatically, such as PSComputerName, to enable multicomputer administrative scenarios.

Single Task to Manage Complex, End-to-End Processes   Administrators can combine related scripts or commands that act upon an entire scenario into a single workflow. The status of activities within the workflow can be viewed at any time.

Automated Failure Recovery   Using Windows PowerShell allows workflows to survive both planned and unplanned interruptions, such as computer restarts. Administrators have the ability to suspend workflow operations and then restart or resume the workflow from the exact point at which it was suspended. Administrators can then create checkpoints as part of their workflow process so that they can resume the workflow from the last persisted task (or checkpoint) instead of restarting the workflow from the beginning.

Activity Retries   Administrators can create workflows that also specify activities that must rerun if the activity does not get completed on one or more managed computers (for example, if a target node was not online at the time the activity was running).

Connect and Disconnect   Administrators can connect and disconnect from the node that is executing the workflow, but the workflow will continue to run.

Configuring Non-Domain Servers   Another advantage of PowerShell is the ability to configure non-domain servers from a Windows Server 2012 R2 server (domain member). When you are running commands on the non-domain machine, you must have access to the non-domain machine's system administrator account. Another way to configure a non-domain server is to connect through remote desktop into the non-domain server and then configure the machine or run PowerShell commands while connected through remote desktop.

Task Scheduling   Workflow tasks have the ability to be scheduled and started when specific conditions are met. This is also true for any other Windows PowerShell cmdlet or script.

Table 4.4 defines a few of the cmdlets available in Windows PowerShell. Again, there are hundreds of cmdlets, and the ones listed in the table are just some of the more common ones. You can retrieve a list of all the cmdlets starting here:

http://technet.microsoft.com/en-us/scriptcenter/dd772285.aspx

TABLE 4.4 Windows PowerShell cmdlets

Cmdlet	Definition
Clear-History	Deletes entries from the command history
Invoke-command	Runs commands on local or remote computers
Start-job	Starts a Windows PowerShell background job
Stop-job	Stops a Windows PowerShell background job
Remove-job	Deletes a Windows PowerShell background job
Import-Module	Adds modules to the current session
Receive-job	Gets the results of a Windows PowerShell background job
Format-table	Shows the results in a table format
Out-file	Sends the job results to a file
Get-Date	Gets the date and time
Set-Date	Sets the system time and date on a computer
Get-event	Gets an event in the event queue
New-event	Creates a new event
Trace-command	Configures and starts a trace of a command on a machine
Get-WindowsFeature	Gets a list of available and installed roles and features on the local server
Get-WindowsFeature -ServerName	Gets a list of available and installed roles and features on a remote server
Get-Help Install-WindowsFeature	Gets the syntax and accepted parameters for the Install-WindowsFeature cmdlet
Uninstall-WindowsFeature	Removes a role or feature
Get-NetIPAddress	Gets information about IP address configuration
Set-NetIPAddress	Modifies IP address configuration properties of an existing IP address
Set-NetIPv4Protocol	Modifies information about the IPv4 protocol configuration

---

Windows PowerShell Commands

I will show you Windows PowerShell commands throughout this book. If I show you how to install a role or feature in Server Manager, I will also include the Windows PowerShell equivalent.

Another advantage of Windows PowerShell is that it allows you to gain access to a file system on a computer and to access the registry, digital certificate stores, and other data stores.

Complete Exercise 4.8 to start the Windows PowerShell utility in the Windows Server 2012 R2 Server Core machine installed in the previous exercise.

EXERCISE 4.8

Starting the Windows PowerShell Utility

1. Type **Start PowerShell** at the Windows Server 2012 R2 Server Core command prompt.

2. When the Windows PowerShell utility starts, type **Help** and press Enter. This will show you the Windows PowerShell syntax and some of the commands included in Windows PowerShell.

3. At the Windows PowerShell command prompt, type **Get-Date**. This will show you the system's date and time.

4. At the Windows command prompt, type **Help** *. This will show you all of the cmdlets you can use.

5. Close the Windows PowerShell utility by typing **Exit**.

Configuring Down-Level Servers

As an administrator, sometimes you might have to configure a Windows Server 2008 R2 server from a Windows Server 2012 R2 machine. This is referred to as configuring a *down-level server*.

When you install Windows Server 2012 R2, Server Manager can be used to configure and manage a down-level server as long as that down-level server is running one of the following operating systems:

- Windows Server 2008 R2 SP1 (either full server or a Server Core installation)
- Windows Server 2008 SP2 (full server only)

To be able to configure the Windows Server 2008/2008 R2 servers remotely, you must first install Windows Management Framework 3.0 (WMF 3.0) and all of its prerequisites on the Windows Server 2008/2008 R2 servers. No special configuration is required on the Windows Server 2012 R2 server.

If you need to install WMF 3.0 on a Windows Server 2008 R2 Server Core installation, you can do this by using the Deployment Image Servicing and Management (DISM) commands. The command names that you would use for these features are as follows:

- MicrosoftWindowsPowerShell
- MicrosoftWindowsPowerShell-WOW64
- NetFx2-ServerCore
- NetFx2-ServerCore-WOW64

To run these commands, you would run the following in Server Core:

```
Dism /online /enable-feature: <Feature Name>
```

 It is important to remember that Dism is case-sensitive in the command shown here.

Configuring Server Core

When configuring servers remotely, an administrator may have to configure a Server Core system. Let's take a look at some of the Server Core commands that can be used to do some basic server configurations.

When configuring Server Core, you may need to set the system for a static TCP/IP address. Use the following Windows PowerShell commands:

- Get-NetIPConfiguration allows you to view your current network configuration.
- Get-NetIPAddress allows you to view the IP addresses you are currently using.

If you want to set your static TCP/IP address, do the following:

1. In Windows PowerShell, run Get-NetIPInterface.
2. Write down the number shown in the IfIndex column of the output for the IP interface or the InterfaceDescription string for the network adapter you want to change.
3. In Windows PowerShell, run New-NetIPAddress -InterfaceIndex 10 -IPAddress -192.168.15.2 -PrefixLength 24 -DefaultGateway -192.168.15.1.
   - InterfaceIndex is the value of IfIndex from step 2 (in this example, 10).

- ▪ IPAddress is the static IP address you intend to set (in this example, 192.168.15.2).

- ▪ PrefixLength is the prefix length (another form of subnet mask) for the IP address you intend to set (in this example, 24).

- ▪ DefaultGateway is the default gateway (in this example, 192.168.15.1).

4. In Windows PowerShell, run Set-DNSClientServerAddress -InterfaceIndex 10 -ServerAddresses 192.168.15.4.

- ▪ InterfaceIndex is the value of IfIndex from step 2.

- ▪ ServerAddresses is the IP address of your DNS server.

5. To add multiple DNS servers, run Set-DNSClientServerAddress -InterfaceIndex 10 -ServerAddresses 192.168.15.4,192.168.15.5.

- ▪ In this example, 192.168.15.4 and 192.168.15.5 are both IP addresses of DNS servers.

Another Server Core task that you may need to configure is setting the server name. In PowerShell, run the following command to rename the server: Rename-Computer.

As an administrator, you may also want to run PowerShell commands on one system to run on another system. You can enable Windows PowerShell Remoting by using the Enable-PSRemoting command.

Configuring the Windows Firewall

The final item to examine is configuring Windows Firewall remotely. Microsoft Server 2012 R2 Windows Firewall will be discussed in full detail in Chapter 6, but since I am discussing remote administration, let's look at the commands needed to configure Windows Firewall remotely.

Netsh advfirewall is a command-line (with Administrator privileges) tool for Windows Firewall with Advanced Security that helps with the creation, administration, and monitoring of Windows Firewall and IPsec settings and provides an alternative to console-based management.

To enter into the netsh advfirewall prompt, you must first type **netsh**. After you enter the netsh prompt, you then type **advfirewall**, which will bring you to the netsh advfirewall prompt. When you enter netsh advfirewall, it enters you into a netsh advfirewall prompt that looks like the following:

netsh advfirewall> prompt

Once you are at the netsh firewall prompt, you can use the question mark to get a list of all available options (netsh advfirewall>?). Figure 4.14 shows you the list of available options.

FIGURE 4.14 Netsh advfirewall options

Summary

In this chapter, I discussed file servers and how they can be effective on your network. I also discussed sharing folders for users to access, and then I discussed how to publish those shared folders to Active Directory.

You learned about NTFS security versus shared folder permissions and how to limit users' hard drive space by setting up disk quotas. The chapter also covered the Encrypting File System (EFS) and how users can encrypt and compress files.

I talked about print servers and configuring printers. I talked about how to share and publish printers within Active Directory as well as print permissions, printer priorities, and print pooling.

You then took a look at remote configuration and a few tools that allow you to configure servers.

- Windows Remote Management lets you configure a server remotely from another machine.

- PowerShell is an important tool in the Windows Server 2012 R2 arsenal. Microsoft has been moving the industry toward PowerShell, and there will be many questions on the exam about PowerShell.

- Netsh allows you to configure Windows Firewall remotely.

Exam Essentials

Learn How Resources Can Be Published   A design goal for Active Directory was to make network resources easier for users to find. With that in mind, you should understand how using published printers and shared folders can simplify network resource management.

Know How to Configure Offline Folders   Offline folders give you the opportunity to set up folders so that users can work on the data while outside the office and later synchronize it with a master copy. You can set up GPOs to help with offline folder synchronization.

Know How to Configure NTFS Security   One of the major advantages of using NTFS over FAT32 is access to additional security features. NTFS allows you to put security at the file and folder layers. NTFS security is in effect whether the user is remote or local to the computer with the data.

Know How to Configure Shared Permissions   Shared permissions allow you to determine the access a user will receive when connecting to a shared folder. Shared permissions are allowed only at the folder layer and are in effect only when the user is remote to the computer with the shared data.

Understand How NTFS and Shared Permissions Work Together   NTFS and shared permissions are individually additive—you get the highest level of security and permissions within each type. NTFS is always in effect, and it is the only security available locally. Shared permissions are in effect only when connecting remotely to access the shared data. When the two types of permissions meet, the most restrictive set of permissions applies.

Know How to Configure Disk Quotas   Disk quotas allow an organization to determine the amount of disk space that users can have on a volume of a server. An administrator can set up disk quotas based on volumes or by users. Each volume must have its own separate set of disk quotas.

Know How to Configure Printing I discussed network printers versus print servers. Understand that when you create a printer, you want to publish the printer within Active Directory so that your users can find it throughout the domain. Understand the different printer permissions and how to install print drivers.

Understand Windows PowerShell Understanding Windows PowerShell is not only important for the exam; it will also allow you to configure Server Core more efficiently. Windows PowerShell is a command-line utility that allows you run single cmdlets as well as run complex tasks to exploit the full power from PowerShell.

Review Questions

1. The company for which you work has a multilevel administrative team that is segmented by departments and locations. There are four major locations, and you are in the Northeast group. You have been assigned to the administrative group that is responsible for creating and maintaining network shares for files and printers in your region. The last place you worked had a large Windows Server 2003 network, where you had a much wider range of responsibilities. You are excited about the chance to learn more about Windows Server 2012 R2.

   For your first task, you have been given a list of file and printer shares that need to be created for the users in your region. You ask how to create them in Windows Server 2012 R2, and you are told that the process of creating a share is the same as with Windows Server 2003. You create the shares and use NETUSE to test them. Everything appears to work fine, so you send out a message that the shares are available. The next day, you start receiving calls from users who say they cannot see any of the resources you created. What is the most likely reason for the calls from the users?

   A. You forgot to enable NetBIOS for the shares.

   B. You need to force replication for the shares to appear in the directory.

   C. You need to publish the shares in the directory.

   D. The shares will appear within the normal replication period.

2. You want to publish a printer to Active Directory. Where would you click in order to accomplish this task?

   A. The Sharing tab

   B. The Advanced tab

   C. The Device Settings tab

   D. The Printing Preferences button

3. A system administrator creates a local Printer object, but it doesn't show up in Active Directory when a user executes a search for all printers. Which of the following are possible reasons for this? (Choose all that apply.)

   A. The printer was not shared.

   B. The printer is offline.

   C. The client does not have permission to view the printer.

   D. The printer is malfunctioning.

4. You are the network administrator for a midsize coffee bean distributor. Your company's network has four Windows 2012 R2 servers, and all of the clients are running either Windows 8 or Windows 7. Most of your end users use laptops to do their work, and many of them work away from the office. What should you configure to help them work on documents when away from the office?

    A. Online file access

    B. Offline file access

    C. Share permissions

    D. NTFS permissions

5. Your company has decided to implement a Windows 2012 R2 server. The company IT manager who came before you always used FAT32 as the system partition. Your company wants to know whether it should move to NTFS. Which of the following are some advantages of NTFS? (Choose all that apply.)

    A. Security

    B. Quotas

    C. Compression

    D. Encryption

6. Will, the IT manager for your company, has been asked to give Moe the rights to read and change documents in the `Stellacon Documents` folder. The following table shows the current permissions on the shared folder:

Group/User	NTFS	Shared
Sales	Read	Change
Marketing	Modify	Change
R&D	Deny	Full Control
Finance	Read	Read
Tylor	Read	Change

Moe is a member of the Sales and Finance groups. When Moe accesses the `Stellacon Documents` folder, he can read all of the files, but the system won't let him change or delete files. What do you need to do to give Moe the minimum amount of rights to do his job?

    A. Give Sales Full Control to shared permissions.

    B. Give Moe Full Control to NTFS security.

    C. Give Finance Change to shared permissions.

    D. Give Finance Modify to NTFS security.

    E. Give Moe Modify to NTFS security.

7. You are the administrator of your network, which consists of two Windows Server 2012 R2 systems. One of the servers is a domain controller, and the other server is a file server for data storage. The hard drive of the file server is starting to fill up. You do not have the ability to install another hard drive, so you decide to limit the amount of space everyone gets on the hard drive. What do you need to implement to solve your problem?

    A. Disk spacing

    B. Disk quotas

    C. Disk hardening

    D. Disk limitations

8. You are the IT manager for your company. You have been asked to give the Admin group the rights to read, change, and assign permissions to documents in the Stellacon Documents folder. The following table shows the current permissions on the Stellacon Documents shared folder:

Group/User	NTFS	Shared
Sales	Read	Change
Marketing	Modify	Change
R&D	Deny	Full Control
Finance	Read	Read
Admin	Change	Change

What do you need to do to give the Admin group the rights to do their job? (Choose all that apply.)

   A. Give Sales Full Control to shared permissions.

   B. Give Full Control to NTFS security.

   C. Give Admin Full Control to shared permissions.

   D. Give Finance Modify to NTFS security.

   E. Give Admin Full Control to NTFS security.

9. You have been asked to configure a Windows Server 2012 R2 Datacenter Server Core machine. Which remote configuration applications can you use to configure this server from your machine? (Choose all that apply.)

   A. Windows Remote Management

   B. Command prompt

   C. Windows PowerShell

   D. Microsoft Remote Admin (MRA)

10. You have been hired by a small company to implement new Windows Server 2012 R2 systems. The company wants you to set up a server for users' home folder locations. What type of server would you be setting up?

   A. PDC server

   B. Web server

   C. Exchange server

   D. File server

Chapter

5

Administer Active Directory

THE FOLLOWING 70-410 EXAM OBJECTIVES ARE COVERED IN THIS CHAPTER:

✓ **Create and manage Active Directory users and computers**

- Automate the creation of Active Directory accounts

- Create, copy, configure, and delete users and computers

- Configure templates

- Perform bulk Active Directory operations

- Configure user rights

- Offline domain join

- Manage inactive and disabled accounts

✓ **Create and manage Active Directory groups and organizational units (OUs)**

- Configure group nesting

- Convert groups including security, distribution, universal, domain local, and domain global

- Manage group membership using Group Policy

- Enumerate group membership

- Delegate the creation and management of Active Directory objects

- Manage default Active Directory containers

- Create, copy, configure, and delete groups and OUs

In previous chapters, you learned how to install Domain Name System (DNS) and Active Directory, but you still haven't been introduced to the lower-level objects that exist in Active Directory.

In this chapter, you will look at the structure of the various components within a domain. You'll see how an organization's business structure can be mirrored within Active Directory through the use of organizational units for ease of use and to create a seamless look and feel. Because the concepts related to organizational units are quite simple, some system administrators may underestimate their importance and not plan to use them accordingly. Make no mistake: one of the fundamental components of a successful Active Directory installation is the proper design and deployment of organizational units.

You'll also see in this chapter the actual steps you need to take to create common Active Directory objects and then learn how to configure and manage them. Finally, you'll look at ways to publish resources and methods for creating user accounts automatically.

An Overview of OUs

An *organizational unit (OU)* is a logical group of Active Directory objects, just as the name implies. OUs serve as containers within which Active Directory objects can be created, but they do not form part of the DNS namespace. They are used solely to create organization within a domain.

OUs can contain the following types of Active Directory objects:

- Users
- Groups
- Computers
- Shared Folder objects
- Contacts
- Printers
- InetOrgPerson objects
- Microsoft Message Queuing (MSMQ) Queue aliases
- Other OUs

Perhaps the most useful feature of OUs is that they can contain other OU objects. As a result, system administrators can hierarchically group resources and objects according to business practices. The OU structure is extremely flexible and, as you will see later in this chapter, can easily be rearranged to reflect business reorganizations.

Another advantage of OUs is that each can have its own set of policies. Administrators can create individual and unique Group Policy objects (GPOs) for each OU. GPOs are rules or policies that can apply to all of the objects within the OU. GPOs are discussed in detail in Chapter 6 "Manage GPOs."

Each type of object has its own purpose within the organization of Active Directory domains. Later in this chapter, you'll look at the specifics of User, Computer, Group, and Shared Folder objects. For now, let's focus on the purpose and benefits of using OUs.

The Purpose of OUs

OUs are mainly used to organize the objects within Active Directory. Before you dive into the details of OUs, however, you must understand how OUs, users, and groups interact. Most important, you should understand that OUs are simply containers that you can use to group various objects logically. They are not, however, groups in the classical sense. That is, they are not used for assigning security permissions. Another way of stating this is that the user accounts, computer accounts, and group accounts that are contained in OUs are considered security principals while the OUs themselves are not.

OUs do not take the place of standard user and group permissions. A good general practice is to assign users to groups and then place the groups within OUs. This enhances the benefits of setting security permissions and of using the OU hierarchy for making settings. Figure 5.1 illustrates this concept.

FIGURE 5.1 Relationships of users, groups, and OUs

An OU contains objects only from within the domain in which it resides. As you'll see in the section "Delegating Administrative Control" later in this chapter, the OU is the finest level of granularity used for group policies and other administrative settings.

Benefits of OUs

There are many benefits to using OUs throughout your network environment.

- OUs are the smallest unit to which you can assign directory permissions.
- You can easily change the OU structure, and it is more flexible than the domain structure.
- The OU structure can support many different levels of hierarchy.
- Child objects can inherit OU settings.
- You can set Group Policy settings on OUs.
- You can easily delegate the administration of OUs and the objects within them to the appropriate users and groups.

Now that you have a good idea of why you should use OUs, take a look at some general practices you can use to plan the OU structure.

Planning the OU Structure

One of the key benefits of Active Directory is the way in which it can bring organization to complex network environments. Before you can begin to implement OUs in various configurations, you must plan a structure that is compatible with business and technical needs. In this section, you'll learn about several factors that you should consider when planning for the structure of OUs.

Logical Grouping of Resources

The fundamental purpose of using OUs is to group resources (which exist within Active Directory) hierarchically. Fortunately, hierarchical groups are quite intuitive and widely used in most businesses. For example, a typical manufacturing business might divide its various operations into different departments as follows:

- Sales
- Marketing
- Engineering
- Research and Development
- Support
- Information Technology (IT)

Each of these departments usually has its own goals and mission. To make the business competitive, individuals within each of the departments are assigned to various roles. The following role types might be used:

- Managers
- Clerical staff
- Technical staff
- Planners

Each of these roles usually entails specific job responsibilities. For example, managers should provide direction to general staff members. Note that the very nature of these roles suggests that employees may fill many different positions. That is, one employee might be a manager in one department and a member of the technical staff in another. In the modern workplace, such situations are quite common.

All of this information helps you plan how to use OUs. First the structure of OUs within a given network environment should map well to the business's needs, including the political and logical structure of the organization as well as its technical needs. Figure 5.2 shows how a business organization might be mapped to the OU structure within an Active Directory domain.

FIGURE 5.2   Mapping a business organization to an OU structure

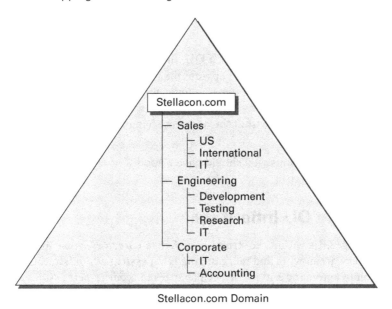

Stellacon.com Domain

When naming OUs for your organization, you should keep several considerations and limitations in mind:

Keep the Names and Descriptions Simple   The purpose of OUs is to make administering and using resources simple. Therefore, it's always a good idea to keep the names of your objects simple and descriptive. Sometimes, finding a balance between these two goals can be a challenge. For example, although a printer name like "The LaserJet located near Bob's cube" might seem descriptive, it is certainly difficult to type. Also, imagine the naming changes that you might have to make if Bob moves (or leaves the company)!

Pay Attention to Limitations   The maximum length for the name of an OU is 64 characters. In most cases, this should adequately describe the OU. Remember, the name of an OU does not have to describe the object uniquely because the OU is generally referenced only as part of the overall hierarchy. For example, you can choose to create an OU named "IT" within two different parent OUs. Even though the OUs have the same name, users and administrators are able to distinguish between them based on their complete pathname.

Pay Attention to the Hierarchical Consistency   The fundamental basis of an OU structure is its position in a hierarchy. From a design standpoint, this means you cannot have two OUs with the same name at the same level. However, you can have OUs with the same name at different levels. For example, you could create an OU named "Corporate" within the North America OU and another one within the South America OU. This is because the fully qualified domain name includes information about the hierarchy. When an administrator tries to access resources in a Corporate OU, they must specify which Corporate OU they mean.

For example, if you create a North America OU, the Canada OU should logically fit under it. If you decide that you want to separate the North America and Canada OUs into completely different containers, then you might want to use other, more appropriate names. For example, you could change North America to "U.S." Users and administrators depend on the hierarchy of OUs within the domain, so make sure that it remains logically consistent.

Based on these considerations, you should have a good idea of how best to organize the OU structure for your domain.

Understanding OU Inheritance

When you rearrange OUs within the structure of Active Directory, you can change several settings. When they are moving and reorganizing OUs, system administrators must pay careful attention to automatic and unforeseen changes in security permissions and other configuration options. By default, OUs inherit the permissions of their new parent container when they are moved.

By using the built-in tools provided with Windows Server 2012 R2 and Active Directory, you can move or copy OUs only within the same domain. You cannot use the Active

Directory Users and Computers tool to move OUs between domains. To do this, use the *Active Directory Migration Tool (ADMT)*. This is one of the many Active Directory support tools.

Delegating Administrative Control

I already mentioned that OUs are the smallest component within a domain to which administrative permissions and group policies can be assigned by administrators. Now you'll take a look specifically at how administrative control is set on OUs.

Real World Scenario

Delegation occurs when a higher security authority assigns permissions to a lesser security authority. As a real-world example, assume that you are the director of IT for a large organization. Instead of doing all of the work yourself, you would probably assign roles and responsibilities to other individuals. For example, if you worked within a multidomain environment, you might make one system administrator responsible for all operations within the Sales domain and another responsible for the Engineering domain. Similarly, you could assign the permissions for managing all printers and print queue objects within your organization to one individual user while allowing another individual user to manage all security permissions for users and groups. In this way, you can distribute the various roles and responsibilities of the IT staff throughout the organization.

Businesses generally have a division of labor that handles all of the tasks involved in keeping the company's networks humming. Network operating systems (NOSs), however, often make it difficult to assign just the right permissions; in other words, they do not support very granular permission assignments. Sometimes, fine granularity is necessary to ensure that only the right permissions are assigned. A good general rule of thumb is to provide users and administrators with the minimum permissions they require to do their jobs. This way, you can ensure that accidental, malicious, and otherwise unwanted changes do not occur.

You can use auditing to log events to the Security log in the Event Viewer. This is a way to ensure that if accidental, malicious, and otherwise unwanted changes do occur, they are logged and traceable.

In the world of Active Directory, you delegate to define responsibilities for OU administrators. As a system administrator, you will occasionally be tasked with having to delegate responsibility to others—you can't do it all, although sometimes administrators believe that they can. You understand the old IT logic of doing all of the tasks yourself for job security, but this can actually make you look worse.

 You can delegate control only at the OU level and not at the object level within the OU.

If you do find yourself in a role where you need to delegate, remember that Windows Server 2012 R2 was designed to offer you the ability to do so. In its simplest definition, *delegation* allows a higher administrative authority to grant specific administrative rights for containers and subtrees to individuals and groups. What this essentially does is to eliminate the need for domain administrators with sweeping authority over large segments of the user population. You can break up this control over branches within your tree, within each OU you create.

 To understand delegation and rights, you should first understand the concept of *access control entries (ACEs)*. ACEs grant specific administrative rights on objects in a container to a user or group. A container's access control list (ACL) is used to store ACEs.

When you are considering implementing delegation, keep these two concerns in mind:

Parent-Child Relationships   The OU hierarchy you create will be important when you consider the maintainability of security permissions. OUs can exist in a parent-child relationship, which means that permissions and group policies set on OUs higher up in the hierarchy (parents) can interact with objects in lower-level OUs (children). When it comes to delegating permissions, this is extremely important. You can allow child containers to inherit the permissions set on parent containers automatically. For example, if the North America division of your organization contains 12 other OUs, you could delegate permissions to all of them at once (saving time and reducing the likelihood of human error) by placing security permissions on the North America division. This feature can greatly ease administration, especially in larger organizations, but it is also a reminder of the importance of properly planning the OU structure within a domain.

Inheritance Settings   Now that you've seen how you can use parent-child relationships for administration, you should consider *inheritance*, the process in which child objects take on the permissions of a parent container. When you set permissions on a parent container, all of the child objects are configured to inherit the same permissions. You can override this behavior, however, if business rules do not lend themselves well to inheritance.

Applying Group Policies

One of the strengths of the Windows operating system is that it offers users a great deal of power and flexibility. From installing new software to adding device drivers, users can make many changes to their workstation configurations. However, this level of flexibility is also a potential problem. For instance, inexperienced users might inadvertently change settings, causing problems that can require many hours to fix.

In many cases (and especially in business environments), users require only a subset of the complete functionality the operating system provides. In the past, however, the difficulty associated with implementing and managing security and policy settings has led to lax security policies. Some of the reasons for this are technical—it can be tedious and difficult to implement and manage security restrictions. Other problems have been political—users and management might feel that they should have full permissions on their local machines, despite the potential problems this might cause.

That's where the idea of group policies comes in. Simply defined, *group policies* are collections of rules that you can apply to objects within Active Directory. Specifically, Group Policy settings are assigned at the site, domain, and OU levels, and they can apply to user accounts and computer accounts. For example, a system administrator can use group policies to configure the following settings:

- Restricting users from installing new programs
- Disallowing the use of the Control Panel
- Limiting choices for display and Desktop settings

Creating OUs

Now that you have looked at several different ways in which OUs can be used to bring organization to the objects within Active Directory, it's time to look at how you can create and manage them.

Through the use of the *Active Directory Users and Computers administrative tool*, also called the *MMC (Microsoft Management Console)*, you can quickly and easily add, move, and change OUs. This graphical tool makes it easy to visualize and create the various levels of hierarchy an organization requires.

Figure 5.3 shows a geographically based OU structure that a multinational company might use. Note that the organization is based in North America and that it has a corporate office located there. In general, the other offices are much smaller than the corporate office located in North America.

FIGURE 5.3 A geographically based OU structure

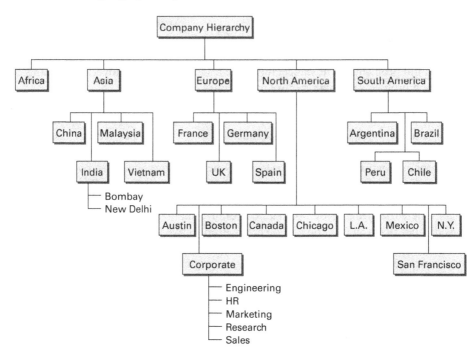

It's important to note that this OU structure could have been designed in several different ways. For example, I could have chosen to group all of the offices located in the United
States within an OU named "U.S." However, because of the large size of these offices,
I chose to place these objects at the same level as the Canada and Mexico OUs. This prevents an unnecessarily deep OU hierarchy while still logically grouping the offices.

One nice feature when creating an OU is the ability to protect the OU from being accidentally deleted. When you create an OU, you can check the Protect Container From Accidental Deletion check box. This check box protects against an administrator deleting the
OU. To delete the OU, you must go into the advanced view of the OU and uncheck the box.

Exercise 5.1 walks you through the process of creating several OUs for a multinational
business. You'll be using this OU structure in later exercises within this chapter.

To perform the exercises included in this chapter, you must have administrative access to a Windows Server 2012 R2 domain controller.

EXERCISE 5.1

Creating an OU Structure

1. Click the Windows key on the keyboard and choose Administrative Tools.

2. Open the Active Directory Users and Computers administrative tool.

3. Right-click the name of the local domain and choose New ➢ Organizational Unit. You will see the dialog box shown here. Notice that this box shows you the current context within which the OU will be created. In this case, you're creating a top-level OU, so the full path is simply the name of the domain.

4. Type **North America** for the name of the first OU. Uncheck the box Protect Container From Accidental Deletion and click OK to create this object.

5. Create the following top-level OUs by right-clicking the name of the domain and choosing New ➢ Organizational Unit. Also make sure to uncheck Protect Container From Accidental Deletion for all OUs in these exercises because you'll be deleting some of these OUs in later ones.

    Africa

    Asia

    Europe

    South America

    Note that the order in which you create the OUs is not important. In this exercise, you are simply using a method that emphasizes the hierarchical relationship.

6. Create the following second-level OUs within the North America OU by right-clicking the North America OU and selecting New ➢ Organizational Unit:

   Austin

   Boston

   Canada

   Chicago

   Corporate

   Los Angeles

   Mexico

   New York

   San Francisco

7. Create the following OUs under the Asia OU:

   China

   India

   Malaysia

   Vietnam

8. Create the following OUs under the Europe OU:

   France

   Germany

   Spain

   UK

9. Create the following OUs under the South America OU:

   Argentina

   Brazil

   Chile

   Peru

10. Create the following third-level OUs under the India OU by right-clicking India within the Asia OU and selecting New ➢ Organizational Unit:

    Bombay

    New Delhi

11. Within the North America Corporate OU, create the following OUs:

Engineering

HR

Marketing

Research

Sales

12. When you have completed creating the OUs, you should have a structure that looks similar to the one in the left pane shown here.

Managing OUs

Managing network environments would still be challenging, even if things rarely changed. However, in the real world, business units, departments, and employee roles change frequently. As business and technical needs change, so should the structure of Active Directory.

Fortunately, changing the structure of OUs within a domain is a relatively simple process. In the following sections, you'll look at ways to delegate control of OUs and make other changes.

Moving, Deleting, and Renaming OUs

The process of moving, deleting, and renaming OUs is a simple one. Exercise 5.2 shows how you can easily modify and reorganize OUs to reflect changes in the business organization. The specific scenario covered in this exercise includes the following changes:

- The Research and Engineering departments have been combined to form a department known as Research and Development (RD).

- The Sales department has been moved from the Corporate headquarters office to the New York office.

- The Marketing department has been moved from the Corporate headquarters office to the Chicago office.

This exercise assumes you have already completed the steps in Exercise 5.1.

EXERCISE 5.2

Modifying OU Structure

1. Click the Windows key on the keyboard and choose Administrative Tools.

2. Open the Active Directory Users and Computers administrative tool.

3. Right-click the Engineering OU (located within North America ➢ Corporate) and click Delete. When you are prompted for confirmation, click Yes. Note that if this OU contained objects, they would have all been automatically deleted as well.

4. Right-click the Research OU and select Rename. Type **RD** to change the name of the OU and press Enter.

5. Right-click the Sales OU and select Move. In the Move dialog box, expand the North America branch and click the New York OU. Click OK to move the OU.

6. You will use an alternate method to move the Marketing OU. Drag the Marketing OU and drop it onto the Chicago OU.

7. When you have finished, you should see an OU structure similar to the one shown here. Close the Active Directory Users and Computers administrative tool.

Administering Properties of OUs

Although OUs are primarily created for organizational purposes within the Active Directory environment, they have several settings that you can modify. To modify the properties of an OU using the Active Directory Users and Computers administrative tool, right-click the name of any OU and select Properties. When you do, the OU Properties dialog box appears. In the example shown in Figure 5.4, you'll see the options on the General tab.

FIGURE 5.4   The General tab of the OU's Properties dialog box

In any organization, it helps to know who is responsible for managing an OU. You can set this information on the Managed By tab (see Figure 5.5). The information specified on this tab is convenient because it is automatically pulled from the contact information on a user record. You should consider always having a contact for each OU within your organization so that other system administrators know whom to contact if they need to make any changes.

FIGURE 5.5   The Managed By tab of the OU's Properties dialog box

Delegating Control of OUs

In simple environments, one or a few system administrators may be responsible for managing all of the settings within Active Directory. For example, a single system administrator could manage all users within all OUs in the environment. In larger organizations, however, roles and responsibilities may be divided among many different individuals. A typical situation is one in which a system administrator is responsible for objects within only a few OUs in an Active Directory domain. Alternatively, one system administrator might manage User and Group objects while another is responsible for managing file and print services.

Fortunately, using the Active Directory Users and Computers tool, you can quickly and easily ensure that specific users receive only the permissions they need. In Exercise 5.3, you will use the Delegation of Control Wizard to assign permissions to individuals. To complete these steps successfully, first you must have created the objects in the previous exercises of this chapter.

EXERCISE 5.3

Using the Delegation of Control Wizard

1. Click the Windows key on the keyboard and choose Administrative Tools.

2. Open the Active Directory Users and Computers administrative tool.

3. Right-click the Corporate OU within the North America OU and select Delegate Control. This starts the Delegation of Control Wizard. Click Next to begin configuring security settings.

4. In the Users Or Groups page, click the Add button. In the Enter The Object Names To Select field, enter **Account Operators** and click the Check Names button. Click OK. Click Next to continue.

5. In the Tasks To Delegate page, select Delegate The Following Common Tasks and place a check mark next to the following items:

    Create, Delete, And Manage User Accounts

    Reset User Passwords And Force Password Change At Next Logon

    Read All User Information

    Create, Delete, And Manage Groups

    Modify The Membership Of A Group

6. Click Next to continue.

EXERCISE 5.3 *(continued)*

7. The Completing The Delegation Of Control Wizard page then provides a summary of the operations you have selected. To implement the changes, click Finish.

Although the common tasks available through the wizard are sufficient for many delegation operations, you may have cases in which you want more control. For example, you might want to give a particular system administrator permissions to modify only Computer objects. Exercise 5.4 uses the Delegation of Control Wizard to assign more granular permissions. To complete these steps successfully, you must have completed the previous exercises in this chapter.

EXERCISE 5.4

Delegating Custom Tasks

1. Click the Windows key on the keyboard and choose Administrative Tools.

2. Open the Active Directory Users and Computers administrative tool.

3. Right-click the Corporate OU within the North America OU and select Delegate Control. This starts the Delegation of Control Wizard. Click Next to begin making security settings.

4. In the Users Or Groups page, click the Add button. In the Enter The Object Names To Select field, enter **Server Operators** and click the Check Names button. Click OK and then click Next to continue.

5. In the Tasks To Delegate page, select the Create A Custom Task To Delegate radio button and click Next to continue.

6. In the Active Directory Object Type page, choose Only The Following Objects In The Folder and place a check mark next to the following items. (You will have to scroll down to see them all.)

User Objects

Computer Objects

Contact Objects

Group Objects

Organizational Unit Objects

Printer Objects

7. Click Next to continue.

8. In the Permissions page, place a check mark next to the General option and make sure the other options are not checked. Note that if the various objects within your Active Directory schema had property-specific settings, you would see those options here. Place a check mark next to the following items:

Create All Child Objects

Read All Properties

Write All Properties

This gives the members of the Server Operators group the ability to create new objects within the Corporate OU and the permissions to read and write all properties for these objects.

9. Click Next to continue.

10. The Completing The Delegation Of Control Wizard page provides a summary of the operations you have selected. To implement the changes, click Finish.

🌐 Real World Scenario

Delegation: Who's Responsible for What?

You're the IT director for a large, multinational organization. You've been with the company for quite a while, that is, since the environment had only a handful of offices and a few network and system administrators. Times have changed, however. Now system administrators must coordinate the efforts of hundreds of IT staffers in 14 countries.

For years now, a debate has been raging among IT administrators on the question of when to create a new child domain and when to make it just an OU. For example, let's say you have a remote office in Concord, New Hampshire. Do you give the remote office its own domain (as a child domain), or do you just make the Concord office an OU? Well, it really depends on who you want to manage the resources in Concord. Do you want to create domains or OUs based on location?

Fortunately, through the proper use of OUs and delegation, you are given a lot of flexibility in determining how to handle the administration. You can structure the administration in several ways. First, if you choose to create OUs based on a geographic business structure, you could delegate control of these OUs based on the job functions of various system administrators. For example, you could use one user account to administer the

Concord OU. Within the Concord OU, this system administrator could delegate control of resources represented by the Printers and Scanners OUs.

Alternatively, the OU structure may create a functional representation of the business. For example, the Engineering OU might contain other OUs that are based on office locations such as New York and Paris. A system administrator of the Engineering domain could delegate permissions based on geography or job functions to the lower OUs. Regardless of whether you build a departmental, functional, or geographical OU model, keep in mind that each model excludes other models. This is one of the most important decisions you need to make. When you are making this decision or modifying previous decisions, your overriding concern is how it will affect the management and administration of the network. The good news is that, because Active Directory has so many features, the model you choose can be based on specific business requirements rather than imposed by architectural constraints.

Troubleshooting OUs

In general, you will find using OUs to be a relatively straightforward and painless process. With adequate planning, you'll be able to implement an intuitive and useful structure for OU objects.

The most common problems with OU configuration are related to the OU structure. When troubleshooting OUs, pay careful attention to the following factors:

Inheritance   By default, Group Policy and other settings are transferred automatically from parent OUs to child OUs and objects. Even if a specific OU is not given a set of permissions, objects within that OU might still get them from parent objects.

Delegation of Administration   If you allow the wrong user accounts or groups to perform specific tasks on OUs, you might be violating your company's security policy. Be sure to verify the delegations you have made at each OU level.

Organizational Issues   Sometimes, business practices do not easily map to the structure of Active Directory. A few misplaced OUs, user accounts, computer accounts, or groups can make administration difficult or inaccurate. In many cases, it might be beneficial to rearrange the OU structure to accommodate any changes in the business organization. In others, it might make more sense to change business processes.

If you regularly consider each of these issues when troubleshooting problems with OUs, you will be much less likely to make errors in the Active Directory configuration.

Creating and Managing Active Directory Objects

Now that you are familiar with the task of creating OUs, you should find creating and managing other Active Directory objects quite simple. The following sections will examine the details.

Overview of Active Directory Objects

When you install and configure a domain controller, Active Directory sets up an organizational structure for you, and you can create and manage several types of objects.

Active Directory Organization

When you are looking at your Active Directory structure, you will see objects that look like folders in Windows Explorer. These objects are containers, or *organizational units (OUs)*. The difference is that an OU is a container to which you can link a GPO. Normal containers cannot have a GPO linked to them. That's what makes an OU a special container.

By default, after you install and configure a domain controller, you will see the following organizational sections within the Active Directory Users and Computers tool (they look like folders):

Built-In   The *Built-In container* includes all of the standard groups that are installed by default when you promote a domain controller. You can use these groups to administer the servers in your environment. Examples include the Administrators group, Backup Operators group, and Print Operators group.

Computers   By default, the *Computers container* contains a list of the workstations in your domain. From here, you can manage all of the computers in your domain.

Domain Controllers   The *Domain Controllers OU* includes a list of all the domain controllers for the domain.

Foreign Security Principals   *Foreign security principals* containers are any objects to which security can be assigned and that are not part of the current domain. *Security principals* are Active Directory objects to which permissions can be applied, and they can be used to manage permissions in Active Directory.

Managed Service Accounts   The *Managed Service Accounts container* is a new Windows Server 2012 R2 container. Service accounts are accounts created to run specific services such as Exchange and SQL Server. Having a Managed Service Accounts container allows you to control the service accounts better and thus allows for better service account security.

Users   The *Users container* includes all the security accounts that are part of the domain. When you first install the domain controller, there will be several groups in this container.

For example, the Domain Admins group and the administrator account are created in this container.

You want to be sure to protect the administrator account. You should rename the admin account and make sure the password is complex. Protected admin accounts can make your network safer. Every hacker knows that there is an administrator account on the server by default. Be sure to make your network safer by protecting the admin account.

Active Directory Objects

You can create and manage several different types of Active Directory objects. The following are specific object types:

Computer *Computer objects* represent workstations that are part of the Active Directory domain. All computers within a domain share the same security database, including user and group information. Computer objects are useful for managing security permissions and enforcing Group Policy restrictions.

Contact *Contact objects* are usually used in OUs to specify the main administrative contact. Contacts are not security principals like users. They are used to specify information about individuals outside the organization.

Group *Group objects* are logical collections of users primarily for assigning security permissions to resources. When managing users, you should place them into groups and then assign permissions to the group. This allows for flexible management without the need to set permissions for individual users.

InetOrgPerson The *InetOrgPerson object* is an Active Directory object that defines attributes of users in Lightweight Directory Access Protocol (LDAP) and X.500 directories.

MSIMaging-PSPs *MSIMaging-PSPs* is a container for all Enterprise Scan Post Scan Process objects.

MSMQ Queue Alias An *MSMQ Queue Alias object* is an Active Directory object for the MSMQ-Custom-Recipient class type. The Microsoft Message Queuing (MSMQ) Queue Alias object associates an Active Directory path and a user-defined alias with a public, private, or direct single-element format name. This allows a queue alias to be used to reference a queue that might not be listed in Active Directory Domain Services (AD DS).

Organizational Unit An *OU object* is created to build a hierarchy within the Active Directory domain. It is the smallest unit that can be used to create administrative groupings, and it can be used to assign group policies. Generally, the OU structure within a domain reflects a company's business organization.

Printer *Printer objects* map to printers.

Shared Folder *Shared Folder objects* map to server shares. They are used to organize the various file resources that may be available on file/print servers. Often, Shared Folder objects are used to give logical names to specific file collections. For example, system administrators might create separate shared folders for common applications, user data, and shared public files.

User   A *User object* is the fundamental security principal on which Active Directory is based. User accounts contain information about individuals as well as password and other permission information.

Creating Objects Using the Active Directory Users and Computers Tool

Exercise 5.5 walks you through the steps necessary to create various objects within an Active Directory domain. In this exercise, you create some basic Active Directory objects. To complete this exercise, you must have access to at least one Active Directory domain controller, and you should have also completed the previous exercises in this chapter.

EXERCISE 5.5

Creating Active Directory Objects

1. Click the Windows key on the keyboard and choose Administrative Tools.

2. Open the Active Directory Users and Computers tool.

3. Expand the current domain to list the objects currently contained within it. For this exercise, you will use the second- and third-level OUs contained within the North America top-level OU, as shown here.

4. Right-click the Corporate OU and select New ➢ User. Fill in the following information:

    First Name: **Maria**

    Initial: **D**

    Last Name: **President**

    Full Name: (leave as default)

    User Logon Name: **mdpresident** (leave default domain)

    Click Next to continue.

5. Enter **P@ssw0rd** for the password for this user and then confirm it. Note that you can also make changes to password settings here. Click Next.

6. You will see a summary of the user information. Click Finish to create the new user.

7. Click the RD container and create another user in that container with the following information:

    First Name: **John**

    Initial: **Q**

    Last Name: **Adams**

    Full Name: (leave as default)

    User Logon Name: **jqadams** (leave default domain)

    Click Next to continue.

8. Assign the password **P@ssw0rd**. Click Next and then click Finish to create the user.

9. Right-click the RD OU and select New ➢ Contact. Use the following information to fill in the properties of the Contact object:

    First Name: **Jane**

    Initials: **R**

    Last Name: **Admin**

    Display Name: **jradmin**

    Click OK to create the new Contact object.

10. Right-click the RD OU and select New ➢ Shared Folder. Enter **Software** for the name and **\\server1\applications** for the network path (also known as the Universal Naming Convention [UNC] path). Note that you can create the object even though this resource (the physical server) does not exist. Click OK to create the Shared Folder object.

11. Right-click the HR OU and select New ➢ Group. Type **All Users** for the group name. Do not change the value in the Group Name (Pre–Windows 2000) field. For Group Scope, select Global, and for Group Type, select Security. To create the group, click OK.

12. Right-click the Sales OU and select New ➤ Computer. Type **Workstation1** for the name of the computer. Notice that the pre–Windows 2000 name is automatically populated and that, by default, the members of the Domain Admins group are the only ones who can add this computer to the domain. Place a check mark in the Assign This Computer Account As A Pre-Windows 2000 Computer box and then click OK to create the Computer object.

13. Close the Active Directory Users and Computers tool.

Configuring the User Principal Name

When you log into a domain, your logon name looks like an email address (for example, wpanek@willpanek.com). This is called your *user principal name (UPN)*. A UPN is the username followed by the @ sign and the domain name. At the time that the user account is created, the UPN suffix is generated by default. The UPN is created as *userName@Domain Name*, but an administrator can alter or change the default UPN. If your forest has multiple domains and you need to change the UPN to a different domain, you have that ability. To change the UPN suffix, in Active Directory Users and Computers, choose a user and go into their properties. Choose the Attribute Editor tab. Scroll down to the userPrincipalName attribute and make your changes. These changes then get replicated to the global catalog.

 If your organization has multiple forests set up by a trust, you can't change the UPN to a domain in the other forest. Global catalogs are used to log on users. Because UPNs get replicated to the local forest global catalog servers, you cannot log onto other forests using the UPN.

Using Templates

Now you are going to dive into user templates. *User templates* allow an Active Directory administrator to create a default account (for example, template_sales) and use that account to create all of the other users who match it (all the salespeople).

If you are creating multiple accounts, this can save you a lot of time and resources. For example, if you need to add 35 new salespeople to your company, you'll create one template for sales and use a copy of that template for all of the other new accounts. This saves you the trouble of filling out many of the same fields over and over again. When you copy a template, some of the information does *not* get copied over. This is because it is user-specific information. Here are some of the fields that do not get copied over from a template:

- Name
- Logon Name
- Password
- Email

- Phone Numbers
- Description
- Office
- Web Page

Many of the important fields such as Member Of (groups to which the user belongs), Profile Path, Department, and Company all get copied over. There is one important item that needs to be done when creating a template: the template account needs to be disabled after creation. You do not want anyone using this account to access your network. In Exercise 5.6, you will create a Sales template to use for your Sales department.

EXERCISE 5.6

Creating a User Template

1. Click the Windows key on the keyboard and choose Administrative Tools.

2. Open the Active Directory Users and Computers snap-in.

3. Expand the current domain to list the objects contained within it. For this exercise, you will use the Sales OU. Right-click the Sales OU and choose New ➢ User.

4. Use the following properties:

    First Name: **Sales**

    Last Name: **Template**

    Username: **sales_template**

    Password: **P@ssw0rd**

5. Click Next and then click Finish.

6. In the right window, double-click the Sales Template user to open the properties.

7. On the General tab, complete the following items:

    Description: **Template Account**

    Office: **Corporate**

    Telephone: **999-999-9999**

    Email: **Salet@abc.com**

    Web: **www.abc.com**

8. Click the Profile tab. In the Profile Path field, type **\\ServerA\%username%**.

9. On the Members Of tab, click the Add button. At the Enter The Object Name To Select box, type **Administrator** and click the Check Names button. (Normally you would not

EXERCISE 5.6 (continued)

add salespeople to the Administrators group, but you are doing so just for this exercise.) Click OK.

10. Click the Account tab. Scroll down in the Account Options box and check the Account Is Disabled check box.

11. Click OK in the user's Properties window to go back to the Sales OU.

12. Right-click the Sales Template account and choose Copy.

13. Enter the following information:

First Name: **Jenny**

Last Name: **Sales**

Username: **jsales**

Password: **P@ssw0rd**

Uncheck the Account Is disabled check box.

14. In the right window, double-click the Jenny Sales user to open the properties.

15. Take a look at the Members Of tab, the General tab, and the Profile tab, and you will see that some of the fields are prefilled (including the Administrators group).

16. Close Jenny Sales Properties and exit Active Directory Users and Computers.

Importing Objects from a File

In Exercise 5.5, you created an account using the Active Directory Users and Computers tool. But what if you need to bulk import accounts? There are two main applications for doing bulk imports of accounts: the ldifde.exe utility and the csvde.exe utility. Both utilities import accounts from files.

The ldifde utility imports from line-delimited files. This utility allows an administrator to export and import data, thus allowing batch operations such as Add, Modify, and Delete to be performed in Active Directory. Windows Server 2012 R2 includes ldifde.exe to help support batch operations.

The csvde.exe utility performs the same export functions as ldifde.exe, but csvde.exe uses a comma-separated value file format. The csvde.exe utility does not allow administrators to modify or delete objects. It only supports adding objects to Active Directory.

Active Directory Migration Tool

Another tool that administrators have used in the past is *Active Directory Migration Tool (ADMT)*. ADMT allows an administrator to migrate users, groups, and computers from a previous version of the server to a current version of the server.

Administrators also used the ADMT to migrate users, groups, and computers between Active Directory domains in different forests (interforest migration) and between Active Directory domains in the same forest (intraforest migration).

At the time this book was written, Microsoft had not yet released a new version of ADMT that is supported by Windows Server 2012 R2. The reason I even mention it in this book is because Microsoft may be releasing a version of it soon, and I wanted you to understand what it can do. Continue to check the Microsoft website to see whether a new version has been released.

Offline Domain Join of a Computer

Offline domain join gives administrators the ability to preprovision computer accounts in the domain to prepare operating systems for deployments. At startup, computers can then join the domain without the need to contact a domain controller. This helps reduce the time it takes to deploy computers in a datacenter.

Let's say your datacenter needs to have multiple virtual machines deployed. This is where offline domain join can be useful. Upon initial startup after the operating system is installed, offline domain join allows the virtual machines to join the domain automatically. No additional steps or restart are needed.

The following are some of the benefits of using offline domain join:

- There is no additional network traffic for Active Directory state changes.

- There is no additional network traffic for computer state changes to the domain controller.

- Changes for both the Active Directory state and the computer state can be completed at a different times.

Managing Object Properties

Once you've created the necessary Active Directory objects, you'll probably need to make changes to their default properties. In addition to the settings you made when you were creating Active Directory objects, you can configure several more properties. You can also access object properties by right-clicking any object and selecting Properties from the pop-up menu.

Each object type contains a unique set of properties.

User Object Properties   The following list describes some of the properties of a User object:

General   General account information about this user

Address   Physical location information about this user

Account   User logon name and other account restrictions, such as workstation restrictions and logon hours

Profile   Information about the user's roaming profile settings

Telephones   Telephone contact information for the user

Organization   The user's title, department, and company information

Member Of   Group membership information for the user

Dial-In   Remote Access Service (RAS) permissions for the user

Environment   Logon and other network settings for the user

Sessions   Session limits, including maximum session time and idle session settings

Remote Control   Remote control options for this user's session

Remote Desktop Services Profile   Information about the user's profile for use with Remote Desktop Services

Personal Virtual Desktop   Allows you to assign a user a specific virtual machine to use as a personal virtual desktop

COM+   Specifies a COM+ partition set for the user

Computer Object Properties

Computer objects have different properties than User objects. Computer objects refer to the systems that clients are operating to be part of a domain. The following list describes some Computer object properties:

General   Information about the name of the computer, the role of the computer, and its description

(You can enable an option to allow the Local System account of this machine to request services from other servers. This is useful if the machine is a trusted and secure computer.)

Operating System   The name, version, and service pack information for the operating system running on the computer

Member Of   Active Directory groups of which this Computer object is a member

Delegation   Allows you to set services that work on behalf of another user

Location   A description of the computer's physical location

Managed By   Information about the User or Contact object that is responsible for managing this computer

Dial-In   Sets dial-in options for the computer

Setting Properties for Active Directory Objects

Now that you have seen the various properties that can be set for the Active Directory objects, let's complete an exercise on how to configure some of these properties. Exercise 5.7 walks you through how to set various properties for Active Directory objects. To complete the steps in this exercise, first you must have completed Exercise 5.5.

Although it may seem a bit tedious, it's always a good idea to enter as much information as you know about Active Directory objects when you create them. Although the name Printer1 may be meaningful to you, users will appreciate the additional information, such as location, when they are searching for objects.

EXERCISE 5.7

Managing Object Properties

1. Click the Windows key on the keyboard and choose Administrative Tools.

2. Open the Active Directory Users and Computers tool.

3. Expand the name of the domain and select the RD container. Right-click the John Q. Adams user account and select Properties.

4. Here you will see the various Properties tabs for the User account. Make some configuration changes based on your personal preferences. Click OK to continue.

5. Select the HR OU. Right-click the All Users group and click Properties. In the All Users Properties dialog box, you will be able to modify the membership of the group.

EXERCISE 5.7 *(continued)*

Click the Members tab and then click Add. Add the Maria D. President and John Q. Admin user accounts to the group. Click OK to save the settings and then OK to accept the group modifications.

6. Select the Sales OU. Right-click the Workstation1 Computer object. Notice that you can choose to disable the account or reset it (to allow another computer to join the domain under that same name). From the context menu, choose Properties. You'll see the properties for the Computer object.

   Examine the various options and make changes based on your personal preference. After you have examined the available options, click OK to continue.

7. Select the Corporate OU. Right-click the Maria D. President user account and choose Reset Password. You will be prompted to enter a new password, and then you'll be asked to confirm it. Note that you can also force the user to change this password upon the next logon, and you can also unlock the user's account from here. For this exercise, do not enter a new password; just click Cancel.

8. Close the Active Directory Users and Computers tool.

By now, you have probably noticed that Active Directory objects have a lot of common options. For example, Group and Computer objects both have a Managed By tab.

Windows Server 2012 R2 allows you to manage many User objects at once. For instance, you can select several User objects by holding down the Shift or Ctrl key while selecting. You can then right-click any one of the selected objects and select Properties to display the properties that are available for multiple users. Notice that not every user property is available because some properties are unique to each user. You can configure the Description field for multiple object selections that include both users and nonusers, such as computers and groups.

An important thing to think about when it comes to accounts is the difference between disabling an account and deleting an account. When you delete an account, the security ID (SID) gets deleted. Even if you later create an account with the same username, it will have a different SID number, and therefore it will be a different account. It is sometimes better to disable an account and place it into a nonactive OU called *Disabled.* This way, if you ever need to reaccess the account, you can do so.

Another object management task is the process of deprovisioning. *Deprovisioning* is the management of Active Directory objects in the container. When you remove an object from an Active Directory container, the deprovisioning process removes the object and synchronizes the container to stay current.

Understanding Groups

Now that you know how to create user accounts, it's time to learn how to create group accounts. As an instructor, I am always amazed when students (who work in the IT field) have no idea why they should use groups. This is something every organization should be using.

To illustrate their usefulness, let's say you have a Sales department user by the name of wpanek. Your organization has 100 resources shared on the network for users to access. Because wpanek is part of the Sales department, he has access to 50 of the resources. The Marketing department uses the other 50. If the organization is not using groups and wpanek moves from Sales to Marketing, how many changes do you have to make? The answer is 100. You have to move him out of the 50 resources he currently can use and place his account into the 50 new resources that he now needs.

Now let's say that you use groups. The Sales group has access to 50 resources, and the Marketing group has access to the other 50. If wpanek moves from Sales to Marketing, you need to make only two changes. You just have to take wpanek out of the Sales group and place him in the Marketing group. Once this is done, wpanek can access everything he needs to do his job.

Group Properties

Now that you understand why you should use groups, let's go over setting up groups and their properties. When you are creating groups, it helps to understand some of the options that you need to use.

Group Type   You can choose from two group types: security groups and distribution groups.

Security Groups   These groups can have rights and permissions placed on them. For example, if you want to give a certain group of users access to a particular printer, but you want to control what they are allowed to do with this printer, you'd create a security group and then apply certain rights and permissions to this group.

Security groups can also receive emails. If someone sent an email to the group, all users within that group would receive it (as long as they have a mail system that allows for mail-enabled groups, like Exchange).

Distribution Groups   These groups are used for email *only* (as long as they have a mail system that allows for mail-enabled groups, like Exchange). You cannot place permissions and rights for objects on this group type.

Group Scope   When it comes to group scopes, you have three choices.

Domain Local Groups   Domain local groups are groups that remain in the domain in which they were created. You use these groups to grant permissions within a single domain. For example, if you create a domain local group named HPLaser, you cannot use that group in any other domain, and it has to reside in the domain in which you created it.

Global Group   Global groups can contain other groups and accounts from the domain in which the group is created. In addition, you can give them permissions in any domain in the forest.

Universal Groups   Universal groups can include other groups and accounts from any domain in the domain tree or forest. You can give universal groups permissions in any domain in the domain trcc or forest.

Creating Group Strategies

When you are creating a group strategy, think of this acronym that Microsoft likes to use in the exam: AGDLP (or AGLP). This acronym stands for a series of actions you should perform. Here is how it expands:

A   Accounts (Create your user accounts.)

G   Global groups (Put user accounts into global groups.)

DL   Domain local groups (Put global groups into domain local groups.)

P   Permissions (Assign permissions such as Deny or Apply on the domain local group.)

Another acronym that stands for a strategy you can use is AGUDLP (or AULP). Here is how it expands:

A   Accounts (Create your user accounts.)

G   Global groups (Put user accounts into global groups.)

U   Universal groups (Put the global groups into universal groups.)

DL   Domain local groups (Put universal groups into domain local groups.)

P   Permissions (Place permissions on the local group.)

Creating a Group

To create a new group, open the Active Directory Users and Computers snap-in. Click the OU where the group is going to reside. Right-click and choose New and then Group. After you create the group, just click the Members tab and choose Add. Add the users you want to reside in that group, and that's all there is to it.

Filtering and Advanced Active Directory Features

The Active Directory Users and Computers tool has a couple of other features that come in quite handy when you are managing many objects. You can access the Filter Options dialog box by clicking the View menu in the MMC and choosing Filter Options. You'll see a dialog box similar to the one shown in Figure 5.6. Here you can choose to filter objects by their specific types within the display. For example, if you are an administrator who works primarily with user accounts and groups, you can select those specific items by placing check marks in the list. In addition, you can create more complex filters by choosing Create Custom. Doing so provides you with an interface that looks similar to that of the Find command.

FIGURE 5.6   The Filter Options dialog box

Another option in the Active Directory Users and Computers tool is to view advanced options. You can enable the advanced options by choosing Advanced Features in the View menu. This adds some top-level folders to the list under the name of the domain. Let's take a look at a couple of the new top-level folders.

The System folder (shown in Figure 5.7) provides additional features that you can configure to work with Active Directory. You can configure settings for the Distributed File System (DFS), IP Security (IPSec) policies, the File Replication Service (FRS), and more. In addition to the System folder, you'll see the LostAndFound folder. This folder contains any files that may not have been replicated properly between domain controllers. You should check this folder periodically for any files so that you can decide whether you need to move them or copy them to other locations.

FIGURE 5.7   Advanced Features in the System folder of the Active Directory Users and Computers tool

As you can see, managing Active Directory objects is generally a simple task. The Active Directory Users and Computers tool allows you to configure several objects. Let's move on to look at one more common administration function: moving objects.

Moving, Renaming, and Deleting Active Directory Objects

One of the extremely useful features of the Active Directory Users and Computers tool is its ability to move users and resources easily.

Exercise 5.8 walks you through the process of moving Active Directory objects. In this exercise, you will make several changes to the organization of Active Directory objects. To complete this exercise, first you must have completed Exercise 5.5.

EXERCISE 5.8

Moving Active Directory Objects

1. Click the Windows key on the keyboard and choose Administrative Tools.

2. Open the Active Directory Users and Computers tool and expand the name of the domain.

3. Select the Sales OU (under the New York OU), right-click Workstation1, and select Move. A dialog box appears. Select the RD OU and click OK to move the Computer object to that container.

4. Click the RD OU and verify that Workstation1 was moved.

5. Close the Active Directory Users and Computers tool.

In addition to moving objects within Active Directory, you can easily rename them by right-clicking an object and selecting Rename. Note that this option does not apply to all objects. You can remove objects from Active Directory by right-clicking them and choosing Delete.

WARNING   Deleting an Active Directory object is an irreversible action. When an object is destroyed, any security permissions or other settings made for that object are removed as well. Because each object within Active Directory contains its own security identifier (SID), simply re-creating an object with the same name does not place any permissions on it. Before you delete an Active Directory object, be sure that you will never need it again. Windows Server 2012 R2 has an Active Directory Recycle Bin to allow an administrator to retrieve a deleted object, but in case the Recycle Bin gets cleared, it's better to be safe than sorry. Also, the AD Recycle Bin is disabled by default, so it will be unavailable unless you turn that feature on. So, what is the moral of this story? Don't delete AD objects unless you are absolutely sure you want them gone.

Windows Server 2012 R2 has a check box called Protect Container From Accidental Deletion for all OUs. If this check box is checked, to delete or move an OU, you must go into the Active Directory Users and Computers advanced options. Once you are in the advanced options, you can uncheck the box to move or delete the OU.

Resetting an Existing Computer Account

Every computer on the domain establishes a discrete channel of communication with the domain controller at logon time. The domain controller stores a randomly selected password (different from the user password) for authentication across the channel. The password is updated every 30 days.

Sometimes the computer's password and the domain controller's password don't match, and communication between the two machines fails. Without the ability to reset the computer account, you wouldn't be able to connect the machine to the domain. Fortunately, you can use the Active Directory Users and Computers tool to reestablish the connection.

Exercise 5.9 shows you how to reset an existing computer account. You should have completed the previous exercises in this chapter before you begin this exercise.

EXERCISE 5.9

Resetting an Existing Computer Account

1. Click the Windows key on the keyboard and choose Administrative Tools.

2. Open the Active Directory Users and Computers tool and expand the name of the domain.

3. Click the RD OU and then right-click the Workstation1 computer account.

4. Select Reset Account from the context menu. Click Yes to confirm your selection. Click OK at the success prompt.

5. When you reset the account, you break the connection between the computer and the domain. So, after performing this exercise, reconnect the computer to the domain if you want it to continue working on the network.

Throughout this book, I have tried to show you the PowerShell way of doing a task shown previously using an MMC snap-in. Well, this is going to be no different.

This example shows you how to reset the secure connection between the local computer and the domain to which it is joined using a PowerShell command. In this example, the domain controller that performs the operation is specified as StellaDC1.Stellacon.com. To execute this PowerShell command, you must run this command on the local computer:

```
Test-ComputerSecureChannel -Repair -Server StellaDC1.Stellacon.com
```

Publishing Active Directory Objects

One of the main goals of Active Directory is to make resources easy to find. Two of the most commonly used resources in a networked environment are server file shares and printers. These are so common, in fact, that most organizations have dedicated file and print servers. When it comes to managing these types of resources, Active Directory makes it easy to determine which files and printers are available to users.

With that being said, take a look at how Active Directory manages to publish shared folders and printers.

Making Active Directory Objects Available to Users

An important aspect of managing Active Directory objects is that a system administrator can control which objects users can see. The act of making an Active Directory object available is known as *publishing*. The two main types of publishable objects are Printer objects and Shared Folder objects.

The general process for creating server shares and shared printers has remained unchanged from previous versions of Windows: you create the various objects (a printer or a file system folder) and then enable them for sharing. To make these resources available via Active Directory, however, there's an additional step: you must publish the resources. Once an object has been published in Active Directory, clients will be able to use it.

When you publish objects in Active Directory, you should know the server name and share name of the resource. When system administrators use Active Directory objects, they can change the resource to which the object points, without having to reconfigure or even notify clients. For example, if you move a share from one server to another, all you need to do is to update the Shared Folder object's properties to point to the new location. Active Directory clients still refer to the resource with the same path and name that they used before.

Publishing Printers

Printers can be published easily within Active Directory. This makes them available to users in your domain.

Exercise 5.10 walks you through the steps you need to take to share and publish a Printer object by having you create and share a printer. To complete the printer installation, you need access to the Windows Server 2012 R2 installation media (via the hard disk, a network share, or the CD-ROM drive).

EXERCISE 5.10

Creating and Publishing a Printer

1. Click the Windows key on the keyboard and choose Control Panel.

2. Click Devices And Printers ➢ Add A Printer. This starts the Add Printer Wizard. Then click the Next button.

3. In the Choose A Local Or Network Printer page, select Add A Local Printer. This should automatically take you to the next page. If it does not, click Next.

4. On the Choose A Printer Port page, select Use An Existing Port. From the drop-down list beside that option, make sure LPT1: (Printer Port) is selected. Click Next.

5. On the Install The Printer Driver page, select Generic for the manufacturer. For the printer, highlight Generic/Text Only. Click Next.

6. On the Type A Printer Name page, type **Text Printer**. Uncheck the Set As The Default Printer box and then click Next.

7. The Installing Printer screen appears. After the system is finished, the Printer Sharing page appears. Make sure the box labeled "Share this printer so that others on your network can find and use it" is selected, and accept the default share name of Text Printer.

8. In the Location section, type **Building 203**, and in the Comment section, add the following comment: **This is a text-only Printer**. Click Next.

9. On the You've Successfully Added Text Printer page, click Finish.

10. Next you need to verify that the printer will be listed in Active Directory. Right-click the Text Printer icon and select Printer Properties.

EXERCISE 5.10 *(continued)*

11. Select the Sharing tab and make sure that the List In The Directory box is checked. Note that you can also add additional printer drivers for other operating systems using this tab. Click OK to accept the settings.

Note that when you create and share a printer this way, an Active Directory Printer object is not displayed within the Active Directory Users and Computers tool. The printer is actually associated with the Computer object to which it is connected.

Publishing Shared Folders

Now that you've created and published a printer, you'll see how the same thing can be done to shared folders.

Exercise 5.11 walks through the steps required to create a folder, share it, and then publish it in Active Directory. This exercise assumes you are using the C: partition; however, you may want to change this based on your server configuration. This exercise assumes you have completed Exercise 5.5.

EXERCISE 5.11

Creating and Publishing a Shared Folder

1. Create a new folder in the root directory of your C: partition and name it Test Share. To do this, click the File Explorer link on the toolbar.

2. Right-click the Test Share folder. Choose Share With ➤ Specific People.

3. In the File Sharing dialog box, enter the names of users with whom you want to share this folder. In the upper box, enter **Everyone** and then click Add. Note that Everyone appears in the lower box. Click in the Permission Level column next to Everyone and choose Read/Write from the pop-up menu. Then click Share.

4. You'll see a message that your folder has been shared. Click Done.

5. Click the Windows key on the keyboard and choose Administrative Tools.

6. Open the Active Directory Users and Computers tool. Expand the current domain and right-click the RD OU. Select New ➢ Shared Folder.

7. In the New Object - Shared Folder dialog box, type **Shared Folder Test** for the name of the folder. Then type the UNC path to the share (for example, **\\server1\Test Share**). Click OK to create the share.

Once you have created and published the Shared Folder object, clients can use the My Network Places icon to find it. The Shared Folder object will be organized based on the OU in which you created it. When you use publication, you can see how this makes it easy to manage shared folders.

Querying Active Directory

So far you've created several Active Directory resources. One of the main benefits of having all of your resource information in Active Directory is that you can easily find what you're looking for using the Find dialog box. Recall that I recommended that you always enter as much information as possible when creating Active Directory objects. This is where that extra effort begins to pay off.

Exercise 5.12 walks you through the steps to find specific objects in Active Directory. To complete this exercise, you must have completed Exercise 5.5.

EXERCISE 5.12

Finding Objects in Active Directory

1. Click the Windows key on the keyboard and choose Administrative Tools.

2. Open the Active Directory Users and Computers tool.

3. Right-click the name of the domain and select Find.

4. In the Find Users, Contacts, And Groups dialog box, select Users, Contacts, And Groups from the Find drop-down list. For the In setting, choose Entire Directory. This searches the entire Active Directory environment for the criteria you enter.

   Note that if this is a production domain and there are many objects, searching the whole directory may be a time-consuming and network-intensive operation.

EXERCISE 5.12 *(continued)*

5. In the Name field, type **admin** and then click Find Now to obtain the results of the search.

6. Now that you have found several results, you can narrow down the list. Click the Advanced tab of the Find Users, Contacts, And Groups dialog box.

In the Field drop-down list, select User ➤ Last Name. For Condition, select Starts With, and for Value, type **admin**. Click Add to add this condition to the search criteria. Click Find Now. Now only the users that have the last name Admin are shown.

7. When you have finished searching, close the Find Users, Contacts, And Groups dialog box and exit the Active Directory Users and Computers tool.

Using the many options available in the Find dialog box, you can usually narrow down the objects for which you are searching quickly and efficiently. Users and system administrators alike find this tool useful in environments of any size. Now that you have seen how to create objects in Active Directory, let's take a look at a new Windows Server 2012 R2 feature called Active Directory Administrative Center.

Using the Active Directory Administrative Center

Windows Server 2012 R2 has a feature called the *Active Directory Administrative Center* (see Figure 5.8). This feature allows you to manage many Active Directory tasks from one central location (see Figure 5.9).

FIGURE 5.8 Active Directory Administrative Center

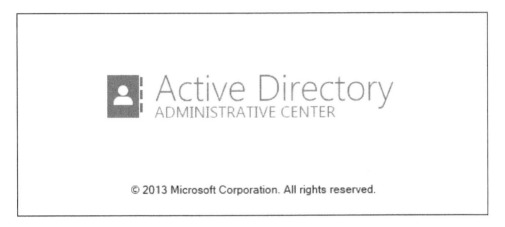

© 2013 Microsoft Corporation. All rights reserved.

FIGURE 5.9 Administrative Center Overview screen

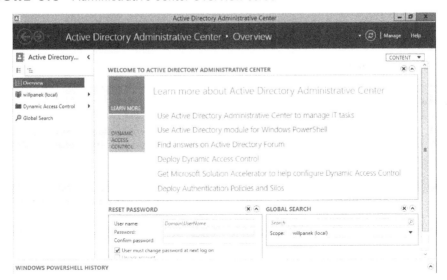

Using the Active Directory Administrative Center, here are some of the tasks that an administrator can perform:

- Reset passwords
- Create new objects
- Delete objects
- Move objects
- Perform global searches
- Configure properties for Active Directory objects

In Windows Server 2012 R2, the Active Directory Administrative Center is just another tool in your Active Directory tool belt. It does not matter which way you create your Active Directory objects as long as you have a good understanding of how to create them.

Using the Command Prompt for Active Directory Configuration

Many IT administrators like to use command-line commands to configure and maintain their Active Directory environment. One advantage of using command-line commands is the ability to do multiple changes at once using batch files.

Another advantage of knowing how to manipulate Active Directory using the command prompt is working with Windows Server 2012 R2 Server Core. Server Core is an installation of Windows Server 2012 R2 that has no GUI windows. One of the ways to configure Server Core is to use commands in the command prompt window.

Table 5.1 shows you many of the command prompt commands and explains how each command affects Active Directory.

TABLE 5.1   Command prompt commands

Command	Explanation
Csvde	This command allows you to import and export data from Active Directory. The data gets stored in a comma-separated value (CSV) format.
Dcdiag	This troubleshooting command checks the state of your domain controllers in your forest and sends back a report of any problems.

Djoin	This command allows a computer account to join a domain, and it runs an offline domain join when a computer restarts.
Dsacls	This command allows you to see and change permissions in the access control list for objects in Active Directory Domain Services (AD DS).
Dsadd	This command allows you to add an object to the AD DS directory.
Dsamain	This command shows the Active Directory data stored in either a snapshot or a backup as if it were in a Lightweight Directory Access Protocol (LDAP) server.
Dsdbutil	This command provides database utilities for Active Directory Lightweight Directory Services (AD LDS).
Dsget	This command shows the properties of an object in the AD DS directory.
Dsmgmt	This command gives an administrator management utilities for AD LDS.
Dsmod	This command allows you to modify an AD DS object.
Dsmove	This command allows you to move an object in an Active Directory domain from its current OU to a new OU within the same forest.
Dsquery	This command allows you to query AD DS.
Dsrm	This command removes an object from the AD DS directory.
Ldifde	This command allows you to import and export data from Active Directory. The data is stored as LDAP Data Interchange Format (LDIF).
Ntdsutil	This is one of the most important commands for Active Directory. It allows you to do maintenance on the Active Directory database.
Repadmin	This command allows administrators to diagnose Active Directory replication problems between domain controllers.

Summary

This chapter covered the fundamentals of administering Active Directory. The most important part of administering Active Directory is learning about how to work with OUs. Therefore, you should be aware of the purpose of OUs; that is, they help you to organize and manage the directory. For instance, think of administrative control. If you wanted to delegate rights to another administrator (such as a sales manager), you could delegate that authority to that user within the Sales OU. As the system administrator, you would retain the rights to the castle.

You also looked at how to design an OU structure from an example. The example showed you how to design a proper OU layout. You can also create, organize, and reorganize OUs if need be.

In addition, you took a look at groups and group strategies. There are different types of groups (domain local, global, and universal groups), and you should know when each group is available and when to use each group.

Finally, this chapter covered how to use the Active Directory Users and Computers tool to manage Active Directory objects. If you're responsible for day-to-day system administration, there's a good chance that you are already familiar with this tool; if not, you should be after reading this chapter. Using this tool, you learned how to work with Active Directory objects such as User, Computer, and Group objects. You also learned how to import users by doing a bulk import, and you studied the two different file types that work for bulk imports. Bulk imports allow you to import multiple users without the need to add one user at a time.

Exam Essentials

Understand the purpose of OUs.   OUs are used to create a hierarchical, logical organization for objects within an Active Directory domain.

Know the types of objects that can reside within OUs.   OUs can contain Active Directory User, Computer, Shared Folder, and other objects.

Understand how to use the Delegation of Control Wizard.   The Delegation of Control Wizard is used to assign specific permissions at the level of OUs.

Understand the concept of inheritance.   By default, child OUs inherit permissions and Group Policy assignments set for parent OUs. However, these settings can be overridden for more granular control of security.

Know groups and group strategies.   You can use three groups in Native mode: domain local, global, and universal. Understand the group strategies and when they apply.

Understand how Active Directory objects work.   Active Directory objects represent some piece of information about components within a domain. The objects themselves have attributes that describe details about them.

Understand how Active Directory objects can be organized.   By using the Active Directory Users and Computers tool, you can create, move, rename, and delete various objects.

Understand how to import bulk users.   You can import multiple accounts by doing a bulk import. Bulk imports use files to import the data into Active Directory. Know the two utilities (`ldifde.exe` and `csvde.exe`) you need to perform the bulk imports and how to use them.

Learn how resources can be published.   A design goal for Active Directory was to make network resources easier for users to find. With that in mind, you should understand how using published printers and shared folders can simplify network resource management.

Review Questions

1. You are the administrator of an organization with a single Active Directory domain. A user who left the company returns after 16 weeks. The user tries to log onto their old computer and receives an error stating that authentication has failed. The user's account has been enabled. You need to ensure that the user is able to log onto the domain using that computer. What do you do?

   A. Reset the computer account in Active Directory. Disjoin the computer from the domain and then rejoin the computer to the domain.

   B. Run the ADadd command to rejoin the computer account.

   C. Run the MMC utility on the user's computer, and add the Domain Computers snap-in.

   D. Re-create the user account and reconnect the user account to the computer account.

2. You are the administrator of an organization with a single Active Directory domain. One of your senior executives tries to log onto a machine and receives the error "This user account has expired. Ask your administrator to reactivate your account." You need to make sure that this doesn't happen again to this user. What do you do?

   A. Configure the domain policy to disable account lockouts.

   B. Configure the password policy to extend the maximum password age to 0.

   C. Modify the user's properties to set the Account Never Expires setting.

   D. Modify the user's properties to extend the maximum password age to 0.

3. You need to create a new user account using the command prompt. Which command would you use?

   A. dsmodify

   B. dscreate

   C. dsnew

   D. dsadd

4. Maria is a user who belongs to the Sales distribution global group. She is not able to access the laser printer that is shared on the network. The Sales global group has full access to the laser printer. How do you fix the problem?

   A. Change the group type to a security group.

   B. Add the Sales global group to the Administrators group.

   C. Add the Sales global group to the Printer Operators group.

   D. Change the Sales group to a local group.

5. You are a domain administrator for a large domain. Recently, you have been asked to make changes to some of the permissions related to OUs within the domain. To restrict security for the Texas OU further, you remove some permissions at that level. Later, a junior system administrator mentions that she is no longer able to make changes to objects within the Austin OU (which is located within the Texas OU). Assuming that no other changes have been made to Active Directory permissions, which of the following characteristics of OUs might have caused the change in permissions?

   A. Inheritance

   B. Group Policy

   C. Delegation

   D. Object properties

6. Isabel, a system administrator, created a new Active Directory domain in an environment that already contains two trees. During the promotion of the domain controller, she chose to create a new Active Directory forest. Isabel is a member of the Enterprise Administrators group and has full permissions over all domains. During the organization's migration to Active Directory, many updates were made to the information stored within the domains. Recently, users and other system administrators have complained about not being able to find specific Active Directory objects in one or more domains (although the objects exist in others). To investigate the problem, Isabel wants to check for any objects that have not been properly replicated among domain controllers. If possible, she would like to restore these objects to their proper place within the relevant Active Directory domains.

   Which two of the following actions should she perform to be able to view the relevant information? (Choose two.)

   A. Change Active Directory permissions to allow object information to be viewed in all domains.

   B. Select the Advanced Features item in the View menu.

   C. Promote a member server in each domain to a domain controller.

   D. Rebuild all domain controllers from the latest backups.

   E. Examine the contents of the LostAndFound folder using the Active Directory Users and Computers tool.

7. You are a consultant hired to evaluate an organization's Active Directory domain. The domain contains more than 200,000 objects and hundreds of OUs. You begin examining the objects within the domain, but you find that the loading of the contents of specific OUs takes a long time. Furthermore, the list of objects can be large. You want to do the following:

   ▪ Use the built-in Active Directory administrative tools and avoid the use of third-party tools or utilities.

   ▪ Limit the list of objects within an OU to only the type of objects that you're examining (for example, only Computer objects).

   ▪ Prevent any changes to the Active Directory domain or any of the objects within it.

Which one of the following actions meets these requirements?

A. Use the Filter option in the Active Directory Users and Computers tool to restrict the display of objects.

B. Use the Delegation of Control Wizard to give yourself permissions over only a certain type of object.

C. Implement a new naming convention for objects within an OU and then sort the results using this new naming convention.

D. Use the Active Directory Domains and Trusts tool to view information from only selected domain controllers.

E. Edit the domain Group Policy settings to allow yourself to view only the objects of interest.

8. You are the administrator for a small organization with four servers. You have one file server named Paniva that runs Windows Server 2012 R2. You have a junior administrator who needs to do backups on this server. You need to ensure that the junior admin can use Windows Server Backup to create a complete backup of Paniva. What should you configure to allow the junior admin to do the backups?

A. The local groups by using Computer Management

B. A task by using Authorization Manager

C. The User Rights Assignment by using the Local Group Policy Editor

D. The Role Assignment by using Authorization Manager

9. Miguel is a junior-level system administrator, and he has basic knowledge about working with Active Directory. As his supervisor, you have asked Miguel to make several security-related changes to OUs within the company's Active Directory domain. You instruct Miguel to use the basic functionality provided in the Delegation of Control Wizard. Which of the following operations are represented as common tasks within the Delegation of Control Wizard? (Choose all that apply.)

A. Reset passwords on user accounts.

B. Manage Group Policy links.

C. Modify the membership of a group.

D. Create, delete, and manage groups.

10. You are the primary system administrator for a large Active Directory domain. Recently, you have hired another system administrator upon whom you intend to offload some of your responsibilities. This system administrator will be responsible for handling help desk calls and for basic user account management. You want to allow the new employee to have permissions to reset passwords for all users within a specific OU. However, for security reasons, it's important that the user not be able to make permissions changes for objects within other OUs in the domain. Which of the following is the best way to do this?

A. Create a special administration account within the OU and grant it full permissions for all objects within Active Directory.

B. Move the user's login account into the OU that the new employee is to administer.

C. Move the user's login account to an OU that contains the OU (that is, the parent OU of the one that the new employee is to administer).

D. Use the Delegation of Control Wizard to assign the necessary permissions on the OU that the new employee is to administer.

Chapter

6

Manage GPOs

THE FOLLOWING 70-410 EXAM OBJECTIVES ARE COVERED IN THIS CHAPTER:

✓ **Create Group Policy Objects (GPOs)**

 ▪ Configure a Central Store

 ▪ Manage starter GPOs

 ▪ Configure GPO links

 ▪ Configure multiple local group policies

 ▪ Configure security filtering

✓ **Configure application restriction policies**

 ▪ Configure rule enforcement

 ▪ Configure applocker rules

 ▪ Configure Software Restriction Policies

For many years, making changes to computer or user environments was a time-consuming process. If you wanted to install a service pack or a piece of software, unless you had a third-party utility, you had to use the *sneakernet* (that is, you had to walk from one computer to another with a disk containing the software).

Installing any type of software or companywide security change was one of the biggest challenges faced by system administrators. It was difficult enough just to deploy and manage workstations throughout the environment. Combine this with the fact that users were generally able to make system configuration changes to their own machines, it quickly became a management nightmare!

For example, imagine that a user noticed that they did not have enough disk space to copy a large file. Instead of seeking assistance from the IT help desk, they may have decided to do a little cleanup on their own. Unfortunately, this cleanup operation may have resulted in deleting critical system files! Or, consider the case of users who changed system settings "just to see what they did." Relatively minor changes, such as modifying TCP/IP bindings or Desktop settings, could cause hours of support headaches. Now multiply these (or other common) problems by hundreds (or even thousands) of end users. Clearly, system administrators needed to have a secure way to limit the options available to users of client operating systems.

How do you prevent problems such as these from occurring in a Windows Server 2012 R2 environment? Fortunately, there's a readily available solution delivered with the base operating system that's easy to implement. Two of the most important system administration features in Windows Server 2012 R2 and Active Directory are *Group Policy* and *Security Policy*. By using *Group Policy objects (GPOs)*, administrators can quickly and easily define restrictions on common actions and then apply them at the site, domain, or organizational unit (OU) level. In this chapter, you will see how group and security policies work, and then you will look at how to implement them within an Active Directory environment.

Introducing Group Policy

One of the strengths of Windows-based operating systems is their flexibility. End users and system administrators can configure many different options to suit the network environment and their personal tastes. However, this flexibility comes at a price—generally, end users on a network should not change many of these options. For example, TCP/IP configuration and security policies should remain consistent for all client computers. In fact, end users really don't need to be able to change these types of settings in the first place because many of them do not understand the purpose of these settings.

Windows Server 2012 R2 *group policies* are designed to provide system administrators with the ability to customize end-user settings and to place restrictions on the types of actions that users can perform. Group policies can be easily created by system administrators and then later applied to one or more users or computers within the environment. Although they ultimately do affect registry settings, it is much easier to configure and apply settings through the use of Group Policy than it is to make changes to the registry manually. To make management easy, Microsoft has set up Windows Server 2008, Windows Server 2008 R2, Windows Server 2012, and Windows Server 2012 R2 so that Group Policy settings are all managed from within the Microsoft Management Console (MMC) in the Group Policy Management Console (GPMC).

Group policies have several potential uses. I'll cover the use of group policies for software deployment, and I'll also focus on the technical background of group policies and how they apply to general configuration management.

Let's begin by looking at how group policies function.

Understanding Group Policy Settings

Group Policy settings are based on *Group Policy administrative templates*. These templates provide a list of user-friendly configuration options and specify the system settings to which they apply. For example, an option for a user or computer that reads Require A Specific Desktop Wallpaper Setting would map to a key in the registry that maintains this value. When the option is set, the appropriate change is made in the registry of the affected users and computers.

By default, Windows Server 2012 R2 comes with several administrative template files that you can use to manage common settings. Additionally, system administrators and application developers can create their own administrative template files to set options for specific functionality.

Most Group Policy items have three different settings options:

Enabled Specifies that a setting for this GPO has been configured. Some settings require values or options to be set.

Disabled Specifies that this option is disabled for client computers. Note that disabling an option *is* a setting. That is, it specifies that the system administrator wants to disallow certain functionality.

Not Configured Specifies that these settings have been neither enabled nor disabled. Not Configured is the default option for most settings. It simply states that this group policy will not specify an option and that other policy settings may take precedence.

The specific options available (and their effects) will depend on the setting. Often, you will need additional information. For example, when setting the Account Lockout policy, you must specify how many bad login attempts may be made before the account is locked out. With this in mind, let's look at the types of user and computer settings that can be managed.

Group Policy settings can apply to two types of Active Directory objects: User objects and Computer objects. Because both users and computers can be placed into groups and organized within OUs, this type of configuration simplifies the management of hundreds, or even thousands, of computers.

The main options you can configure within user and computer group policies are as follows:

Software Settings   The *Software Settings* options apply to specific applications and software that might be installed on the computer. System administrators can use these settings to make new applications available to end users and to control the default configuration for these applications.

Windows Settings   The *Windows Settings* options allow system administrators to customize the behavior of the Windows operating system. The specific options that are available here are divided into two types: user and computer. User-specific settings let you configure Internet Explorer (including the default home page and other settings). Computer settings include security options, such as Account Policy and Event Log options.

Administrative Templates   *Administrative templates* are used to configure user and computer settings further. In addition to the default options available, system administrators can create their own administrative templates with custom options.

Group Policy Preferences   The Windows Server 2012 R2 operating system includes *Group Policy preferences (GPPs)*, which give you more than 20 new Group Policy extensions. These extensions, in turn, give you a vast range of configurable settings within a Group Policy object. Included in the new Group Policy preference extensions are settings for folder options, mapped drives, printers, the registry, local users and groups, scheduled tasks, services, and the Start menu.

Besides providing easier management, Group Policy preferences give an administrator the ability to deploy settings for client computers without restricting the users from changing the settings. This gives an administrator the flexibility needed to decide which settings to enforce and which not to enforce.

Figure 6.1 shows some of the options you can configure with Group Policy.

ADMX Central Store   Another consideration in GPO settings is whether to set up an *ADMX Central Store*. GPO administrative template files are saved as ADMX (.admx) files and AMXL (.amxl) for the supported languages. To get the most benefit out of using administrative templates, you should create an ADMX Central Store.

You create the Central Store in the SYSVOL folder on a domain controller. The Central Store is a repository for all of your administrative templates, and the Group Policy tools check it. The Group Policy tools then use any ADMX files that they find in the Central Store. These files then replicate to all domain controllers in the domain.

If you want your clients to be able to edit domain-based GPOs by using the ADMX files that are stored in the ADMX Central Store, you must be using Windows Vista, Windows 7, Windows 8, Server 2008, Server 2008 R2, Server 2012, or Server 2012 R2.

Security Template   *Security templates* are used to configure security settings through a GPO. Some of the security settings that can be configured are settings for account policies, local policies, event logs, restricted groups, system services, and the registry.

FIGURE 6.1   Group Policy configuration options

Starter GPOs   *Starter Group Policy objects* give administrators the ability to store a collection of administrative template policy settings in a single object. Administrators then have the ability to import and export starter GPOs to distribute the GPOs easily to other environments. When a GPO is created from a starter GPO, as with any template, the new GPO receives the settings and values that were defined from the administrative template policy in the starter GPO.

> Group Policy settings do not take effect immediately. You must run the gpupdate command at the command prompt or wait for the regular update cycle in order for the policy changes to take effect.

The Security Settings Section of the GPO

One of the most important sections of a GPO is the Security Settings section. The Security Settings section, under the Windows Settings section, allows an administrator to secure many aspects of the computer and user policies. The following are some of the configurable options for the Security Settings section:

Computer Section Only of the GPO

- Account Policies
- Local Policies
- Event Policies

- Restricted Groups
- System Services
- Registry
- File System
- Wired Network
- Windows Firewall with Advanced Security
- Network List Manager Policies
- Wireless Networks
- Network Access Protection
- Application Control Policies
- IP Security Policies
- Advanced Audit Policy Configuration

Computer and User Sections of the GPO

- Public Key Policies
- Software Restriction Policy

Restricted Groups

The *Restricted Groups* settings allow you to control group membership by using a GPO. The group membership I am referring to is the normal Active Directory groups (domain local, global, and universal). The settings offer two configurable properties: Members and Members Of.

The users on the Members list do not belong to the restricted group. The users on the Members Of list do belong to the restricted group. When you configure a Restricted Group policy, members of the restricted group that are not on the Members list are removed. Users who are on the Members list who are not currently a member of the restricted group are added.

Software Restriction Policy

Software restriction policies allow administrators to identify software and to control its ability to run on the user's local computer, organizational unit, domain, or site. This prevents users from installing unauthorized software. Software Restriction Policy is discussed in greater detail in this chapter in the "Implementing Software Deployment" section.

Group Policy Objects

So far, I have discussed what group policies are designed to do. Now it's time to drill down to determine exactly how you can set up and configure them.

To make them easier to manage, group policies may be placed in items called *Group Policy objects (GPOs)*. GPOs act as containers for the settings made within Group Policy files, which simplifies the management of settings. For example, as a system administrator, you might have different policies for users and computers in different departments. Based on these requirements, you could create a GPO for members of the Sales department and another for members of the Engineering department. Then you could apply the GPOs to the OU for each department. Another important concept you need to understand is that Group Policy settings are hierarchical; that is, system administrators can apply Group Policy settings at four different levels. These levels determine the GPO processing priority.

Local Every Windows operating system computer has one Group Policy object that is stored locally. This GPO functions for both the computer and user Group Policy processing.

Sites At the highest level, system administrators can configure GPOs to apply to entire sites within an Active Directory environment. These settings apply to all of the domains and servers that are part of a site. Group Policy settings managed at the site level may apply to more than one domain within the same forest. Therefore, they are useful when you want to make settings that apply to all of the domains within an Active Directory tree or forest.

Domains Domains are the third level to which system administrators can assign GPOs. GPO settings placed at the domain level will apply to all of the User and Computer objects within the domain. Usually, system administrators make master settings at the domain level.

Organizational Units The most granular level of settings for GPOs is the OU level. By configuring Group Policy options for OUs, system administrators can take advantage of the hierarchical structure of Active Directory. If the OU structure is planned well, you will find it easy to make logical GPO assignments for various business units at the OU level.

Based on the business need and the organization of the Active Directory environment, system administrators might decide to set up Group Policy settings at any of these four levels. Because the settings are cumulative by default, a User object might receive policy settings from the site level, from the domain level, and from the OUs in which it is contained.

You can also apply Group Policy settings to the local computer (in which case Active Directory is not used at all), but this limits the manageability of the Group Policy settings.

Group Policy Inheritance

In most cases, Group Policy settings are cumulative. For example, a GPO at the domain level might specify that all users within the domain must change their password every 60 days, and a GPO at the OU level might specify the default desktop background for all users and computers within that OU. In this case, both settings apply, so users within the OU are forced to change their password every 60 days and have the default Desktop setting.

What happens if there's a conflict in the settings? For example, suppose you create a scenario where a GPO at the site level specifies that users are to use red wallpaper and another GPO at the OU level specifies that they must use green wallpaper. The users at the OU layer would have green wallpaper by default. Although hypothetical, this raises an important point about *inheritance*. By default, the settings at the most specific level (in this case, the OU that contains the User object) override those at more general levels. As a friend of mine from Microsoft always says, "Last one to apply wins."

Although the default behavior is for settings to be cumulative and inherited, system administrators can modify this behavior. They can set two main options at the various levels to which GPOs might apply.

Block Policy Inheritance   The *Block Policy Inheritance* option specifies that Group Policy settings for an object are not inherited from its parents. You might use this, for example, when a child OU requires completely different settings from a parent OU. Note, however, that you should manage blocking policy inheritance carefully because this option allows other system administrators to override the settings made at higher levels.

Force Policy Inheritance   The *Enforced option* (sometimes referred as *No Override*) can be placed on a parent object, and it ensures that all lower-level objects inherit these settings. In some cases, system administrators want to ensure that Group Policy inheritance is not blocked at other levels. For example, suppose it is corporate policy that all network accounts are locked out after five incorrect password attempts. In this case, you would not want lower-level system administrators to override the option with other settings.

System administrators generally use this option when they want to enforce a specific setting globally. For example, if a password expiration policy should apply to all users and computers within a domain, a GPO with the *Force Policy Inheritance* option enabled could be created at the domain level.

You must consider one final case: If a conflict exists between the computer and user settings, the user settings take effect. If, for instance, a system administrator applies a default desktop setting for the Computer policy and a different default desktop setting for the User policy, the one they specify in the User policy takes effect. This is because the user settings are more specific, and they allow system administrators to make changes for individual users regardless of the computer they're using.

Planning a Group Policy Strategy

Through the use of Group Policy settings, system administrators can control many different aspects of their network environment. As you'll see throughout this chapter, system administrators can use GPOs to configure user settings and computer configurations. Windows Server 2012 R2 includes many different administrative tools for performing these tasks. However, it's important to keep in mind that, as with many aspects of using Active Directory, a successful Group Policy strategy involves planning.

Because there are thousands of possible Group Policy settings and many different ways to implement them, you should start by determining the business and technical needs of your organization. For example, you should first group your users based on their work functions. You might find, for example, that users in remote branch offices require particular network configuration options. In that case, you might implement Group Policy settings best at the site level. In another instance, you might find that certain departments have varying requirements for disk quota settings. In this case, it would probably make the most sense to apply GPOs to the appropriate department OUs within the domain.

The overall goal should be to reduce complexity (for example, by reducing the overall number of GPOs and GPO links) while still meeting the needs of your users. By taking into account the various needs of your users and the parts of your organization, you can often determine a logical and efficient method of creating and applying GPOs. Although it's rare that you'll come across a right or wrong method of implementing Group Policy settings, you will usually encounter some that are either better or worse than others.

By implementing a logical and consistent set of policies, you'll also be well prepared to troubleshoot any problems that might come up or to adapt to your organization's changing requirements. Later in this chapter, you'll learn about some specific methods for determining effective Group Policy settings before you apply them.

Implementing Group Policy

Now that I've covered the basic layout and structure of group policies and how they work, let's look at how you can implement them in an Active Directory environment. In the following sections, you'll start by creating GPOs. Then you'll apply these GPOs to specific Active Directory objects, and you'll take a look at how to use administrative templates.

Creating GPOs

In Windows Server 2000 and Windows Server 2003, you could create GPOs from many different locations. For example, you could use Active Directory Users and Computers to create GPOs on your OUs along with other GPO tools. In Windows Server 2012 R2, things are simpler. You can create GPOs for OUs in only one location: the Group Policy Management Console (GPMC). You have your choice of three applications for setting up policies on your Windows Server 2012 R2 computers.

Local Computer Policy Tool   This administrative tool allows you to quickly access the Group Policy settings that are available for the local computer. These options apply to the local machine and to users who access it. You must be a member of the local Administrators group to access and make changes to these settings.

Administrators may need the ability to work on multiple local group policy objects (MLGPOs) at the same time. To do this, you would complete the following steps. (You can't configure MLGPOs on domain controllers.)

1. Open the MMC by typing **MMC** in the Run command box.
2. Click File and then click Add/Remove Snap-in.
3. From the available snap-ins list, choose Group Policy Object Editor and click Add.
4. In the Select Group Policy Object dialog box, click the Browse button.
5. Click the Users tab in the Browse For The Group Policy Object dialog box.
6. Click the user or group for which you want to create or edit a local Group Policy and click OK.
7. Click Finish and then click OK.
8. Configure the multiple policy settings.

Group Policy Management Console You must use the GPMC to manage Group Policy deployment. The GPMC provides a single solution for managing all Group Policy–related tasks, and it is also best suited to handle enterprise-level tasks, such as forest-related work.

The GPMC allows administrators to manage Group Policy and GPOs all from one easy-to-use console whether their enterprise solution spans multiple domains and sites within one or more forests or is local to one site. The GPMC adds flexibility, manageability, and functionality. Using this console, you can also perform other functions, such as backup and restore, importing, and copying.

Auditpol.exe Auditpol.exe is a command-line utility that works with Windows Vista, Windows 7, Windows 8, Windows Server 2008, Windows Server 2008 R2, Windows Server 2012, and Windows Server 2012 R2. An administrator has the ability to display information about policies and also to perform some functions to manipulate audit policies. Table 6.1 shows some of the switches available for auditpol.exe.

TABLE 6.1 Auditpol.exe switches

Switch	Description
/?	This is the Auditpol.exe help command.
/get	This allows you to display the current audit policy.
/set	This allows you to set a policy.
/list	This displays selectable policy elements.
/backup	This allows you to save the audit policy to a file.
/restore	This restores a policy from previous backup.
/clear	This clears the audit policy.
/remove	This removes all per-user audit policy settings and disables all system audit policy settings.
/ResourceSACL	This configures the Global Resource SACL.

WARNING You should be careful when making Group Policy settings because certain options might prevent the proper use of systems on your network. Always test Group Policy settings on a small group of users before you deploy them throughout your organization. You'll probably find that some settings need to be changed to be effective.

Exercise 6.1 walks you through the process of installing the Group Policy Management MMC snap-in for editing Group Policy settings and creating a GPO.

Creating a Group Policy Object Using the GPMC

1. Click the Windows button and choose Administrative Tools ➢ Group Policy Management. The Group Policy Management tool opens.

2. Expand the Forest, Domains, *your domain name,* and North America containers. Right-click the Corporate OU and then choose Create A GPO In This Domain, And Link It Here.

3. When the New GPO dialog box appears, type **Warning Box** in the Name field. Click OK.

4. The New GPO will be listed on the right side of the Group Policy Management window. Right-click the GPO and choose Edit.

5. In the Group Policy Management Editor, expand the following: Computer Configuration ➢ Policies ➢ Windows Settings ➢ Security Settings ➢ Local Policies ➢ Security Options. On the right side, scroll down and double-click Interactive Logon: Message Text For Users Attempting To Log On.

6. Click the box Define This Policy Setting In The Template. In the text box, type **Unauthorized use of this machine is prohibited** and then click OK. Close the GPO and return to the GPMC main screen.

EXERCISE 6.1 *(continued)*

7. Under the domain name (in the GPMC), right-click Group Policy Objects and choose New.

8. When the New GPO dialog box appears, type **Unlinked Test GPO** in the Name field. Click OK.

9. On the right side, the new GPO will appear. Right-click Unlinked Test GPO and choose Edit.

10. Under the User Configuration section, click Policies ➢ Administrative Templates ➢ Desktop. On the right side, double-click Hide And Disable All Items On The Desktop and then click Enabled. Click OK and then close the GPMC.

Note that Group Policy changes may not take effect until the next user logs in (some settings may even require that the machine be rebooted). That is, users who are currently working on the system will not see the effects of the changes until they log off and log in again. GPOs are reapplied every 90 minutes with a 30-minute offset. In other words, users who are logged in will have their policies reapplied every 60 to 120 minutes. Not all settings are reapplied (for example, software settings and password policies).

Linking Existing GPOs to Active Directory

Creating a GPO is the first step in assigning group policies. The second step is to link the GPO to a specific Active Directory object. As mentioned earlier in this chapter, GPOs can be linked to sites, domains, and OUs.

Exercise 6.2 walks you through the steps that you must take to assign an existing GPO to an OU within the local domain. In this exercise, you will link the Test Domain Policy GPO to an OU. To complete the steps in this exercise, you must have completed Exercise 6.1.

EXERCISE 6.2

Linking Existing GPOs to Active Directory

1. Open the Group Policy Management Console.

2. Expand the Forest and Domain containers and right-click the Africa OU.

3. Choose Link An Existing GPO.

4. The Select GPO dialog box appears. Click Unlinked Test GPO and click OK.

5. Close the Group Policy Management Console.

Note that the GPMC tool offers a lot of flexibility in assigning GPOs. You can create new GPOs, add multiple GPOs, edit them directly, change priority settings, remove links, and delete GPOs all from within this interface. In general, creating new GPOs using the GPMC tool is the quickest and easiest way to create the settings you need.

To test the Group Policy settings, you can simply create a user account within the Africa OU that you used in Exercise 6.2. Then, using another computer that is a member of the same domain, you can log on as the newly created user.

Managing Group Policy

Now that you have implemented GPOs and applied them to sites, domains, and OUs within Active Directory, it's time to look at some ways to manage them. In the following sections, you'll look at how multiple GPOs can interact with one another and ways that you can provide security for GPO management. Using these features is an important part of work-ing with Active Directory, and if you properly plan Group Policy, you can greatly reduce the time the help desk spends troubleshooting common problems.

Managing GPOs

One of the benefits of GPOs is that they're modular and can apply to many different objects and levels within Active Directory. This can also be one of the drawbacks of GPOs if they're not managed properly. A common administrative function related to using GPOs is finding all of the Active Directory links for each of these objects. You can do this when you are viewing the Linked Group Policy Objects tab of the site, domain, or OU in the GPMC (shown in Figure 6.2).

FIGURE 6.2 Viewing GPO links to an Active Directory OU

In addition to the common action of delegating permissions on OUs, you can set permissions regarding the modification of GPOs. The best way to accomplish this is to add users to the Group Policy Creator/Owners built-in security group. The members of this group are able to modify security policy. You saw how to add users to groups back in Chapter 5, "Administer Active Directory."

Windows Management Instrumentation

Windows Management Instrumentation (WMI) scripts are used to gather information or to help GPOs deploy better. The best way to explain this is to give an example. Let's say you wanted to deploy Microsoft Office 2013 to everyone in the company. You would first set up a GPO to deploy the Office package (explained later in the section "Deploying Software Through a GPO").

You can then place a WMI script on the GPO stating that only computers with 10GB of hard disk space actually deploy Office. Now if a computer has 10GB of free space, the Office GPO would get installed. If the computer does not have the 10GB of hard disk space, the GPO will not deploy. You can use WMI scripts to check for computer information such as MAC addresses. WMI is a powerful tool because if you know how to write scripts, the possibilities are endless. The following script is a sample of a WMI that is checking for at least 10GB of free space on the C: partition/volume:

```
Select * from Win32_LogicalDisk where FreeSpace > 10737418240 AND
Caption = "C:"
```

Security Filtering of a Group Policy

Another method of securing access to GPOs is to set permissions on the GPOs themselves. You can do this by opening the GPMC, selecting the GPO, and clicking the Advanced button in the Delegation tab. The Unlinked Test GPO Security Settings dialog box appears (see Figure 6.3).

FIGURE 6.3   A GPO's Security Settings dialog box

The following permissions options are available:

- Full Control
- Read
- Write

- Create All Child Objects
- Delete All Child Objects
- Apply Group Policy

You might have to scroll the Permissions window to see the Apply Group Policy item. Of these, the Apply Group Policy setting is particularly important because you use it to filter the scope of the GPO. *Filtering* is the process by which selected security groups are included or excluded from the effects of the GPOs. To specify that the settings should apply to a GPO, you should select the Allow check box for both the Apply Group Policy setting and the Read setting. These settings will be applied only if the security group is also contained within a site, domain, or OU to which the GPO is linked. To disable GPO access for a group, choose Deny for both of these settings. Finally, if you do not want to specify either Allow or Deny, leave both boxes blank. This is effectively the same as having no setting.

In Exercise 6.3, you will filter Group Policy using security groups. To complete the steps in this exercise, you must have completed Exercises 6.1 and 6.2.

EXERCISE 6.3

Filtering Group Policy Using Security Groups

1. Open the Active Directory Users and Computers administrative tool.

2. Create a new OU called **Group Policy Test**.

3. Create two new global security groups within the Group Policy Test OU and name them **PolicyEnabled** and **PolicyDisabled**.

4. Exit Active Directory Users and Computers and open the GPMC.

5. Right-click the Group Policy Test OU and select Link An Existing GPO.

6. Choose Unlinked Test GPO and click OK.

7. Expand the Group Policy Test OU so that you can see the GPO (Unlinked Test GPO) underneath the OU.

8. Click the Delegation tab and then click the Advanced button in the lower-right corner of the window.

9. Click the Add button and type **PolicyEnabled** in the Enter The Object Names To Select field. Click the Check Names button. Then click OK.

10. Add a group named **PolicyDisabled** in the same way.

11. Highlight the PolicyEnabled group and select Allow for the Read and Apply Group Policy permissions. This ensures that users in the PolicyEnabled group will be affected by this policy.

12. Highlight the PolicyDisabled group and select Deny for the Read and Apply Group Policy permissions. This ensures that users in the PolicyDisabled group will not be affected by this policy.

13. Click OK. You will see a message stating that you are choosing to use the Deny permission and that the Deny permission takes precedence over the Allow entries. Click the Yes button to continue.

14. When you have finished, close the GPMC tool.

Delegating Administrative Control of GPOs

So far, you have learned about how to use Group Policy to manage user and computer settings. What you haven't done yet is to determine who can modify GPOs. It's important to establish the appropriate security on GPOs themselves for two reasons.

- If the security settings aren't set properly, users and system administrators can easily override them. This defeats the purpose of having the GPOs in the first place.

- Having many different system administrators creating and modifying GPOs can become extremely difficult to manage. When problems arise, the hierarchical nature of GPO inheritance can make it difficult to pinpoint the problem.

Fortunately, through the use of delegation, determining security permissions for GPOs is a simple task. Exercise 6.4 walks you through the steps that you must take to grant the appropriate permissions to a user account. Specifically, the process involves delegating the ability to manage Group Policy links on an Active Directory object (such as an OU). To complete this exercise, you must have completed Exercises 6.1 and 6.2.

EXERCISE 6.4

Delegating Administrative Control of Group Policy

1. Open the Active Directory Users and Computers tool.

2. Expand the local domain and create a user named **Policy Admin** within the Group Policy Test OU.

3. Exit Active Directory Users and Computers and open the GPMC.

4. Click the Group Policy Test OU and select the Delegation tab.

5. Click the Add button. In the field Enter The Object Name To Select, type **Policy Admin** and click the Check Names button.

6. The Add Group Or User dialog box appears. In the Permissions drop-down list, make sure that the item labeled Edit Settings, Delete, Modify Security is chosen. Click OK.

EXERCISE 6.4 *(continued)*

7. At this point you should be looking at the Group Policy Test Delegation window. Click the Advanced button in the lower-right corner.

8. Highlight the Policy Admin account and check the Allow Full Control box. This user now has full control of these OUs and all child OUs and GPOs for these OUs. Click OK.

    If you just want to give this user individual rights, then, in the Properties window (step 8), click the Advanced button and then the Effective Permissions tab. This is where you can also choose a user and give them only the rights that you want them to have.

9. When you have finished, close the GPMC tool.

Understanding Delegation

Although I have talked about delegation throughout the book, it's important to discuss it again in the context of OUs, Group Policy, and Active Directory.

Once configured, Active Directory administrative delegation allows an administrator to delegate tasks (usually administration related) to specific user accounts or groups. What this means is that if you don't manage it all, the user accounts (or groups) you choose will be able to manage their portions of the tree.

It's important to be aware of the benefits of Active Directory Delegation (AD Delegation). *AD Delegation* will help you manage the assigning of administrative control over objects in Active Directory, such as users, groups, computers, printers, domains, and sites. AD Delegation is used to create more administrators, which essentially saves time.

For example, let's say you have a company whose IT department is small and situated in a central location. The central location connects three other smaller remote sites. These sites do not each warrant a full-time IT person, but the manager on staff (for example) at each remote site can become an administrator for their portion of the tree. If that manager administers the user accounts for the staff at the remote site, this reduces the burden on the system administrator of doing trivial administrative work, such as unlocking user accounts or changing passwords, and thus it reduces costs.

Controlling Inheritance and Filtering Group Policy

Controlling inheritance is an important function when you are managing GPOs. Earlier in this chapter, you learned that, by default, GPO settings flow from higher-level Active Directory objects to lower-level ones. For example, the effective set of Group Policy settings for a user might be based on GPOs assigned at the site level, at the domain level, and in the OU hierarchy. In general, this is probably the behavior you would want.

In some cases, however, you might want to block Group Policy inheritance. You can accomplish this easily by selecting the object to which a GPO has been linked. Right-click the object and choose Block Inheritance (see Figure 6.4). By enabling this option, you are effectively specifying that this object starts with a clean slate; that is, no other Group Policy settings will apply to the contents of this Active Directory site, domain, or OU.

FIGURE 6.4   Blocking GPO inheritance

System administrators can also force inheritance. By setting the Enforced option, they can prevent other system administrators from making changes to default policies. You can set the Enforced option by right-clicking the GPO and choosing the Enforced item (see Figure 6.5).

FIGURE 6.5   Setting the Enforced GPO option

Assigning Script Policies

System administrators might want to make several changes and implement certain settings that would apply while the computer is starting up or the user is logging on. Perhaps the most common operation that logon scripts perform is mapping network drives. Although users can manually map network drives, providing this functionality within login scripts ensures that mappings stay consistent and that users only need to remember the drive letters for their resources.

Script policies are specific options that are part of Group Policy settings for users and computers. These settings direct the operating system to the specific files that should be processed during the startup/shutdown or logon/logoff processes. You can create the scripts by using the *Windows Script Host (WSH)* or with standard batch file commands. WSH allows developers and system administrators to create scripts quickly and easily using Visual Basic Scripting Edition (VBScript) or JScript (Microsoft's implementation of JavaScript). Additionally, WSH can be expanded to accommodate other common scripting languages.

To set script policy options, you simply edit the Group Policy settings. As shown in Figure 6.6, there are two main areas for setting script policy settings.

Startup/Shutdown Scripts   These settings are located within the Computer Configuration ➢ Windows Settings ➢ Scripts (Startup/Shutdown) object.

Logon/Logoff Scripts   These settings are located within the User Configuration ➢ Windows Settings ➢ Scripts (Logon/Logoff) object.

FIGURE 6.6   Viewing Startup/Shutdown script policy settings

To assign scripts, simply double-click the setting, and its Properties dialog box appears. For instance, if you double-click the Startup setting, the Startup Properties dialog box appears (see Figure 6.7). To add a script filename, click the Add button. When you do, you will be asked to provide the name of the script file (such as `MapNetworkDrives.vbs` or `ResetEnvironment.bat`).

FIGURE 6.7   Setting scripting options

Note that you can change the order in which the scripts are run by using the Up and Down buttons. The Show Files button opens the directory folder in which you should store the Logon script files. To ensure that the files are replicated to all domain controllers, you should be sure you place the files within the SYSVOL share.

Understanding the Loopback Policy

There may be times when the user settings of a Group Policy object should be applied to a computer based on its location instead of the user object. Usually, the user Group Policy processing dictates that the GPOs be applied in order during computer startup based on the computers located in their organizational unit. User GPOs, on the other hand, are applied in order during logon, regardless of the computer to which they log on.

In some situations, this processing order may not be appropriate. A good example is a kiosk machine. You would not want applications that have been assigned or published to a user to be installed when the user is logged on to the kiosk machine. *Loopback Policy* allows two ways to retrieve the list of GPOs for any user when they are using a specific computer in an OU.

Merge Mode   The GPOs for the computer are added to the end of the GPOs for the user. Because of this, the computer's GPOs have higher precedence than the user's GPOs.

Replace Mode   In Replace mode, the user's GPOs are not used. Only the GPOs of the Computer object are used.

Managing Network Configuration

Group policies are also useful in network configuration. Although administrators can handle network settings at the protocol level using many different methods, such as Dynamic Host Configuration Protocol (DHCP), Group Policy allows them to set which functions and operations are available to users and computers.

Figure 6.8 shows some of the features that are available for managing Group Policy settings. The paths to these settings are as follows:

Computer Network Options   These settings are located within the Computer Configuration ➢ Administrative Templates ➢ Network ➢ Network Connections folder.

User Network Options   These settings are located within User Configuration ➢ Administrative Templates ➢ Network.

Here are some examples of the types of settings available:

- The ability to allow or disallow the modification of network settings.

  In many environments, the improper changing of network configurations and protocol settings is a common cause of help desk calls.

- The ability to allow or disallow the creation of Remote Access Service (RAS) connections.

FIGURE 6.8   Viewing Group Policy User network configuration options

This option is useful, especially in larger networked environments, because the use of modems and other WAN devices can pose a security threat to the network.

- The ability to set offline files and folders options.

  This is especially useful for keeping files synchronized for traveling users, and it is commonly configured for laptops.

Each setting includes detailed instructions in the description area of the GPO Editor window. By using these configuration options, system administrators can maintain consistency for users and computers and avoid many of the most common troubleshooting calls.

Automatically Enrolling User and Computer Certificates in Group Policy

You can also use Group Policy to enroll user and computer certificates automatically, making the entire certificate process transparent to your end users. Before proceeding, you should understand what certificates are and why they are an important part of network security.

Think of a digital certificate as a carrying case for a public key. A certificate contains the public key and a set of attributes, including the key holder's name and email address.

These attributes specify something about the holder: their identity, what they're allowed to do with the certificate, and so on. The attributes and the public key are bound together because the certificate is digitally signed by the entity that issued it. Anyone who wants to verify the certificate's contents can verify the issuer's signature.

Certificates are one part of what security experts call a *public-key infrastructure (PKI)*. A PKI has several different components that you can mix and match to achieve the desired results. Microsoft's PKI implementation offers the following functions:

Certificate Authorities   CAs issue certificates, revoke certificates they've issued, and publish certificates for their clients. Big CAs like Thawte and VeriSign do this for millions of users. If you want, you can also set up your own CA for each department or workgroup in your organization. Each CA is responsible for choosing which attributes it will include in a certificate and what mechanism it will use to verify those attributes before it issues the certificate.

Certificate Publishers   They make certificates publicly available, inside or outside an organization. This allows widespread availability of the critical material needed to support the entire PKI.

PKI-Savvy Applications   These allow you and your users to do useful things with certificates, such as encrypt email or network connections. Ideally, the user shouldn't have to know (or even be aware of) what the application is doing—everything should work seamlessly and automatically. The best-known examples of PKI-savvy applications are web browsers such as Internet Explorer and Firefox and email applications such as Outlook.

Certificate Templates   These act like rubber stamps. By specifying a particular template as the model you want to use for a newly issued certificate, you're actually telling the CA which optional attributes to add to the certificate as well as implicitly telling it how to fill some of the mandatory attributes. Templates greatly simplify the process of issuing certificates because they keep you from having to memorize the names of all of the attributes you may potentially want to put in a certificate.

Learn More About PKI

When discussing certificates, it's also important to mention PKI and its definition. The exam doesn't go deeply into PKI, but I recommend you do some extra research on your own because it is an important technology and shouldn't be overlooked. PKI is actually a simple concept with a lot of moving parts. When broken down to its bare essentials, PKI is nothing more than a server and workstations utilizing a software service to add security to your infrastructure. When you use PKI, you are adding a layer of protection. The auto-enrollment Settings policy determines whether users and/or computers are automatically enrolled for the appropriate certificates when necessary. By default, this policy is enabled if a certificate server is installed, but you can make changes to the settings, as shown in Exercise 6.5.

In Exercise 6.5, you will learn how to configure automatic certificate enrollment in Group Policy. You must have first completed the other exercises in this chapter in order to proceed with Exercise 6.5.

EXERCISE 6.5

Configuring Automatic Certificate Enrollment in Group Policy

1. Open the Group Policy Management Console tool.

2. Right-click the North America OU that you created in the previous exercises in this book.

3. Choose Create A GPO In This Domain And Link It Here and name it **Test CA**. Click OK.

4. Right-click the Test CA GPO and choose Edit.

5. Open Computer Configuration ➢ Policies ➢ Windows Settings ➢ Security Settings ➢ Public Key Policies.

6. Double-click Certificate Services Client – Auto-Enrollment in the right pane.

7. The Certificate Services Client – Auto-Enrollment Properties dialog box will appear.

8. For now, don't change anything. Just become familiar with the settings in this dialog box. Click OK to close it.

Redirecting Folders

Another set of Group Policy settings that you will learn about are the *folder redirection settings*. Group Policy provides a means for redirecting the Documents, Desktop, and Start Menu folders, as well as cached application data, to network locations. Folder redirection is particularly useful for the following reasons:

- When they are using roaming user profiles, a user's Documents folder is copied to the local machine each time they log on. This requires high bandwidth consumption and time if the Documents folder is large. If you redirect the Documents folder, it stays in the redirected location, and the user opens and saves files directly to that location.

- Documents are always available no matter where the user logs on.

- Data in the shared location can be backed up during the normal backup cycle without user intervention.

- Data can be redirected to a more robust server-side administered disk that is less prone to physical and user errors.

When you decide to redirect folders, you have two options: basic and advanced.

- Basic redirection redirects everyone's folders to the same location (but each user gets their own folder within that location).

- Advanced redirection redirects folders to different locations based on group membership. For instance, you could configure the Engineers group to redirect their folders to //Engineering1/Documents/ and the Marketing group to //Marketing1/Documents/. Again, individual users still get their own folder within the redirected location.

To configure folder redirection, follow the steps in Exercise 6.6. You must have completed the other exercises in this chapter to proceed with this exercise.

EXERCISE 6.6

Configuring Folder Redirection in Group Policy

1. Open the GPMC tool.

2. Open the North America OU and then edit the Test CA GPO.

3. Open User Configuration ➢ Policies ➢ Windows Settings ➢ Folder Redirection ➢ Documents.

4. Right-click Documents, and select Properties.

5. On the Target tab of the Documents Properties dialog box, choose the Basic – Redirect Everyone's Folder To The Same Location selection from the Settings drop-down list.

6. Leave the default option for the Target Folder Location drop-down list and specify a network path in the Root Path field.

7. Click the Settings tab. All of the default settings are self-explanatory and should typically be left at the default setting. Click OK when you have finished.

Folder Redirection Facts

Try not to mix up the concepts of *folder redirection* and *offline folders*, especially in a world with ever-increasing numbers of mobile users. Folder redirection and offline folders are different features.

Windows Server 2012 R2 folder redirection works as follows: The system uses a pointer that moves the folders you want to a location you specify. Users do not see any of this—it is transparent to them. One problem with folder redirection is that it does not work for mobile users (users who will be offline and who will not have access to files they may need).

Offline folders, however, are copies of folders that were local to you. Files are now available locally to you on the system you have with you. They are also located back on the server where they are stored. The next time you log in, the folders are synchronized so that both folders contain the latest data. This is a perfect feature for mobile users, whereas folder redirection provides no benefit for the mobile user.

Managing GPOs with Windows PowerShell Group Policy Cmdlets

As stated earlier in this book, *Windows PowerShell* is a Windows command-line shell and scripting language. Windows PowerShell can also help an administrator automate many of the same tasks that you perform using the Group Policy Management Console.

Windows Server 2012 R2 helps you perform many of the Group Policy tasks by providing more than 25 cmdlets. Each of these cmdlets is a simple, single-function command-line tool.

The Windows PowerShell Group Policy cmdlets can help you perform some of the following tasks for domain-based Group Policy objects:

- Maintain, create, remove, back up, and import GPOs

- Create, update, and remove GPO links to Active Directory containers

- Set Active Directory OUs and domain permissions and inheritance flags

- Configure Group Policy registry settings

- Create and edit Starter GPOs

The requirement for Windows PowerShell Group Policy cmdlets is Windows Server 2012 R2 on either a domain controller or a member server that has the GPMC installed. Windows 7 and Windows 8 also have the ability to use Windows PowerShell Group Policy cmdlets if they have Remote Server Administration Tools (RSAT) installed. RSAT includes the GPMC and its cmdlets. PowerShell is also a requirement.

Deploying Software Through a GPO

It's difficult enough to manage applications on a stand-alone computer. It seems that the process of installing, configuring, and uninstalling applications is never finished. Add in the hassle of computer reboots and reinstalling corrupted applications, and the reduction in productivity can be substantial.

Software administrators who manage software in network environments have even more concerns.

- First, they must determine which applications specific users require.

- Then, IT departments must purchase the appropriate licenses for the software and acquire any necessary media.

- Next, the system administrators need to install the applications on users' machines. This process generally involves help desk staff visiting computers, or it requires end users to install the software themselves. Both processes entail several potential problems, including installation inconsistency and lost productivity from downtime experienced when applications were installed.

- Finally, software administrators still need to manage software updates and remove unused software.

One of the key design goals for Active Directory was to reduce some of the headaches involved in managing software and configurations in a networked environment. To that end, Windows Server 2012 R2 offers several features that can make the task of deploying software easier and less error prone. Before you dive into the technical details, however, you need to examine the issues related to software deployment.

The Software Management Life Cycle

Although it may seem that the use of a new application requires only the installation of the necessary software, the overall process of managing applications involves many more steps. When managing software applications, there are three main phases to their life cycle, as follows:

Phase 1: Deploying Software   The first step in using applications is to install them on the appropriate client computers. Generally, some applications are deployed during the initial configuration of a PC, and others are deployed when they are requested. In the latter case, this often used to mean that system administrators and help desk staffs have to visit client computers and manually walk through the installation process. With Windows Server 2012 R2 and GPOs, the entire process can be automated.

Before You Install, Stop

It is important to understand that just because you can easily deploy software, it does not necessarily mean you have the right to do so. Before you install software on client computers, you must make sure you have the appropriate licenses for the software. Furthermore, it's important to take the time to track application installations. As many system administrators have discovered, it's much more difficult to inventory software installations after they've been performed. Another issue you may encounter is that you lack available resources (for instance, your system does not meet the minimum hardware requirements) and that you face problems such as limited hard disk space or memory that may not be able to handle the applications that you want to load and use. You may also find that your user account does not have the permission to install software. It's important to consider not only how you will install software but also whether you can.

Phase 2: Maintaining Software   Once an application is installed and in use on client computers, you need to ensure that the software is maintained. You must keep programs up-to-date by applying changes due to bug fixes, enhancements, and other types of updates. This is normally done with service packs, hot fixes, and updates. As with the initial software deployment, software maintenance can be tedious. Some programs require older versions to be uninstalled before updates are added. Others allow for automatically upgrading over existing installations. Managing and deploying software updates can consume a significant amount of the IT staff's time.

Using Windows Update

Make sure that you learn about Windows Update, a service that allows you to connect to Microsoft's website and download what your system may need to bring it up to compliance. This tool is helpful if you are running a stand-alone system, but if you want to deploy software across the enterprise, the best way to accomplish this is first to test the updates you are downloading and make sure you can use them and that they are not bug ridden. Then you can use a tool such as the Windows Server Update Service (WSUS), which was formerly called the Software Update Services (SUS).

You can check for updates at Microsoft's website (http://update.microsoft.com). Microsoft likes to ask many types of questions about WSUS on its certification exams. WSUS is described in detail in other Sybex certification books.

Phase 3: Removing Software   The end of the life cycle for many software products involves the actual removal of unused programs. Removing software is necessary when applications become outdated or when users no longer require their functionality. One of the traditional problems with uninstalling applications is that many of the installed files may not be removed. Furthermore, the removal of shared components can sometimes cause other programs to stop functioning properly. Also, users often forget to uninstall applications that they no longer need, and these programs continue to occupy disk space and consume valuable system resources.

The Microsoft Windows Installer (MSI) manages each of these three phases of the software maintenance life cycle. Now that you have an overview of the process, let's move forward to look at the steps involved in deploying software using Group Policy.

The *Microsoft Windows Installer* (sometimes referred to as Microsoft Installer or Windows Installer) is an application installation and configuration service. An instruction file (the Microsoft Installer package) contains information about what needs to be done to install a product. It's common to confuse the two.

The Windows Installer

If you've installed newer application programs (such as Microsoft Office 2013), you've probably noticed the updated setup and installation routines. Applications that comply with the updated standard use the *Windows Installer specification* and MSI software packages for deployment. Each package contains information about various setup options and the files required for installation. Although the benefits may not seem dramatic on the surface, there's a lot of new functionality under the hood.

The Windows Installer was created to solve many of the problems associated with traditional application development. It has several components, including the Installer service (which runs on Windows 2000, XP, Vista, Windows 7, Windows 8, Windows Server 2003, Windows Server 2008, Windows Server 2008 R2, Windows Server 2012, and Windows Server 2012 R2 computers), the Installer program (`msiexec.exe`) that is responsible for executing the instructions in a *Windows Installer package*, and the specifications third-party developers use to create their own packages. Within each installation package file is a relational structure (similar to the structure of tables in databases) that records information about the programs contained within the package.

To appreciate the true value of the Windows Installer, you'll need to look at some of the problems with traditional software deployment mechanisms and then at how the Windows Installer addresses many of them.

Application Installation Issues

Before the Windows Installer, applications were installed using a setup program that managed the various operations required for a program to operate. These operations included copying files, changing registry settings, and managing any other operating system changes that might be required (such as starting or stopping services). However, this method had several problems:

- The setup process was not robust, and aborting the operation often left many unnecessary files in the file system.

- The process included uninstalling an application (this also often left many unnecessary files in the file system) and remnants in the Windows registry and operating system folders. Over time, these remnants would result in reduced overall system performance and wasted disk space.

- There was no standard method for applying upgrades to applications, and installing a new version often required users to uninstall the old application, reboot, and then install the new program.

- Conflicts between different versions of *dynamic link libraries (DLLs)*—shared program code used across different applications—could cause the installation or removal of one application to break the functionality of another.

Benefits of the Windows Installer

Because of the many problems associated with traditional software installation, Microsoft created the *Windows Installer*. This system provides for better manageability of the software installation process and allows system administrators more control over the deployment process. Specifically, the Windows Installer provides the following benefits:

Improved Software Removal   The process of removing software is an important one because remnants left behind during the uninstall process can eventually clutter up the registry and file system. During the installation process, the Windows Installer keeps track of all of the changes made by a setup package. When it comes time to remove an application, all of these changes can then be rolled back.

More Robust Installation Routines   If a typical setup program is aborted during the software installation process, the results are unpredictable. If the actual installation hasn't yet begun, then the installer generally removes any temporary files that may have been created. However, if the file copy routine starts before the system encounters an error, it is likely that the files will not be automatically removed from the operating system. In contrast, the Windows Installer allows you to roll back any changes when the application setup process is aborted.

Ability to Use Elevated Privileges   Installing applications usually requires the user to have Administrator permissions on the local computer because file system and registry changes are required. When installing software for network users, system administrators have two options. First, they can log off of the computer before installing the software and then log back on as a user who has Administrator permissions on the local computer. This method is tedious and time-consuming. The second option is to give users Administrator permissions temporarily on their own machines. This method could cause security problems and requires the attention of a system administrator.

Through the use of the Installer service, the Windows Installer is able to use temporarily elevated privileges to install applications. This allows users, regardless of their security settings, to execute the installation of authorized applications. This saves time and preserves security.

Support for Repairing Corrupted Applications   Regardless of how well a network environment is managed, critical files are sometimes lost or corrupted. Such problems can prevent applications from running properly and can cause crashes. Windows Installer packages provide you with the ability to verify the installation of an application and, if necessary, replace any missing or corrupted files. This support saves time and lessens end-user headaches associated with removing and reinstalling an entire application to replace just a few files.

Prevention of File Conflicts   Generally, different versions of the same files should be compatible with each other. In the real world, however, this isn't always the case. A classic problem in the Windows world is the case of one program replacing DLLs that are used by several other programs. Windows Installer accurately tracks which files are used by certain programs and ensures that any shared files are not improperly deleted or overwritten.

Automated Installations   A typical application setup process requires end users or system administrators to respond to several prompts. For example, a user may be able to choose the program group in which icons will be created and the file system location to which the program will be installed. Additionally, they may be required to choose which options are installed. Although this type of flexibility is useful, it can be tedious when you are rolling out multiple applications. By using features of the Windows Installer, however, users are able to specify setup options before the process begins. This allows system administrators to ensure consistency in installations, and it saves users time.

Advertising and On-Demand Installations   One of the most powerful features of the Windows Installer is its ability to perform on-demand software installations. Prior to the

Windows Installer, application installation options were quite basic—either a program was installed or it was not. When setting up a computer, system administrators would be required to guess which applications the user might need and install all of them.

The Windows Installer supports a function known as advertising. *Advertising* makes applications appear to be available via the Start menu. However, the programs themselves may not actually be installed on the system. When a user attempts to access an advertised application, the Windows Installer automatically downloads the necessary files from a server and installs the program. The result is that applications are installed only when they are needed, and the process requires no intervention from the end user. We'll cover the details of this process later in this chapter.

To anyone who has managed many software applications in a network environment, all of these features of the Windows Installer are likely welcome ones. They also make life easier for end users and application developers; they can focus on the "real work" that their jobs demand.

Windows Installer File Types

When performing software deployment with the Windows Installer in Windows Server 2012 R2, you may encounter several different file types.

Microsoft Windows Installer Packages   To take full advantage of Windows Installer functionality, applications must include Microsoft Windows Installer packages. Third-party application vendors and software developers normally create these packages, and they include the information required to install and configure the application and any supporting files.

Microsoft Transformation Files   *Microsoft Transformation (MST) files* are useful when you are customizing the details of how applications are installed. When a system administrator chooses to assign or publish an application, they may want to specify additional options for the package. For example, if a system administrator wants to allow users to install only the Microsoft Word and Microsoft PowerPoint components of Office 2013, they could specify these options within a transformation file. Then, when users install the application, they will be provided only with the options related to these components.

Microsoft Patches   To maintain software, patches are often required. Patches may make registry and/or file system changes. *Patch files (MSP)* are used for minor system changes and are subject to certain limitations. Specifically, a patch file cannot remove any installed program components and cannot delete or modify any shortcuts created by the user.

Initialization Files   To provide support for publishing non-Windows Installer applications, *initialization files* can be used. These files provide links to a standard executable file that is used to install an application. An example might be \\server1\software\program1\ setup.exe. These files can then be published and advertised, and users can access the *Add Or Remove Programs* icon to install them over the network.

Application Assignment Scripts *Application assignment scripts (AAS)* store information regarding assigning programs and any settings that the system administrator makes. These files are created when Group Policy is used to create software package assignments for users and computers.

Each of these types of files provides functionality that allows the system administrator to customize software deployment. Windows Installer packages have special properties that you can view by right-clicking the file in Windows Explorer and choosing Properties (see Figure 6.9).

FIGURE 6.9 Viewing the properties of an MSI package file

Deploying Applications

The functionality provided by Windows Installer offers many advantages to end users who install their own software. However, that is just the beginning in a networked environment. As you'll see later in this chapter, the various features of Windows Installer and compatible packages allow system administrators to determine centrally applications that users will be able to install.

There are two main methods of making programs available to end users using Active Directory: assigning and publishing. Both assigning and publishing applications greatly ease the process of deploying and managing applications in a network environment.

In the following sections, you'll look at how the processes of assigning and publishing applications can make life easier for IT staff and users alike. The various settings for assigned and published applications are managed through the use of GPOs.

Assigning Applications

Software applications can be assigned to users and computers. *Assigning* a software package makes the program available for automatic installation. The applications advertise their availability to the affected users or computers by placing icons within the Programs folder of the Start menu for Windows 8 (and before) and Windows Server 2012, and within the Apps area on Windows 8.1 and Windows Server 2012 R2.

When applications are assigned to a user, programs will be advertised to the user regardless of which computer they are using. That is, icons for the advertised program will appear regardless of whether the program is installed on that computer. If the user clicks an icon for a program that has not yet been installed on the local computer, the application will automatically be accessed from a server and it will be installed.

When an application is assigned to a computer, the program is made available to any users of the computer. For example, all users who log on to a computer that has been assigned Microsoft Office 2013 will have access to the components of the application. If the user did not previously install Microsoft Office 2013, they will be prompted for any required setup information when the program first runs.

Generally, applications that are required by the vast majority of users should be assigned to computers. This reduces the amount of network bandwidth required to install applications on demand and improves the end-user experience by preventing the delay involved when installing an application the first time it is accessed. Any applications that may be used by only a few users (or those with specific job tasks) should be assigned to users.

Publishing Applications

When applications are *published*, they are advertised, but no icons are automatically created. Instead, the applications are made available for installation using the Add Or Remove Programs icon in Control Panel.

Windows Vista, Windows 7, and Windows 8 do not have the Add Or Remove Programs feature. They use the Programs icon in Control Panel to install the software.

Implementing Software Deployment

So far, you have become familiar with the issues related to software deployment and management from a theoretical level. Now it's time to drill down into the actual steps required to deploy software using the features of Active Directory and the GPMC. In the following sections, you will walk through the steps required to create an application distribution share point, to publish and assign applications, to update previously installed applications, to verify the installation of applications, and to update Windows operating systems.

Preparing for Software Deployment

Before you can install applications on client computers, you must make sure that the necessary files are available to end users. In many network environments, system administrators create shares on file servers that include the installation files for many applications. Based on security permissions, either end users or system administrators can then connect to these shares from a client computer and install the needed software. The efficient organization of these shares can save the help desk from having to carry around a library of DVDs, and it allows you to install applications easily on many computers at once.

One of the problems in network environments is that users frequently install applications whether or not they really need them. They may stumble upon applications that are stored on common file servers and install them out of curiosity. These actions can often decrease productivity and may violate software licensing agreements. You can help avoid this by placing all of your application installation files in hidden shares (for example, software$).

Exercise 6.7 walks you through the process of creating a software distribution share point. In this exercise, you will prepare for software deployment by creating a directory share and placing certain types of files in this directory. To complete the steps in this exercise, you must have access to the Microsoft Office 2010 or Microsoft Office 2013 installation files (via DVD or through a network share) and have 2,000MB of free disk space. For this exercise, I used Microsoft Office 2013.

EXERCISE 6.7

Creating a Software Deployment Share

1. Using Windows Explorer, create a folder called Software that you can use with application sharing. Be sure that the volume on which you create this folder has at least 2,000MB of available disk space.

2. Create a folder called Office 2013 within the Software folder.

3. Copy all of the installation files for Microsoft Office 2013 from the DVD or network share containing the files to the Office 2013 folder you created in step 2. If you prefer, you can use switches to install all of the Office 2013 installation files. You can find these switches at http://technet.microsoft.com/en-us/library/ee624360.aspx.

4. Right-click the Software folder (created in step 1) and select Share. In the Choose People On Your Network To Share With dialog box, type **Everyone**, and click the Add button. Next click the Share button. When you see a message that the sharing process is complete, click Done.

Once you have created an application distribution share, it's time to publish and assign the applications. This topic is covered next.

Software Restriction Policies

One of the biggest problems that we face as IT managers is users downloading and installing software. Many software packages don't cause any issues and are completely safe. Unfortunately, many software packages do have viruses and can cause problems. This is where software restriction policies can help. Software restriction policies help to identify software and to control its ability to run on a local computer, organizational unit, domain, or site.

Software restriction policies give administrators the ability to regulate unknown or untrusted software. Software restriction policies allow you to protect your computers from unwanted software by identifying and also specifying what software packages are allowed to be installed.

When configuring software restriction policies, an administrator is able to define a default security level of Unrestricted (software is allowed) or Disallowed (software is not allowed to run) for a GPO. Administrators can make exceptions to this default security level. They can create software restriction policy rules for specific software.

To create a software policy using the Group Policy Management Console, create a new GPO. In the GPO, expand the Windows Settings for either the user or computer configuration section, expand Security, right-click Software Restriction Policy, and choose New Software Restriction Policy. Set the policy for the level of security that you need.

Using AppLocker

AppLocker is a feature in Windows 7, Windows 8, Windows Server 2012, and Windows Server 2012 R2. It is the replacement for software restriction policies. *AppLocker* allows you to configure a Denied list and an Accepted list for applications. Applications that are configured on the Denied list will not run on the system, whereas applications on the Accepted list will operate properly.

The new capabilities and extensions of the AppLocker feature help reduce administrative overhead and help administrators control how users can access and use files, such as EXE files, scripts, Windows Installer files (MSI and MSP files), and DLLs.

Group Policy Slow Link Detection

When setting up GPOs, most of us assume that the connection speeds between servers and clients are going to be fast. In today's world, it is unlikely to see slow connections between locations, but they are still out there. Sometimes connection speeds can cause issues with the deployment of GPOs, specifically ones that are deploying software.

A setting in the Computer and User section of the GPO called *Group Policy Slow Link Detection* defines a slow connection for the purposes of applying and updating GPOs. If the data transfer rate from the domain controller providing the GPO to the computer is slower than what you have specified in this setting, the connection is considered to be a slow connection. If a connection is considered slow, the system response will vary depending on the policy. For example, if a GPO is going to deploy software and the connection is considered slow, the software may not be installed on the client computer. If you configure this option as 0, all connections are considered fast connections.

Publishing and Assigning Applications

As mentioned earlier in this section, system administrators can make software packages available to users by using publishing and assigning operations. Both of these operations allow system administrators to leverage the power of Active Directory and, specifically, GPOs to determine which applications are available to users. Additionally, OUs can provide the organization that can help group users based on their job functions and software requirements.

The general process involves creating a GPO that includes software deployment settings for users and computers and then linking this GPO to Active Directory objects.

Exercise 6.8 walks you through the steps required to publish and assign applications. In this exercise, you will create applications and assign them to specific Active Directory objects using GPOs. To complete the steps in this exercise, you must have completed Exercise 6.7.

EXERCISE 6.8

Publishing and Assigning Applications Using Group Policy

1. Open the Active Directory Users and Computers tool from the Administrative Tools program group (using the Windows key).

2. Expand the domain and create a new top-level OU called **Software**.

3. Within the Software OU, create a user named **Jane User** with a login name of **juser** (choose the defaults for all other options).

4. Exit Active Directory Users and Computers and open the Group Policy Management Console.

5. Right-click the Software OU and choose Create A GPO In This Domain And Link It Here.

6. For the name of the new GPO, type **Software Deployment**.

7. To edit the Software Deployment GPO, right-click it and choose Edit. Expand the Computer Configuration ➤ Policies ➤ Software Settings object.

8. Right-click the Software Installation item and select New ➢ Package.

9. Navigate to the Software share you created in Exercise 6.7.

10. Within the Software share, double-click the Office 2013 folder and select the appropriate MSI file depending on the version of Office 2013 you have. Office 2013 Professional is being used in this example, so you'll see that the OFFICEMUI.MSI file is chosen. Click Open.

11. In the Deploy Software dialog box, choose Advanced. (Note that the Published option is unavailable because applications cannot be published to computers.) Click OK to return to the Deploy Software dialog box.

12. To examine the deployment options of this package, click the Deployment tab. Accept the default settings by clicking OK.

13. Within the Group Policy Object Editor, expand the User Configuration ➢ Software Settings object.

14. Right-click the Software Installation item and select New ➢ Package.

15. Navigate to the Software share you created in Exercise 6.7.

16. Within the Software share, double-click the Office 2013 folder and select the appropriate MSI file. Click Open.

17. For the Software Deployment option, select Published in the Deploy Software dialog box and click OK.

18. Close the GPMC.

The overall process involved with deploying software using Active Directory is quite simple. However, you shouldn't let the intuitive graphical interface fool you—there's a lot of power under the hood of these software deployment features! Once you've properly assigned and published applications, it's time to see the effects of your work.

Applying Software Updates

The steps described in the previous section work only when you are installing a new application. However, software companies often release updates that you need to install on top of existing applications. These updates usually consist of bug fixes or other changes that are required to keep the software up-to-date. You can apply software updates in Active Directory by using the Upgrades tab of the software package Properties dialog box found in the Group Policy Object Editor.

In Exercise 6.9, you will apply a software update to an existing application. You should add the upgrade package to the GPO in the same way you added the original application in steps 8 through 12 of Exercise 6.8. You should also have completed Exercise 6.8 before attempting this exercise.

EXERCISE 6.9

Applying Software Updates

1. Open the Group Policy Management Console from the Administrative Tools program group.

2. Click the Software OU, right-click the Software Deployment GPO, and choose Edit.

3. Expand the Computer Configuration ➤ Policies ➤ Software Settings ➤ Software Installation object.

4. Right-click the software package and select Properties from the context menu to bring up the Properties dialog box.

5. Select the Upgrades tab and click the Add button.

6. Click the Current Group Policy Object (GPO) radio button in the Choose A Package From section of the dialog box or click the Browse button to select the GPO to which you want to apply the upgrade. Consult your application's documentation to see whether you should choose the Uninstall The Existing Package, Then Install The Upgrade Package radio button or the Package Can Upgrade Over The Existing Package radio button.

7. Click Cancel to close the Add Upgrade Package dialog box.

8. Click Cancel and exit the GPMC.

You should understand that not all upgrades make sense in all situations. For instance, if the Paniva 2010 files are incompatible with the Paniva 2013 application, then your Paniva 2010 users might not want you to perform the upgrade without taking additional steps to ensure that they can continue to use their files. In addition, users might have some choice about which version they use when it doesn't affect the support of the network.

Regardless of the underlying reason for allowing this flexibility, you should be aware that there are two basic types of upgrades that are available for administrators to provide to the users:

Mandatory Upgrade   Forces everyone who currently has an existing version of the program to upgrade according to the GPO. Users who have never installed the program for whatever reason will be able to install only the new, upgraded version.

Nonmandatory Upgrade   Allows users to choose whether they would like to upgrade. This upgrade type also allows users who do not have their application installed to choose which version they would like to use.

Verifying Software Installation

To ensure that the software installation settings you make in a GPO have taken place, you can log into the domain from a Windows 8, Windows 7, or Windows Vista computer that is within the OU to which the software settings apply. When you log in, you will notice two changes. First the application is installed on the computer (if it was not installed already). To access the application, a user needs to click one of the icons within the Program group of the Start menu. Note also that applications are available to any of the users who log on to this machine. Second, the settings apply to any computers that are contained within the OU and to any users who log on to these computers.

If you publish an application to users, the change may not be as evident, but it is equally useful. When you log on to a Windows 8, Windows 7, or Windows Vista computer that is a member of the domain, and when you use a user account from the OU where you published the application, you will be able to install any of the published applications automatically. On a Windows 8 or Windows 7 computer, you can do this by accessing the Programs icon in Control Panel. By clicking Add New Programs, you access a display of the applications available for installation. By clicking the Add button in the Add New Programs section of the Programs dialog box, you will automatically begin the installation of the published application.

Configuring Automatic Updates in Group Policy

So far you've seen the advantages of deploying application software in a group policy. Group policies also provide a way to install operating system updates across the network for Windows 2000, XP, Vista, Windows 7, Windows 8, Windows Server 2003, Windows Server 2008, Windows Server 2008 R2, Windows Server 2012, and Windows Server 2012 R2 machines using Windows Update in conjunction with Windows Server Update Service. WSUS is the newer version of SUS, and it is used on a Windows Server 2012 R2 system to update systems. As you may remember, WSUS and SUS are patch-management tools that help you deploy updates to your systems in a controlled manner.

Windows Update is available through the Microsoft website, and it is used to provide the most current files for Windows operating systems. Examples of updates include security fixes, critical updates, updated help files, and updated drivers. You can access Windows Update by clicking the Windows Update icon in the system tray.

WSUS is used to leverage the features of Windows Update within a corporate environment by downloading Windows updates to a corporate server, which in turn provides the updates to the internal corporate clients. This allows administrators to test and have full control over what updates are deployed within the corporate environment.

Within an enterprise network that is using Active Directory, you would typically see automatic updates configured through Group Policy. Group policies are used to manage configuration and security settings via Active Directory. Group Policy is also used to specify what server a client will use for automatic updates.

If the WSUS client were part of an enterprise network that is using Active Directory, you would configure the client via a group policy.

Configuring Software Deployment Settings

In addition to the basic operations of assigning and publishing applications, you can use several other options to specify the details of how software is deployed. In the following sections, you will examine the various options that are available and their effects on the software installation process.

The Software Installation Properties Dialog Box

The most important software deployment settings are contained in the Software Installation Properties dialog box, which you can access by right-clicking the Software Installation item and selecting Properties from the context menu. The following sections describe the features contained on the various tabs of the dialog box.

Managing Package Defaults

On the Deployment tab of the Software Installation Properties dialog box, you'll be able to specify some defaults for any packages that you create within this GPO. Figure 6.10 shows the Deployment options for managing software installation settings.

FIGURE 6.10   Deployment tab of the Software Installation Properties dialog box

The following options are used for managing software installation settings:

Default Package Location   This setting specifies the default file system or network location for software installation packages. This is useful if you are already using a specific share on a file server for hosting the necessary installation files.

New Packages   These settings specify the default type of package assignment that will be used when you add a new package to either the user or computer settings. If you'll be assigning or publishing multiple packages, you may find it useful to set a default here. Selecting the Advanced option (see Figure 6.11) enables Group Policy to display the package's Properties dialog box each time a new package is added.

FIGURE 6.11   Advanced Deployment dialog box

Installation User Interface Options   When installing an application, system administrators may or may not want end users to see all of the advanced installation options. If Basic is chosen, the user will be able to configure only the minimal settings (such as the installation location). If Maximum is chosen, all of the available installation options will be displayed. The specific installation options available will depend on the package itself.

Uninstall Applications When They Fall Out Of The Scope of Management   So far, you have seen how applications can be assigned and published to users or computers. But what happens when effective GPOs change? For example, suppose User A is currently located within the Sales OU. A GPO that assigns the Microsoft Office 2013 suite of applications is linked to the Sales OU. You decide to move User A to the Engineering OU, which has no software deployment settings. Should the application be uninstalled or should it remain?

If the Uninstall Applications When They Fall Out Of The Scope of Management option is checked, applications will be removed if they are not specifically assigned or published within GPOs. In this example, this means Office 2013 would be uninstalled for User A. If this box is left unchecked, however, the application will remain installed.

Managing File Extension Mappings

One of the potential problems associated with using many different file types is that it's difficult to keep track of which applications work with which files. For example, if you received a file with the filename extension .abc, you would have no idea which application you would need to view it.

Fortunately, through software deployment settings, system administrators can specify mappings for specific *filename extensions*. For example, you could specify that whenever users attempt to access a file with the extension .vsd, the operating system should attempt to open the file using Visio diagramming software. If Visio is not installed on the user's machine, the computer can automatically download and install it (assuming that the application has been properly advertised).

This method allows users to have applications automatically installed when they are needed. The following is an example of a sequence of events that might occur:

1. A user receives an email message that contains a PDF (.pdf) file attachment.

2. The computer realizes that the PDF file does not have the appropriate viewing application for this type of file installed. However, it also realizes that a filename extension mapping is available within the Active Directory software deployment settings.

3. The client computer automatically requests the PDF software package from the server, and it uses the Microsoft Windows Installer to install the application automatically.

4. The computer opens the attachment for the user.

Notice that all of these steps were carried out without any further interaction with the user.

You can manage filename extension mappings by right-clicking the Software Installation item, selecting Properties, and then clicking the File Extensions tab.

Creating Application Categories

In many network environments, the list of supported applications can include hundreds of items. For users who are looking for only one specific program, searching through a list of all of these programs can be difficult and time-consuming.

Fortunately, methods for categorizing the applications are available on your network. You can easily manage the application categories for users and computers by right-clicking the Software Installation item, selecting Properties, and then clicking the Categories tab.

Figure 6.12 shows you the categories tab of the Software Installation package. When creating categories, it is a good idea to use category names that are meaningful to users because it will make it easier for them to find the programs they're seeking.

Once the software installation categories have been created, you can view them by clicking the Programs or Programs And Features icon in Control Panel. When you click Add New Programs, you'll see that several options appear in the Category drop-down list. Now when you select the properties for a package, you will be able to assign the application to one or more of the categories.

FIGURE 6.12   The Categories tab of the Software Installation Properties dialog box

Removing Programs

As discussed in the beginning of the chapter, an important phase in the software management life cycle is the removal of applications. Fortunately, if you use the GPMC and the Windows Installer packages, the process is simple. To remove an application, you can right-click the package within the Group Policy settings and select All Tasks ➢ Remove (see Figure 6.13).

When choosing to remove a software package from a GPO, you have two options, shown here:

Immediately Uninstall The Software From Users And Computers   System administrators can choose this option to ensure that an application is no longer available to users who are affected by the GPO. When this option is selected, the program will be uninstalled automatically from users and/or computers that have the package. This option might be useful, for example, if the license for a certain application has expired or if a program is no longer on the approved applications list.

Allow Users To Continue To Use The Software, But Prevent New Installations   This option prevents users from making new installations of a package, but it does not remove the software if it has already been installed for users. This is a good option if the company has run out of additional licenses for the software but the existing licenses are still valid. Figure 6.14 shows these two removal options.

If you no longer require the ability to install or repair an application, you can delete it from your software distribution share point by deleting the appropriate Windows Installer package files. This will free up additional disk space for newer applications.

FIGURE 6.13   Removing a software package

FIGURE 6.14   Software removal options

Microsoft Windows Installer Settings

Several options influence the behavior of the Windows Installer; you can set them within a GPO. You can access these options by navigating to User Configuration ➢ Administrative Templates ➢ Windows Components ➢ Windows Installer (see Figure 6.15).
The options are as follows:

Always Install With Elevated Privileges   This policy allows users to install applications that require elevated privileges. For example, if a user does not have the permissions necessary to modify the registry but the installation program must make registry changes, this policy will allow the process to succeed.

FIGURE 6.15   GPO settings for Windows Installer

Prevent Removable Media Source For Any Install   This option disallows the installation of software using removable media (such as a CD-ROM or DVD-ROM). It is useful for ensuring that users install only approved applications.

Prohibit Rollback   When this option is enabled, the Windows Installer does not store the system state information that is required to roll back the installation of an application. System administrators may choose this option to reduce the amount of temporary disk space required during installation and to increase the performance of the installation operation. However, the drawback is that the system cannot roll back to its original state if the installation fails and the application needs to be removed.

Specify The Order In Which Windows Installer Searches   This setting specifies the order in which the Windows Installer will search for installation files. The options include *n* (for network shares), *m* (for searching removal media), and *u* (for searching the Internet for installation files).

With these options, system administrators can control how the Windows Installer operates for specific users who are affected by the GPO.

Troubleshooting Group Policies

Because of the wide variety of configurations that are possible when you are establishing GPOs, you should be aware of some common troubleshooting methods. These methods will help isolate problems in policy settings or GPO links.

One possible problem with GPO configuration is that logons and system startups may take a long time. This occurs especially in large environments when the Group Policy settings must be transmitted over the network and, in many cases, slow WAN links. In general, the number of GPOs should be limited because of the processing overhead and network requirements during logon. By default, GPOs are processed in a synchronous manner. This means that the processing of one GPO must be completed before another one is applied (as opposed to asynchronous processing, where they can all execute at the same time).

When a group policy gets processed on a Windows-based operating system, client-side extensions are the mechanisms that interpret the stored policy and then make the appropriate changes to the operating system environment. When an administrator is troubleshooting a given extension's application of policy, the administrator can view the configuration parameters for that extension in the operating system's registry. To view the extension in the registry, you would view the following key:

```
HKEY_LOCAL_MACHINE\Software\Microsoft\Windows \CurrentVersion\Group Policy
```

The most common issue associated with Group Policy is the unexpected setting of Group Policy options. In Windows Server 2000, administrators spent countless hours analyzing inheritance hierarchy and individual settings to determine why a particular user or computer was having policy problems. For instance, say a user named wpanek complains that the Run option is missing from his Start menu. The wpanek user account is stored in the New Hampshire OU, and you've applied group policies at the OU, domain, and site levels. To determine the source of the problem, you would have to sift through each GPO manually to find the Start menu policy as well as to figure out the applicable inheritance settings.

Windows Server 2012 R2 has a handy feature called *Resultant Set of Policy (RSoP)* that displays the exact settings that actually apply to individual users, computers, OUs, domains, and sites after inheritance and filtering have taken effect. In the example just described, you could run RSoP on the wpanek account and view a single set of Group Policy settings that represent the settings that apply to that account. In addition, each setting's Properties dialog box displays the GPO from which the setting is derived as well as the order of priority, the filter status, and other useful information, as you will see a bit later.

RSoP actually runs in two modes.

Logging Mode   *Logging mode* displays the actual settings that apply to users and computers, as shown in the example in the preceding paragraph.

Planning Mode   *Planning mode* can be applied to users, computers, OUs, domains, and sites, and you use it before you apply any settings. As its name implies, planning mode is used to plan GPOs.

Additionally, you can run the command-line utility `gpresult.exe` to get a quick snapshot of the Group Policy settings that apply to a user and/or computer. Let's take a closer look at the two modes and the `gpresult.exe` command.

RSoP in Logging Mode

RSoP in logging mode can query policy settings only for users and computers. The easiest way to access RSoP in logging mode is through the Active Directory Users and Computers tool, although you can run it as a stand-alone MMC snap-in if you want.

To analyze the policy settings for wpanek from the earlier example, you would right-click the user icon in Active Directory Users and Computers and select All Tasks ➢ Resultant Set of Policy (Logging). The Group Policy Results Wizard appears. The wizard walks you through the steps necessary to view the RSoP for wpanek.

The Computer Selection page, shown in Figure 6.16, requires you to select a computer for which to display settings. Remember that a GPO contains both user and computer settings, so you must choose a computer to which the user is logged on in order to continue with the wizard. If the user has never logged on to a computer, then you must run RSoP in planning mode because there is no logged policy information yet for that user.

The User Selection page, shown in Figure 6.17, requires you to select a user account to analyze. Because I selected a user from the Active Directory Users and Computers tool, the username is filled in automatically. This page is most useful if you are running RSoP in MMC mode and don't have the luxury of selecting a user contextually.

FIGURE 6.16   The Computer Selection page of the Group Policy Results Wizard

FIGURE 6.17 The User Selection page of the Group Policy Results Wizard

The Summary Of Selections page, shown in Figure 6.18, summarizes your choices and provides an option for gathering extended error information. If you need to make any changes before you begin to analyze the policy settings, you should click the Back button on the Summary screen. Otherwise, click Next.

FIGURE 6.18 The Summary Of Selections page of the Group Policy Results Wizard

After the wizard is complete, you will see the window shown in Figure 6.19. This window displays only the policy settings that apply to the user and computer that you selected in the wizard. You can see these users and computers at the topmost level of the tree.

FIGURE 6.19   The User Selection page for the administrator on computer SERVER1

Any warnings or errors appear as a yellow triangle or red X over the applicable icon at the level where the warning or error occurred. To view more information about the warning or error, right-click the icon and select Properties, as shown in Figure 6.20.

You cannot make changes to any of the individual settings because RSoP is a diagnostic tool and not an editor, but you can get more information about settings by clicking a setting and selecting Properties from the context menu.

The Details tab of the user's Properties window, shown in Figure 6.21, displays the actual setting that applies to the user in question based on GPO inheritance.

RSoP in Planning Mode

Running RSoP in planning mode isn't much different from running RSoP in logging mode, but the RSoP Wizard asks for a bit more information than you saw earlier.

In the former example, wpanek couldn't see the Run option in the Start menu because his user account is affected by the New Hampshire GPO in the San Jose OU. As an administrator, you could plan to move his user account to the North America OU. Before doing so, you could verify his new policy settings by running RSoP in planning mode. Run the RSoP on the user wpanek under the scenario that you've already moved him from the San Jose OU to the North America OU. At this point, you haven't actually moved the user, but you can see what his settings would be if you did.

FIGURE 6.20 Details of event pertaining to the administrator account on computer SERVER1

FIGURE 6.21 The Details tab of the object's Properties window

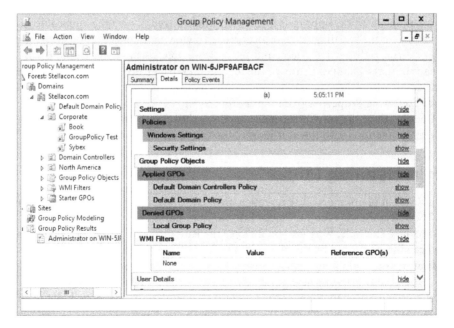

Using the *gpresult.exe* Command

The command-line utility gpresult.exe is included as part of the RSoP tool. Running the command by itself without any switches returns the following Group Policy information about the local user and computer:

- The name of the domain controller from which the local machine retrieved the policy information
- The date and time at which the policies were applied
- Which policies were applied
- Which policies were filtered out
- Group membership

You can use the switches shown in Table 6.2 to get information for remote users and computers and to enable other options.

Table 6.2 is not a complete list. To see a complete list of the gpresult.exe command, visit Microsoft at www.microsoft.com.

TABLE 6.2 gpresult switches

Switch	Description
/S *systemname*	Generates RSoP information for a remote computer name.
/USER *username*	Generates RSoP information for a remote username.
/x /h *filename*	Generates a report in either XML (/x) or HTML (/h) format. The filename and location is specified by the *filename* parameter.
/V	Specifies verbose mode, which displays more verbose information such as user rights information.
/Z	Specifies an even greater level of verbose information.
/SCOPE MACHINE	Displays maximum information about the computer policies applied to this system.
/SCOPE USER	Displays maximum information about the user policies applied to this system.
>*textfile.txt*	Writes the output to a text file.

For example, to obtain information about user wpanek in a system called STELLACON, you would use the command gpresult/S STELLACON/USERwpanek.

Through the use of these techniques, you should be able to track down even the most elusive Group Policy problems. Remember, however, that good troubleshooting skills do not replace planning adequately and maintaining GPO settings!

Summary

In this chapter, you examined Active Directory's solution to a common headache for many systems administrators: policy settings. Specifically, I discussed topics that covered Group Policy.

I covered the fundamentals of Group Policy including its fundamental purpose. You can use Group Policy to enforce granular permissions for users in an Active Directory environment. Group policies can restrict and modify the actions allowed for users and computers within the Active Directory environment.

Certain Group Policy settings may apply to users, computers, or both. Computer settings affect all users who access the machines to which the policy applies. User settings affect users regardless of the machines to which they log on.

You learned that you can link Group Policy objects to Active Directory sites, domains, or OUs. This link determines to which objects the policies apply. GPO links can interact through inheritance and filtering to result in an effective set of policies.

The chapter covered inheritance and how GPOs filter down. I showed you how to use the Enforced option on a GPO issued from a parent and how to block a GPO from a child.

You can also use administrative templates to simplify the creation of GPOs. There are some basic default templates that come with Windows Server 2012 R2.

In addition, administrators can delegate control over GPOs in order to distribute administrative responsibilities. Delegation is an important concept because it allows for distributed administration.

You can also deploy software using GPOs. This feature can save time and increase productivity throughout the entire software management life cycle by automating software installation and removal on client computers. The Windows Installer offers a more robust method for managing installation and removal, and applications that support it can take advantage of new Active Directory features. Make sure you are comfortable using the Windows Installer.

You learned about publishing applications via Active Directory and the difference between publishing and assigning applications. You can assign some applications to users and computers so that they are always available. You can also publish them to users so that the user can install them with minimal effort when required.

You also learned how to prepare for software deployment. Before your users can take advantage of automated software installation, you must set up an installation share and provide the appropriate permissions.

The final portion of the chapter covered the Resultant Set of Policy (RSoP) tool, which you can use in logging mode or planning mode to determine exactly which set of policies applies to users, computers, OUs, domains, and sites.

Exam Essentials

Understand the purpose of Group Policy. System administrators use Group Policy to enforce granular permissions for users in an Active Directory environment.

Understand user and computer settings. Certain Group Policy settings may apply to users, computers, or both. Computer settings affect all users that access the machines to which the policy applies. User settings affect users, regardless of which machines they log on to.

Know the interactions between Group Policy objects and Active Directory. GPOs can be linked to Active Directory objects. This link determines to which objects the policies apply.

Understand filtering and inheritance interactions between GPOs. For ease of administration, GPOs can interact via inheritance and filtering. It is important to understand these interactions when you are implementing and troubleshooting Group Policy.

Know how Group Policy settings can affect script policies and network settings. You can use special sets of GPOs to manage network configuration settings.

Understand how delegation of administration can be used in an Active Directory environment. Delegation is an important concept because it allows for distributed administration.

Know how to use the Resultant Set of Policy (RSoP) tool to troubleshoot and plan Group Policy. Windows Server 2012 R2 includes the RSoP feature, which you can run in logging mode or planning mode to determine exactly which set of policies applies to users, computers, OUs, domains, and sites.

Identify common problems with the software life cycle. IT professionals face many challenges with client applications, including development, deployment, maintenance, and troubleshooting.

Understand the benefits of the Windows Installer. Using the Windows Installer is an updated way to install applications on Windows-based machines. It offers a more robust method for making the system changes required by applications, and it allows for a cleaner uninstall. Windows Installer–based applications can also take advantage of new Active Directory features.

Understand the difference between publishing and assigning applications. Some applications can be assigned to users and computers so that they are always available.

Applications can be published to users so that the user may install the application with a minimal amount of effort when it is required.

Know how to prepare for software deployment.   Before your users can take advantage of automated software installation, you must set up an installation share and provide the appropriate permissions.

Know how to configure application settings using Active Directory and Group Policy.   Using standard Windows Server 2012 R2 administrative tools, you can create an application policy that meets your requirements. You can use automatic, on-demand installation of applications as well as many other features.

Create application categories to simplify the list of published applications.   It's important to group applications by functionality or the users to whom they apply, especially in organizations that support a large number of programs.

Review Questions

1. You are the network administrator for a large organization that uses Windows Server 2012 R2 domain controllers and DNS servers. All of your client machines currently have the Windows XP operating system. You want to be able to have client computers edit the domain-based GPOs by using the ADMX files that are located in the ADMX Central Store. How do you accomplish this task? (Choose all that apply.)

    A. Upgrade your clients to Windows 8.

    B. Upgrade your clients to Windows 7.

    C. Add the client machines to the ADMX edit utility.

    D. In the ADMX store, choose the box Allow All Client Privileges.

2. You work for an organization with a single Windows Server 2012 R2 Active Directory domain. The domain has OUs for Sales, Marketing, Admin, R&D, and Finance. You need only the users in the Finance OU to get Windows Office 2013 installed automatically onto their computers. You create a GPO named OfficeApp. What is the next step in getting all of the Finance users Office 2013?

    A. Edit the GPO, and assign the Office application to the user's account. Link the GPO to the Finance OU.

    B. Edit the GPO, and assign the Office application to the user's account. Link the GPO to the domain.

    C. Edit the GPO, and assign the Office application to the computer account. Link the GPO to the domain.

    D. Edit the GPO, and assign the Office application to the computer account. Link the GPO to the Finance OU.

3. You are hired as a consultant to the ABC Company. The owner of the company complains that she continues to have desktop wallpaper that she did not choose. When you speak with the IT team, you find out that a former employee created 20 GPOs and they have not been able to figure out which GPO is changing the owner's desktop wallpaper. How can you resolve this issue?

    A. Run the RSoP utility against all forest computer accounts.

    B. Run the RSoP utility against the owner's computer account.

    C. Run the RSoP utility against the owner's user account.

    D. Run the RSoP utility against all domain computer accounts.

4. You are the network administrator for a large organization that has multiple sites and multiple OUs. You have a site named SalesSite that is for the sales building across the street. In the domain, there is an OU for all salespeople called Sales. You set up a GPO for the SalesSite, and you need to be sure that it applies to the Sales OU. The Sales OU GPOs cannot override the SalesSite GPO. What do you do?

    A. On the GPO, disable the Block Child Inheritance setting.

    B. On the GPO, set the Enforce setting.

    C. On the GPO, set the priorities to 1.

    D. On the Sales OU, set the Inherit Parent Policy settings.

5. You are the administrator for an organization that has multiple locations. You are running Windows Server 2012 R2, and you have only one domain with multiple OUs set up for each location. One of your locations, Boston, is connected to the main location by a 256Kbps ISDN line. You configure a GPO to assign a sales application to all computers in the entire domain. You have to be sure that Boston users receive the GPO properly. What should you do?

    A. Disable the Slow Link Detection setting in the GPO.

    B. Link the GPO to the Boston OU.

    C. Change the properties of the GPO to publish the application to the Boston OU.

    D. Have the users in Boston run the GPResult/force command.

6. To disable GPO settings for a specific security group, which of the following permissions should you apply?

    A. Deny Write

    B. Allow Write

    C. Enable Apply Group Policy

    D. Deny Apply Group Policy

7. GPOs assigned at which of the following level(s) will override GPO settings at the domain level?

    A. OU

    B. Site

    C. Domain

    D. Both OU and site

8. A system administrator wants to ensure that only the GPOs set at the OU level affect the Group Policy settings for objects within the OU. Which option can they use to do this (assuming that all other GPO settings are the defaults)?

    A. The Enforced option

    B. The Block Policy Inheritance option

    C. The Disable option

    D. The Deny permission

9. A system administrator is planning to implement Group Policy objects in a new Windows Server 2012 R2 Active Directory environment. In order to meet the needs of the organization, he decides to implement a hierarchical system of Group Policy settings. At which of the following levels is he able to assign Group Policy settings? (Choose all that apply.)

   A. Sites

   B. Domains

   C. Organizational units

   D. Local system

10. Ann is a system administrator for a medium-sized Active Directory environment. She has determined that several new applications that will be deployed throughout the organization use registry-based settings. She would like to do the following:

   ▪ Control these registry settings using Group Policy

   ▪ Create a standard set of options for these applications and allow other system administrators to modify them using the standard Active Directory tools

   Which of the following options can she use to meet these requirements? (Choose all that apply.)

   A. Implement the inheritance functionality of GPOs.

   B. Implement delegation of specific objects within Active Directory.

   C. Implement the No Override functionality of GPOs.

   D. Create administrative templates.

   E. Provide administrative templates to the system administrators who are responsible for creating Group Policy for the applications.

Chapter

7

Manage Security

THE FOLLOWING 70-410 EXAM OBJECTIVES ARE COVERED IN THIS CHAPTER:

✓ **Configuring security policies**

  ▪ Configure User Rights Assignment

  ▪ Configure Security Options settings

  ▪ Configure Security templates

  ▪ Configure Audit Policy

  ▪ Configure Local Users and Groups

  ▪ Configure User Account Control (UAC)

✓ **Configuring Windows Firewall**

  ▪ Configure rules for multiple profiles using Group Policy

  ▪ Configure connection security rules

  ▪ Configure Windows Firewall to allow or deny applications, scopes, ports, and users

  ▪ Configure authenticated firewall exceptions

  ▪ Import and export settings

As an IT Director and Microsoft Trainer, I can explain the importance of every chapter in this book, but some chapters are more important for real-world use. This is one of them.

Setting up security so that only people who need access to resources are the ones who get access to those resources is one of the most important jobs an IT member can have. This helps protect your data from hackers and, believe it or not, your own users.

In this chapter, you will learn how to protect data on your network. I will also discuss how to protect your individual system by using Windows Firewall.

Managing Security

One of the fundamental design goals for Active Directory is to define a single, centralized repository of users and information resources. Active Directory records information about all of the users, computers, and resources on your network. Each domain acts as a logical boundary, and members of the domain (including workstations, servers, and domain controllers) share information about the objects within them.

The information stored within Active Directory determines which resources are accessible to which users. Through the use of *permissions* that are assigned to Active Directory objects, you can control all aspects of network security.

You should be sure that you have implemented appropriate access control settings for the file system, network devices, and other resources. Let's look at the various components of network security, which include working with security principals and managing security and permissions, access control lists (ACLs), User Account Control (UAC), and access control entries (ACEs).

When you are setting up a network, you should always keep in mind that 90 percent of all hacks on a network are internal. This means internal permissions and security (as well as external security) need to be as strong as possible while still allowing users to do their jobs.

Understanding Security Principals

Security principals are Active Directory objects that are assigned *security identifiers (SIDs)*. An SID is a unique identifier that is used to manage any object to which permissions can be assigned. Security principals are assigned permissions to perform certain actions and access certain network resources.

The following basic types of Active Directory objects serve as security principals:

User Accounts   User accounts identify individual users on your network by including information such as the user's name and their password. User accounts are the fundamental unit of security administration.

Groups   There are two main types of groups: *security groups* and *distribution groups*. Both types can contain user accounts. System administrators use security groups to ease the management of security permissions. They use distribution groups, on the other hand, solely to send email. Distribution groups are not security principals. You'll see the details of groups in the next section.

Computer Accounts   *Computer accounts* identify which client computers are members of particular domains. Because these computers participate in the Active Directory database, system administrators can manage security settings that affect the computer. They use computer accounts to determine whether a computer can join a domain and for authentication purposes. As you'll see later in this chapter, system administrators can also place restrictions on certain computer settings to increase security. These settings apply to the computer and, therefore, also apply to any user who is using it (regardless of the permissions granted to the user account).

Note that other objects, such as organizational units (OUs), do not function as security principals. What this means is that you can apply certain settings (such as Group Policy) on all of the objects within an OU; however, you cannot specifically set permissions with respect to the OU. The purpose of OUs is to organize other Active Directory objects logically based on business needs, add a needed level of control for security, and create an easier way to delegate.

You can manage security by performing the following actions with security principals:

- You can assign them permissions to access various network resources.

- You can give them user rights.

- You can track their actions through auditing (covered later in this chapter).

The major types of security principals—user accounts, groups, and computer accounts—form the basis of the Active Directory security architecture. As a system administrator, you will likely spend a portion of your time managing permissions for these objects.

 It is important to understand that since a unique SID defines each security principal, deleting a security principal is an irreversible process. For example, if you delete a user account and then later re-create one with the same name, you'll need to reassign permissions and group membership settings for the new account. Once a user account is deleted, its SID is deleted.

Users and groups are two types of fundamental security principals employed for security administration. In the following sections, you'll learn how users and groups interact. You'll also learn about the different types of groups you can create.

Types of Groups

When dealing with groups, you should make the distinction between local security principals and domain security principals, as follows:

Local Users and Groups   You use *local users and groups* to assign the permissions necessary to access the local machine. For example, you may assign the permissions you need to reboot a domain controller to a specific domain local group.

Domain Users and Groups   *Domain users and groups*, on the other hand, are used throughout the domain. These objects are available on any of the computers within the Active Directory domain and between domains that have a trust relationship.

Here are the two main types of groups used in Active Directory:

Security Groups   *Security groups* are considered security principals. They can contain user accounts, computers, or groups. To make administration simpler, system administrators usually grant permissions to groups. This allows you to change permissions easily at the Active Directory level (instead of at the level of the resource on which the permissions are assigned).

You can also place Active Directory Contact objects within security groups, but security permissions will not apply to them.

Distribution Groups   Distribution groups are not considered security principals because they do not have SIDs. As mentioned earlier, they are used only for the purpose of sending email messages. You can add users to distribution groups just as you would add them to security groups. You can also place distribution groups within OUs so that they are easier to manage. You will find them useful, for example, if you need to send email messages to an entire department or business unit within Active Directory.

Understanding the differences between security and distribution groups is important in an Active Directory environment. For the most part, system administrators use security groups for the daily administration of permissions. On the other hand, system administrators who are responsible for maintaining email distribution lists generally use distribution groups to group members of departments and business units logically. (A system administrator can also email all of the users within a security group, but to do so, they would have to specify the email addresses for the accounts.)

When you are working in Windows Server 2003, Server 2008, Server 2008 R2, Windows Server 2012, or Windows Server 2012 R2 functional-level domains, you can convert security groups to or from distribution groups.

It is vital that you understand group types when you are getting ready to take the Microsoft exams. Microsoft likes to include trick questions about putting permissions on distribution groups. Remember, only security groups can have permissions assigned to them.

Group Scope

In addition to being classified by type, each group is given a specific scope. The scope of a group defines two characteristics. First, it determines the level of security that applies to a group. Second, it determines which users can be added to the group. *Group scope* is an important concept in network environments because it ultimately defines which resources users are able to access.

The three types of group scope are as follows:

Domain Local   The scope of *domain local groups* extends as far as the local domain. When you're using the Active Directory Users and Computers tool, domain local accounts apply to the computer for which you are viewing information. Domain local groups are used to assign permissions to local resources, such as files and printers. They can contain domain locals, global groups, universal groups, and user accounts.

Global   The scope of *global groups* is limited to a single domain. Global groups may contain any of the users who are a part of the Active Directory domain in which the global groups reside or other global groups. Global groups are often used for managing domain security permissions based on job functions. For example, if you need to specify permissions for the Engineering department, you could create one or more global groups (such as EngineeringManagers and EngineeringDevelopers). You could then assign security permissions to each group.

Universal   *Universal groups* can contain accounts or other universal groups from any domains within an Active Directory forest. Therefore, system administrators use them to manage security across domains. When you are managing multiple domains, it often helps to group global groups within universal groups. For instance, if you have an Engineering global group in the `research.stellacon.com` domain and an Engineering global group in the `asia.stellacon.com` domain, you can create a universal AllEngineers group that contains both of the global groups. Now whenever you must assign security permissions to all engineers within the organization, you need only assign permissions to the AllEngineers universal group.

For domain controllers to process authentication between domains, information about the membership of universal groups is stored in the global catalog (GC). Keep this in mind if you ever plan to place users directly into universal groups and bypass global groups because all of the users will be enumerated in the GC, which will impact size and performance.

Fortunately, universal group credentials are cached on domain controllers that universal group members use to log on. This process is called *universal group membership caching*. The domain controller obtains the cached data whenever universal group members log on, and then it is retained on the domain controller for eight hours by default. This is especially useful for smaller locations, such as branch offices, that run less expensive domain controllers. Most domain controllers at these locations cannot store a copy of the entire GC, and frequent calls to the nearest GC would require an inordinate amount of network traffic.

When you create a new group using the Active Directory Users and Computers tool, you must specify the scope of the group. Figure 7.1 shows the New Object – Group dialog box and the available options for the group scope.

Changing group scope, however, can be helpful when your security administration or business needs change. You can change group scope easily using the Active Directory Users and Computers tool. To do so, access the properties of the group. As shown in Figure 7.2, you can make a group scope change by clicking one of the options.

FIGURE 7.1 The New Object – Group dialog box

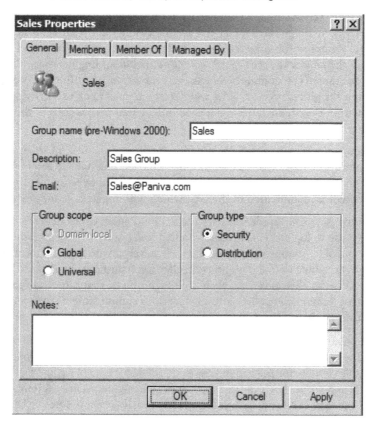

FIGURE 7.2 The Sales Security Group's Properties dialog box

Built-in Domain Local Groups

System administrators use built-in domain local groups to perform administrative functions on the local server. Because these have pre-assigned permissions and privileges, they allow system administrators to assign common management functions easily. Figure 7.3 shows the default built-in groups that are available on a Windows Server 2012 R2 domain controller.

FIGURE 7.3 Default built-in local groups

The list of built-in local groups includes some of the following:

Account Operators   These users can create and modify domain user and group accounts. Members of this group are generally responsible for the daily administration of Active Directory.

Administrators   By default, members of the Administrators group are given full permissions to perform any functions within the Active Directory domain and on the local computer. This means they can access all files and resources that reside on any server within the domain. As you can see, this is a powerful account.

In general, you should restrict the number of users who are included in this group because most common administration functions do not require this level of access.

Backup Operators   One of the problems associated with backing up data in a secure network environment is that you need to provide a way to bypass standard file system security so that you can copy files. Although you could place users in the Administrators group, doing so usually provides more permissions than necessary. Members of the Backup Operators group can bypass standard file system security for the purpose of backup and recovery only. They cannot, however, directly access or open files within the file system.

Generally, backup software applications and data use the permissions assigned to the Backup Operators group.

Certificate Service DCOM Access   Members of the Certificate Service DCOM Access group can connect to certificate authority servers in the enterprise.

Cryptographic Operators   Members of the Cryptographic Operators group are authorized to perform cryptographic operations. *Cryptography* allows the use of codes to convert data, which then allows a specific recipient to read it using a key.

Guests   Typically, you use the Guests group to provide access to resources that generally do not require security. For example, if you have a network share that provides files that should be made available to all network users, you can assign permissions to allow members of the Guests group to access those files.

Print Operators   By default, members of the Print Operators group are given permissions to administer all of the printers within a domain. This includes common functions such as changing the priority of print jobs and deleting items from the print queue.

Replicator   The Replicator group allows files to be replicated among the computers in a domain. You can add accounts used for replication-related tasks to this group to provide those accounts with the permissions they need to keep files synchronized across multiple computers.

Server Operators   A common administrative task is managing server configuration. Members of the Server Operators group are granted the permissions they need to manage services, shares, and other system settings.

Users   The Users built-in domain local group is used to administer security for most network accounts. Usually, you don't give this group many permissions, and you use it to apply security settings for most employees within an organization.

Windows Server 2012 R2 also includes many different default groups, which you can find in the Users folder. As shown in Figure 7.4, these groups are of varying scopes, including domain local, global, and universal groups. You'll see the details of these groups in the next section.

FIGURE 7.4 Contents of the default Users folder

Three important user accounts are created during the promotion of a domain controller, described here:

Administrator Account The Administrator account is assigned the password a system administrator provides during the promotion process, and it has full permissions to perform all actions within the domain.

Guest Account The Guest account is disabled by default. The purpose of the *Guest account* is to provide anonymous access to users who do not have an individual logon and password to use within the domain. Although the Guest account might be useful in some situations, it is generally recommended that this account be disabled to increase security.

Krbtgt, or Key Distribution Center Service, Account Only the operating system uses the *krbtgt*, or *Key Distribution Center Service*, *account* for Kerberos authentication while it is using DCPromo.exe. This account is disabled by default. Unlike other user accounts, the krbtgt account cannot be used to log on to the domain, and therefore it does not need to be enabled. Since only the operating system uses this account, you do not need to worry about hackers gaining access by using this account.

Predefined Global Groups

As mentioned earlier in this chapter, you use global groups to manage permissions at the domain level. Members of each of these groups can perform specific tasks related to managing Active Directory.

The following predefined global groups are installed in the Users folder:

Cert Publishers   Certificates are used to increase security by allowing for strong authentication methods. User accounts are placed within the *Cert Publishers group* if they must publish security certificates. Generally, Active Directory security services use these accounts.

Domain Computers   All of the computers that are members of the domain are generally members of the *Domain Computers group*. This includes any workstations or servers that have joined the domain, but it does not include the domain controllers.

Domain Admins   Members of the *Domain Admins group* have full permissions to manage all of the Active Directory objects for this domain. This is a powerful account; therefore, you should restrict its membership only to those users who require full permissions.

Domain Controllers   All of the domain controllers for a given domain are generally included within the *Domain Controllers group*.

Domain Guests   Generally, by default, members of the *Domain Guests group* are given minimal permissions with respect to resources. System administrators may place user accounts in this group if they require only basic access or temporary permissions within the domain.

Domain Users   The *Domain Users group* usually contains all of the user accounts for the given domain. This group is generally given basic permissions to resources that do not require higher levels of security. A common example is a public file share.

Enterprise Admins   Members of the *Enterprise Admins group* are given full permissions to perform actions within the entire forest. This includes functions such as managing trust relationships and adding new domains to trees and forests.

Group Policy Creator Owners   Members of the *Group Policy Creator Owners group* are able to create and modify Group Policy settings for objects within the domain. This allows them to enable security settings on OUs (and the objects they contain).

Schema Admins   Members of the *Schema Admins group* are given permissions to modify the Active Directory schema. As a member of Schema Admins, you can create additional fields of information for user accounts. This is a powerful function because any changes to the schema will be propagated to all the domains and domain controllers within an Active Directory forest. Furthermore, you cannot undo changes to the schema (although you can disable some).

In addition to these groups, you can create new ones for specific services and applications that are installed on the server. Specifically, services that run on domain controllers and servers will be created as security groups with domain local scope. For example, if a domain controller is running the DNS service, the DnsAdmins and DnsUpdateProxy groups become available. In addition, there are two read-only domain controller (RODC) local groups: the Allowed RODC Password Replication and the Denied RODC Password Replication groups. Similarly, if you install the DHCP service, it automatically creates the

DHCP Users and DHCP Administrators groups. The purpose of these groups depends on the functionality of the applications being installed.

Foreign Security Principals

In environments that have more than one domain, you may need to grant permissions to users who reside in multiple domains. Generally, you manage this using Active Directory trees and forests. However, in some cases, you may want to provide resources to users who belong to domains that are not part of the forest.

Active Directory uses the concept of *foreign security principals* to allow permissions to be assigned to users who are not part of an Active Directory forest. This process is automatic and does not require the intervention of system administrators. You can then add the foreign security principals to domain local groups for which, in turn, you can grant permissions for resources within the domain. You can view a list of foreign security principals by using the Active Directory Users and Computers tool. Figure 7.5 shows the contents of the ForeignSecurityPrincipals folder.

FIGURE 7.5 The ForeignSecurityPrincipals folder

Managing Security and Permissions

Now that you understand the basic issues, terms, and Active Directory objects that pertain to security, it's time to look at how you can apply this information to secure your network resources. The general practice for managing security is to assign users to groups and then grant permissions and logon parameters to the groups so that they can access certain resources.

For management ease and to implement a hierarchical structure, you can place groups within OUs. You can also assign Group Policy settings to all of the objects contained within an OU. By using this method, you can combine the benefits of a hierarchical structure (through OUs) with the use of security principals. Figure 7.6 provides a diagram of this process.

FIGURE 7.6 An overview of security management

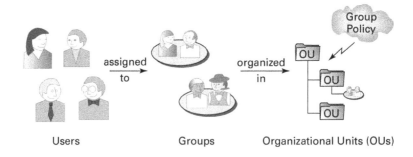

Users   Groups   Organizational Units (OUs)

The primary tool you use to manage security permissions for users, groups, and computers is the Active Directory Users and Computers tool. Using this tool, you can create and manage Active Directory objects and organize them based on your business needs. Common tasks for many system administrators might include the following:

- Resetting a user's password (for example, in cases where they forget their password)
- Creating new user accounts (when, for instance, a new employee joins the company)
- Modifying group memberships based on changes in job requirements and functions
- Disabling user accounts (when, for example, users will be out of the office for long periods of time and will not require network resource access)

Once you've properly grouped your users, you need to set the actual permissions that affect the objects within Active Directory. The actual permissions available vary based on the type of object. Table 7.1 provides an example of some of the permissions that you can apply to various Active Directory objects and an explanation of what each permission does.

TABLE 7.1 Permissions of Active Directory objects

Permission	Explanation
Control Access	Changes security permissions on the object
Create Child	Creates objects within an OU (such as other OUs)
Delete Child	Deletes child objects within an OU

Delete Tree	Deletes an OU and the objects within it
List Contents	Views objects within an OU
List Object	Views a list of the objects within an OU
Read	Views properties of an object (such as a username)
Write	Modifies properties of an object

Using ACLs and ACEs

Each object in Active Directory has an *access control list (ACL)*. The ACL is a list of user accounts and groups that are allowed to access the resource. For each ACL, there is an access control entry (ACE) that defines what a user or a group can actually do with the resource. Deny permissions are always listed first. This means that if users have Deny permissions through user or group membership, they will not be allowed to access the object, even if they have explicit Allow permissions through other user or group permissions. Figure 7.7 shows an ACL for the Sales OU.

FIGURE 7.7   The ACL for an OU named Sales

 The Security tab is enabled only if you selected the Advanced Features option from the View menu in the Active Directory Users and Computers tool.

Configuring User Account Control

One issue that many users have run into is as follows: When they log into their standard Windows user account and they need to make a change on their local machines or run a program that requires a higher level of security, they can't complete the task. This is where User Account Controls can help.

User Account Control (UAC) allows your domain users to log into their machines using their standard Windows user account and then execute processes that may require additional user group access.

Some applications may require additional security permissions to run successfully. These types of programs are normally referred to as *legacy applications*. Some applications, however, such as installing new software or making configuration changes, require more permissions than what is available to a standard user account. This is where UAC can help.

When an executable or program needs to function properly with more than just standard user rights, UAC can give that user's token additional user groups. This token allows the executable or program to function properly by giving the standard user account the rights to complete the task.

To configure the UAC, an administrator can go into the system's Control Panel and then User Accounts. Inside the User Accounts snap-in, choose Change User Account Control Settings.

Delegating Control of Users and Groups

A common administrative function related to the use of Active Directory involves managing users and groups. You can use OUs to group objects logically so that you can easily manage them. Once you have placed the appropriate Active Directory objects within OUs, you are ready to delegate control of these objects.

Delegation is the process by which a higher-level security administrator assigns permissions to other users. For example, if Admin A is a member of the Domain Admins group, they are able to delegate control of any OU within the domain to Admin B. You can access the Delegation Of Control Wizard through the Active Directory Users and Computers tool. You can use it to perform common delegation tasks quickly and easily. The wizard walks you through the steps of selecting the objects for which you want to perform delegation, what permission you want to allow, and which users will have those permissions.

Exercise 7.1 walks through the steps required to delegate control of OUs.

EXERCISE 7.1

Delegating Control of Active Directory Objects

1. Open the Active Directory Users and Computers tool.

2. Create a new user within the Engineering OU using the following information (use the default settings for any fields not specified):

First Name: **Robert**

Last Name: **Admin**

User Logon Name: **radmin**

Password: **P@ssw0rd**

3. Right-click the Sales OU and select Delegate Control. This starts the Delegation Of Control Wizard. Click Next.

4. To add users and groups to which you want to delegate control, click the Add button. In the Add dialog box, enter **Robert Admin** for the name of the user to add. Note that you can specify multiple users or groups using this option.

5. Click OK to add the account to the delegation list, which is shown in the Users Or Groups page. Click Next to continue.

6. On the Tasks To Delegate page, you must specify which actions you want to allow the selected user to perform within this OU. Select the Delegate The Following Common Tasks option and place a check mark next to the following options:

    Create, Delete, And Manage User Accounts

    Reset User Passwords And Force Password Change At Next Logon

    Read All User Information

    Create, Delete And Manage Groups

    Modify The Membership Of A Group

7. Click Next to continue. The wizard provides you with a summary of the selections that you have made on the Completing The Delegation Of Control Wizard page. To complete the process, click Finish to have the wizard commit the changes.

    Now when the user Robert Admin logs on (using *radmin* as his logon name), he will be able to perform common administrative functions for all the objects contained within the Sales OU.

8. When you have finished, close the Active Directory Users and Computers tool.

Understanding Dynamic Access Control

One of the advantages of Windows Server 2012 R2 is the ability to apply data governance to your file server. This will help control who has access to information and auditing. You get these advantages through the use of Dynamic Access Control (DAC). DAC allows you to identify data by using data classifications (both automatic and manual) and then to control access to these files based on these classifications.

DAC also gives administrators the ability to control file access by using a central access policy. This central access policy will also allow an administrator to set up audit access to files for reporting and forensic investigation.

DAC allows an administrator to set up Active Directory Rights Management Service (AD RMS) encryption for Microsoft Office documents. For example, you can set up encryption for any documents that contain financial information.

DAC gives an administrator the flexibility to configure file access and auditing to domain-based file servers. To do this, DAC controls claims in the authentication token, resource properties, and conditional expressions within permission and auditing entries.

Administrators have the ability to give users access to files and folders based on Active Directory attributes. For example, a user named Dana is given access to the file server share because in the user's Active Directory (department attribute) properties, the value contains the value Sales.

For DAC to function properly, an administrator must enable Windows 8 computers and Windows Server 2012/2012 R2 file servers to support claims and compound authentication.

Using Group Policy for Security

Through the use of Group Policy settings, system administrators can assign thousands of different settings and options for users, groups, and OUs. Specifically, in relation to security, you can use many different options to control how important features, such as password policies, user rights, and account lockout settings, can be configured.

The general process for making these settings is to create a Group Policy object (GPO) with the settings that you want and then link it to an OU or other Active Directory object.

Table 7.2 lists many Group Policy settings, which are relevant to creating a secure Active Directory environment. Note that this list is not comprehensive—many other options are available through Windows Server 2012 R2 administrative tools.

TABLE 7.2 Group Policy settings used for security purposes

Setting section	Setting name	Purpose
Account Policies ➢ Password Policy	Enforce Password History	Specifies how many passwords will be remembered. This option prevents users from reusing the same passwords whenever they're changed.
Account Policies ➢ Password Policy	Minimum Password Length	Prevents users from using short, weak passwords by specifying the minimum number of characters that the password must include.

Account Policies ➢ Account Lockout Policy	Account Lockout Threshold	Specifies how many bad password attempts can be entered before the account gets locked out.
Account Policies ➢ Account Lockout Policy	Account Lockout Duration	Specifies how long an account will remain locked out after too many bad password attempts have been entered. By setting this option to a reasonable value (such as 30 minutes), you can reduce administrative overhead while still maintaining fairly strong security.
Account Policies ➢ Account Lockout Policy	Reset Account Lockout Counter After	Specifies how long the Account Lockout Threshold counter will hold failed logon attempts before resetting to 0.
Local Policies ➢ Security Options	Accounts: Rename Administrator Account	Often, when trying to gain unauthorized access to a computer, individuals attempt to guess the administrator password. One method for increasing security is to rename this account so that no password allows entry using this logon.
Local Policies ➢ Security Options	Domain Controller: Allow Server Operators To Schedule Tasks	This option specifies whether members of the built-in Server Operators group are allowed to schedule tasks on the server.
Local Policies ➢ Security Options	Interactive Logon: Do Not Display Last User Name	Increases security by not displaying the name of the last user who logged onto the system.
Local Policies ➢ Security Options	Shutdown: Allow System To Be Shut Down Without Having To Log On	Allows system administrators to perform remote shutdown operations without logging on to the server.

Implementing an Audit Policy

One of the most important aspects of controlling security in networked environments is ensuring that only authorized users are able to access specific resources. Although system administrators often spend much time managing security permissions, it is almost always possible for a security problem to occur.

Sometimes, the best way to find possible security breaches is actually to record the actions that specific users take. Then, in the case of a security breach (the unauthorized shutdown of a server, for example), system administrators can examine the log to find the cause of the problem.

The Windows Server 2012 R2 operating system and Active Directory offer you the ability to audit a wide range of actions. In the following sections, you'll see how to implement auditing for Active Directory.

Overview of Auditing

The act of *auditing* relates to recording specific actions. From a security standpoint, auditing is used to detect any possible misuse of network resources. Although auditing does not necessarily prevent resources from being misused, it does help determine when security violations have occurred (or were attempted). Furthermore, just the fact that others know that you have implemented auditing may prevent them from attempting to circumvent security.

You need to complete several steps in order to implement auditing using Windows Server 2012 R2:

1. Configure the size and storage settings for the audit logs.

2. Enable categories of events to audit.

3. Specify which objects and actions should be recorded in the audit log.

Note that there are trade-offs to implementing auditing. First, recording auditing information can consume system resources. This can decrease overall system performance and use up valuable disk space. Second, auditing many events can make the audit log impractical to view. If too much detail is provided, system administrators are unlikely to scrutinize all of the recorded events. For these reasons, you should always be sure to find a balance between the level of auditing details provided and the performance-management implications of these settings.

Implementing Auditing

Auditing is not an all-or-none type of process. As is the case with security in general, system administrators must choose specifically which objects and actions they want to audit.

The main categories for auditing include the following:

- Audit account logon events
- Audit account management
- Audit directory service access
- Audit logon events
- Audit object access
- Audit policy change
- Audit privilege use
- Audit process tracking
- Audit system events

In this list of categories, four of the categories are related to Active Directory. Let's discuss these auditing categories in a bit more detail.

Audit Account Logon Events You enable this auditing event if you want to audit when a user authenticates with a domain controller and logs onto the domain. This event is logged in the security log on the domain controller.

Audit Account Management This auditing event is used when you want to watch what changes are being made to Active Directory accounts. For example, when another administrator creates or deletes a user account, it would be an audited event.

Audit Directory Service Access This auditing event occurs whenever a user or administrator accesses Active Directory objects. Let's say that an administrator opens Active Directory and clicks a user account; even if nothing is changed on that account, an event is logged.

Audit Logon Events Account logon events are created for domain account activity. For example, you have a user who logs on to a server so that they can access files; the act of logging onto the server creates this audit event.

Audit Object Access Audit object access allows you to audit objects within your network such as folders, files, and printers. If you suspect someone is trying to hack into an object (for example, the finance folder), this is the type of auditing that you would use. You still would need to enable auditing on the actual object (for example, the finance folder).

Audit Policy Change Audit policy change allows you to audit changes to user rights assignment policies, audit policies, or trust policies. This auditing allows you to see whether anyone changes any of the other audit policies.

Audit Privilege Use Setting the audit privilege use allows an administrator to audit each instance of a user exercising a user right. For example, if a user changes the system time on a machine, this is a user right. Logging on locally is another common user right.

To audit access to objects stored within Active Directory, you must enable the Audit Directory Service Access option. Then you must specify which objects and actions should be tracked.

Exercise 7.2 walks through the steps you must take to implement auditing of Active Directory objects on domain controllers.

EXERCISE 7.2

Enabling Auditing of Active Directory Objects

1. Open the Local Security Policy tool (located in the Administrative Tools program group).

2. Expand Local Policies ➤ Audit Policy.

3. Double-click the setting for Audit Directory Service Access.

4. In the Audit Directory Service Access Properties dialog box, place check marks next to Success and Failure. Click OK to save the settings.

5. Close the Local Security Policy tool.

Using the *Auditpol.exe* Command

There may be a time when you need to look at your actual auditing policies set on a user or a system. This is where an administrator can use the `Auditpol.exe` command. *Auditpol* allows administrators the ability not only to view an audit policy but also to set, configure, modify, restore, and even remove an audit policy. Auditpol is a command-line utility, and there are multiple switches that can be used with Auditpol. The following is the syntax used with Auditpol; Table 7.3 describes some of the switches:

```
Auditpol command [<sub-command><options>]
```

Here's an example:

```
Auditpol /get /user:wpanek /category:"Detailed Tracking" /r
```

TABLE 7.3 Auditpol commands

Command	Description
/backup	Allows an administrator to save the audit policy to a file
/clear	Allows an administrator to clear an audit policy
/get	Gives administrators the ability to view the current audit policy
/list	Allows you to view selectable policy elements
/remove	Removes all per-user audit policy settings and disables all system audit policy settings
/restore	Allows an administrator to restore an audit policy from a file that was previously created by using `auditpol /backup`
/set	Gives an administrator the ability to set an audit policy
/?	Displays help

Features of Windows Server 2012 R2 Auditing

Microsoft continues to increase the level of detail in the security auditing logs. Microsoft has also simplified the deployment and management of auditing policies. The following list includes some of the features:

Global Object Access Auditing Administrators using Windows Server 2012 R2 and Windows 8 now have the ability to define computer-wide system access control lists (SACLs). Administrators can define SACLs for either the file system or the registry. After the specified SACL is defined, the SACL is then applied automatically to every object of that type. This can be helpful to administrators for verifying that all critical files, folders, and registry settings on a computer are protected. This is also helpful for identifying when an issue occurs with a system resource.

"Reason For Access" Reporting   When an administrator is performing auditing in Windows Server 2012 R2 and Windows 8, they can now see the reason why an operation was successful or unsuccessful. Previously, they lacked the ability to see the reason why an operation succeeded or failed.

Advanced Audit Policy Settings   In Windows Server 2012 R2, there are many new Advanced Audit Policy settings that can be used in place of the nine basic auditing settings. These advanced audit settings also help eliminate the unnecessary auditing activities that can make audit logs difficult to manage and decipher.

Expression-Based Audit Policies   Administrators have the ability, because of Dynamic Access Control, to create targeted audit policies by using expressions based on user, computer, and resource claims. For example, an administrator has the ability to create an audit policy that tracks all Read and Write operations for files that are considered high-business impact. Expression-based audit policies can be directly created on a file or folder or created through the use of a Group Policy.

Removable Storage Device Auditing   Administrators have the ability to monitor attempts to use a removable storage device on your network. If an administrator decides to implement this policy, an audit event is created every time one of your users attempts to copy, move, or save a network resource onto a removable storage device.

Configuring Windows Firewall Options

Another security aspect to look into is Windows Firewall. Before I can start talking about firewall options, you must first understand what a firewall does. A *firewall* is a software or hardware device that checks the information that is received from an outside (Internet) or external network and uses that information to determine whether the packet should be accepted or declined.

Depending on the firewall, you have the ability to check all potential remote users against Active Directory to verify that the remote user has an authorized domain account. This process is called *Active Directory account integration.*

Microsoft Windows Server 2012 R2 has a built-in firewall. The following are some of the configuration options included in the Windows Firewall Settings dialog box:

Domain Profile Tab   On the Domain Profile tab, you have the ability to turn the firewall on or off by using the Firewall State drop-down menu. When setting the Firewall State option on this tab, it's for turning the firewall on or off for the domain only. When turning the firewall on, you also have the ability to block inbound and outbound connections (see Figure 7.8). Administrators also have the ability to control the Windows Firewall behavior along with setting up logging.

FIGURE 7.8 Domain Profile tab of Windows Firewall Settings

Private Profile Tab On the Private Profile tab, you have the ability to turn the firewall on or off by using the Firewall State drop-down menu. When setting the Firewall State in this tab, it's for turning the firewall on or off for the Private Profile only. When turning the firewall on, you also have the ability to block inbound and outbound connections (see Figure 7.9). Administrators also have the ability to control the Windows Firewall Private Profile behavior along with setting up logging.

FIGURE 7.9 Private Profile tab of Windows Firewall Settings

Public Profile On the Public Profile tab, you have the ability to turn the firewall on or off by using the Firewall State drop-down menu. When setting the Firewall State in this tab, it's for turning the firewall on or off for the Public Profile only. When turning the firewall on, you also have the ability to block inbound and outbound connections (see Figure 7.10). Administrators also have the ability to control the Windows Firewall Public Profile behavior along with setting up logging.

FIGURE 7.10 Public Profile tab of Windows Firewall

IPsec Settings Tab The IPsec Setting tab allows you to set up the IPsec defaults, IPsec exemptions, and IPsec tunnel authorization. The IPsec defaults button allows you to specify settings used by IPsec to establish secured connections. The IPsec exemptions allow you to set up ICMP exemptions from IPsec. Finally, you can set up IPsec tunnel authorization, which allows you to specify the users and computers that are authorized to establish an IPsec tunnel (see Figure 7.11).

Windows Server 2012 R2 takes firewalls a step further than just the normal firewall settings in Control Panel. An MMC snap-in called *Windows Firewall with Advanced Security* (see Figure 7.12) can block all incoming and outgoing connections based on its configuration.

One of the major advantages to using the Windows Firewall with Advanced Security snap-in is the ability to set firewall configurations on remote computers using group policies. Another advantage to using this MMC is the ability to set up firewalls using IPsec security. Windows Firewall with Advanced Security snap-in allows an administrator to set more in-depth rules for Microsoft Active Directory users and groups, source and destination Internet Protocol (IP) addresses, IP port numbers, ICMP settings, IPsec settings, specific types of interfaces, and services.

FIGURE 7.11   IPsec Settings tab of Windows Firewall Settings

FIGURE 7.12   Windows Firewall with Advanced Security snap-in

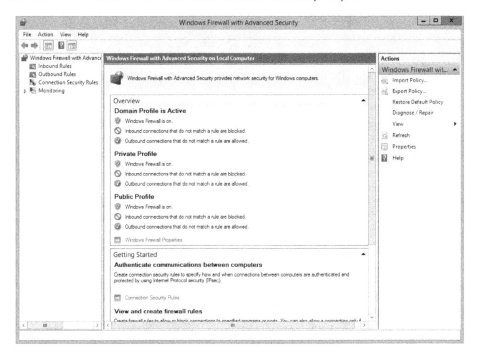

You can configure more advanced settings by configuring Windows Firewall with Advanced Security. To access Windows Firewall with Advanced Security, press the Windows key and choose Control Panel ➢ Large Icons View ➢ Windows Firewall, and click the Advanced Settings link.

The scope pane to the left shows that you can set up specific inbound and outbound rules, connection security rules, and monitoring rules. The central area shows an overview of the firewall's status as well as the current profile settings. Let's take a look at these in more detail.

Inbound and Outbound Rules

Inbound and outbound rules consist of many preconfigured rules that can be enabled or disabled. Obviously, inbound rules (see Figure 7.13) monitor inbound traffic, and outbound rules monitor outbound traffic. By default, many are disabled. Double-clicking a rule will bring up its Properties dialog box, as shown in Figure 7.14.

You can filter the rules to make them easier to view. Filtering can be performed based on the profile the rule affects or whether the rule is enabled or disabled or based on the rule group.

If you can't find a rule that is appropriate to your needs, you can create a new rule by right-clicking Inbound Rules or Outbound Rules in the scope pane and then selecting New Rule. The New Inbound (or Outbound) Rule Wizard will launch, and you will be asked whether you want to create a rule based on a particular program, protocol or port, predefined category, or custom settings.

FIGURE 7.13   Inbound rules

FIGURE 7.14 An inbound rule's Properties dialog box for WSUS

When setting up rules, you can also set up firewall exceptions. These exceptions allow you to work around a particular rule that you may be setting up. Firewall exceptions can be handy when an authenticated user or service needs to get around a firewall setting. These exceptions can be also set under the advanced firewall settings under the Connection Security Rules link.

Exercise 7.3 will walk you through the steps needed to create a new inbound rule that will allow only encrypted TCP traffic. In this exercise, you will have the ability to create a custom rule and then specify which authorized users and computers can connect using this rule.

EXERCISE 7.3

Configuring Windows Firewall

1. Press the Windows key and select Control Panel ➢ Large Icon View ➢ Windows Firewall.

2. Click Advanced Settings on the left side.

3. Right-click Inbound Rules and select New Rule.

4. Choose a rule type. For this exercise, choose Custom so that you can see all of the options available to you; then click Next.

5. Choose the programs or services that are affected by this rule. For this exercise, choose All Programs; then click Next.

6. Choose the protocol type as well as the local and remote port numbers that are affected by this rule. For this exercise, choose TCP and make sure All Ports is selected for both Local Port and Remote Port. Click Next to continue.

7. Choose the local and remote IP addresses that are affected by this rule. Choose Any IP Address for both local and remote; then click Next.

8. Specify whether this rule will allow the connection, allow the connection only if it is secure, or block the connection. Select the option Allow The Connection If It Is Secure; then click Next.

9. Specify whether connections should be allowed only from certain users. You can experiment with these options if you want. Then click Next to continue.

10. Specify whether connections should be allowed only from certain computers. Again, you can experiment with these options if you want. Then click Next to continue.

11. Choose those profiles that will be affected by this rule. Select one or more profiles; then click Next to continue.

12. Give your profile a name and description; then click Finish. Your custom rule will appear in the list of Inbound Rules, and the rule will be enabled.

13. Double-click your newly created rule. Notice that you can change the options you previously configured.

14. Disable the rule by right-clicking the rule and choosing Disable Rule.

15. Close Windows Firewall.

Now let's take a look at setting up Connection Security Rules through Windows Firewall with Advanced Security.

Configuring Windows Firewall with a GPO

If you wanted to configure Windows Firewall on all of your client machines, you have two options. You can either configure each machine manually or set up a GPO to configure the Windows Firewall. To set up the Windows Firewall using a GPO, configure the Computer section ➢ Windows Settings ➢ Security ➢ Windows Firewall With Advanced Security.

One of the advantages of using a GPO when configuring the Windows firewall is that you can configure multiple profiles and multiple firewall settings using the Group Policy.

Another even bigger advantage is being able to configure thousands of computers by setting just one GPO. It saves an IT administrator from going around the company from machine to machine to set up the firewall.

Import/Export Policies

One advantage of configuring Windows Firewall is the ability to export and import policy settings. For example, I set up a policy for 35 machines; I created the policy on one of the 35 machines and then exported the policy. I then imported the policy to the other

34 machines so that I did not have to re-create the policy over and over again. To export a policy, right-click Windows Firewall With Advanced Security and choose Export Policy. Choose Import Policy on the other machines to import the policy.

IPsec Policy Settings in Windows Firewall

When configuring options for Windows Firewall with Advanced Security, you have the ability to configure some IPsec policies. The three options are as follows:

IPsec Defaults   Specify settings used by IPsec to establish secure connections.

IPsec Exemptions   Exempting ICMP from all IPsec requirements can simplify troubleshooting of network connectivity issues.

IPsec Tunnel Authorization   Specify the computers or users authorized to establish IPsec tunnel connections to this computer.

Monitoring

The Monitoring section shows detailed information about the firewall configurations for the Domain Profile, Private Profile, and Public Profile settings. These network location profiles determine which settings are enforced for private networks, public networks, and networks connected to a domain.

 Real World Scenario

Firewalls

When I'm consulting, it always makes me laugh when I see small to midsize companies using Microsoft Windows Firewall and no other protection.

Microsoft Windows Firewall should be your *last* line of defense, not your only one. You need to make sure that you have good hardware firewalls that separate your network from the world.

Also watch Windows Firewall when it comes to printing. I have run into many situations where a printer that needs to talk to the operating system has issues when Windows Firewall is enabled. If this happens, make sure that the printer is allowed in the Allowed Programs section.

Summary

In this chapter, you examined server security and saw why it's one of the most important aspects of Windows Server 2012 R2. As a system administrator, Windows security is something that every administrator should be using but many don't know how it works properly.

I explained how to set up groups and group security as well as how to set up the permissions for those groups. I also covered auditing. I showed you how to set up and monitor auditing to see who has successfully, or unsuccessfully, accessed resources, machines, Active Directory, and all aspects of network security.

I finished the chapter by looking into Windows Firewall. I showed you how to configure the firewall and add exclusions and rules. I also showed you how to view and monitor the firewall results.

Exam Essentials

Understand group types and group scope.   The two major types of groups are security and distribution groups, and they have different purposes. Groups can be local, global, or universal. Domain local groups are used to assign permissions to local resources, such as files and printers. The scope of global groups is limited to a single domain. Universal groups can contain users from any domains within an Active Directory forest.

Understand the purpose and permissions of built-in groups.   The Active Directory environment includes several built-in local and global groups that are designed to simplify common system administration tasks. For instance, members of the Administrators group are given full permissions to perform any functions within the Active Directory domain and on the local computer.

Understand how to use Group Policy to manage security-related policies.   Through the use of Group Policy settings, you can configure password and account-related options. You can also specify to which users, groups, and OUs many of the settings apply.

Understand how to use auditing.   Through the use of auditing, an administrator can see who has been successfully and unsuccessfully accessing resources and Active Directory.

Understand Windows Firewall.   Windows Server 2012 R2 includes Windows Firewall. Windows Firewall gives you secure access to a machine by allowing or denying which applications or users can access a system.

Review Questions

1. You are the network administrator for your organization. A new company policy has been released wherein if a user enters their password incorrectly three times within five minutes, they are locked out for 30 minutes. What three actions do you need to set to comply with this policy? (Choose all that apply.)

   A. Set Account Lockout Duration to five minutes.

   B. Set Account Lockout Duration to 30 minutes.

   C. Set the Account Lockout Threshold setting to three invalid logon attempts.

   D. Set the Account Lockout Threshold setting to 30 minutes.

   E. Set the Reset Account Lockout Counter setting to five minutes.

   F. Set the Reset Account Lockout Counter setting to three times.

2. You create a GPO and link it to the Sales OU. You want to monitor users in the Sales OU who connect to the file server. What type of auditing do you enable?

   A. Audit Object Access

   B. Audit Logon Events

   C. Audit System Events

   D. Audit Process Tracking

3. Alexis is a system administrator for an Active Directory environment that contains four domains. Recently, several managers have reported suspicions about user activities and have asked her to increase security in the environment. Specifically, the requirements are as follows:

   - Audit changes to User objects that are contained within a specific OU.

   - Allow a special user account called Audit to view and modify all security-related information about objects in that OU.

   Which of the following steps should Alexis take to meet these requirements? (Choose all that apply.)

   A. Convert all volumes on which Active Directory information resides to NTFS.

   B. Enable auditing with the Active Directory Users and Computers tool.

   C. Create a new Active Directory domain and create restrictive permissions for the suspected users within this domain.

   D. Reconfigure trust settings using the Active Directory Domains and Trusts tool.

   E. Specify auditing options for the OU using the Active Directory Users and Computers tool.

   F. Use the Delegation of Control Wizard to grant appropriate permissions to view and modify objects within the OU to the Audit user account.

4. Crystal is a system administrator for an Active Directory environment that is running in Native mode. Recently, several managers have reported suspicions about user activities and have asked her to increase security in the environment. Specifically, the requirements are as follows:

- The accessing of certain sensitive files must be logged.

- Modifications to certain sensitive files must be logged.

- System administrators must be able to provide information about which users accessed sensitive files and when they were accessed.

- All logon attempts for specific shared machines must be recorded.

Which of the following steps should Crystal take to meet these requirements? (Choose all that apply.)

A. Enable auditing with the Computer Management tool.

B. Enable auditing with the Active Directory Users and Computers tool.

C. Enable auditing with the Active Directory Domains and Trusts tool.

D. Enable auditing with the Event Viewer tool.

E. View the audit log using the Event Viewer tool.

F. View auditing information using the Computer Management tool.

G. Enable failure and success auditing settings for specific files stored on NTFS volumes.

H. Enable failure and success auditing settings for logon events on specific computer accounts.

5. You create a GPO and link it to the Sales OU. You want to monitor users in the Sales OU who connect to the file server. What type of auditing do you enable?

A. Audit Object Access

B. Audit Logon Events

C. Audit System Events

D. Audit Process Tracking

Chapter

8

Configure TCP/IP

THE FOLLOWING 70-410 EXAM OBJECTIVES ARE COVERED IN THIS CHAPTER:

✓ **Configure IPv4 and IPv6 addressing**

- ▪ Configure IP address options
- ▪ Configure IPv4 or IPv6 subnetting
- ▪ Configure supernetting
- ▪ Configure interoperability between IPv4 and IPv6
- ▪ Configure ISATAP
- ▪ Configure Teredo

In this chapter, I will discuss the most important protocol used in a Microsoft Windows Server 2012 R2 network: *Transmission Control Protocol/Internet Protocol (TCP/IP)*.

TCP/IP is actually two sets of protocols bundled together: the Transmission Control Protocol (TCP) and the Internet Protocol (IP). TCP/IP is a suite of protocols developed by the U.S. Department of Defense's Advanced Research Projects Agency in 1969.

This chapter is divided into two main topics: First I'll talk about TCP/IP version 4, and then I'll discuss TCP/IP version 6. TCP/IP version 4 is still used in Windows Server 2012 R2, and it was the primary version of TCP/IP in all previous versions of Windows. However, TCP/IP version 6 is the new release of TCP/IP, and it has been incorporated into Windows Server 2012 R2.

Understanding TCP/IP

I mentioned that TCP/IP is actually two sets of protocols bundled together: TCP and IP. These protocols sit on a four-layer TCP/IP model.

Details of the TCP/IP Model

The four layers of the TCP/IP model are as follows (see Figure 8.1):

Application Layer The *Application layer* is where the applications that use the protocol stack reside. These applications include File Transfer Protocol (FTP), Trivial File Transfer Protocol (TFTP), Simple Mail Transfer Protocol (SMTP), and Hypertext Transfer Protocol (HTTP).

Transport Layer The *Transport layer* is where the two Transport layer protocols reside. These are TCP and the User Datagram Protocol (UDP). TCP is a connection-oriented protocol, and delivery is guaranteed. UDP is a connectionless protocol. This means that UDP does its best job to deliver the message, but there is no guarantee.

Internet Layer The *Internet layer* is where IP resides. *IP* is a connectionless protocol that relies on the upper layer (Transport layer) for guaranteeing delivery. *Address Resolution Protocol (ARP)* also resides on this layer. ARP turns an IP address into a Media Access Control (MAC) address. All upper and lower layers travel through the IP protocol.

Link Layer The data link protocols like Ethernet and Token Ring reside in the *Link layer*. This layer is also referred to as the *Network Access layer*.

FIGURE 8.1   TCP/IP model

How TCP/IP Layers Communicate

When an application like FTP is called upon, the application moves down the layers and TCP is retrieved. TCP then connects itself to the IP protocol and gets released onto the network through the Link layer (see Figure 8.2). This is a connection-oriented protocol because TCP is the protocol that guarantees delivery.

When an application like TFTP gets called, the application moves down the layers and UDP is retrieved. UDP then connects itself to the IP protocol and gets released onto the network through the Link layer. This is a connectionless protocol because UDP does not have guaranteed delivery.

Understanding Port Numbers

TCP and UDP rely on port numbers assigned by the *Internet Assigned Numbers Authority (IANA)* to forward packets to the appropriate application process. Port numbers are 16-bit integers that are part of a message header. They identify the application software process with which the packet should be associated. For example, let's say that a client has a copy of Internet Explorer and a copy of Mail open at the same time. Both applications are sending TCP requests across the Internet to retrieve web pages and email, respectively. How does the computer know which return packets to forward to Internet Explorer and which packets to forward to Mail?

FIGURE 8.2 TCP/IP process

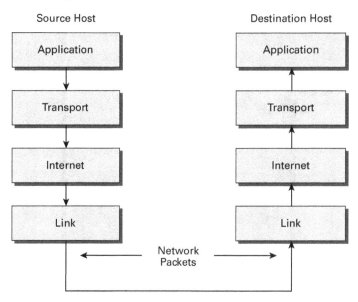

When making a connection, the client chooses a source port for the communication that is usually in the range 1024–65535 (or sometimes in the range 1–65535). This source port then communicates with a destination port of 80 or 110 on the server side. Every packet destined for Internet Explorer has a source port number of 80 in the header, and every packet destined for Mail has a source port number of 110 in the header.

Table 8.1 describes the most common port numbers (you might need to know these for the exam). You can visit www.iana.org to get the most current and complete list of port numbers. It's good to become familiar with specific port numbers because it's a benefit to be able to determine from memory the ports that, for example, allow or block specific protocols in a firewall. Allowing only port 80, for instance, does not ensure that all web traffic will be allowed. You must also allow port 443 for certain secure web traffic.

Simply because a port is "well known" doesn't mean that a given service must run on it. It's technically valid to run any service on any port, but doing so is usually a bad idea. For example, if you chose to run your web server on TCP port 25, clients would need to type www.example.com:25 to reach your website from most browsers.

TABLE 8.1 Common port numbers

Port number	Description
20	FTP data
21	FTP control
23	Telnet
25	Simple Mail Transfer Protocol (SMTP)
53	Domain Name System (DNS)
80	Hypertext Transfer Protocol (HTTP), Web
88	Kerberos
110	Post Office Protocol v3 (POP3)
443	Secure HTTP (HTTPS)

Understanding IP Addressing

Understanding IP addressing is critical to understanding how IP works. An IP address is a numeric identifier assigned to each device on an IP network. This type of address is a logical software address that designates the device's location on the network. It isn't the physical hardware address hard-coded in the device's network interface card.

In the following sections, you will see how IP addresses are used to identify uniquely every machine on the network (MAC address).

The Hierarchical IP Addressing Scheme

An IP address consists of 32 bits of information. These bits are divided into four sections (sometimes called *octets* or *quads*) containing 1 byte (8 bits) each. There are three common methods for specifying an IP address:

- Dotted-decimal, as in 130.57.30.56
- Binary, as in 10000010.00111001.00011110.00111000
- Hexadecimal, as in 82 39 1E 38

All of these examples represent the same IP address.

The 32-bit IP address is a structured, or hierarchical, address as opposed to a flat, or nonhierarchical, address. Although IP could have used either *flat addressing* or *hierarchical addressing*, its designers elected to use the latter for a very good reason, as you will now see.

 Real World Scenario

Why Hierarchical Addressing Is Used

What's the difference between flat and hierarchical addressing? A good example of a flat addressing scheme is a U.S. state driver's license number. There's no partitioning to it; the range of legal numbers isn't broken up in any meaningful way (say, by county of residence or date of issue). If this method had been used for IP addressing, every machine on the Internet would have needed a totally unique address, just as each driver's license number in a particular state is unique.

The good news about flat addressing is that it can handle a large number of addresses in 32 bits of data, namely, 4.3 billion. A 32-bit address space with two possible values for each position—either 0 (zero) or 1 (one)—gives you 2^{32} values, which equals approximately 4.3 billion.

The bad news—and the reason flat addressing isn't used in IP—relates to routing. If every address were totally unique, every router on the Internet would need to store the address of every other machine on the Internet. It would be fair to say that this would make efficient routing impossible, even if only a fraction of the possible addresses were used.

The solution to this dilemma is to use a hierarchical addressing scheme that breaks the address space into ordered chunks. Telephone numbers are a great example of this type of addressing. The first section of a U.S. telephone number, the area code, designates a very large area. The area code is followed by the prefix, which narrows the scope to a local calling area. The final segment, the customer number, zooms in on the specific connection. By looking at a number such as 603-766-xxxx, you can quickly determine that the number is located in the southern part of New Hampshire (area code 603) in the Portsmouth area (the 766 exchange).

IP Address Structure

IP addressing works the same way. Instead of the entire 32 bits being treated as a unique identifier, one part of the IP address is designated as the network address (or network ID) and the other part as a node address (or host ID), giving it a layered, hierarchical structure. Together, the IP address, the network address, and the node address uniquely identify a device within an IP network.

The network address—the first two sets of numbers in an IP address—uniquely identifies each network. Every machine on the same network shares that network address as part of its IP address, just as the address of every house on a street shares the same street name. In the IP address 130.57.30.56, for example, 130.57 is the network address.

The node address—the second two sets of numbers—is assigned to, and uniquely identifies, each machine in a network, just as each house on the same street has a different house number. This part of the address must be unique because it identifies a particular machine—an individual, as opposed to a network. This number can also be referred to as a *host address*. In the sample IP address 130.57.30.56, the node address is .30.56.

Understanding Network Classes

The designers of the Internet decided to create classes of networks based on network size. For the small number of networks possessing a very large number of nodes, they created the Class A network. At the other extreme is the Class C network, reserved for the numerous networks with small numbers of nodes. The class of networks in between the very large and very small ones is predictably called the Class B network.

The default subdivision of an IP address into a network and node address is determined by the class designation of your network. Table 8.2 summarizes the three classes of networks, which will be described in more detail in the following sections.

TABLE 8.2 Network address classes

Class	Mask bits	Leading bit pattern	Decimal range of first octet of IP address	Assignable networks	Maximum nodes per network
A	8	0	1–126	126	16,777,214
B	16	10	128–191	16,384	65,534
C	24	110	192–223	2,097,152	254

Classless Inter-Domain Routing (CIDR), explained in detail later in this chapter, has effectively done away with these class designations. You will still hear and should still know the meaning behind the class designations of addresses because they are important to understanding IP addressing. However, when you're working with IP addressing in practice, CIDR is more important to know.

To ensure efficient routing, Internet designers defined a mandate for the leading bits section of the address for each different network class. For example, because a router knows that a Class A network address always starts with a 0, it can quickly apply the default mask, if necessary, after reading only the first bit of the address. Table 8.2 illustrates how the leading bits of a network address are defined. When considering the subnet masking between network and host addresses, the number of bits to mask is important. For example, in a Class A network, 8 bits are masked, making the default subnet mask 255.0.0.0; in a Class C, 24 bits are masked, making the default subnet mask 255.255.255.0.

Some IP addresses are reserved for special purposes and shouldn't be assigned to nodes. Table 8.3 describes some of the reserved IP addresses. See RFC 3330 for others.

TABLE 8.3   Special network addresses

Address	Function
Entire IP address set to all 0s	Depending on the mask, this network (that is, the network or subnet of which you are currently a part) or this host on this network.
A routing table entry of all 0s with a mask of all 0s	Used as the default gateway entry. Any destination address masked by all 0s produces a match for the all 0s reference address. Because the mask has no 1s, this is the least desirable entry, but it will be used when no other match exists.
Network address 127	Reserved for loopback tests. Designates the local node, and it allows that node to send a test packet to itself without generating network traffic.
Node address of all 0s	Used when referencing a network without referring to any specific nodes on that network. Usually used in routing tables.
Node address of all 1s	Broadcast address for all nodes on the specified network, also known as a *directed broadcast*. For example, 128.2.255.255 means all nodes on the Class B network 128.2. Routing this broadcast is configurable on certain routers.
169.254.0.0 with a mask of 255.255.0.0	The "link-local" block used for autoconfiguration and communication between devices on a single link. Communication cannot occur across routers. Microsoft uses this block for Automatic Private IP Addressing (APIPA).
Entire IP address set to all 1s (same as 255.255.255.255) 10.0.0.0/8 172.16.0.0 to 172.31.255.255	Broadcast to all nodes on the current network; sometimes called a *limited broadcast* or an *all-1s broadcast*. This broadcast is not routable.
192.168.0.0/16	The private-use blocks for Classes A, B, and C. As noted in RFC 1918, the addresses in these blocks must never be allowed into the Internet, making them acceptable for simultaneous use behind NAT servers and non-Internet-connected IP networks.

In the following sections, you will look at the three network types.

Class A Networks

In a Class A network, the first byte is the network address, and the three remaining bytes are used for the node addresses. The Class A format is Network.Node.Node.Node.

For example, in the IP address 49.22.102.70, 49 is the network address, and 22.102.70 is the node address. Every machine on this particular network would have the distinctive network address of 49. Within that network, however, you could have a large number of machines.

There are 126 possible Class A network addresses. Why? The length of a Class A network address is 1 byte, and the first bit of that byte is reserved, so 7 bits in the first byte remain available for manipulation. This means that the maximum number of Class A networks is 128. (Each of the 7 bit positions that can be manipulated can be either a 0 or a 1, and this gives you a total of 2^7 positions, or 128.) But to complicate things further, it was also decided that the network address of all 0s (0000 0000) would be reserved. This means that the actual number of usable Class A network addresses is 128 minus 1, or 127. Also, 127 is a reserved number (a network address of 0 followed by all 1s [0111 1111], so you actually start with 128 addresses minus the 2 reserved, and you're left with 126 possible Class A network addresses.

Each Class A network has 3 bytes (24 bit positions) for the node address of a machine, which means that there are 2^{24}, or 16,777,216, unique combinations. Because addresses with the two patterns of all 0s and all 1s in the node bits are reserved, the actual maximum usable number of nodes for a Class A network is 2^{24} minus 2, which equals 16,777,214.

Class B Networks

In a Class B network, the first 2 bytes are assigned to the network address, and the remaining 2 bytes are used for node addresses. The format is Network.Network.Node.Node.

For example, in the IP address 130.57.30.56, the network address is 130.57, and the node address is 30.56.

The network address is 2 bytes, so there would be 2^{16} unique combinations. But the Internet designers decided that all Class B networks should start with the binary digits 10. This leaves 14 bit positions to manipulate; therefore, there are 16,384 (or 2^{14}) unique Class B networks.

This gives you an easy way to recognize Class B addresses. If the first 2 bits of the first byte can be only 10, that gives you a decimal range from 128 up to 191 in the first octet of the IP address. Remember that you can always easily recognize a Class B network by looking at its first byte, even though there are 16,384 different Class B networks. If the first octet in the address falls between 128 and 191, it is a Class B network, regardless of the value of the second octet.

A Class B network has 2 bytes to use for node addresses. This is 2^{16} minus the two patterns in the reserved-exclusive club (all 0s and all 1s in the node bits) for a total of 65,534 possible node addresses for each Class B network.

Class C Networks

The first 3 bytes of a Class C network are dedicated to the network portion of the address, with only 1 byte remaining for the node address. The format is Network.Network.Network.Node.

In the example IP address 198.21.74.102, the network address is 198.21.74, and the node address is 102.

In a Class C network, the first three bit positions are always binary 110. Three bytes, or 24 bits, minus 3 reserved positions leaves 21 positions. There are therefore 2^{21} (or 2,097,152) possible Class C networks.

The lead bit pattern of 110 equates to decimal 192 and runs through 223. Remembering our handy easy-recognition method, this means you can always spot a Class C address if the first byte is in the range 192–223, regardless of the values of the second and third bytes of the IP address.

Each unique Class C network has 1 byte to use for node addresses. This leads to 2^8, or 256, minus the two special patterns of all 0s and all 1s, for a total of 254 node addresses for each Class C network.

Class D networks, used for multicasting only, use the address range 224.0.0.0 to 239.255.255.255 and are used, as in broadcasting, as destination addresses only. Class E networks (reserved for future use at this point) cover 240.0.0.0 to 255.255.255.255. Addresses in the Class E range are considered within the experimental range.

Subnetting a Network

If an organization is large and has lots of computers or if its computers are geographically dispersed, it makes good sense to divide its colossal network into smaller ones connected by routers. These smaller networks are called *subnets*. The benefits of using subnets are as follows:

Reduced Network Traffic   We all appreciate less traffic of any kind, and so do networks. Without routers, packet traffic could choke the entire network. Most traffic will stay on the local network—only packets destined for other networks will pass through the router and to another subnet. This traffic reduction also improves overall performance.

Simplified Management   It's easier to identify and isolate network problems in a group of smaller networks connected together than within one gigantic one.

Understanding the Benefits of Subnetting

To understand one benefit of subnetting, consider a hotel or office building. Say that a hotel has 1,000 rooms with 75 rooms to a floor. You could start at the first room on the first floor and number it 1; then when you get to the first room on the second floor, you could number it 76 and keep going until you reach room 1,000. But someone looking for room 521 would have to guess on which floor that room is located. If you were to "subnet" the hotel, you would identify the first room on the first floor with the number 101 (1 = Floor 1 and 01 = Room 1), the first room on the second floor with 201, and so on. The guest looking for room 521 would go to the fifth floor and look for room 21.

An organization with a single network address (comparable to the hotel building mentioned in the sidebar "Understanding the Benefits of Subnetting") can have a subnet address for each individual physical network (comparable to a floor in the hotel building). Each subnet is still part of the shared network address, but it also has an additional identifier denoting its individual subnetwork number. This identifier is called a *subnet address*.

Subnetting solves several addressing problems:

- If an organization has several physical networks but only one IP network address, it can handle the situation by creating subnets.

- Because subnetting allows many physical networks to be grouped together, fewer entries in a routing table are required, notably reducing network overhead.

- These things combine collectively to yield greatly enhanced network efficiency.

The original designers of the Internet Protocol envisioned a small Internet with only tens of networks and hundreds of hosts. Their addressing scheme used a network address for each physical network. As you can imagine, this scheme and the unforeseen growth of the Internet created a few problems. The following are two examples:

Not Enough Addresses   A single network address can be used to refer to multiple physical networks, but an organization can request individual network addresses for each one of its physical networks. If all of these requests were granted, there wouldn't be enough addresses to go around.

Gigantic Routing Tables   If each router on the Internet needed to know about every physical network, routing tables would be impossibly huge. There would be an overwhelming amount of administrative overhead to maintain those tables, and the resulting physical overhead on the routers would be massive (CPU cycles, memory, disk space, and so on). Because routers exchange routing information with each other, an additional, related consequence is that a terrific overabundance of network traffic would result.

Although there's more than one way to approach these problems, the principal solution is the one that I'll cover in this book—subnetting. As you might guess, *subnetting* is the process of carving a single IP network into smaller logical subnetworks. This trick is achieved by subdividing the host portion of an IP address to create a subnet address. The actual subdivision is accomplished through the use of a subnet mask (covered later in the chapter).

In the following sections, you will see exactly how to calculate and apply subnetting.

Implementing Subnetting

Before you can implement subnetting, you need to determine your current requirements and plan on how best to implement your subnet scheme.

How to Determine Your Subnetting Requirements

Follow these guidelines to calculate the requirements of your subnet:

1. Determine the number of required network IDs: one for each subnet and one for each wide area network (WAN) connection.

2. Determine the number of required host IDs per subnet: one for each TCP/IP device, including, for example, computers, network printers, and router interfaces.

3. Based on these two data points, create the following:

   - One subnet mask for your entire network

   - A unique subnet ID for each physical segment

   - A range of host IDs for each unique subnet

How to Implement Subnetting

Subnetting is implemented by assigning a subnet address to each machine on a given physical network. For example, in Figure 8.3, each machine on subnet 1 has a subnet address of 1.

The default network portion of an IP address can't be altered without encroaching on another administrative domain's address space, unless you are assigned multiple consecutive classful addresses. To maximize the efficient use of the assigned address space, machines on a particular network share the same network address. In Figure 8.3, you can see that all of the Widget Inc. machines have a network address of 130.57. That principle is constant. In subnetting, it's the host address that's manipulated—the network address doesn't change. The subnet address scheme takes a part of the host address and recycles it as a subnet address. Bit positions are stolen from the host address to be used for the subnet identifier. Figure 8.4 shows how an IP address can be given a subnet address.

FIGURE 8.3   A sample subnet

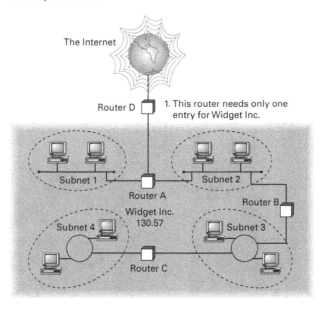

FIGURE 8.4   Network vs. host addresses

Because the Widget Inc. network is a Class B network, the first two bytes specify the network address and are shared by all machines on the network, regardless of their particular subnet. Here every machine's address on the subnet must have its third byte read 0000 0001. The fourth byte, the host address, is the unique number that identifies the actual host within that subnet. Figure 8.5 illustrates how a network address and a subnet address can be used together.

FIGURE 8.5 The network address and its subnet

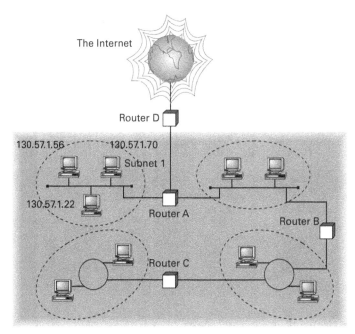

When implementing subnetting, you need some type of hardware installed onto the network. Most of us will just use a router. But if you do not want to purchase an expensive router, there is another way.

One way that you can implement subnetting is by using a Windows Server 2012 R2 machine with multiple NIC adapters configured with routing enabled on the server. This type of router is called a *multihomed router*. This is an inexpensive way to set up a router using a Microsoft server, but it may not be the best way. Many companies specialize in routers, and these routers offer many more features and more flexibility than a multihomed router.

How to Use Subnet Masks

For the subnet address scheme to work, every machine on the network must know which part of the host address will be used as the network address. This is accomplished by assigning each machine a subnet mask.

The network administrator creates a 32-bit subnet mask comprising 1s and 0s. The 1s in the subnet mask represent the positions in the IP address that refer to the network and subnet addresses. The 0s represent the positions that refer to the host part of the address. Figure 8.6 illustrates this combination.

In the Widget Inc. example, the first two bytes of the subnet mask are 1s because Widget's network address is a Class B address, formatted as Network.Network.Node.Node. The third byte, normally assigned as part of the host address, is now used to represent the subnet address. Hence, those bit positions are represented with 1s in the subnet mask. The fourth byte is the only part of the example that represents the host address.

FIGURE 8.6 The subnet mask revealed

Subnet mask code

1s = Positions representing network or subnet addresses
0s = Positions representing the host address

Subnet mask for Widget, Inc.

1111 1111. 1111 1111. 1111 1111. 0000 0000

Network address   Subnet   Host
positions   positions   positions

The subnet mask can also be expressed using the decimal equivalents of the binary patterns. The binary pattern of 1111 1111 is the same as decimal 255. Consequently, the subnet mask in the example can be denoted in two ways, as shown in Figure 8.7.

FIGURE 8.7 Different ways to represent the same mask

Subnet mask in binary: 1111 1111. 1111 1111. 1111 1111. 0000 0000

Subnet mask in decimal: 255   .   255   .   255   .   0

(The spaces in the above example are only for illustrative purposes.
The subnet mask in decimal would actually appear as 255.255.255.0.)

Not all networks need to have subnets, and therefore they don't need to use custom subnet masks. In this case, they are said to have a *default* subnet mask. This is basically the same as saying that they don't have any subnets except for the one main subnet on which the network is running. Table 8.4 shows the default subnet masks for the different classes of networks.

TABLE 8.4 Default subnet masks

Class	Format	Default Subnet Mask
A	Network.Node.Node.Node	255.0.0.0
B	Network.Network.Node.Node	255.255.0.0
C	Network.Network.Network.Node	255.255.255.0

Once the network administrator has created the subnet mask and has assigned it to each machine, the IP software applies the subnet mask to the IP address to determine its subnet address. The word *mask* carries the implied meaning of "lens" in this case; that is, the IP software looks at its IP address through the lens of its subnet mask to see its subnet address. Figure 8.8 illustrates an IP address being viewed through a subnet mask.

FIGURE 8.8 Applying the subnet mask

In this example, the IP software learns through the subnet mask that, instead of being part of the host address, the third byte of its IP address is now going to be used as a subnet address. The IP software then looks in its IP address at the bit positions that correspond to the mask, which are 0000 0001.

The final step is for the subnet bit values to be matched up with the binary numbering convention and converted to decimal. In the Widget Inc. example, the binary-to-decimal conversion is simple, as illustrated in Figure 8.9.

FIGURE 8.9 Converting the subnet mask to decimal

Binary numbering convention	
Position/value: ←——(continued)	128 64 32 16 8 4 2 1
Widget third byte:	0 0 0 0 0 0 0 1
Decimal equivalent:	0 + 1 = 1
Subnet address:	1

By using the entire third byte of a Class B address as the subnet address, it is easy to set and determine the subnet address. For example, if Widget Inc. wants to have a subnet 6, the third byte of all machines on that subnet will be 0000 0110 (decimal 6 in binary).

Using the entire third byte of a Class B network address for the subnet allows for a fair number of available subnet addresses. One byte dedicated to the subnet provides eight bit positions. Each position can be either a 1 or a 0, so the calculation is 2^8, or 256. Thus, Widget Inc. can have up to 256 total subnetworks, each with up to 254 hosts.

Although RFC 950 prohibits the use of binary all 0s and all 1s as subnet addresses, today almost all products actually permit this usage. Microsoft's TCP/IP stack allows it, as does the software in most routers (provided you enable this feature, which sometimes is not the case by default). This gives you two additional subnets. However, you should not use a subnet of 0 (all 0s) unless all the software on your network recognizes this convention.

How to Calculate the Number of Subnets

The formulas for calculating the maximum number of subnets and the maximum number of hosts per subnet are as follows:

$2 \times$ number of masked bits in subnet mask = maximum number of subnets

$2 \times$ number of unmasked bits in subnet mask − 2 = maximum number of hosts per subnet

In the formulas, *masked* refers to bit positions of 1, and *unmasked* refers to bit positions of 0. The downside to using an entire byte of a node address as your subnet address is that you reduce the possible number of node addresses on each subnet. As explained earlier, without a subnet, a Class B address has 65,534 unique combinations of 1s and 0s that can be used for node addresses. The question then is why would you ever want 65,534 hosts on a single physical network?

The trade-off is acceptable to most who ask themselves this question. If you use an entire byte of the node address for a subnet, you then have only 1 byte for the host addresses, leaving only 254 possible host addresses. If any of your subnets are populated with more than 254 machines, you'll have a problem. To solve it, you would then need to shorten the subnet mask, thereby lengthening the number of host bits and increasing the number of host addresses. This gives you more available host addresses on each subnet. A side effect of this solution is that it shrinks the number of possible subnets.

Figure 8.10 shows an example of using a smaller subnet address. A company called Acme Inc. expects to need a maximum of 14 subnets. In this case, Acme does not need to take an entire byte from the host address for the subnet address. To get its 14 different subnet addresses, it needs to snatch only 4 bits from the host address (2^4 = 16). The host portion of the address has 12 usable bits remaining (2^{12} − 2 = 4094). Each of Acme's 16 subnets could then potentially have a total of 4,094 host addresses, and 4,094 machines on each subnet should be plenty.

FIGURE 8.10 An example of a smaller subnet address

Acme, Inc.

Network address: 132.8 (Class B; net.net.host.host)

Example IP address: 1000 0100. 0000 1000. 0001 0010. 0011 1100

Decimal: 132 . 8 . 18 . 60

Subnet Mask Code

1s = Positions representing network or subnet addresses
0s = Positions representing the host address

Subnet mask:
Binary: 1111 1111. 1111 1111. 1111 0000. 0000 0000
Decimal: 255 . 255 . 240 . 0
(The decimal 240 is equal to the binary 1111 0000.)

Positions relating to the subnet address

Subnet mask: 1111 1111. 1111 1111. 1111 0000. 0000 0000

IP address of a Acme machine: 1000 0100. 0000 1000. 0001 0010. 0011 1100
(Decimal: 132.8.18.60)

Bits relating to the subnet address

Binary-to-Decimal Conversions for Subnet Address

Subnet mask positions:	1	1	1	1	0	0	0	0
Position/value: ⟵(continue)	128	64	32	16	8	4	2	1
Third byte of IP address:	0	0	0	1	0	0	1	0
Decimal equivalent:				0 + 16 = 16				
Subnet address for this IP address:				16				

An Easier Way to Apply Subnetting

Now that you have the basics of how to subnet down, you'll learn an easier way. If you have learned a different way and it works for you, stick with it. It does not matter how you get to the finish line, just as long as you get there. But if you are new to subnetting, Figure 8.11 will make it easier for you.

This chart may look intimidating, but it's really simple to use once you have done it a few times.

Remember that, on this chart, 1s equal subnets, and 0s equal hosts. If you get this confused, you will get wrong answers in the following exercises.

FIGURE 8.11   TCP/IP v4 subnetting chart

$2^{(X)}-2=Y$	128	64	32	16	8	4	2	1
255	1	1	1	1	1	1	1	1
254	1	1	1	1	1	1	1	0
252	1	1	1	1	1	1	0	0
248	1	1	1	1	1	0	0	0
240	1	1	1	1	0	0	0	0
224	1	1	1	0	0	0	0	0
192	1	1	0	0	0	0	0	0
128	1	0	0	0	0	0	0	0
0	0	0	0	0	0	0	0	0

0 = Hosts, 1 = Subnets

X (POWER)			X		Y
2^X	3	=	8	−2	6
2^X	4	=	16	−2	14
2^X	5	=	32	−2	30
2^X	6	=	64	−2	62
2^X	7	=	128	−2	126
2^X	8	=	256	−2	254
2^X	9	=	512	−2	510
2^X	10	=	1024	−2	1022
2^X	11	=	2048	−2	2046
2^X	12	=	4096	−2	4094
2^X	13	=	8192	−2	8190
2^X	14	=	16384	−2	16382
2^X	15	=	32768	−2	32766
2^X	16	=	65536	−2	65534
2^X	17	=	131072	−2	131070

Watch the Y column on the lower end of the chart. This represents the number of addresses available to you after the two reserved addresses have been removed. The following exercises provide some examples.

SUBNET MASK EXERCISE 8.1

Class C, 10 Hosts per Subnet

You have a Class C address, and you require 10 hosts per subnet.

1. Write down the following:

   255.255.255.___

   The blank is the number you need to fill in.

2. Look under the Y column and choose the first number that is larger than 10 (the number of hosts per subnet you need). You should have come up with 14.

3. Move across the page and look at number in the X (Power) column. The power number is 4.

4. Go to the top of the chart and look for the row with exactly four 0s (hosts). Find the number at the beginning of the row.

The number at the beginning of the row is 240. That's your answer. The subnet mask should be 255.255.255.240.

SUBNET MASK EXERCISE 8.2

Class C, 20 Hosts per Subnet

You have a Class C address, and you need 20 hosts per subnet.

1. Write down the following:

   255.255.255.___

2. Look under the Y column and find the first number that covers 20. (This should be 30.)

3. Go across to the power number (5).

4. Go to the top part of the chart and find the row with exactly five 0s from right to left.

The number at the beginning of the row is 224. Your answer should be 255.255.255.224.

SUBNET MASK EXERCISE 8.3

Class C, Five Subnets

Now you have a Class C address, and you need five subnets. Remember that subnets are represented by 1s in the chart.

1. Write down the following:

   255.255.255.___

2. Look under the Y column and find the first number that covers 5. (This should be 6.)

3. Go across to the power number. (This should be 3.)

4. Go to the top part of the chart and find out which row has exactly three 1s (remember, 1s are for subnets) from left to right.

Your answer should be 255.255.255.224.

SUBNET MASK EXERCISE 8.4

Class B, 1,500 Hosts per Subnet

This one is a bit harder. You have a Class B address, and you need 1,500 hosts per subnet. Because you have a Class B address, you need to fill in the third octet of numbers. The fourth octet contains eight 0s.

1. Write down the following:

   255.255.___.0

2. Look at the Y column and find the first number that covers 1,500. (This should be 2,046.)

3. Go across and find the power number. (This should be 11.)

4. Remember, you already have eight 0s in the last octet. So, you need only three more. Find the row with three 0s.

You should come up with an answer of 255.255.248.0. This actually breaks down to 11111111. 11111111.11111000.00000000, and that's how you got the 11 zeros.

SUBNET MASK EXERCISE 8.5

Class B, 3,500 Hosts per Subnet

You have a Class B address, and you need 3,500 hosts per subnet.

1. Write down the following:

   255.255.___.0

2. Look at the Y column and find the first number that covers 3,500. (This should be 4,094.)

3. Go across and find the power number. (This should be 12.)

4. Remember, you already have eight 0s in the last octet, so you need only four more. Count for four zeros from right to left.

You should come up with an answer of 255.255.240.0. Again, this actually breaks down to 111 11111.11111111.11110000.00000000, and that's how you got the 12 zeros.

If you get a question that gives you both the hosts and the subnets, always figure out the larger number first. Then, depending on the mask you have decided to use, make sure that the lower number is also correct with that mask.

Now try some more subnet mask exercises using the data that follows:

Class B address	Class B address
1,000 hosts per subnet	25 subnets
Class C address	Class B address
45 hosts per subnet	4,000 hosts per subnet
192.168.0.0	Class B address
10 subnets	2,000 hosts per subnet
	25 subnets

Here are the answers. If any of your answers are wrong, follow the previous examples and try to work through them again.

Class B address	Class B address
1,000 hosts per subnet 255.255.252.0	25 subnets 255.255.248.0
Class C address	Class B address
45 hosts per subnet 255.255.255.192	4,000 hosts per subnet 255.255.240.0
192.168.0.0	Class B address
10 subnets 255.255.255.240	2,000 hosts per subnet
	25 subnets 255.255.248.0

Applying Subnetting the Traditional Way

Sometimes subnetting can be confusing. After all, it can be quite difficult to remember all of those numbers. You can step back a minute and take a look at the primary classes of networks and how to subnet each one. Let's start with Class C because it uses only 8 bits for the node address, so it's the easiest to calculate. In the following sections, I will explain how to subnet the various types of networks.

Subnetting Class C

If you recall, a Class C network uses the first 3 bytes (24 bits) to define the network address. This leaves you 1 byte (8 bits) with which to address hosts. So if you want to create subnets, your options are limited because of the small number of bits available.

If you break down your subnets into chunks smaller than the default Class C, then figuring out the subnet mask, network number, broadcast address, and router address can be confusing. To build a sturdy base for subnetting, study the following techniques for determining these special values for each subnet, but also learn and use the more efficient technique presented in the later section "Quickly Identifying Subnet Characteristics Using CIDR" and the earlier section "An Easier Way to Apply Subnetting." Table 8.5 summarizes how you can break down a Class C network into one, two, four, or eight smaller subnets, and it gives you the subnet masks, network numbers, broadcast addresses, and router addresses. The first three bytes have simply been designated x.y.z. (Note that the table assumes you can use the all-0s and all-1s subnets too.)

TABLE 8.5 Setting up Class C subnets

Number of desired subnets	Subnet mask	Network number	Router address	Broadcast address	Remaining number of IP addresses
1	255.255.255.0	x.y.z.0	x.y.z.1	x.y.z.255	253
2	255.255.255.128	x.y.z.0	x.y.z.1	x.y.z.127	125
	255.255.255.128	x.y.z.128	x.y.z.129	x.y.z.255	125
4	255.255.255.192	x.y.z.0	x.y.z.1	x.y.z.63	61
	255.255.255.192	x.y.z.64	x.y.z.65	x.y.z.127	61
	255.255.255.192	x.y.z.128	x.y.z.129	x.y.z.191	61
	255.255.255.192	x.y.z.192	x.y.z.193	x.y.z.255	61
8	255.255.255.224	x.y.z.0	x.y.z.1	x.y.z.31	29
	255.255.255.224	x.y.z.32	x.y.z.33	x.y.z.63	29
	255.255.255.224	x.y.z.64	x.y.z.65	x.y.z.95	29
	255.255.255.224	x.y.z.96	x.y.z.97	x.y.z.127	29
	255.255.255.224	x.y.z.128	x.y.z.129	x.y.z.159	29
	255.255.255.224	x.y.z.160	x.y.z.161	x.y.z.191	29
	255.255.255.224	x.y.z.192	x.y.z.193	x.y.z.223	29
	255.255.255.224	x.y.z.224	x.y.z.225	x.y.z.255	29

For example, suppose you want to chop up a Class C network, 200.211.192.x, into two subnets. As you can see in the table, you'd use a subnet mask of 255.255.255.128 for each subnet. The first subnet would have the network number 200.211.192.0, router address 200.211.192.1, and broadcast address 200.211.192.127. You could assign IP addresses 200.211.192.2 through 200.211.192.126—that's 125 additional different IP addresses.

Heavily subnetting a network results in the loss of a progressively greater percentage of addresses to the network number, broadcast address, and router address.

The second subnet would have the network number 200.211.192.128, router address 200.211.192.129, and broadcast address 200.211.192.255.

Why It's Best to Use Routers That Support Subnet 0

When subnetting a Class C network using the method in Table 8.5, if you use the $2^x - 2$ calculation, the subnet 128 in the table doesn't make sense. It turns out that there's a legitimate and popular reason to do it this way, however.

- Remember that using subnet 0 is not allowed according to the RFC standards, but by using it you can subnet your Class C network with a subnet mask of 128. This uses only 1 bit, and according to your calculator $2^1 - 2 = 0$, giving you zero subnets.

- By using routers that support subnet 0, you can assign 1–126 for hosts and 129–254 for hosts, as stated in the table. This saves a bunch of addresses! If you were to stick to the method defined by the RFC standards, the best you could gain is a subnet mask of 192 (2 bits), which allows you only two subnets ($2^2 - 2 = 2$).

Determining the Subnet Numbers for a Class C Subnet

The first subnet always has a 0 in the interesting octet. In the example, it would be 200.211.192.0, the same as the original nonsubnetted network address. To determine the subnet numbers for the additional subnets, first you have to determine the incremental value:

1. Begin with the octet that has an interesting value (other than 0 or 255) in the subnet mask. Then subtract the interesting value from 256. The result is the incremental value.

   If again you use the network 200.211.192.x and a mask of 255.255.255.192, the example yields the following equation: $256 - 192 = 64$. Thus, 64 is your incremental value in the interesting octet—the fourth octet in this case. Why the fourth octet? That's the octet with the interesting value, 192, in the mask.

2. To determine the second subnet number, add the incremental value to the 0 in the fourth octet of the first subnet.

   In the example, it would be 200.211.192.64.

3. To determine the third subnet number, add the incremental value to the interesting octet of the second subnet number.

   In the example, it would be 200.211.192.128.

4. Keep adding the incremental value in this fashion until you reach the actual subnet mask number.

For example, 0 + 64 = 64, so your second subnet is 64. And 64 + 64 is 128, so your third subnet is 128. And 128 + 64 is 192, so your fourth subnet is 192. Because 192 is the subnet mask, this is your last subnet. If you tried to add 64 again, you'd come up with 256, an unusable octet value, which is always where you end up when you've gone too far. This means your valid subnets are 0, 64, 128, and 192.

The numbers between the subnets are your valid host and broadcast addresses. For example, the following are valid hosts for two of the subnets in a Class C network with a subnet mask of 192:

- The valid hosts for subnet 64 are in the range 65–126, which gives you 62 hosts per subnet.

    (You can't use 127 as a host because that would mean your host bits would be all 1s. The all-1s format is reserved as the broadcast address for that subnet.)

- The valid hosts for subnet 128 are in the range 129–190, with a broadcast address of 191.

As you can see, this solution wastes a few addresses—six more than not subnetting at all, to be exact. In a Class C network, this should not be hard to justify. The 255.255.255.128 subnet mask is an even better solution if you need only two subnets and expect to need close to 126 host addresses per subnet.

Calculating Values for an Eight-Subnet Class C Network

What happens if you need eight subnets in your Class C network?

By using the calculation of 2^x, where x is the number of subnet bits, you would need 3 subnet bits to get eight subnets ($2^3 = 8$). What are the valid subnets, and what are the valid hosts of each subnet? Let's figure it out.

11100000 is 224 in binary, and it would be the interesting value in the fourth octet of the subnet mask. This must be the same on all workstations.

> You're likely to see test questions that ask you to identify the problem with a given configuration. If a workstation has the wrong subnet mask, the router could "think" that the workstation is on a different subnet than it actually is. When that happens, the misguided router won't forward packets to the workstation in question. Similarly, if the mask is incorrectly specified in the workstation's configuration, that workstation will observe the mask and send packets to the default gateway when it shouldn't.

To figure out the valid subnets, subtract the interesting octet value from 256 (256 – 224 = 32), so 32 is your incremental value for the fourth octet. Of course, the 0 subnet is your first subnet, as always. The other subnets would be 32, 64, 96, 128, 160, 192, and 224. The valid hosts are the numbers between the subnet numbers, except the numbers that equal all 1s in the host bits. These numbers would be 31, 63, 95, 127, 159, 191, 223, and 255. Remember that using all 1s in the host bits is reserved for the broadcast address of each subnet.

The valid subnets, hosts, and broadcasts are as follows:

Subnet	Hosts	Broadcast
0	1–30	31
32	33–62	63
64	65–94	95
96	97–126	127
128	129–158	159
160	161–190	191
192	193–222	223
224	225–254	255

You can add one more bit to the subnet mask just for fun. You were using 3 bits, which gave you 224. By adding the next bit, the mask now becomes 240 (11110000).

By using 4 bits for the subnet mask, you get 14 subnets because $2^4 = 16$. This subnet mask also gives you only 4 bits for the host addresses, or $2^4 - 2 = 14$ hosts per subnet. As you can see, the number of hosts per subnet gets reduced rather quickly for each host bit that gets reallocated for subnet use.

The first valid subnet for subnet 240 is 0, as always. Because $256 - 240 = 16$, your remaining subnets are then 16, 32, 48, 64, 80, 96, 112, 128, 144, 160, 176, 192, 208, 224, and 240. Remember that the actual interesting octet value also represents the last valid subnet, so 240 is the last valid subnet number. The valid hosts are the numbers between the subnets, except for the numbers that are all 1s—the broadcast address for the subnet.

Table 8.6 shows the numbers in the interesting (fourth) octet for a Class C network with eight subnets.

TABLE 8.6 Fourth octet addresses for a Class C network with eight subnets

Subnet	Hosts	Broadcast
0	1–14	15
16	17–30	31
32	33–46	47
48	49–62	63
64	65–78	79

80	81–94	95
96	97–110	111
112	113–126	127
128	129–142	143
144	145–158	159
160	161–174	175
176	177–190	191
192	193–206	207
208	209–222	223
224	225–238	239
240	241–254	255

Subnetting Class B

Because a Class B network has 16 bits for host addresses, you have plenty of available bits to play with when figuring out a subnet mask. Remember that you have to start with the leftmost bit and work toward the right. For example, a Class B network would look like x.y.0.0, with the default mask of 255.255.0.0. Using the default mask would give you one network with 65,534 hosts.

The default mask in binary is 11111111.11111111.00000000.00000000. The 1s represent the corresponding network bits in the IP address, and the 0s represent the host bits. When you're creating a subnet mask, the leftmost bit(s) will be borrowed from the host bits (0s will be turned into 1s) to become the subnet mask. You then use the remaining bits that are still set to 0 for host addresses.

If you use only 1 bit to create a subnet mask, you have a mask of 255.255.128.0. If you use 2 bits, you have a mask of 255.255.192.0, or 11111111.11111111.11000000.00000000.

As with subnetting a Class C address, you now have three parts of the IP address: the network address, the subnet address, and the host address. You figure out the subnet mask numbers the same way as you did with a Class C network (see the previous section, "Calculating Values for an Eight-Subnet Class C Network"), but you'll end up with a lot more hosts per subnet.

There are four subnets, because $2^2 = 4$. The valid third-octet values for the subnets are 0, 64, 128, and 192 (256 – 192 = 64, so the incremental value of the third octet is 64). However, there are 14 bits (0s) left over for host addressing. This gives you 16,382 hosts per subnet ($2^{14} – 2 = 16,382$).

The valid subnets and hosts are as follows:

Subnet	Hosts	Broadcast
x.y.0.0	x.y.0.1 through x.y. 63.254	x.y.63.255
x.y.64.0	x.y.64.1 through x.y.127.254	x.y.127.255
x.y.128.0	x.y.128.1 through x.y.191.254	x.y.191.255
x.y.192.0	x.y.192.1 through x.y.255.254	x.y.255.255

You can add another bit to the subnet mask, making it 11111111.11111111.11100000. 00000000, or 255.255.224.0. This gives you eight subnets ($2^3 = 8$) and 8,190 hosts. The valid subnets are 0, 32, 64, 96, 128, 160, 192, and 224 (256 – 224 = 32). The subnets, valid hosts, and broadcasts are listed here:

Subnet	Hosts	Broadcast
x.y.0.0	x.y.0.1 through x.y.31.254	x.y.31.255
x.y.32.0	x.y.32.1 through x.y.63.254	x.y.63.255
x.y.64.0	x.y.64.1 through x.y.95.254	x.y.95.255
x.y.96.0	x.y.96.1 through x.y.127.254	x.y.127.255
x.y.128.0	x.y.128.1 through x.y.159.254	x.y.159.255
x.y.160.0	x.y.160.1 through x.y.191.254	x.y.191.255
x.y.192.0	x.y.192.1 through x.y.223.254	x.y.223.255
x.y.224.0	x.y.224.1 through x.y.255.254	x.y.255.255

The following are the breakdowns for a 9-bit mask and a 14-bit mask:

- If you use 9 bits for the mask, it gives you 512 subnets (2^9). With only 7 bits for hosts, you still have 126 hosts per subnet ($2^7 – 2 = 126$). The mask looks like this:

  11111111.11111111.11111111.10000000, or 255.255.255.128

- If you use 14 bits for the subnet mask, you get 16,384 subnets (2^{14}) but only two hosts per subnet ($2^2 – 2 = 2$). The subnet mask would look like this:

  11111111.11111111.11111111.11111100, or 255.255.255.252

Real World Scenario

Subnet Mask Use in an ISP

You may be wondering why you would use a 14-bit subnet mask with a Class B address. This approach is actually very common. Let's say you have a Class B network and use a subnet mask of 255.255.255.0. You'd have 256 subnets and 254 hosts per subnet. Imagine also that you are an Internet service provider (ISP) and have a network with many WAN links, a different one between you and each customer. Typically, you'd have a direct connection between each site. Each of these links must be on its own subnet or network. There will be two hosts on these subnets—one address for each router port. If you used the mask described earlier (255.255.255.0), you would waste 252 host addresses per subnet. But by using the 255.255.255.252 subnet mask, you have more subnets available, which means more customers—each subnet with only two hosts, which is the maximum allowed on a point-to-point circuit.

You can use the 255.255.255.252 subnet mask only if you are running a routing algorithm such as Enhanced Interior Gateway Routing Protocol (EIGRP) or Open Shortest Path First (OSPF). These routing protocols allow what is called *variable-length subnet masking (VLSM)*. VLSM allows you to run the 255.255.255.252 subnet mask on your interfaces to the WANs and run 255.255.255.0 on your router interfaces in your local area network (LAN) using the same classful network address for all subnets. It works because these routing protocols transmit the subnet mask information in the update packets that they send to the other routers. Classful routing protocols, such as RIP version 1, don't transmit the subnet mask and therefore cannot employ VLSM.

Subnetting Class A

Class A networks have even more bits available than Class B and Class C networks. A default Class A network subnet mask is only 8 bits, or 255.0.0.0, giving you a whopping 24 bits for hosts to play with. Knowing which hosts and subnets are valid is a lot more complicated than it was for either Class B or Class C networks.

If you use a mask of 11111111.1111111.00000000.00000000, or 255.255.0.0, you'll have 8 bits for subnets, or 256 subnets (2^8). This leaves 16 bits for hosts, or 65,534 hosts per subnet ($2^{16} - 2 = 65534$).

If you split the 24 bits evenly between subnets and hosts, you would give each one 12 bits. The mask would look like this: 11111111.11111111.11110000.00000000, or 255.255.240.0. How many valid subnets and hosts would you have? The answer is 4,096 subnets each with 4,094 hosts ($2^{12} - 2 = 4094$).

The second octet will be somewhere between 0 and 255. However, you will need to figure out the third octet. Because the third octet has a 240 mask, you get 16

(256 – 240 = 16) as your incremental value in the third octet. The third octet must start with 0 for the first subnet, the second subnet will have 16 in the third octet, and so on. This means that some of your valid subnets are as follows (not in order):

Subnet	Hosts	Broadcast
x.0-255.0.0	x.0-255.0.1 through x.0-255.15.254	x.0-255.15.255
x.0-255.16.0	x.0-255.16.1 through x.0-255.31.254	x.0-255.31.255
x.0-255.32.0	x.0-255.32.1 through x.0-255.47.254	x.0-255.47.255
x.0-255.48.0	x.0-255.48.1 through x.0-255.63.254	x.0-255.63.255

They go on in this way for the remaining third-octet values through 224 in the subnet column.

Working with Classless Inter-Domain Routing

Microsoft uses an alternate way to write address ranges, called *Classless Inter-Domain Routing (CIDR;* pronounced "cider"). CIDR is a shorthand version of the subnet mask. For example, an address of 131.107.2.0 with a subnet mask of 255.255.255.0 is listed in CIDR as 131.107.2.0/24 because the subnet mask contains 24 1s. An address listed as 141.10.32.0/19 would have a subnet mask of 255.255.224.0, or 19 1s (the default subnet mask for Class B plus 3 bits). This is the nomenclature used in all Microsoft exams (see Figure 8.12).

FIGURE 8.12   Subnet mask represented by 1s

Subnet mask in binary: 1111 1111. 1111 1111. 1111 1111. 0000 0000

Subnet mask in decimal: 255   .   255   .   255   .   0

(The spaces in the above example are only for illustrative purposes.
The subnet mask in decimal would actually appear as 255.255.255.0.)

Let's say an Internet company has assigned you the following Class C address and CIDR number: 192.168.10.0/24. This represents the Class C address of 192.168.10.0 and a subnet mask of 255.255.255.0.

Again, CIDR represents the number of 1s turned on in a subnet mask. For example, a CIDR number of /16 stands for 255.255.0.0 (11111111.11111111.00000000.00000000).

The following is a list of all of the CIDR numbers (starting with a Class A default subnet mask) and their corresponding subnet masks:

CIDR	Mask	CIDR	Mask	CIDR	Mask
/8	255.0.0.0	/17	255.255.128.0	/25	255.255.255.128
/9	255.128.0.0	/18	255.255.192.0	/26	255.255.255.192
/10	255.192.0.0	/19	255.255.224.0	/27	255.255.255.224
/11	255.224.0.0	/20	255.255.240.0	/28	255.255.255.240
/12	255.240.0.0	/21	255.255.248.0	/29	255.255.255.248
/13	255.248.0.0	/22	255.255.252.0	/30	255.255.255.252
/14	255.252.0.0	/23	255.255.254.0	/31	255.255.255.254
/15	255.254.0.0	/24	255.255.255.0	/32	255.255.255.255
/16	255.255.0.0				

Quickly Identifying Subnet Characteristics Using CIDR

Given the limited time you have to dispatch questions in the structured environment of a Microsoft certification exam, every shortcut to coming up with the correct answer is a plus. The following method, using CIDR notation, can shave minutes off the time it takes you to complete a single question. Since you already understand the underlying binary technology at the heart of subnetting, you can use the following shortcuts, one for each address class, to come up with the correct answer without working in binary.

Identifying Class C Subnet Characteristics

Consider the host address 192.168.10.50/27. The following steps flesh out the details of the subnet of which this address is a member:

1. Obtain the CIDR-notation prefix length for the address by converting the dotted-decimal mask to CIDR notation.

   In this case, /27 corresponds to a mask of 255.255.255.224. Practice converting between these notations until it becomes second nature.

2. Using the closest multiple of 8 that is greater than or equal to the prefix length, compute the interesting octet (the octet that increases from one subnet to the next in increments other than 1 or 0). Divide this multiple by 8. The result is a number corresponding to the octet that is interesting.

   In this case, the next multiple of 8 greater than 27 is 32. Dividing 32 by 8 produces the number 4, pointing to the fourth octet as the interesting one.

3. To compute the incremental value in the interesting octet, subtract the prefix length from the next higher multiple of 8, which in this case is 32. The result (32 – 27) is 5. Raise 2 to the computed value ($2^5 = 32$). The result is the incremental value of the interesting octet.

4. Recall the value of the interesting octet from the original address (50 in this case). Starting with 0, increment by the incremental value until the value is exceeded. The values then are 0, 32, 64, and so on.

5. The subnet in question extends from the increment that is immediately less than or equal to the address's interesting octet value to the address immediately before the next increment. In this example, 192.168.10.50/27 belongs to the subnet 192.168.10.32, and this subnet extends to the address immediately preceding 192.168.10.64, which is its broadcast address, 192.168.10.63.

   Note that if the interesting octet is not the fourth octet, all octets after the interesting octet must be set to 0 for the subnet address.

6. The usable range of addresses for the subnet in question extends from one higher than the subnet address to one less than the broadcast address, making the range for the subnet in question 192.168.10.33 through 192.168.10.62. As you can see, 192.168.10.50/27 definitely falls within the subnet 192.168.10.32/27.

Identifying Class B Subnet Characteristics

Using the steps in the previous section, find the subnet in which the address 172.16.76.12 with a mask of 255.255.240.0 belongs.

1. The corresponding CIDR notation prefix length is /20.

2. The next multiple of 8 that is greater than 20 is 24. 24 × 8 = 3. Octet 3 is interesting.

3. 24 − 20 = 4, so the incremental value is 2^4 = 16.

4. The increments in the third octet are 0, 16, 32, 48, 64, 80, and so on.

5. The increments of 64 and 80 bracket the address's third-octet value of 76, making the subnet in question 172.16.64.0, after setting all octets after the interesting octet to 0. This subnet's broadcast address is 172.16.79.255, which comes right before the next subnet address of 172.16.80.0.

6. The usable address range then extends from 172.16.64.1 through 172.16.79.254.

Identifying Class A Subnet Characteristics

Try it one more time with 10.6.127.255/14. Combine some of the related steps if possible:

1. The prefix length is 14. The next multiple of 8 that is greater than or equal to 14 is 16. 16 × 8 = 2, so the second octet is interesting.

2. 16 − 14 = 2, so the incremental value in the second octet is 2^2 = 4.

3. The corresponding second-octet value of 6 in the address falls between the 4 and 8 increments. This means that the subnet in question is 10.4.0.0 (setting octets after the second one to 0) and its broadcast address is 10.7.255.255.

4. The usable address range is from 10.4.0.1 through 10.7.255.254.

Determining Quantities of Subnets and Hosts

The general technique described in the previous section is also useful when trying to determine the total number of subnets and hosts produced by a given mask with respect to the default mask of the class of address in question.

For example, consider the Class B address 172.16.0.0 with a subnet mask of 255.255.254.0.

This is a prefix length of 23 bits. When you subtract the default prefix length for a Class B address of 16 from 23, you get the value 7. Raising 2 to the 7th power results in the value 128, which is the number of subnets you get when you subnet a Class B address with the 255.255.254.0 mask.

Determining the number of hosts available in each of these 128 subnets is simple because you always subtract the prefix length that the subnet mask produces, 23 in this example, from the value 32, which represents the total number of bits in any IP address. The difference, 9, represents the remaining number of 0s, or host bits, in the subnet mask. Raising 2 to this value produces the total possible number of host IDs per subnet that this subnet mask allows. Remember to subtract 2 from this result to account for the subnet and broadcast addresses for each subnet. This gives you the actual number of usable host IDs per subnet. In this case, this value is $2^9 - 2 = 510$.

Repeated practice with this technique will reduce your time to obtain the desired answer to mere seconds, leaving time for the more challenging tasks in each question. You have a wealth of examples and scenarios in this chapter, as well as in the review questions, on which to try your technique and build your trust in this faster method.

Supernetting

Let's take a look at a different type of subnetting. Class B addresses give you 65,534 addresses, but let's say that you have 1,000 users. Would you really need a Class B address? Not if you use supernetting.

Supernetting allows you to have two or more blocks of contiguous subnetwork addresses. So what does that actually mean? Class C addresses give you 254 useable addresses. So if you needed 1,000 users, you could set up supernetting of 4 Class C addresses that are contiguous.

Example:
192.168.16.0
192.168.17.0
192.168.18.0
192.168.19.0

When you set up supernetting for a Class C, you would use a Class B subnet mask. When you set up supernetting for a Class B, you would use a Class A subnet mask. This allows you to use multiple classes to get a larger number of hosts without taking up an entire class.

So the subnet mask for the above example would be 255.255.252.0 or /22. The reason we used this subnet mask is because a 252 subnet mask allows for 4 subnets. Each of the above Class C numbers would equal one subnet on this network.

Understanding IPv6

Internet Protocol version 6 (IPv6) is the first major revamping of IP since RFC 791 was accepted in 1981. Yes, the operation of IP has improved, and there have been a few bells and whistles added (such as NAT, for example), but the basic structure is still being used as it was originally intended. IPv6 has actually been available to use in Microsoft operating systems since NT 4.0, but it always had to be manually enabled. Windows Vista was the first Microsoft operating system to have it enabled by default. It is also enabled by default in Windows 7, Windows 8, Windows Server 2008, Windows Server 2008 R2, and Windows Server 2012 R2, and it probably will be in all Microsoft operating systems from this point on.

TCP and UDP—as well as the IP applications, such as HTTP, FTP, SNMP, and the rest—are still being used in IPv4. So, you might ask, why change to the new version? What does IPv6 bring to your networking infrastructure? What is the structure of an IPv6 address? How is it implemented and used within Windows Server 2012 R2? I'll answer all of those questions and more in the following sections.

IPv6 History and Need

In the late 1970s, as the IP specifications were being put together, the vision of the interconnected devices was limited compared to what we actually have today. To get an idea of the growth of the Internet, take a look at Hobbes' Internet Timeline in RFC 2235 (www.faqs.org/rfcs/rfc2235.html). As you can see, in 1984, the number of hosts finally surpassed 1,000—two years after TCP and IP were introduced. With 32 bits of addressing available in IPv4, it handled the 1,000+ hosts just fine. And even with the number of hosts breaking the 10,000 mark in 1987 and then 100,000 in 1989, there were still plenty of IP addresses to go around. But when the number of hosts exceeded 2 million in 1992 and 3 million in 1994, concern in the industry started to build. So in 1994, a working group was formed to come up with a solution to the quickly dwindling usable address availability in the IPv4 space. Internet Protocol next generation (IPng) was started.

Have you heard of IP address depletion being a problem today? Probably not as much. When the working group realized that it could not have IPv6 standardized before the available addresses might run out, they developed and standardized *Network Address Translation (NAT)* as an interim solution. NAT, or more specifically an implementation of NAT called *Port Address Translation (PAT)*, took care of a big portion of the problem.

NAT works very well, but it does have some limitations, including issues of peer-to-peer applications with their IPv4 addresses embedded in the data, issues of end-to-end traceability, and issues of overlapping addresses when two networks merge. Because all devices in an IPv6 network will have a unique address and no network address translation will take place, the global addressing concept of IPv4 will be brought back (the address put on by the source device will stay all the way to the destination). Thus, with the new-and-improved functionality of IPv6, the drawbacks of NAT and the limitations of IPv4 will be eliminated.

New and Improved IPv6 Concepts

Several elements of the IPv4 protocol could use some enhancements. Fortunately, IPv6 incorporates those enhancements as well as new features directly into the protocol specification to provide better and additional functionality.

The following list includes new concepts and new implementations of old concepts in IPv6:

- Larger address space (128-bit vs. 32-bit).

- Autoconfiguration of Internet-accessible addresses with or without DHCP. (Without DHCP, it's called *stateless autoconfiguration*.)

- More efficient IP header (fewer fields and no checksum).

- Fixed-length IP header (the IPv4 header is variable length) with extension headers beyond the standard fixed length to provide enhancements.

- Built-in IP mobility and security. (Although available in IPv4, the IPv6 implementation is a much better implementation.)

- Built-in transition schemes to allow integration of the IPv4 and IPv6 spaces.

- ARP broadcast messages replaced with multicast request.

Here are more details about these features:

128-Bit Address Space   The new 128-bit address space will provide unique addresses for the foreseeable future. Although I would like to say that we will never use up all of the addresses, history may prove me wrong. The number of unique addresses in the IPv6 space is 2^{128}, or 3.4×10^{38}, addresses. How big is that number? It's enough for toasters and refrigerators (and maybe even cars) to all have their own addresses.

As a point of reference, the nearest black hole to Earth is 1,600 light years away. If you were to stack 4mm BB pellets from here to the nearest black hole and back, you would need 1.51×10^{22} BBs. This means you could uniquely address each BB from Earth to the black hole and back and still have quite a few addresses left over.

Another way to look at it is that the IPv6 address space is big enough to provide more than 1 million addresses per square inch of the surface area of the earth (oceans included).

Autoconfiguration and Stateless Autoconfiguration   Autoconfiguration is another added/improved feature of IPv6. We've used DHCP for a while to assign IP addresses to client machines. You should even remember that APIPA can be used to assign addresses automatically to Microsoft DHCP client machines in the absence of a DHCP server. The problem with APIPA is that it confines communication between machines to a local LAN (no default gateway). What if a client machine could ask whether there was a router on the LAN and what network it was on? If the client machine knew that, it could not only assign itself an address, it could also choose the appropriate network and default gateway. The stateless autoconfiguration functionality of IPv6 allows the clients to do this.

Improved IPv6 Header   The IPv6 header is more efficient than the IPv4 header because it is fixed length (with extensions possible) and has only a few fields. The IPv6 header consists of a total of 40 bytes:

32 bytes   Source and destination IPv6 addresses

8 bytes   Version field, traffic class field, flow label field, payload length field, next header field, and hop limit field

You don't have to waste your time with a checksum validation anymore, and you don't have to include the length of the IP header (it's fixed in IPv6; the IP header is variable length in IPv4, so the length must be included as a field).

IPv6 Mobility   IPv6 is only a replacement of the OSI layer 3 component, so you'll continue to use the TCP (and UDP) components as they currently exist. IPv6 addresses a TCP issue, though. Specifically, TCP is connection oriented, meaning that you establish an end-to-end communication path with sequencing and acknowledgments before you ever send any data, and then you have to acknowledge all of the pieces of data sent. You do this through a combination of an IP address, port number, and port type (socket).

If the source IP address changes, the TCP connection may be disrupted. But then how often does this happen? Well, it happens more and more often because more people are walking around with a wireless laptop or a wireless Voice over IP (VoIP) telephone. IPv6 mobility establishes a TCP connection with a home address and, when changing networks, it continues to communicate with the original endpoint from a care-of address as it changes LANs, which sends all traffic back through the home address. The handing off of network addresses does not disrupt the TCP connection state (the original TCP port number and address remain intact).

Improved Security   Unlike IPv4, IPv6 has security built in. *Internet Protocol Security (IPsec)* is a component used today to authenticate and encrypt secure tunnels from a source to a destination. This can be from the client to the server or between gateways. IPv4 lets you do this by enhancing IP header functionality (basically adding a second IP header while encrypting everything behind it). In IPv6, you add this as standard functionality by using extension headers. Extension headers are inserted into the packet only if they are needed. Each header has a "next header" field, which identifies the next piece of information. The extension headers currently identified for IPv6 are Hop-By-Hop Options, Routing, Fragment, Destination Options, Authentication, and Encapsulating Security Payload. The Authentication header and the Encapsulating Security Payload header are the IPsec-specific control headers.

IPv4 to IPv6 Interoperability   Several mechanisms in IPv6 make the IPv4-to-IPv6 transition easy.

- A simple dual-stack implementation where both IPv4 and IPv6 are installed and used is certainly an option. In most situations (so far), this doesn't work so well because most of us aren't connected to an IPv6 network and our Internet connection is not IPv6 even if we're using IPv6 internally. Therefore, Microsoft includes other mechanisms that can be used in several different circumstances.

- *Intra-Site Automatic Tunnel Addressing Protocol (ISATAP)* is an automatic tunneling mechanism used to connect an IPv6 network to an IPv4 address space (not using NAT). ISATAP treats the IPv4 space as one big logical link connection space.

- *6to4* is a mechanism used to transition to IPv4. This method, like ISATAP, treats the IPv4 address space as a logical link layer with each IPv6 space in transition using a 6to4 router to create endpoints using the IPv4 space as a point-to-point connection (kind of like a WAN, eh?). 6to4 implementations still do not work well through a NAT, although a 6to4 implementation using an Application layer gateway (ALG) is certainly doable.

- *Teredo* is a mechanism that allows users behind a NAT to access the IPv6 space by tunneling IPv6 packets in UDP.

Pseudo-interfaces are used in these mechanisms to create a usable interface for the operating system. Another interesting feature of IPv6 is that addresses are assigned to interfaces (or pseudo-interfaces), not simply to the end node. Your Windows Server 2012 R2 will have several unique IPv6 addresses assigned.

New Broadcast Methods   IPv6 has moved away from using broadcasting. The three types of packets used in IPv6 are unicast, multicast, and anycast. IPv6 clients then must use one of these types to get the MAC address of the next Ethernet hop (default gateway). IPv6 makes use of multicasting for this along with the new functionality called *neighbor discovery*. Not only does ARP utilize new functionality, but ICMP (also a layer 3 protocol) has been redone and is now known as ICMP6. *ICMP6* is used for messaging (packet too large, time exceeded, and so on) as it was in IPv4, but now it's also used for the messaging of IPv6 mobility. ICMP6 echo request and ICMP6 echo reply are still used for ping.

IPv6 Addressing Concepts

You need to consider several concepts when using IPv6 addressing. For starters, the format of the address has changed. Three types of addresses are used in IPv6 with some predefined values within the address space. You need to get used to seeing these addresses and be able to identify their uses.

IPv6 Address Format

For the design of IPv4 addresses, you present addresses as octets or the decimal (base 10) representation of 8 bits. Four octets add up to the 32 bits required. IPv6 expands the address space to 128 bits, and the representation is for the most part shown in hexadecimal (a notation used to represent 8 bits using the values 0–9 and A–F). Figure 8.13 compares IPv4 to IPv6.

A full IPv6 address looks like this example:

2001:0DB8:0000:0000:1234:0000:A9FE:133E

You can tell the implementation of DNS will make life a lot easier even for those who like to ping the address in lieu of the name. Fortunately, DNS already has the ability to handle IPv6 addresses with the use of an AAAA record. (*A* is short for *alias*.) An A record in IPv4's addressing space is 32 bits, so an AAAA record, or four *A*s, is 128 bits. The Windows Server 2012 R2 DNS server handles the AAAA and the reverse pointer (PTR) records for IPv6.

FIGURE 8.13   IPv4/IPv6 comparison

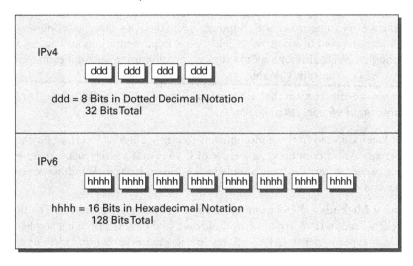

IPv6 Address Shortcuts

There are several shortcuts for writing an IPv6 address. These are described in the following list:

- :0: stands for :0000:.

- You can omit preceding 0s in any 16-bit word. For example, :DB8: and :0DB8: are equivalent.

- :: is a variable standing for enough zeros to round out the address to 128 bits. :: can be used only once in an address.

   You can use these shortcuts to represent the example address 2001:0DB8:0000:0000:1234:0000:A9FE:133E, as shown here:

- Compress :0000: into :0::

   2001:0DB8:0000:0000:1234:0:A9FE:133E

- Eliminate preceding zeros:

   2001:DB8:0000:0000:1234:0:A9FE:133E

- Use the special variable shortcut for multiple 0s:

   2001:DB8::1234:0:A9FE:133E

   You now also use prefix notation or slash notation when discussing IPv6 networks. For example, the network of the previous address can be represented as 2001:DB8:0000:0000:0000:0000:0000:0000. This can also be expressed as 2001:DB8:: /32. The /32 indicates 32 bits of network, and 2001:DB8: is 32 bits of network.

IPv6 Address Assignment

So, do you subnet IPv6? The answer depends on your definition of subnetting. If you are given 32 bits of network from your ISP, you have 96 bits with which to work. If you use some of the 96 bits to route within your network infrastructure, then you are subnetting. In this context, you do subnet IPv6. However, given the huge number of bits you have available, you will no longer need to implement VLSM. For example, Microsoft has a network space of 2001:4898:: /32. That gives the administrators a space of 96 bits ($2^{96} = 79,228,162,514,264,337,593,543,950,336$ unique addresses using all 96 bits) with which to work.

You can let Windows Server 2012 R2 dynamically/automatically assign its IPv6 address, or you can still assign it manually (see Figure 8.14). With dynamic/automatic assignment, the IPv6 address is assigned either by a DHCPv6 server or by the Windows Server 2012 R2 machine. If no DHCPv6 server is configured, the Windows Server 2012 R2 machine can query the local LAN segment to find a router with a configured IPv6 interface. If so, the server will assign itself an address on the same IPv6 network as the router interface and set its default gateway to the router interface's IPv6 address. Figure 8.14 shows that you have the same dynamic and manual choices as you do in IPv4; however, the input values for IPv6 must conform to the new format.

FIGURE 8.14   TCP/IPv6 Properties window

To see your configured IP addresses (IPv4 and IPv6), you can still use the ipconfig command. For example, I have configured a static IPv4 address and an IPv6 address on my server. The IPv6 address is the same as the one used in the earlier IPv6 example address. Figure 8.15 shows the result of this command on Windows Server 2012 R2 for my server.

FIGURE 8.15   IPv6 configuration as seen from the command prompt

IPv6 Address Types

As stated earlier, there are three types of addresses in IPv6: anycast, unicast, and multicast. A description of each of these types of IPv6 addresses follows.

> **NOTE**   Note the absence of the broadcast type, which is included in IPv4. You can't use broadcasts in IPv6; they've been replaced with multicasts.

Anycast Addresses   Anycast addresses are not really new. The concept of anycast existed in IPv4 but was not widely used. An *anycast address* is an IPv6 address assigned to multiple devices (usually different devices). When an anycast packet is sent, it is delivered to one of the devices, usually the closest one.

Unicast Addresses   A *unicast packet* uniquely identifies an interface of an IPv6 device. The interface can be a virtual or pseudo-interface or a real (physical) interface.

Unicast addresses come in several types, as described in the following list:

Global Unicast Address   As of this writing, the global unicast address space is defined as 2000:: /3. The 2001::/32 networks are the IPv6 addresses currently being issued to business entities. As mentioned, Microsoft has been allocated 2001:4898:: /32. A Microsoft DHCPv6 server would be set up with scopes (ranges of addresses to be assigned) within this address space. There are some special addresses and address formats that you will see in use as well. You'll find most example addresses listed as 2001:DB8:: /32; this space has been reserved for documentation. Do you remember the loopback address in IPv4, 127.0.0.1? In IPv6 the loopback address is ::1 (or 0:0:0:0:0:0:0:0001). You may also see an address with dotted-decimal used. A dual-stack Windows Server 2012 machine may also show you FE80::5EFE:192.168.1.200. This address form is used in an integration/migration model of IPv6 (or if you just can't leave the dotted-decimal era, I suppose).

Link-Local Address   Link-local addresses are defined as FE80:: /10. If you refer to Figure 8.15 showing the ipconfig command, you will see the link-local IPv6 address as fe80::a425:ab9d:7da4:ccba. The last 8 bytes (64 bits) are random to ensure a high probability of randomness for the link-local address. The link-local address is to be used on a single link (network segment) and should never be routed.

There is another form of the local-link IPv6 address called the *Extended User Interface 64-bit (EUI-64)* format. This is derived by using the MAC address of the physical interface and inserting an FFFE between the third and fourth bytes of the MAC. The first byte is also made 02 (this sets the universal/local or U/L bit to 1 as defined in IEEE 802 frame specification). Again looking at Figure 8.15, the EUI-64 address would take the physical (MAC) address 00-03-FF-11-02-CD and make the link-local IPv6 address FE80::0203:FFFF:FE11:02CD. (I've left the preceding zeros in the link-local IPv6 address to make it easier for you to pick out the MAC address with the FFFE inserted.)

AnonymousAddress   Microsoft Server 2012 R2 uses the random address by default instead of EUI-64. The random value is called the *AnonymousAddress* in Microsoft Server 2012 R2. It can be modified to allow the use of EUI-64.

Unique Local Address   The *unique local address* can be Fc00 or FD00, and it is used like the private address space of IPv4. RFC 4193 describes unique local addresses. They are not expected to be routable on the global Internet. They are used for private routing within an organization.

Multicast Address   *Multicast addresses* are one-to-many communication packets. Multicast packets are identifiable by their first byte (most significant byte, leftmost byte, leftmost 2 nibbles, leftmost 8 bits, and so on). A multicast address is defined as FF00::/8.

In the second byte shown (the 00 of FF00), the second 0 is what's called the *scope*. Interface-local is 01, and link-local is 02. FF01:: is an interface-local multicast.

There are several well-known (already defined) multicast addresses. For example, if you want to send a packet to all nodes in the link-local scope, you send the packet to FF02::1 (also shown as FF02:0:0:0:0:0:0:1). The all-routers multicast address is FF02::2.

You can also use multicasting to get the logical link layer address (MAC address) of a device with which you are trying to communicate. Instead of using the ARP mechanism of IPv4, IPv6 uses the ICMPv6 neighbor solicitation (NS) and neighbor advertisement (NA) messages. The NS and NA ICMPv6 messages are all part of the new *Neighbor Discovery Protocol (NDP)*. This new ICMPv6 functionality also includes router solicitation and router advertisements as well as redirect messages (similar to the IPv4 redirect functionality). Table 8.7 outlines the IPv6 address space known prefixes and some well-known addresses.

Unicast vs. Anycast

Unicast and anycast addresses look the same and may be indistinguishable from each other; it just depends on how many devices have the same address. If only one device has a globally unique IPv6 address, it's a unicast address. If more than one device has the same address, it's an anycast address. Both unicast and anycast are considered one-to-one communication, although you could say that anycast is one-to-"one of many."

TABLE 8.7 IPv6 address space known prefixes and addresses

Address Prefix	Scope of Use
2000:: /3	Global unicast space prefix
FE80:: /10	Link-local address prefix
FC00:: /7	Unique local unicast prefix
FD00:: /8	Unique local unicast prefix
FF00:: /8	Multicast prefix
2001:DB8:: /32	Global unicast prefix used for documentation
::1	Reserved local loopback address
2001:0000: /32	Teredo prefix (discussed later in this chapter)
2002:: /16	6to4 prefix

IPv6 Integration/Migration

It's time to get into the mind-set of integrating IPv6 into your existing infrastructure with the longer goal of migrating to IPv6. In other words, this is not going to be an "OK, Friday the Internet is changing over" rollout. You have to bring about the change as a controlled implementation. It could easily take three to five years before a solid migration occurs and probably longer. I think the migration will take slightly less time than getting the world to migrate to the metric system on the overall timeline. The process of integration/migration consists of several mechanisms.

Dual Stack   Simply running both IPv4 and IPv6 on the same network, utilizing the IPv4 address space for devices using only IPv4 addresses and utilizing the IPv6 address space for devices using IPv6 addresses

Tunneling   Using an encapsulation scheme for transporting one address space inside another

Address Translation   Using a higher-level application to change one address type (IPv4 or IPv6) to the other transparently so that end devices are unaware one address space is talking to another

I elaborate on these three mechanisms in the following sections.

IPv6 Dual Stack

The default implementation in Windows Server 2012 R2 is an enabled IPv6 configuration along with IPv4; this is dual stack. The implementation can be dual IP layer or dual TCP/IP stack. Windows Server 2012 R2 uses the dual IP layer implementation (see Figure 8.16). When an application queries a DNS server to resolve a hostname to an IP address, the DNS server may respond with an IPv4 address or an IPv6 address. If the DNS server responds with both, Windows Server 2012 R2 will prefer the IPv6 address. Windows Server 2012 R2 can use both IPv4 and IPv6 addresses as necessary for network communication. When looking at the output of the `ipconfig` command, you will see both address spaces displayed.

FIGURE 8.16   IPv6 dual IP layer diagram

IPv6 Tunneling

Windows Server 2012 R2 includes several tunneling mechanisms for tunneling IPv6 through the IPv4 address space. They include the following:

- Intra-Site Automatic Tunnel Addressing Protocol (ISATAP), which is used for unicast IPv6 communication across an IPv4 infrastructure. ISATAP is enabled by default in Windows Server 2012 R2.

- 6to4, which is used for unicast IPv6 communication across an IPv4 infrastructure.

- Teredo, which is used for unicast IPv6 communication with an IPv4 NAT implementation across an IPv4 infrastructure.

   With multiple tunneling protocols available and enabled by default, you might ask, what's the difference, and why is one used over the others? They all allow you to tunnel IPv6 packets through the IPv4 address space (a really cool thing if you're trying to integrate/migrate). Here are the details of these tunneling mechanisms:

ISATAP   *Intra-Site Automatic Tunnel Addressing Protocol (ISATAP)* is the automatic tunnel addressing protocol providing IPv6 addresses based on the IPv4 address of the end interface (node). The IPv6 address is automatically configured on the local device, and the dual stack machine can use either its IPv4 or IPv6 address to communicate on the local network (within the local network infrastructure). ISATAP can use the neighbor discovery mechanism to determine the router ID and network prefix where the device is located, thus making intrasite communication possible even in a routed infrastructure.

The format of an ISATAP address is as follows:

[64bits of prefix] [32bits indicating ISATAP] [32bits IPv4 Address]

The center 32 bits indicating ISATAP are actually 0000:5EFE (when using private IPv4 addresses). The ISATAP address of the example Windows Server 2012 R2 machine using the link-local IPv6 address is FE80::5EFE:192.168.1.200. Each node participating in the ISATAP infrastructure must support ISATAP. If you're routing through an IPv4 cloud, a border router (a router transitioning from an IPv6 to IPv4 space) must support ISATAP. Windows Server 2012 R2 can be configured as a border router, and it will forward ISATAP packets. ISATAP is experimental and is defined in RFC 4214.

6to4 *6to4* specifies a procedure for IPv6 networks to communicate with each other through an IPv4 space without the IPv6 nodes having to know what's happening. The IPv6 nodes do not need to be dual stacked to make this happen. The border router is the device responsible for knowing about the IPv6-to-IPv4 transition. The IPv6 packets are encapsulated at the border router (and decapsulated at the other end or on the way back). There is an assigned prefix for the 6to4 implementation: 2002:: /16. 6to4 is defined in RFC 3056.

Teredo *Teredo* (named after a kind of shipworm that drills holes in the wood of ships) is a protocol designed to allow IPv6 addresses to be available to hosts through one or more layers of NAT. Teredo uses a process of tunneling packets through the IPv4 space using UDP. The Teredo service encapsulates the IPv6 data within a UDP segment (packet) and uses IPv4 addressing to get through the IPv4 cloud. Having a layer 4 (Transport layer) available to use as translation functionality is what gives you the ability to be behind a NAT. Teredo provides host-to-host communication and dynamic addressing for IPv6 nodes (dual stack), allowing the nodes to have access to resources in an IPv6 network and the IPv6 devices to have access to the IPv6 devices that have only connectivity to the IPv4 space (like home users who have an IPv6-enabled operating system connecting to IPv6 resources while their home ISP has only IPv4 capabilities). Teredo is defined in RFC 4380.

In Windows Server 2012 R2, an IPv4 Teredo server is identified and configured (using the netsh command interface). The Teredo server provides connectivity resources (address) to the Teredo client (the node that has access to the IPv4 Internet and needs access to an IPv6 network/Internet). A Teredo relay is a component used by the IPv6 router to receive traffic destined for Teredo clients and forward the traffic appropriately. The defined prefix for Teredo address is 2001:0000:: /32. Teredo does add overhead like all the other implementations discussed. It is generally accepted that you should use the simplest model available. However, in the process of integration/migration for most of us behind a NAT, Teredo will be the process to choose.

From Windows Server 2012 R2, use the ipconfig /all command to view the default configurations including IPv4 and IPv6. You may notice a notation that I didn't discuss, the percent sign at the end of the IPv6 address (see Figure 8.17). The number after the percent sign is the virtual interface identifier used by Windows Server 2012 R2.

FIGURE 8.17 IPv6 interface identifier for `ipconfig` display

```
Link-local IPv6 Address . . . . . : fe80::a425:ab9d:7da4:ccba%10
```

Useful IPv6 Information Commands

You can use numerous commands to view, verify, and configure the network parameters of Windows Server 2012 R2. Specifically, you can use the `netsh` command set and the `route` command set as well as the standard `ping` and `tracert` functions.

Use the `netsh` command interface (as well as the provided dialog boxes, if you want) to examine and configure IPv6 functionality. The `netsh` command issued from the command interpreter changes into a network shell (netsh) where you can configure and view both IPv4 and IPv6 components.

Don't forget to use the ever-popular `route print` command to see the Windows Server 2012 R2 routing tables (IPv4 and IPv6). The other diagnostic commands are still available for IPv4 as well as IPv6. In previous versions of Microsoft operating systems, `ping` was the IPv4 command, and `ping6` was the IPv6 command. This has changed in Windows Server 2012 R2; `ping` works for both IPv4 and IPv6 to test layer 3 connectivity to remote devices. The IPv4 `tracert` command was `tracert6` for IPv6. The command is now `tracert` for both IPv4 and IPv6, and it will show you every layer 3 (IP) hop from source to destination. (This assumes that all of the administrators from here to there want you to see the hops and are not blocking ICMP. It also assumes that there are no IP tunnels, which your packets are traversing; you won't see the router hops in the tunnel either.)

Overall, the consortium of people developing the Internet and the Internet Protocol have tried to make all of the changes to communication infrastructures easy to implement. (This is a daunting task with the many vendors and various infrastructures currently in place.) The goal is not to daze and confuse administrators; it's designed to provide maximum flexibility with the greatest functionality. IPv6 is going to provide the needed layer 3 (Network layer, global addressing layer, logical addressing layer...call it what you like) functionality for the foreseeable future.

Subnetting with IPv6

Subnetting with IPv6 is a lot like subnetting with IPv4. You need to know how many bits you are going to use for the network mask to subnet it correctly.

For example, let's say you have an IPv6 prefix of 2001:DB8:BBCC:0000::/53 and you need to set up your network so that your IPv6 addressing scheme can handle 1,500 more subnets. How would you figure this out?

When determining any number of hosts or subnets, the calculation is 2 to the power (2^x). The first power number that is greater than or equal to the number you need is the power number that you add to the current network mask. Thus, in the previous question, to get to 1,500 subnets, you would need to determine which 2^x is the first one that is greater than or equal to 1,500. If you calculate your powers correctly, 2^{11} ($2^{11} = 2,048$) is the first one that is greater than or equal to 1,500. So, you would add the power of 11 to the /53 in the previous address, and you would now use /64 as your network mask. Table 8.8 shows you some of the power numbers for the power of 2.

TABLE 8.8 Powers of 2

Power	Equals
2^2	4
2^3	8
2^4	16
2^5	32
2^6	64
2^7	128
2^8	256
2^9	512
2^{10}	1024
2^{11}	2048
2^{12}	4096

Summary

Why TCP/IP is the primary protocol in use today is one of the important topics covered in this chapter. You also learned that the 32-bit IPv4 address is a structured and hierarchical one that is used to identify uniquely every machine on a network. You learned how to determine available IP addresses and implement subnetting. In addition, you learned how the new layer 3 IPv6 protocol is implemented, including the structure of the IPv6 address. Finally, I discussed the new functionality included in IPv6 addressing as well as several Windows Server 2012 R2 integration/migration implementations.

Exam Essentials

Understand what subnetting is and when to use it.   If an organization is large and has many computers or if its computers are geographically dispersed, it's sensible to divide its large network into smaller ones connected by routers. These smaller networks are called *subnets*. Subnetting is the process of carving a single IP network into smaller, logical subnetworks.

Understand subnet masks.   For the subnet address scheme to work, every machine on the network must know which part of the host address will be used as the subnet address. The network administrator creates a 32-bit subnet mask consisting of 1s and 0s. The 1s in the subnet mask represent the positions that refer to the network or subnet addresses. The 0s represent the positions that refer to the host portion of the address.

Understand IPv6.   Understand the structure of an IPv6 address and how it's displayed. Know the shortcuts and rules (such as for displaying 0s) for writing IPv6 addresses. Know the integration/migration components for IPv6 included in Windows Server 2012 R2, including tunneling and dual stack.

Review Questions

1. You are the network administrator for ABC Company. You have an IPv6 prefix of 2001:DB8:BBCC:0000::/53, and you need to set up your network so that your IPv6 addressing scheme can handle 1,000 more subnets. Which network mask would you use?

   A. /60

   B. /61

   C. /62

   D. /63

   E. /64

2. You are the network administrator for Stellacon Corporation. Stellacon has a Windows Server 2012 R2 machine that needs to be able to communicate with all of the computers on the internal network. Stellacon has decided to add 15 new segments to its IPv6 network. How would you configure the IPv6 address so that the server can communicate with all the segments?

   A. Configure the IPv6 address as fd00::2b0:e0ff:dee9:4143/8.

   B. Configure the IPv6 address as fe80::2b0:e0ff:dee9:4143/32.

   C. Configure the IPv6 address as ff80::2b0:e0ff:dee9:4143/64.

   D. Configure the IPv6 address as fe80::2b0:e0ff:dee9:4143/64.

3. You are the network administrator for a midsize organization that has installed Windows Server 2012 R2 onto the network. You are thinking of moving all machines to Windows 8 and IPv6. You decide to set up a test environment with four subnets. What type of IPv6 addresses do you need set up?

   A. Global addresses

   B. Link-local addresses

   C. Unique local addresses

   D. Site-local addresses

4. You have a large IP-routed network using the address 137.25.0.0; it is composed of 20 subnets, with a maximum of 300 hosts on each subnet. Your company continues on a merger-and-acquisitions spree, and your manager has told you to prepare for an increase to 50 subnets with some containing more than 600 hosts. Using the existing network address, which of the following subnet masks would work for the requirement set by your manager?

   A. 255.255.252.0

   B. 255.255.254.0

   C. 255.255.248.0

   D. 255.255.240.0

5. Your company is growing dramatically via acquisitions of other companies. As the network administrator, you need to keep up with the changes because they affect the workstations, and you need to support them. When you started, there were 15 locations connected via routers, and now there are 25. As new companies are acquired, they are migrated to Windows Server 2012 R2 and brought into the same domain as another site. Management says that they are going to acquire at least 10 more companies in the next two years. The engineers have also told you that they are redesigning the company's Class B address into an IP addressing scheme that will support these requirements and that there will never be more than 1,000 network devices on any subnet. What is the appropriate subnet mask to support this network when the changes are completed?

   A. 255.255.252.0

   B. 255.255.248.0

   C. 255.255.255.0

   D. 255.255.255.128

6. You work for a small printing company that has 75 workstations. Most of them run standard office applications such as word processing, spreadsheet, and accounting programs. Fifteen of the workstations are constantly processing huge graphics files and then sending print jobs to industrial-sized laser printers. The performance of the network has always been an issue, but you have never addressed it. You have now migrated your network to Windows 8 and Windows Server 2012 R2 and have decided to take advantage of the routing capability built into Windows Server 2012 R2. You choose the appropriate server and place two NICs in the machine, but you realize that you have only one network address, 201.102.34.0, which you obtained years ago. How should you subnet this address to segment the bandwidth hogs from the rest of the network while giving everyone access to the entire network?

   A. 255.255.255.192

   B. 255.255.255.224

   C. 255.255.255.252

   D. 255.255.255.240

7. You work for Carpathian Worldwide Enterprises, which has more than 50 administrative and manufacturing locations around the world. The size of these organizations varies greatly, with the number of computers per location ranging from 15 to slightly fewer than 1,000. The sales operations use more than 1,000 facilities, each of which contains 2 to 5 computers. Carpathian is also in merger talks with another large organization. If the merger materializes as planned, you will have to accommodate another 100 manufacturing and administrative locations, each with a maximum of 600 computers, as well as 2,000 additional sales facilities. You don't have any numbers for the future growth of the company, but you are told to keep growth in mind. You decide to implement a private addressing plan for the entire organization. More than half of your routers don't support variable-length subnet masking. Which subnet masks would work for this situation? (Choose all that apply.)

   A. 255.255.224.0

   B. 255.255.240.0

   C. 255.255.248.0

   D. 255.255.252.0

   E. 255.255.254.0

8. Which of the following subnet masks are represented with the CIDR of /27?

   A. 255.255.255.254

   B. 255.255.255.248

   C. 255.255.255.224

   D. 255.255.255.240

9. You are the administrator for a Windows Server 2012 R2 network that uses DHCP. You notice that your DHCP database is getting too large, and you want to reduce the size of the database. What should you do?

   A. From the folder containing the DHCP database, run `jetpack.exe dhcp.mdb temp.mdb`.

   B. From the folder containing the DHCP database, run `shrinkpack.exe dhcp.mdb temp.mdb`.

   C. From the folder containing the DHCP database, run `jetshrink.exe dhcp.mdb temp.mdb`.

   D. From the folder containing the DHCP database, run `shrinkjet.exe dhcp.mdb temp.mdb`.

10. You ask one of your technicians to get the IPv6 address of a new Windows Server 2012 R2 machine, and she hands you a note with FE80::0203:FFFF:FE11:2CD on it. What can you tell from this address? (Choose two.)

   A. This is a globally unique IPv6 address.

   B. This is a link-local IPv6 address.

   C. This is a multicast IPv6 address.

   D. In EUI-64 format, you can see the MAC address of the node.

   E. In EUI-64 format, you can see the IPv4 address of the node.

Chapter

9

Use Virtualization in Windows Server 2012

THE FOLLOWING 70-410 EXAM OBJECTIVES ARE COVERED IN THIS CHAPTER:

✓ **Create and configure virtual machine settings**

- Configure dynamic memory
- Configure smart paging
- Configure Resource Metering
- Configure guest integration services
- Create and configure Generation 1 and 2 virtual machines
- Configure and use extended session mode
- Configure remoteFX

✓ **Create and configure virtual machine storage**

- Create VHDs and VHDX
- Configure differencing drives
- Modify VHDs
- Configure pass-through disks
- Manage checkpoints
- Implement a virtual Fibre Channel adapter
- Configure storage Quality of Service

✓ **Create and configure virtual networks**

- Configure Hyper-V virtual switches
- Optimize network performance
- Configure MAC addresses
- Configure network isolation
- Configure synthetic and legacy virtual network adapters
- Configure NIC teaming in virtual machines

Hyper-V is a server role in Windows Server 2012 R2 that allows you to virtualize your environment and therefore run multiple virtual operating system instances simultaneously on a physical server. This not only helps you to improve server utilization but also helps you to create a more cost-effective and dynamic system.

In this chapter, you will learn the basic concepts and features of Hyper-V that a Windows Server 2012 R2 technical specialist must know. You will also get a solid understanding of what is important in virtualization and in what areas of your work life you can use it.

Hyper-V Overview

In the following sections, I'll introduce you to Hyper-V. To begin, you'll take a look at virtualization and what types of virtualization exist. I will then discuss Hyper-V features and the Hyper-V architecture before finishing up with the Hyper-V requirements for software and hardware.

What Is Virtualization?

Virtualization is a method for abstracting physical resources from the way that they interact with other resources. For example, if you abstract the physical hardware from the operating system, you get the benefit of being able to move the operating system between different physical systems.

This is called *server virtualization*. But there are also other forms of virtualization available, such as presentation virtualization, desktop virtualization, and application virtualization. I will now briefly explain the differences between these forms of virtualization:

Server Virtualization   This basically enables multiple servers to run on the same physical server. Hyper-V is a server virtualization tool that allows you to move physical machines to virtual machines and manage them on a few physical servers. Thus, you will be able to consolidate physical servers.

Presentation Virtualization   When you use *presentation virtualization*, your applications run on a different computer, and only the screen information is transferred to your computer. An example of presentation virtualization is Microsoft Remote Desktop Services in Windows Server 2012 R2.

Desktop Virtualization   *Desktop virtualization* provides you with a virtual machine on your desktop, comparable to server virtualization. You run your complete operating system and applications in a virtual machine so that your local physical machine just needs to run a very basic operating system. An example of this form of virtualization is Microsoft Virtual PC.

Application Virtualization   *Application virtualization* helps prevent conflicts between applications on the same PC. Thus, it helps you to isolate the application running environment from the operating system installation requirements by creating application-specific copies of all shared resources. It also helps reduce application-to-application incompatibility and testing needs. An example of an application virtualization tool is Microsoft Application Virtualization (App-V).

Hyper-V Features

As a lead-in to the virtualization topic and Hyper-V, I will start with a list of key features, followed by a list of supported guest operating systems. This should provide you with a quick, high-level view of this feature before you dig deeper into the technology.

Key Features of Hyper-V

The following are the key features of Hyper-V:

New Architecture   The hypervisor-based architecture, which has a 64-bit micro-kernel, provides a new array of device support as well as performance and security improvements.

Operating System Support   Both 32-bit and 64-bit operating systems can run simultaneously in Hyper-V. Also, different platforms like Windows, Linux, and others are supported.

Support for Symmetric Multiprocessors   Support for up to 64 processors in a virtual machine environment provides you with the ability to run applications as well as multiple virtual machines faster.

Network Load Balancing   Hyper-V provides support for *Windows Network Load Balancing (NLB)* to balance the network load across virtual machines on different servers.

New Hardware Architecture   Hyper-V's new architecture provides improved utilization of resources such as networking and disks.

Quick Migration   Hyper-V's *quick migration* feature provides you with the functionality to run virtual machines in a clustered environment with switchover capabilities when there is a failure. Thus, you can reduce downtime and achieve higher availability of your virtual machines.

Virtual Machine Snapshot   You can take snapshots of running virtual machines, which provides you with the capability to recover to any previous virtual machine snapshot state quickly and easily.

Resource Metering   Hyper-V *resource metering* allows an organization to track usage within the businesses departments. It allows an organization to create a usage-based billing solution that adjusts to the provider's business model and strategy.

Scripting   Using the Windows Management Instrumentation (WMI) interfaces and APIs, you can easily build custom scripts to automate processes in your virtual machines.

RemoteFX   Windows Server 2012 R2 Hyper-V RemoteFX allows for an enhanced user experience for RemoteFX desktops by providing a 3D virtual adapter, intelligent codecs, and the ability to redirect USB devices in virtual machines.

Fibre Channel   The virtual Fibre Channel feature allows you to connect to the Fibre Channel storage unit from within the virtual machine. *Virtual Fibre Channel* allows an administrator to use their existing Fibre Channel to support virtualized workloads. Hyper-V users have the ability to use Fibre Channel storage area networks (SANs) to virtualize the workloads that require direct access to SAN logical unit numbers (LUNs).

Enhanced Session Mode   *Enhanced Session Mode* enhances the interactive session of the Virtual Machine Connection for Hyper-V administrators who want to connect to their virtual machines. It gives administrators the same functionality as a remote desktop connection when the administrator is interacting with a virtual machine.

In previous versions of Hyper-V, the virtual machine connection gave you limited functionality while you connected to the virtual machine screen, keyboard, and mouse. An administrator could use an RDP connection to get full redirection abilities, but that would require a network connection to the virtual machine host.

Enhanced Session Mode gives administrators the following benefits for local resource redirection:

- Display configuration
- Audio
- Printers
- Clipboard
- Smart cards
- Drives
- USB devices
- Supported Plug and Play devices

Shared Virtual Hard Disk   Windows Server 2012 R2 Hyper-V has a new feature called Shared Virtual Hard Disk. *Shared Virtual Hard Disk* allows an administrator to cluster virtual machines by using shared virtual hard disk (VHDX) files.

Shared virtual hard disks allow an administrator to build a high availability infrastructure, which is important if you are setting up either a private cloud deployment or a cloud-hosted environment for managing large workloads. Shared virtual hard disks allow two or more virtual machines to access the same virtual hard disk (VHDX) file.

Automatic Virtual Machine Activation (AVMA)   *Automatic Virtual Machine Activation (AVMA)* is a new feature that allows administrators to install virtual machines on a properly activated Windows Server 2012 R2 system without the need to manage individual product keys for each virtual machine. When using AVMA, virtual machines get bound to the licensed Hyper-V server as soon as the virtual machine starts.

Network Isolation One nice feature of using Microsoft Hyper-V network virtualization is the ability of Hyper-V to keep virtual networks isolated from the physical network infrastructure of the hosted system. Because administrators can set up Hyper-V software–defined virtualization policies, you are no longer limited by the IP address assignment or VLAN isolation requirements of the physical network. Hyper-V allows for built-in network isolation to keep the virtual network separated from the virtual network.

Dynamic Memory *Dynamic Memory* is a feature of Hyper-V that allows it to balance memory automatically among running virtual machines. Dynamic Memory allows Hyper-V to adjust the amount of memory available to the virtual machines in response to the needs of the virtual machines. It is currently available for Hyper-V in Windows Server 2012 R2.

Supported Guest Operating Systems

The following guest operating systems have been successfully tested on Hyper-V and are hypervisor-aware. Table 9.1 shows all of the guest server operating systems and the maximum number of virtual processors. Table 9.2 shows all of the guest client operating systems and the maximum number of virtual processors.

TABLE 9.1   Hyper-V guest server operating systems

Guest Operating System (Server)	Maximum Number of Virtual Processors
Windows Server 2012 and Server 2012 R2	64
Windows Server 2008 R2 with Service Pack 1 (SP1)	64
Windows Server 2008 R2	64
Windows Server 2008 with Service Pack 2 (SP2)	8
Windows Home Server 2011	4
Windows Small Business Server 2011	Essentials edition: 2 Standard edition: 4
Windows Server 2003 R2 with Service Pack 2 (SP2)	2
Windows Server 2003 with Service Pack 2 (SP2)	2

TABLE 9.1 Hyper-V guest server operating systems *(continued)*

Guest Operating System (Server)	Maximum Number of Virtual Processors
Red Hat Enterprise Linux 5.7 and 5.8	64
Red Hat Enterprise Linux 6.0–6.3	64
SUSE Linux Enterprise Server 11 SP2	64
Open SUSE 12.1	64
Ubuntu 12.04	64

TABLE 9.2 Hyper-V guest client operating systems

Guest Operating System (Client)	Maximum Number of Virtual Processors
Windows 8	32
Windows 7 with Service Pack 1 (SP1)	4
Windows 7	4
Windows Vista with Service Pack 2 (SP2)	2
Windows XP with Service Pack 3 (SP3)	2
Windows XP x64 Edition with Service Pack 2 (SP2)	2
CentOS 5.7 and 5.8	64
CentOS 6.0–6.3	64
Red Hat Enterprise Linux 5.7 and 5.8	64
Red Hat Enterprise Linux 6.0–6.3	64
SUSE Linux Enterprise Server 11 SP2	64
Open SUSE 12.1	64
Ubuntu 12.04	64

The list of supported guest operating systems may always be extended. Please check the official Microsoft Hyper-V site to obtain a current list of supported operating systems: www.microsoft.com/virtualization.

Hyper-V Architecture

This section will provide you with an overview of the Hyper-V architecture (see Figure 9.1). I'll explain the differences between a hypervisor-aware and a non-hypervisor-aware child partition.

FIGURE 9.1 Hyper-V architecture

As you can see, Hyper-V is based on the new microkernel architecture. Hyper-V provides a virtualization layer called a *hypervisor* that runs directly on the system hardware. You can see that the hypervisor is similar to what the kernel is to Windows. It is a software layer responsible for the interaction with the core hardware and works in conjunction with an optimized instance of Windows Server 2012 R2 that allows running multiple operating systems on a physical server simultaneously. The Hyper-V architecture consists of the hypervisor and parent and child partitions.

The Windows Server 2012 R2 operating system runs in the parent partition, and it delivers the WMI provider for scripting as well as the VM service.

Virtual machines each run in their own child partitions. Child partitions do not have direct access to hardware resources; instead, they have a virtual view of the resources, which are called *virtual devices.*

If you're running a hypervisor-aware operating system like Windows Server 2003, Windows Server 2008, Windows Server 2008 R2, Windows Server 2012, or Windows Server 2012 R2 in your virtual machine, any request to the virtual devices is redirected via the high-speed bus to the devices in the parent partition, which will manage the requests.

By default, only Windows Server 2008 R2, Server 2012, and Server 2012 R2 are hypervisor-aware operating systems. Once you install Hyper-V Integration Components on an operating system other than Windows Server 2008 R2 and newer, it will be hypervisor-aware. Microsoft provides a hypervisor adapter to make Linux hypervisor aware.

Non-hypervisor-aware operating systems (for example, Windows NT 4.0) use an emulator to communicate with the Windows hypervisor, which is slower than molasses in the winter.

Hyper-V Requirements

The following sections will describe the hardware and software requirements for installing the Hyper-V server role. It is important to understand these requirements for obtaining your software license as well as for planning for server hardware. When you understand the requirements, you can design and configure a Hyper-V solution that will meet the needs of your applications.

Hardware Requirements

In addition to the basic hardware requirements for Windows Server 2012 R2, there are requirements for running the Hyper-V server role on your Windows server. They are listed in Table 9.3.

TABLE 9.3 Hardware requirements for Hyper-V

Requirement Area	Definition
CPU	x64-compatible processor with Intel VT or AMD-V technology enabled. Hardware Data Execution Prevention (DEP), specifically Intel XD bit (execute disable bit) or AMD NX bit (no execute bit), must be available and enabled. Minimum: 1.4GHz. Recommended: 2GHz or faster.
Memory	Minimum: 1GB RAM. Recommended: 2GB RAM or greater. (Additional RAM is required for each running guest operating system.) Maximum: 1TB.
Hard disk	Minimum: 8GB. Recommended: 20GB or greater. (Additional disk space needed for each guest operating system.)

The Add Roles Wizard in Server Manager additionally verifies the hardware requirements. A good starting point is to check your hardware against the Microsoft hardware list to make sure that Windows Server 2012 R2 supports your hardware. If you try to install the Hyper-V server role on a computer that does not meet the CPU requirements, you'll get a warning window that looks like Figure 9.2.

FIGURE 9.2   Warning window that Hyper-V cannot be installed

Software Requirements

To use virtualization in Windows Server 2012 R2, you need to consider the basic software requirements for Hyper-V. Hyper-V runs only on the following editions of the Windows Server 2012 R2 operating system:

- Windows Server 2012 R2 Standard edition
- Windows Server 2012 R2 Datacenter edition
- Microsoft Hyper-V Server 2012 R2 edition

Hyper-V Installation and Configuration

The following sections explain how to install the Hyper-V role using Server Manager in Windows Server 2012 R2 Full installation mode or the command line mode in Windows Server 2012 R2 Server Core. We will then take a look at Hyper-V as part of Server Manager before discussing how to use the Hyper-V Manager. Finally, we will look at the Hyper-V server settings and then cover two important areas for Hyper-V: virtual networks and virtual hard disks.

Install the Hyper-V Role

Now it's time to see how to install the Hyper-V server role on the two installation options of Windows Server 2012 R2, namely, a Full installation and a Server Core installation.

Installing Hyper-V in Full Installation Mode

You can install the Hyper-V server role on any Windows Server 2012 R2 installation for which the Full option was chosen. In addition, the server must meet both the hardware and software requirements. The installation process is simple, as Exercise 9.1 demonstrates.

EXERCISE 9.1

Installing Hyper-V in Full Installation Mode

1. Open Server Manager.

2. In Server Manager, choose option 2, Add Roles And Features.

3. At the Select Installation Type page, choose the role-based or feature-based installation. Click Next.

4. On the Select Destination Server screen, choose Select A Server From The Server Pool and choose the server to which you want to add this role. Click Next.

5. On the Select Server Roles screen, click the check box next to Hyper-V. When the Add Features dialog box appears, click the Add Features button. Then click Next.

6. At the Select Features screen, click Next.

7. At the Hyper-V introduction screen, click Next.

8. At the Create Virtual Switches screen, choose your adapter and click Next.

9. At the Virtual Machine Migration screen, click Next. You want to use migration only if you have multiple Hyper-V servers. Since we will have only one for this exercise, just skip this screen.

10. At the Default Stores screen, accept the defaults and click Next.

11. At the Confirmation screen, click the Install button.

12. After the installation is complete, click the Close button.

13. Restart your server.

Installing Hyper-V in Server Core

The Server Core installation option is introduced in Windows Server 2012 R2. It creates an operating system installation without a GUI shell. You can either manage the server remotely from another system or use the Server Core's command-line interface.

This installation option provides the following benefits:

- Reduces attack surface (because fewer applications are running on the server)
- Reduces maintenance and management (because only the required options are installed)
- Requires less disk space and produces less processor utilization
- Provides a minimal parent partition
- Reduces system resources required by the operating system as well as the attack surface

By using Hyper-V on a Server Core installation, you can fundamentally improve availability because the attack surface is reduced and the downtime required for installing patches is optimized. It will thus be more secure and reliable with less management.

To install Hyper-V for a Windows Server 2012 R2 installation, you must execute the following command in the command-line interface:

```
Dism /online /enable-feature /featurename:Microsoft-Hyper-V
```

Hyper-V in Server Manager

As with all of the other Windows Server 2012 R2 roles, the Hyper-V role neatly integrates into Server Manager. Server Manager filters the information just for the specific role and thus displays only the required information. As you can see in Figure 9.3, the Hyper-V Summary page shows related event log entries, the state of the system services for Hyper-V, and useful resources and support.

FIGURE 9.3   Hyper-V in Server Manager

Using Hyper-V Manager

Hyper-V Manager is the central management console to configure your server and create and manage your virtual machines, virtual networks, and virtual hard disks. Unlike Virtual Server 2005, where you managed all virtual machines through a web interface, Hyper-V Manager is managed through a Microsoft Management Console (MMC) snap-in. You can access it either in Server Manager or by using Administrative Tools ➢ Hyper-V Manager. Figure 9.4 shows how Hyper-V Manager looks once you start it.

FIGURE 9.4   Hyper-V Manager

Hyper-V Manager is available for the following operating systems:

- Windows Server 2012 R2
- Windows Server 2008 R2
- Windows Server 2008
- Windows 8
- Windows 7
- Windows Vista with Service Pack 1 (SP1)

Hyper-V Manager is installed on a Windows Server 2012 R2 machine only when you install Hyper-V on it. On Windows Server 2008/2008 R2, Server 2003, Windows Vista, Windows 7, or Windows 8, you will need to install the Hyper-V Manager MMC.

You can use Hyper-V Manager to connect to any Full or Server Core installation remotely. Besides Hyper-V Manager, you can use the WMI interface for scripting Hyper-V.

Configure Hyper-V Settings

In this section, you will get an overview of the available Hyper-V settings for the server. You configure all server-side default configuration settings like default locations of your configuration files or the release key. You can open the Hyper-V Settings page (see Figure 9.5) in Hyper-V Manager by clicking Hyper-V Settings in the Actions pane.

FIGURE 9.5   Hyper-V Settings

The Hyper-V Settings page includes the following settings:

Virtual Hard Disks   Specifies the default location of your virtual hard disk files (.vhd and .vdhx).

Virtual Machines   Specifies the default location of your virtual machine configuration files. It includes the Virtual Machine XML configuration files (part of the Virtual Machines folder) as well as related snapshots (part of the Snapshot folder).

Physical GPUs   This feature allows for graphical processing unit (GPU) accelerated video within a virtual machine. The GPU will allow you to support 3D GPU accelerated graphics.

NUMA Spanning   An administrator can configure Hyper-V to allow virtual machines to span nonuniform memory architecture (NUMA) nodes. When the physical computer has NUMA nodes, this setting provides virtual machines with additional computing resources. Spanning NUMA nodes can help you run more virtual machines at the same time. However, using NUMA can decrease overall performance.

Live Migrations   *Live migration* allows a Hyper-V administrator to relocate running virtual machines easily from one node of the failover cluster to another node in the same cluster. Live Migration is explained in more detail later in this chapter.

Storage Migrations   *Storage Migration* allows an administrator to move their virtual machine storage from one location to another. This setting allows you to specify how many storage migrations can be performed at the same time on this system.

Replication Configuration   This setting allows you to configure this computer as a Replica Server to another Hyper-V server. Hyper-V Replica allows administrators to replicate their Hyper-V virtual machines from one Hyper-V host at a primary site to another Hyper-V host at the Replica site.

Each node of the failover cluster that is involved in Replica must have the Hyper-V server role installed. One of the servers in the Hyper-V replication needs to be set up as a Replica Broker to allow the replication to work properly.

Keyboard   Defines how to use Windows key combinations. Options are Physical Computer, Virtual Machine, and Virtual Machine Only When Running Full Screen.

Mouse Release Key   Specifies the key combination to release the mouse in your virtual machine. Options are Ctrl+Alt+left arrow, Ctrl+Alt+right arrow, Ctrl+Alt+space, and Ctrl+Alt+Shift.

Reset Check Boxes   Resets any check boxes that hide pages and messages when checked. This will bring any window up again on which you checked the Do Not Show This Window Again check box.

Manage Virtual Switches

A *virtual network* provides the virtual links between nodes in either a virtual or physical network. Virtual networking in Hyper-V is provided in a secure and dynamic way because you can granularly define virtual network switches for their required usage. For example, you can define a private or internal virtual network if you don't want to allow your virtual machines to send packages to the physical network.

To allow your virtual machines to communicate with each other, you need virtual networks. Just like normal networks, virtual networks exist only on the host computer and allow you to configure how virtual machines communicate with each other, with the host, and with the network or the Internet. You manage virtual networks in Hyper-V using Virtual Switch Manager, as shown in Figure 9.6.

FIGURE 9.6 Virtual Network Manager

Using *Virtual Switch Manager*, you can create, manage, and delete virtual switches. You can define the network type as external, internal only, or private.

External Any virtual machine connected to this virtual switch can access the physical network. You would use this option if you want to allow your virtual machines to access, for example, other servers on the network or the Internet. This option is used in production environments where your clients connect directly to the virtual machines.

Internal This option allows virtual machines to communicate with each other as well as the host system but not with the physical network. When you create an internal network, it also creates a local area connection in Network Connections that allows the host machine to communicate with the virtual machines. You can use this if you want to separate your host's network from your virtual networks.

Private When you use this option, virtual machines can communicate with each other but not with the host system or the physical network; thus, no network packets are hitting the wire. You can use this to define internal virtual networks for test environments or labs, for example.

On the external and internal-only virtual networks, you also can enable virtual LAN (VLAN) identification. You can use VLANs to partition your network into multiple subnets using a VLAN ID. When you enable virtual LAN identification, the NIC that is connected to the switch will never see packets tagged with VLAN IDs. Instead, all packets traveling from the NIC to the switch will be tagged with the access mode VLAN ID as they leave the switch port. All packets traveling from the switch port to the NIC will have their VLAN tags removed. You can use this if you are already logically segmenting your physical machines and also use it for your virtual ones.

Exercise 9.2 explains how to create an internal-only virtual switch.

EXERCISE 9.2

Creating an Internal Virtual Network

1. Click the Windows Key ➢ Administrative Tools ➢ Hyper-V Manager.

2. In Hyper-V Manager, in the Actions pane, choose Virtual Switch Manager.

3. On the Virtual Switch page, select Private and click the Create Virtual Switch button.

4. On the New Virtual Switch page, enter **Private Virtual Network** in the Name field.

5. Click OK.

When you create the internal virtual switch, a network device is created in Network Connections, as shown in Figure 9.7.

FIGURE 9.7   Virtual network card

This is also the case when you create an external virtual network because it will replace the physical network card of the host machine to give the parent partition a virtual network card that is also used in the child partitions.

Unlike with Virtual Server 2005, Hyper-V binds the virtual network service to a physical network adapter only when an external virtual network is created. The benefit of this is that the performance is better if you do not use the external virtual network option. The downside, however, is that there will be a network disruption when you create or delete an external virtual network.

 Communication between the virtual machine and the local host computer is not configured automatically. Once you install a virtual machine, you need to make sure that the TCP/IP settings are in agreement with the settings you define in the virtual network card. Start with a ping from your host machine to the virtual machines to verify that communication is working.

Managing Virtual Hard Disks

In addition to virtual networks, you need to manage virtual hard disks that you attach to your virtual machines. A virtual hard disk in Hyper-V, apart from a pass-through disk, is a VHD or VHDX file that basically simulates a hard drive on your virtual machine.

The following sections will first show you what types of virtual hard disks are available and then show you how to create them. You will also learn about what options are available to manage virtual hard disks.

Types of Hard Disks

Depending on how you want to use the disk, Hyper-V offers various types, as described in Table 9.4.

TABLE 9.4   Virtual hard disks in Hyper-V

Type of disk	Description	When to use it
Dynamically expanding	This disk starts with a small VHD file and expands it on demand once an installation takes place. It can grow to the maximum size you defined during creation. You can use this type of disk to clone a local hard drive during creation.	This option is effective when you don't know the exact space needed on the disk and when you want to preserve hard disk space on the host machine. Unfortunately, it is the slowest disk type.

Fixed size	The size of the VHD file is fixed to the size specified when the disk is created. This option is faster than a dynamically expanding disk. However, a fixed-size disk uses up the maximum defined space immediately. This type is ideal for cloning a local hard drive.	A fixed-size disk provides faster access than dynamically expanding or differencing disks, but it is slower than a physical disk.
Differencing	This type of disk is associated in a parent-child relationship with another disk. The differencing disk is the child, and the associated virtual disk is the parent. Differencing disks include only the differences to the parent disk. By using this type, you can save a lot of disk space in similar virtual machines. This option is suitable if you have multiple virtual machines with similar operating systems.	Differencing disks are most commonly found in test environments and should not be used in production environments.
Physical (or pass-through disk)	The virtual machine receives direct pass-through access to the physical disk for exclusive use. This type provides the highest performance of all disk types and thus should be used for production servers where performance is the top priority. The drive is not available for other guest systems.	This type is used in high-end datacenters to provide optimum performance for VMs. It's also used in failover cluster environments.

Creating Virtual Hard Disks

To help you gain practice in creating virtual hard disks, the following three exercises will teach you how to create a differencing hard disk, how to clone an existing disk by creating a new disk, and how to configure a physical or pass-through disk to your virtual machine. First, in Exercise 9.3, you will learn how to create a differencing virtual hard disk.

EXERCISE 9.3

Creating a Differencing Hard Disk

1. Open Hyper-V Manager.

2. In Hyper-V Manager, on the Actions pane, choose New ➢ Hard Disk.

3. In the New Virtual Hard Disk Wizard, click Next on the Before You Begin page.

EXERCISE 9.3 *(continued)*

4. At the Choose Disk Format screen, choose VHDX and click Next. The size of your VHDs depends on which format you choose. If you're going to have a VHD larger than 2,040GB, use VHDX. If your VHD is less than 2,040GB, then you should use VHD.

5. On the Choose Disk Type page, select Fixed Size and click Next.

6. On the Specify Name And Location page, enter the new name of the child disk (for example, **newvirtualharddisk.vhd**). You can also modify the default location of the new VHD file if you want. Click Next to continue.

7. Next, on the Configure Disk page, you need to specify the size of the VHD file. Choose a size based on your hard disk and then click Next to continue. I used 60GB as our test size.

8. On the Completing The New Virtual Hard Disk Wizard page, verify that all settings are correct and click Finish to create the hard disk.

The process to add a physical or pass-through disk to a virtual machine is quite different. For this, first you need to create the virtual machine, and then you open the virtual machine settings to configure the physical disk. If you want to add a physical disk to a virtual machine, the physical disk must be set as Offline in Disk Management, as shown in Figure 9.8.

FIGURE 9.8   In Disk Management, you can set disks as Offline.

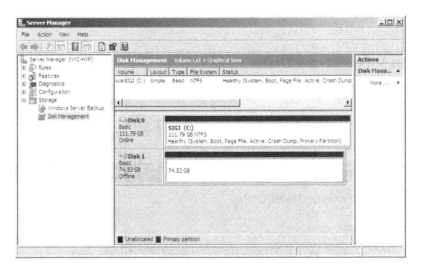

To access Disk Management, click the Windows key, choose Administrative Tools ➢ Computer Management, expand Storage in the left pane, and click Disk Management.

You cannot share a physical disk among multiple virtual machines or with the host system.

Physical or pass-through disks might not be that important if your use of virtualization is based on test environments, but they become crucial when you need to plan for highly available virtual datacenters. This is especially true if you consider using failover clusters to provide the Quick Migration feature, which is when you should consider matching one logical unit number (LUN) from your enterprise storage system or storage area network (SAN) as one physical disk. This provides you with the optimum performance you need in such an environment.

Managing Virtual Hard Disks

Hyper-V also provides two tools to manage virtual hard disks: Inspect Disk and Edit Disk. These tools are available on the Actions pane in Hyper-V Manager.

Inspect Disk   This provides you with information about the virtual hard disk. It shows you not only the type of the disk but also information such as the maximum size for dynamically expanding disks and the parent VHD for differencing disks.

Edit Disk   This provides you with the Edit Virtual Hard Disk Wizard, which you can use to compact, convert, expand, merge, or reconnect hard disks. Figure 9.9 shows you the wizard's options when you select a dynamically expanding disk.

FIGURE 9.9   The Edit Virtual Hard Disk Wizard

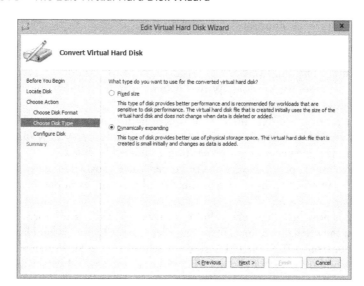

Table 9.5 provides you with an overview of what you can do with the wizard.

TABLE 9.5 Edit Disk overview

Action	Description
Compact	Reduces the size of a dynamically expanding or differencing disk by removing blank space from deleted files.
Convert	Converts a dynamically expanding disk to a fixed disk or vice versa.
Expand	Increases the storage capacity of a dynamically expanding disk or a fixed virtual hard disk.
Merge	Merges the changes from a differencing disk into either the parent disk or another disk (applies to differencing disks only!).
Reconnect	If a differencing disk no longer finds its referring parent disk, this option can reconnect the parent to the disk.

Generation 1 vs. Generation 2 VHDs

Previous versions of Hyper-V had some pretty major drawbacks. One big drawback was that Hyper-V could not boot a virtual machine from a virtual hard drive that was SCSI. Believe it or not, SCSI controllers were not even recognized by Hyper-V unless you installed the Integration Services component.

Another issue that the previous versions of Hyper-V had was the inability to copy files from the Hyper-V host to the virtual machines without the use of a network connection in the virtual machine. The older versions of Hyper-V, prior to Windows Server 2012 R2, are now considered generation 1 versions. Why is it so important to know which generations of Hyper-V you should use or need to use?

Hyper-V generations help determine what functionality and what virtual hardware you can use in your virtual machine. Windows Server 2012 R2 Hyper-V now supports two different virtual machine generations: generation 1 and generation 2.

As already explained, previous versions of Hyper-V are considered generation 1, and this provides the same virtual hardware to the virtual machine as in previous versions of Hyper-V.

Generation 2 is now included with Windows Server 2012 R2, and it provides new functionality on the virtual machines including secure boot (which is enabled by default), the ability to boot from a SCSI virtual hard disk or boot from a SCSI virtual DVD, the ability to use a standard network adapter to PXE boot, and Unified Extensible Firmware

Interface (UEFI) firmware support. Generation 2 now gives you the ability to support UEFI firmware instead of BIOS-based firmware.

So when you create VHDs in Windows Server 2012 R2, one of your choices will be the ability to create the VHDs as a generation 1 or generation 2 VHD. If you need the ability to have your VHDs run on older versions of Hyper-V, make them a generation 1 VHD. If they are going to run only on Windows Server 2012 R2, make your VHDs generation 2 and take advantage of all the new features and functionality.

Configuring Virtual Machines

The following sections cover the topics of creating and managing virtual machines as well as how to back up and restore virtual machines using features such as Import and Export and Snapshot. You'll also briefly look at Hyper-V's Live Migration feature.

Creating and Managing Virtual Machines

It is important to learn how to create a virtual machine, how to change its configuration, and how to delete it. You will take a look at the Virtual Machine Connection tool and install the Hyper-V Integration Components onto a virtual machine.

Virtual Machines

Virtual machines define the child partitions in which you run operating system instances. Each virtual machine is separate and can communicate with the others only by using a virtual network. You can assign hard drives, virtual networks, DVD drives, and other system components to it. A virtual machine is similar to an existing physical server, but it no longer runs on dedicated hardware—it shares the hardware of the host system with the other virtual machines that run on the host.

Exercise 9.4 shows you how to create a new virtual machine.

EXERCISE 9.4

Creating a New Virtual Machine

1. Open Hyper-V Manager.

2. In Hyper-V Manager, on the Actions pane, choose New ➢ Virtual Machine.

3. In the New Virtual Machine Wizard, click Next on the Before You Begin page.

4. On the Specify Name And Location page, give your virtual machine a name and change the default location of the virtual machine configuration files. Click Next to continue.

5. On the Assign Memory page, define how much of your host computer's memory you want to assign to this virtual machine. Remember that once your virtual machine uses up all of your physical memory, it will start swapping to disk, thus reducing the performance of all virtual machines. Click Next to continue.

6. On the Configure Networking page, select the virtual network that you previously configured using Virtual Network Manager. Click Next to continue.

7. On the next page, you configure your virtual hard disk. You can create a new virtual hard disk, select an existing disk, or choose to attach the hard disk later. Be aware that you can create only a dynamically expanding virtual disk on this page; you cannot create a differencing, physical, or fixed virtual hard disk there. However, if you created the virtual hard disk already, you can, of course, select it. Click Next to continue.

8. On the Installation Options page, you can select how you want to install your operating system. You have the option to install an operating system later, install the operating system from a boot CD/DVD-ROM where you can select a physical device or an image file (ISO file), install an operating system from a floppy disk image (VFD file, or a virtual boot floppy disk), or install an operating system from a network-based installation server. The last option will install a legacy network adapter to your virtual machine so that you can boot from the network adapter. Select Install An Operating System Later and then click Next.

9. On the Completing The New Virtual Machine Wizard summary page, verify that all settings are correct. You also have the option to start the virtual machine immediately after creation. Click Next to create the virtual machine.

10. Repeat this process and create a few more virtual machines.

11. If you want to install an operating system on one of the VMs, start the VM, load a Windows Server 2012 R2 installation disk into the DVD drive, and then, under the Media menu, choose DVD and Capture. Then just do a normal install.

After completing Exercise 9.4, you will have a virtual machine available in Hyper-V Manager. Initially, the state of the virtual machine will be Off. Virtual machines can have the following states: Off, Starting, Running, Paused, and Saved. You can change the state of a virtual machine in the Virtual Machines pane by right-clicking the virtual machine's name, as shown in Figure 9.10, or by using the Virtual Machine Connection window.

Here is a list of some of the state options (when the VM is running) available for a virtual machine:

Start Turn on the virtual machine. This is similar to pressing the power button when the machine is turned off. This option is available when your virtual machine is Off or in Saved state.

Turn Off Turn off the virtual machine. This is similar to pressing the power-off button on the computer. This option is available when your virtual machine is in Running, Saved, or Paused state.

FIGURE 9.10   Options available when right-clicking a virtual machine

Shut Down   This option shuts down your operating system. You need to have the Hyper-V Integration Components installed on the operating system; otherwise, Hyper-V will not be able to shut down the system.

Save   The virtual machine is saved to disk in its current state. This option is available when your virtual machine is in Running or Paused state.

Pause   Pause the current virtual machine, but do not save the state to disk. You can use this option to release processor utilization quickly from this virtual machine to the host system.

Reset   Reset the virtual machine. This is like pressing the reset button on your computer. You will lose the current state and any unsaved data in the virtual machine. This option is available when your virtual machine is in Running or Paused state.

Resume   When your virtual machine is paused, you can resume it and bring it online again.

Changing Configuration on an Existing Virtual Machine

To change the configuration settings on an existing virtual machine, you right-click your virtual machine's name in the Virtual Machines pane in Hyper-V Manager and choose Settings. You can change settings such as memory allocation and hard drive configuration. All items that you can configure are described in the following list:

Add Hardware   Add devices to your virtual machine, namely, a SCSI controller, a network adapter, or a legacy network adapter. A legacy network adapter is required if you want to perform a network-based installation of an operating system.

BIOS   This is the replacement of the virtual machine's BIOS. Because you can no longer enter the BIOS during startup, you need to configure it with this setting. You can turn Num Lock on or off and change the basic startup order of the devices.

Memory   Change the amount of random access memory (RAM) allocated to the virtual machine.

Processor   Change the number of logical processors this virtual machine can use and define resource control to balance resources among virtual machines by using a relative weight.

IDE Controller   Add/change and remove devices from the IDE controller. You can have hard drives or DVD drives as devices. Every IDE controller can have up to two devices attached, and by default, you have two IDE controllers available.

Hard Drive   Select a controller to attach to this device as well as to specify the media to use with your virtual hard disk. The available options are Virtual Hard Disk File (with additional buttons labeled New, Edit, Inspect, and Browse that are explained in the virtual hard disk section) and Physical Hard Disk. You can also remove the device here.

DVD Drive   Select a controller to attach to this device and specify the media to use with your virtual CD/DVD drive. The available options are None, Image File (ISO Image), and Physical CD/DVD Drive Connected To The Host Computer. You also can remove the device here.

SCSI Controller   Configure all hard drives that are connected to the SCSI controller. You can add up to 63 hard drives to each SCSI controller, and you can have multiple SCSI controllers available.

Network Adapter   Specify the configuration of the network adapter or remove it. You can also configure the virtual network and MAC address for each adapter and enable virtual LAN identification.

COM1 and COM2   Configure the virtual COM port to communicate with the physical computer through a named pipe. You have COM1 and COM2 available.

Diskette   Specify a virtual floppy disk file to use.

Name   Edit the name of the virtual machine and provide some notes about it.

Integration Services   Define what integration services are available to your virtual machine. Options are Operating System Shutdown, Time Synchronization, Data Exchange, Heartbeat, and Backup (Volume Snapshot).

Snapshot File Location   Define the default file location of your snapshot files.

Smart Paging File Location   This area allows you to set up a paging file for your virtual machine.

Windows Server 2012 R2 has a Hyper-V feature called *Smart Paging*. If you have a virtual machine that has a smaller amount of memory than what it needs for startup memory, when the virtual machine gets restarted, Hyper-V then needs additional memory to restart the virtual machine. Smart Paging is used to bridge the memory gap between minimum memory and startup memory. This allows your virtual machines to restart properly.

Automatic Start   Define what this virtual machine will do when the physical computer starts. Options are Nothing, Automatically Start If The Service Was Running, and Always Start This Virtual Machine. You also can define a start delay here.

Automatic Stop   Define what this virtual machine will do when the physical computer shuts down. Options are Save State, Turn Off, and Shut Down.

> Please be aware that only some settings can be changed when the virtual machine's state is Running. It is best practice to shut down the virtual machine before you modify any setting.

Deleting Virtual Machines

You can also delete virtual machines using Hyper-V Manager. This deletes all of the configuration files, as shown in Figure 9.11.

FIGURE 9.11   Delete Virtual Machine warning window

Make sure you manually delete any virtual disks that were part of the virtual machines to free up disk space. Virtual disks are *not* deleted when you delete a virtual machine.

Virtual Machine Connection

Similar to the Virtual Machine Remote Control (VMRC) client that was available with Virtual Server 2005 R2 and previous versions, Hyper-V comes with Virtual Machine Connection to connect to virtual machines that run on a local or remote server.

You can use it to log onto the virtual machine and use your computer's mouse and keyboard to interact with the virtual machine. You can open Virtual Machine Connection in Hyper-V Manager by double-clicking a virtual machine or by right-clicking a virtual machine and selecting Connect. If your virtual machine is turned off, you might see a window similar to the one in Figure 9.12.

FIGURE 9.12 Virtual Machine Connection window when the machine is turned off

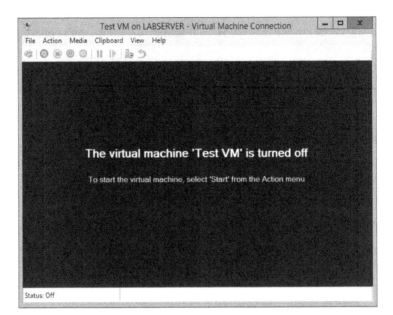

Virtual Machine Connection not only provides you with functionality similar to that of Hyper-V Manager, such as being able to change the state of a virtual machine, but it also provides you with additional features that are especially useful when you want to work with a virtual machine.

File Access Settings or Exit Virtual Machine Connection   Change the state of a virtual machine and create or revert a snapshot. Additionally, you have the options to send Ctrl+Alt+Delete to your virtual machine and Insert Integration Services Setup Disk.

Context-Sensitive Buttons Provide Quick Access to Key Features   These buttons are available under the menu bar to provide you with fast access to the most important features, as you can see in Figure 9.13. It shows the connection of a running VM, but the VM has not had an operating system installed yet, so the figure shows the Windows Setup screen.

NIC Teaming

NIC Teaming, also known as load balancing and failover (LBFO), gives an administrator the ability to allow multiple network adapters on a system to be placed into a team. Independent hardware vendors (IHVs) have required NIC Teaming, but until Windows Server 2012, NIC Teaming was *not* part of the Windows Server operating system.

To be able to use NIC Teaming, the computer system must have at least one Ethernet adapter. If you want to provide fault protection, an administrator must have a minimum of two Ethernet adapters. One advantage of Windows Server 2012 R2 is that an administrator can set up 32 network adapters in a NIC team.

FIGURE 9.13   Virtual Machine Connection window showing a running Windows Server 2012 virtual machine

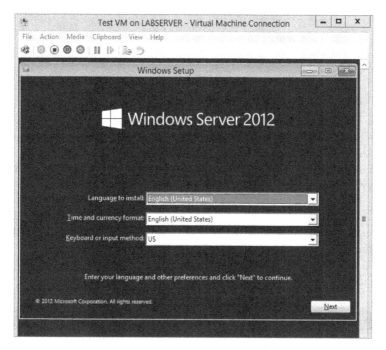

NIC Teaming is a common practice when setting up virtualization. This is one way that you can have load balancing with Hyper-V.

NIC Teaming gives an administrator the ability to allow a virtual machine to use virtual network adapters in Hyper-V. The advantage of using NIC Teaming in Hyper-V is that the administrator can use NIC Teaming to connect to more than one Hyper-V switch. This allows Hyper-V still to have connectivity even if the network adapter under the Hyper-V switch gets disconnected.

An administrator can configure NIC Teaming in either Server Manager or PowerShell.

Storage Quality of Service

Windows Server 2012 R2 Hyper-V includes a new feature called *Storage Quality of Service (QoS)*. Storage QoS allows a Hyper-V administrator to manage how virtual machines access storage throughput for virtual hard disks.

Storage QoS gives an administrator the ability to guarantee that the storage throughput of a single VHD cannot adversely affect the performance of another VHD on the same host. It does this by giving administrators the ability to specify the maximum and minimum I/O loads based on I/O operations per second (IOPS) for each virtual disk in your virtual machines.

To configure Storage QoS, you would set the maximum IOPS values (or limits) and set the minimum values (or reserves) on virtual hard disks for virtual machines.

 If you are using shared virtual hard disks, Storage QoS will not be available.

Installing Hyper-V Integration Components

Hyper-V *Integration Components*, also called *Integration Services*, are required to make your guest operating system hypervisor-aware. Similar to the VM Additions that were part of Microsoft Virtual Server 2005, these components improve the performance of the guest operating system once they are installed. From an architectural perspective, virtual devices are redirected directly via the VMBus; thus, quicker access to resources and devices is provided.

If you do not install the Hyper-V Integration Components, the guest operating system uses emulation to communicate with the host's devices, which of course makes the guest operating system slower.

Exercise 9.5 shows you how to install Hyper-V Integration Components on one of your virtual machines running Windows Server 2012.

EXERCISE 9.5

Installing Hyper-V Integration Components

1. Open Hyper-V Manager.

2. In Hyper-V Manager, in the Virtual Machines pane, right-click the virtual machine on which you want to install Hyper-V Integration Components and click Start.

3. Right-click the virtual machine again and click Connect. Meanwhile, your virtual machine should already be booting.

4. If you need to log into the operating system of your virtual machine, you should do so.

5. Once the Windows Desktop appears, you need to select Insert Integration Services Setup Disk from the Actions menu of your Virtual Machine Connection window.

6. Once the Hyper-V Integration Components are installed, you are asked to perform a reboot.

After the reboot, Hyper-V Integration Components are installed on your operating system, and you will be able to use them.

Summary

Virtualization is quickly becoming a hot topic in information technology. The potential for consolidation is tremendous, and thus it will become more and more important.

After reading this chapter, you should have a good understanding of the Hyper-V architecture and what is required to install Hyper-V.

The section about installation and configuration covered various basic aspects of configuring the virtualization environment. You learned about the different types of virtual networks that are available, the options for installing the Hyper-V role, and the various types of virtual hard disks that you can use to optimize virtualization for your specific scenario.

You also learned how to configure virtual machines using the Hyper-V environment and how to create your own virtual datacenter on top of your Hyper-V machines. I showed you how to create and manage virtual machines, how to use Virtual Machine Connection to control a virtual machine remotely, and how to install Hyper-V Integration Components. You also learned how to export and import virtual machines as well as how to do snapshots of your virtual machine.

If you have never worked with virtualization software before, the information in this chapter may have been completely new to you. You should now be well prepared to try Hyper-V in your own environment.

Exam Essentials

Understand Hyper-V's architecture.   When you have a good understanding of Hyper-V's architecture, especially when an operating system in a virtual machine is hypervisor aware versus non-hypervisor aware, you have a solid understanding of what is important from an architectural perspective.

You should know about the Hyper-V Integration Components and how they change the behavior of a virtual machine. Also know for which operating systems the integration components are available.

Know Hyper-V's requirements and how to install it.   Know the hardware and software requirements as well as how to install Hyper-V. Hyper-V requires an x64-based processor and Data Execution Protection (DEP). Hardware-assisted virtualization must be enabled—don't forget this! Also remember that you can install Hyper-V two ways: using Server Manager or using the command line in Server Core.

Understand virtual networks and virtual hard disks.   Virtual networks and hard disks are the two most tested topics. You definitely should know the types of virtual networks available (that is, external, internal only, and private virtual network) as well as all types of virtual hard disks (namely, dynamically expanding, fixed size, differential, and physical or pass-through). You should be able to apply the correct one when needed. Don't forget the Edit Virtual Hard Disk Wizard, which is also a good source for questions in the exam.

Know how to create and manage virtual machines.   You should be able to explain how to create a virtual machine, what options are available to install an operating system in a virtual machine, and how to install the Hyper-V Integration Components on a virtual machine. Don't forget about the virtual machine states and the virtual machine settings!

Understand how to back up and restore virtual machines.   Have a good understanding of the concept of exporting and importing virtual machines, how snapshots work, and what lies behind a quick migration. Understand how you can export a virtual machine, what you should consider when moving it to a new host machine, and what happens after importing it to the import folder. The same applies to snapshots: You need to know what options you have available and what each option will do. Especially recognize the difference between applying and reverting a snapshot.

Review Questions

1. On which of the following x64 editions of Windows Server 2012 R2 does Hyper-V run? (Choose all that apply.)

   A. Windows Server 2012 R2 Web Edition

   B. Windows Server 2012 R2 Standard Edition

   C. Windows Server 2012 R2 Itanium Edition

   D. Windows Server 2012 R2 Datacenter Edition

2. You want to build a test environment based on virtual machines on a single Windows Server 2012 R2 machine, but you also want to make sure that the virtual machines communicate only with each other. What type of virtual network do you need to configure?

   A. External

   B. Internal only

   C. Private virtual machine network

   D. Public virtual machine network

3. Andy wants to change the memory of a virtual machine that is currently powered up. What does he need to do?

   A. Shut down the virtual machine, use the virtual machine's settings to change the memory, and start it again.

   B. Use the virtual machine's settings to change the memory.

   C. Pause the virtual machine, use the virtual machine's settings to change the memory, and resume it.

   D. Save the virtual machine, use the virtual machine's settings to change the memory, and resume it.

4. You want to make sure that the hard disk space for your virtual machines is occupied only when needed. What type of virtual hard disk would you recommend?

   A. Dynamically expanding disk

   B. Fixed-size disk

   C. Differencing disk

   D. Physical or pass-through disk

5. How do you add a physical disk to a virtual machine?

   A. Use the Virtual Hard Disk Wizard.

   B. Use the Edit Virtual Hard Disk Wizard.

   C. Use the virtual machine's settings.

   D. Use the New Virtual Machine Wizard.

6. Rich bought a new server with an Itanium IA-64 processor, 4GB RAM, and a SAN that provides 1TB hard disk space. After installing Windows Server 2012 R2 for Itanium-based systems, he wants to install Hyper-V on this server. Can Hyper-V be installed on this system?

A. Yes

B. No

7. What are the minimum CPU requirements for running Hyper-V on a machine? (Choose all that apply.)

A. An x64-based processor (Intel or AMD).

B. Hardware Data Execution Protection (DEP) must be enabled.

C. Hardware-assisted virtualization must be enabled.

D. The processor must at least have a dual core.

8. What is the command to install Hyper-V on a Windows Server 2008 machine that was installed in Server Core?

A. `start /w ocsetup Hyper-V`

B. `start /w ocsetup microsoft-hyper-v`

C. `start /w ocsetup Microsoft-Hyper-V`

D. `start /w ocsetup hyper-v`

9. On what operating systems can you install the Hyper-V Manager MMC? (Choose all that apply.)

A. Windows Server 2008 R2

B. Windows Server 2003

C. Windows XP SP3

D. Windows 7, Windows 8

10. What statement is correct for an external virtual network?

A. The virtual machines can communicate with each other and with the host machine.

B. The virtual machines can communicate with each other only.

C. The virtual machines can communicate with each other, with the host machine, and with an external network.

D. The virtual machines cannot communicate with each other.

Appendix A

Answers to Review Questions

Chapter 1: Install Windows Server 2012 R2

1. B. Windows Server 2012 R2 Server Core is a more secure, slimmed-down version of Windows Server. Web versions of Windows Server 2012 R2 are not available. You would use Windows Server 2012 R2 Standard as a web server.

2. C. One of the new advantages of Windows Server 2012 R2 is that you can convert Server Core and GUI versions without the need to reinstall the operating system files completely.

3. B. Microsoft recommends that you upgrade your Windows Server 2008 or Windows Server 2008 R2 web server to Windows Server 2012 R2 Standard.

4. A. Windows Server 2012 R2 Datacenter was designed for organizations that are seeking to migrate to a highly virtualized, private cloud environment. Windows Server 2012 R2 Datacenter has full Windows Server functionality with unlimited virtual instances.

5. D. Windows Server 2012 R2 Foundation was designed for smaller companies that need a Windows Server experience for as few as 15 users. Windows Server 2012 R2 Foundation is general-purpose server with basic server functionality and no virtualization rights.

6. C. Windows Server 2012 R2 Essentials is ideal for small businesses that have as many as 25 users and 50 devices. It has a simple interface, preconfigured connectivity to cloud-based services, and no virtualization rights.

7. A, B, C and D. All four answers are advantages of using Windows Server 2012 R2 Server Core. Server Core is a smaller installation of Windows Server, and therefore all four answers apply.

8. B. Windows Server 2012 R2 Features On Demand allows an administrator not only to disable a role or feature but also to remove the role or feature's files completely from the hard disk.

9. D. New to Windows Server 2012 R2, an administrator has the ability to turn a Windows GUI installation into a Server Core installation.

10. C. Windows Server 2012 R2 has a type of domain controller called a read-only domain controller (RODC). This gives an organization the ability to install a domain controller in an area or location (onsite or offsite) where security is a concern.

Chapter 2: Configure Network Services

1. B. Because of the `.(root)` zone, users will not be able to access the Internet. The DNS forwarding option and DNS root hints will not be configurable. If you want your users to access the Internet, you must remove the `.(root)` zone.

2. C. Active Directory Integrated zones store their records in Active Directory. Because this company has only one Active Directory forest, it's the same Active Directory that both DNS servers are using. This allows ServerA to see all of the records of ServerB and ServerB to see all the records of ServerA.

3. D. The Secure Only option is for DNS servers that have an Active Directory Integrated zone. When a computer tries to register with DNS dynamically, the DNS server checks Active Directory to verify that the computer has an Active Directory account. If the computer that is trying to register has an account, DNS adds the host record. If the computer trying to register does not have an account, the record gets tossed away, and the database is not updated.

4. A. If you need to complete a zone transfer from Microsoft DNS to a BIND (Unix) DNS server, you need to enable BIND secondaries on the Microsoft DNS server.

5. B. Conditional forwarding allows you to send a DNS query to different DNS servers based on the request. Conditional forwarding lets a DNS server on a network forward DNS queries according to the DNS domain name in the query.

6. B. On a Windows Server 2012 R2 DNS machine, debug logging is disabled by default. When it is enabled, you have the ability to log DNS server activity, including inbound and outbound queries, packet type, packet content, and transport protocols.

7. D. Active Directory Integrated zones give you many benefits over using primary and secondary zones including less network traffic, secure dynamic updates, encryption, and reliability in the event of a DNS server going down. The Secure Only option is for dynamic updates to a DNS database.

8. A. Windows Server 2012 R2 DNS supports two features called DNS Aging and DNS Scavenging. These features are used to clean up and remove stale resource records. DNS zone or DNS server aging and scavenging flags old resource records that have not been updated in a certain amount of time (determined by the scavenging interval). These stale records will be scavenged at the next cleanup interval.

9. C. The `dnscmd /zoneexport` command creates a file using the zone resource records. This file can then be given to the Compliance department as a copy.

10. D. Stub zones are useful for slow WAN connections. These zones store only three types of resource records: NS records, glue host (A) records, and SOA records. These three records are used to locate authoritative DNS servers.

Chapter 3: Plan and Install Active Directory

1. B, C and D. The forest and function levels have to be Windows 2003 or newer to install an RODC.

2. B. A domain controller can contain Active Directory information for only one domain. If you want to use a multidomain environment, you must use multiple domain controllers configured in either a tree or a forest setting.

3. D. NTFS has file-level security, and it makes efficient usage of disk space. Since this machine is to be configured as a domain controller, the configuration requires at least one NTFS partition to store the Sysvol information.

4. A and D. To convert the system partition to NTFS, you must first use the CONVERT command-line utility and then reboot the server. During the next boot, the file system will be converted.

5. B and E. The use of LDAP and TCP/IP is required to support Active Directory. TCP/IP is the network protocol favored by Microsoft, which determined that all Active Directory communication would occur on TCP/IP. DNS is required because Active Directory is inherently dependent on the domain model. DHCP is used for automatic address assignment and is not required. Similarly, NetBEUI and IPX/SPX are not available network protocols in Windows Server 2012 R2.

6. A and C. The Sysvol directory must be created on an NTFS partition. If such a partition is not available, you will not be able to promote the server to a domain controller. An error in the network configuration might prevent the server from connecting to another domain controller in the environment.

7. B and C. You need to run the Adprep command when installing your first Windows Server 2012 R2 domain controller onto a Windows Server 2008 R2 domain. Adprep /rodcprep actually gets the network ready to install a read-only domain controller and not a GUI version.

8. A. You'll need to use Active Directory Federation Services (AD FS) in order to implement federated identity management. Federated identity management is a standards-based and information technology process that will enable distributed identification, authentication, and authorization across organizational and platform boundaries. The AD FS solution in

Windows Server 2012 R2 helps administrators address these challenges by enabling organizations to share a user's identity information securely.

9. B. The HOSTS file is a text-file-based database of mappings between hostnames and IP addresses. It works like a file-based version of DNS. DNS resolves a hostname to an IP address.

10. A. You only need to give them rights to the Stellacon.com zone using the DNS snap-in. If they do not have any rights to the Stellatest.com zone, they will not be able to configure this zone in any way.

Chapter 4: Configure Windows Server 2012 R2

1. C. You need to publish shares in the directory before they are available to the users of the directory. If NetBIOS is still enabled on the network, the shares will be visible to the NetBIOS tools and clients, but you do not have to enable NetBIOS on shares. Although replication must occur before the shares are available in the directory, it is unlikely that the replication will not have occurred by the next day. If this is the case, then you have other problems with the directory as well.

2. A. The Sharing tab contains a check box that you can use to list the printer in Active Directory.

3. A and C. A printer may not show up within Active Directory if the printer has not been shared or if the client does not have permission to view the printer. The printer will appear as an object in Active Directory even if it is offline or malfunctioning.

4. B. Offline files give you the opportunity to set up files and folders so that users can work on the data while outside the office.

5. A, B, C and D. Improved security, quotas, compression, and encryption are all advantages of using NTFS over FAT32. These features are not available in FAT32. The only security you have in FAT32 is shared folder permissions.

6. E. By giving Moe Modify on the NTFS security setting, you're giving him just enough to do his job. You could also give Sales or Finance the Modify permission, but then everyone in those groups would be able to delete, change, and do more than they all need to do. Also, Moe does not need Full Control to change or delete files.

7. B. Disk quotas allow you to limit the amount of space on a volume or partition. You can set an umbrella quota for all users and then implement individual users' quotas to bypass the umbrella quota.

8. C and E. The Admin group needs Full Control on the NTFS security and shared permission settings in order to do their job. To be able to give other users permissions, you must have the Full Control permission.

9. A and C. Windows Remote Management and Windows PowerShell allow an administrator to configure a Windows Server 2012 R2 machine remotely. The command prompt is used locally on a Windows Server 2012 R2 Server Core system, and there is no application called Microsoft Remote Admin (MRA).

10. D. File servers are used for storage of data, especially for users' home folders. Home folders are folder locations for your users to store data that is important and that needs to be backed up.

Chapter 5: Administer Active Directory

1. A. A computer account and the domain authenticate each other by using a password. The password resets every 30 days. Since the machine has not connected to the domain for 16 weeks, the computer needs to be rejoined to the domain.

2. C. Checking the box Account Never Expires will prevent this user's account from expiring again.

3. D. The dsadd command allows you to add an object (user's account) to the Active Directory database.

4. A. Distribution groups are for emails only, and distribution groups cannot be assigned rights and permissions to objects.

5. A. Inheritance is the process by which permissions placed on parent OUs affect child OUs. In this example, the permissions change for the higher-level OU (Texas) automatically caused a change in permissions for the lower-level OU (Austin).

6. B and E. Enabling the Advanced Features item in the View menu will allow Isabel to see the LostAndFound and System folders. The LostAndFound folder contains information about objects that could not be replicated among domain controllers.

7. A. Through the use of filtering, you can choose which types of objects you want to see using the Active Directory Users and Computers tool. Several of the other choices may work, but they require changes to Active Directory settings or objects.

8. A. To allow the junior admin to do backups, their account needs to be part of the Backup Operators local group. To add their account to the local group, you need to use Computer Management.

9. A, B, C and D. All of the options listed are common tasks presented in the Delegation of Control Wizard.

10. D. The Delegation of Control Wizard is designed to allow administrators to set up permissions on specific Active Directory objects.

Chapter 6: Manage GPOs

1. A and B. If you want your clients to be able to edit domain-based GPOs by using the ADMX files that are stored in the ADMX Central Store, you must be using Windows Vista, Windows 7, Windows 8, or Windows Server 2003/2008/2008 R2/2012/2012 R2.

2. D. If you assign an application to a user, the application does not get automatically installed. To have an application installed automatically, you must assign the application to the computer account. Since Finance is the only OU that should receive this application, you would link the GPO to Finance only.

3. C. The Resultant Set of Policy (RSoP) utility displays the exact settings that apply to individual users, computers, OUs, domains, and sites after inheritance and filtering have taken effect. Desktop wallpaper settings are under the User section of the GPO, so you would run the RSoP against the user account.

4. B. The Enforced option can be placed on a parent GPO, and this option ensures that all lower-level objects inherit these settings. Using this option ensures that Group Policy inheritance is not blocked at other levels.

5. A. If the data transfer rate from the domain controller providing the GPO to the computer is slower than what you have specified in the slow link detection setting, the connection is considered to be a slow connection and the application will not install properly.

6. D. To disable the application of Group Policy on a security group, you should deny the Apply Group Policy option. This is particularly useful when you don't want GPO settings to apply to a specific group, even though that group may be in an OU that includes the GPO settings.

7. A. GPOs at the OU level take precedence over GPOs at the domain level. GPOs at the domain level, in turn, take precedence over GPOs at the site level.

8. B. The Block Policy Inheritance option prevents group policies of higher-level Active Directory objects from applying to lower-level objects as long as the Enforced option is not set.

9. A, B, C and D. GPOs can be set at all of the levels listed. You cannot set GPOs on security principals such as users or groups.

10. D and E. Administrative templates are used to specify the options available for setting Group Policy. By creating new administrative templates, Ann can specify which options are available for the new applications. She can then distribute these templates to other system administrators in the environment.

Chapter 7: Manage Security

1. B, C and E. The Account Lockout Duration setting states how long an account will be locked out if the password is entered incorrectly. Account Lockout Threshold is the number of bad password attempts, and Account Lockout Counter is the time in which the bad password attempts are made. Once the Account Lockout Counter value reaches 0, the number of bad password attempts returns to 0.

2. B. Account logon events are created for domain account activity. For example, you have a user who logs onto a server so that they can access files; the act of logging onto the server creates this audit event.

3. B, E and F. The first step is to enable auditing. With auditing enabled, Alexis can specify which actions are recorded. To give permissions to the Audit user account, she can use the Delegation of Control Wizard.

4. B, E, G and H. The Active Directory Users and Computers tool allows system administrators to change auditing options and to choose which actions are audited. At the file system level, Crystal can specify exactly which actions are recorded in the audit log. She can then use Event Viewer to view the recorded information and provide it to the appropriate managers.

5. B. Account logon events are created for domain account activity. For example, you have a user who logs on to a server so that they can access files; the act of logging on to the server creates this audit event.

Chapter 8: Configure TCP/IP

1. D. To calculate the network mask, you need to figure out which power number (2^x) is greater than or equal to the number you need. Since you are looking for 1000, $2^{10} = 1024$. You then add the power (10) to the current network mask (53 + 10 = 63).

2. A. When you look at an IPv6 address, the first sections tell you the IPv6 address space prefix. Fd00:: /8 is the unique local unicast prefix, and this allows the server to communicate with all local machines within your intranet.

3. C. The unique local address can be FC00 or FD00, and it is used like the private address space of IPv4. Unique local addresses are not expected to be routable on the global Internet, but they are used for private routing within an organization.

4. A. A Class B address with a default subnet mask of 255.255.0.0 will support up to 65,534 hosts. To increase the number of networks that this network will support, you need to subnet the network by borrowing bits from the host portion of the address. The subnet mask 255.255.252.0 uses 6 bits from the host's area, and it will support 64 subnets while leaving enough bits to support 1,022 hosts per subnet. The subnet mask 255.255.248.0 uses 5 bits from the hosts and will support 32 subnetworks while leaving enough bits to support 2,046 hosts per subnet. 255.255.252.0 is the better answer because it leaves quite a bit of room for further growth in the number of networks while still leaving room for more than 1,000 hosts per subnet, which is a fairly large number of devices on one subnet. The subnet mask 255.255.254.0 uses 7 bits from the host's area and will support more than 120 networks, but it will leave only enough bits to support 500 hosts per subnet. The subnet mask 255.255.240.0 uses 4 bits from the hosts and will support only 16 subnetworks, even though it will leave enough bits to support more than 4,000 hosts per subnet.

5. A. The network mask applied to an address determines which portion of that address reflects the number of hosts available to that network. The balance with subnetting is always between the number of hosts and individual subnetworks that can be uniquely represented within one encompassing address. The number of hosts and networks that are made available depends on the number of bits that can be used to represent them. This scenario requires more than 35 networks and fewer than 1,000 workstations on each network. If you convert the subnet masks as described in the chapter, you will see that the mask in option A allows for more than 60 networks and more than 1,000 hosts. All of the other options are deficient in either the number of networks or the number of hosts that they represent.

6. A. The subnet mask 255.255.255.192 borrows 2 bits from the hosts, which allows you to build four separate networks that you can route through the Windows server. This will allow you to have 62 hosts on each segment. A mask of 255.255.255.128 would have been even better, with two subnets of 126 hosts each, but that wasn't an option, and this solution gives you room for growth in the number of subnets. The subnet mask 255.255.255.224 borrows 3 bits from the hosts. This allows you to create 8 networks, which you don't need, and it leaves only enough bits for 30 hosts. The subnet mask 255.255.255.252 borrows 6 bits from the hosts. This allows you to create more than 60 networks, which you don't need, and it leaves only enough bits for 2 hosts. The subnet mask 255.255.255.240 borrows 4 bits from the hosts. This allows you to create 16 networks, which you don't need, and it leaves only enough bits for 14 hosts per subnet.

7. B, C and D. When you add up the locations that currently need to be given a network address, the total is 3,150, and the maximum number of hosts at any one of these locations is fewer than 1,000. The subnet masks need to support those requirements. Assuming that you choose the Class A private address space 10.0.0.0/8, the subnet masks given in options B, C, and D will provide the address space to support the outlined requirements. The subnet mask 255.255.240.0 supports more than 4,000 subnets and more than 4,000 hosts.

The subnet mask 255.255.248.0 supports more than 8,000 subnets and more than 2,000 hosts. The subnet mask 255.255.252.0 supports more than 16,000 subnets and more than 1,000 hosts. Although each of these subnet masks will work, at the rate that this company is growing, 255.255.252.0 is probably the best mask to prepare for the future. It's unlikely that there will ever be more than 1,000 hosts on any given network. In fact, that number would probably cause performance problems on that subnet. Therefore, it's better to have more subnets available to deploy as the company grows. The subnet mask 255.255.224.0 supports more than 2,000 subnets—an insufficient number to cover the locations. The subnet mask 255.255.254.0 supports more than 32,000 subnets, but only 500 hosts per subnet, which are not enough hosts to cover all of the locations.

8. C. The CIDR /27 tells you that 27 1s are turned on in the subnet mask. Twenty-seven 1s equals 11111111.11111111.11111111.11100000. This would then equal 255.255.255.224.

   The network address 192.168.11.192 with a subnet mask of 255.255.255.224 is perfect for Subnet A because it supports up to 30 hosts. The network address 192.168.11.128 with a subnet mask of 255.255.255.192 is perfect for Subnet B because it supports up to 62 hosts. The network address 192.168.11.0 with a subnet mask of 255.255.255.128 is perfect for Subnet C because it supports up to 126 hosts.

9. A. Microsoft's `jetpack.exe` utility allows you to compact a JET database. Microsoft JET databases are used for WINS and DHCP databases.

10. B and D. If the first word of an IPv6 address is FE80 (actually the first 10 bits of the first word yields `1111 1110 10` or FE80:: /10), then the address is a link-local IPv6 address. If it's in EUI-64 format, then the MAC address is also available (unless it's randomly generated). The middle FF:FE is the filler and indicator of the EUI-64 space, with the MAC address being 00:03:FF:11:02:CD. Remember also the 00 of the MAC becomes 02 in the link-local IPv6 address, flipping a bit to call it local.

Chapter 9: Use Virtualization in Windows Server 2012

1. B and D. Hyper-V can be installed on the Standard or Datacenter Editions of Windows Server 2012 R2. Itanium, x86, and Web Editions are not supported.

2. C. The external virtual network type will allow the virtual machine to communicate with the external network as it would with the Internet, so A is wrong. The internal-only network type allows communication between the virtual machines and the host machine. Because the question says that only communication between the virtual machines should be allowed, the only valid answer is private virtual machine network. The last option, public virtual machine network, does not exist in Hyper-V.

3. A. This question focuses on the fact that you cannot change the memory if the virtual machine is running, paused, or saved. The only valid answer is to shut it down and then change the memory.

4. A. The only virtual hard disk that increases in size is the dynamically expanding disk. Thus, this is the only valid answer to this question. The fixed-size disk creates a disk of the size you specify, the differencing disk is a special disk that stores only the differences between it and a parent disk, and the physical disk uses a physical drive and makes it available to the virtual machine.

5. C. Physical hard disks cannot be configured using the Virtual Hard Disk Wizard, the Edit Virtual Hard Disk Wizard, or the New Virtual Machine Wizard. You can configure and attach a physical disk only by using the virtual machine's settings.

6. B. Hyper-V is not supported on Itanium-based systems; thus, he cannot install it.

7. A, B and C. The minimum CPU requirement for running Hyper-V is a x64-based processor (Itanium is not supported), hardware Data Execution Protection must be enabled, and hardware-assisted virtualization must be enabled. There is no minimum requirement for a dual-core processor.

8. C. This question relates to the setup command used to install the Hyper-V server role on a Windows Server 2008 Server Core machine. It's important to remember that these commands are case sensitive and that the correct command is start /wocsetup Microsoft-Hyper-V, which is option C. All of the other commands will fail to install Hyper-V on a Server Core machine. If you were using a Windows Server 2012 R2 machine, you would use the DISM command.

9. A and D. The Hyper-V Manager is available only for Windows Server 2008, Windows 7, and Windows 8. There is no version available that runs on Windows Server 2003 or on Windows XP SP3.

10. C. The virtual network type in which the machines communicate with each other and with the host machine is called *internal only*. In a private virtual network, the virtual machines can communicate only with each other, not with the network or the host machine. The external network type defines a network where the virtual machines can communicate with each other, with the host machine, and with an external network like the Internet.

Appendix B

About the Additional Study Tools

IN THIS APPENDIX:

- Additional Study Tools
- System requirements
- Using the Study Tools
- Troubleshooting

Additional Study Tools

The following sections are arranged by category and summarize the software and other goodies you'll find from the companion website. If you need help with installing the items, refer to the installation instructions in the "Using the Study Tools" section of this appendix.

The additional study tools can be found at www.sybex.com/go/ mcsawin2012r2install. Here, you will get instructions on how to download the files to your hard drive.

Sybex Test Engine

The files contain the Sybex test engine, which includes two bonus practice exams, as well as the Assessment Test and the Chapter Review Questions, which are also included in the book itself.

Electronic Flashcards

These handy electronic flashcards are just what they sound like. One side contains a question, and the other side shows the answer.

PDF of Glossary of Terms

We have included an electronic version of the Glossary in .pdf format. You can view the electronic version of the Glossary with Adobe Reader.

Adobe Reader

We've also included a copy of Adobe Reader so you can view PDF files that accompany the book's content. For more information on Adobe Reader or to check for a newer version, visit Adobe's website at www.adobe.com/products/reader/

System Requirements

Make sure your computer meets the minimum system requirements shown in the following list. If your computer doesn't match up to most of these requirements, you may have problems using the software and files. For the latest and greatest information, please refer to the ReadMe file located in the downloads.

- A PC running Microsoft Windows 98, Windows 2000, Windows NT4 (with SP4 or later), Windows Me, Windows XP, Windows Vista, or Windows 7
- An Internet connection

Using the Study Tools

To install the items, follow these steps:

1. Download the .ZIP file to your hard drive, and unzip to an appropriate location. Instructions on where to download this file can be found here: www.sybex.com/go/mcsawin2012r2install

2. Click the Start.EXE file to open up the study tools file.

3. Read the license agreement, and then click the Accept button if you want to use the study tools.

The main interface appears. The interface allows you to access the content with just one or two clicks.

Troubleshooting

Wiley has attempted to provide programs that work on most computers with the minimum system requirements. Alas, your computer may differ, and some programs may not work properly for some reason.

The two likeliest problems are that you don't have enough memory (RAM) for the programs you want to use or you have other programs running that are affecting installation or running of a program. If you get an error message such as "Not enough memory" or "Setup cannot continue," try one or more of the following suggestions and then try using the software again:

Turn off any antivirus software running on your computer. Installation programs sometimes mimic virus activity and may make your computer incorrectly believe that it's being infected by a virus.

Close all running programs. The more programs you have running, the less memory is available to other programs. Installation programs typically update files and programs; so if you keep other programs running, installation may not work properly.

Have your local computer store add more RAM to your computer. This is, admittedly, a drastic and somewhat expensive step. However, adding more memory can really help the speed of your computer and allow more programs to run at the same time.

Customer Care

If you have trouble with the book's companion study tools, please call the Wiley Product Technical Support phone number at (800) 762-2974. 74, or email them at `http:/sybex .custhelp.com/`

Index

Note to the Reader: Throughout this index **boldfaced** page numbers indicate primary discussions of a topic. *Italicized* page numbers indicate illustrations.

H

N

Q

Z

Free Interactive Online Study Environment